❖

INTRODUCTION

TO CHRISTIANITY

SECOND EDITION

❖

Of related interest . . .

THE WADSWORTH SERIES IN RELIGIOUS STUDIES

America: Religious and Religion, Catherine L. Albanese
Ways to the Center: An Introduction to World Religions, third edition,
    Denise L. and John T. Carmody
Exploring Religion, second edition, Roger Schmidt
New Testament Story: An Introduction, David Barr
The New Testament: A Critical Introduction, second edition, Edwin D. Freed
Unspoken Worlds: Women's Religious Lives, Nancy Falk and Rita Gross

THE RELIGIOUS LIFE OF MAN SERIES   Frederick Streng, editor

Understanding Religious Life, third edition, Frederick Streng
The House of Islam, third edition, Kenneth Cragg
The Way of Torah, fourth edition, Jacob Neusner
The Hindu Religious Tradition, Thomas J. Hopkins
The Christian Religious Tradition, Stephen Reynolds
Chinese Religion, fourth edition, Laurence G. Thompson
Chinese Way in Religion, Laurence G. Thompson
Japanese Religion, third edition, H. Byron Earhart
Religion in the Japanese Experience, H. Byron Earhart
The Buddhist Religion, third edition, Richard H. Robinson and
    Willard L. Johnson
The Buddhist Experience, Stephan Beyer
Native American Religions, Sam Gill
Native American Traditions, Sam Gill
Islam from Within, Kenneth Cragg and R. Marston Speight
Life of Torah, Jacob Neusner

✦

INTRODUCTION

TO CHRISTIANITY

SECOND EDITION

✦

Mary Jo Weaver

Indiana University

Wadsworth Publishing Company
Belmont, California
A Division of Wadsworth, Inc.

Religion Editor: Sheryl Fullerton
Editorial Assistant: Andrea Varni
Production Editor: Richard Lynch, Bookman Productions
Print Buyer: Martha Branch
Designers: Wendy Calmenson, Judith Levinson
Indexer: Katherine Stimson
Compositor: G&S Typesetters, Inc.
Cover: Vargas/Williams/Design

Printed in the United States of America

1 2 3 4 5 6 7 8 9 10—95 94 93 92 91

Library of Congress Cataloging-in-Publication Data

Weaver, Mary Jo.
  Introduction to Christianity / Mary Jo Weaver.—2nd ed.
    p.   cm.
  Includes bibliographical references.
  ISBN 0-534-13662-1
  1. Christianity.   I. Title.
BR121.2.w35   1990
200—dc20   89-78413
                                                                  CIP

Dedicated to
my colleagues in the Religious Studies Department
Indiana University
with thanks

CONTENTS

INTRODUCTION FOR TEACHERS

This revised introductory textbook has the same modest intentions as its predecessor: it is an intentionally general introduction to Christianity meant to relieve the frustration of having to lay a substantial foundation then having too little time to build on it. My experience with students has not changed: I still notice that many of them come to religions classes knowing very little about Christianity. We cannot assume a general knowledge on their part and so must begin with basic information. Students who enroll in a class in Christianity because they believe they already know what it is often come from narrow confessional backgrounds that need to be expanded, and those who enroll because they know nothing need to begin simply.

As I said in the previous edition, I searched for years for a small, inexpensive book that gave general information in a straightfoward style, something students could read easily with little or no help from me. I found that I could not rely on histories of Christianity because students were often bored with too much historical information, unable to see its relevance to their lives. I also found that I did not have the luxury of assigning several books in a one-semester class. Accordingly, I set out to write my dream textbook and have now revised it to make it more useful. I have many of the same goals in this revised text that I had the first time. The book is historical, but not simply historical: I use the material to raise contemporary questions and to challenge the assumptions many of my students bring with them to class.

I begin by situating Christianity clearly within its Judaic context so that students can see what Christianity had in common with ancient Judaism and where it differed from the Jewish tradition. I am eager for my students to see the integrity of Judaism and I want to make it impossible for them to think of the Jews as "too stubborn" or "too blind" to recognize Jesus as the Messiah. I have tried to make references to Judaism throughout the historical sections and to introduce some aspects of the Jewish-Christian dialogue so students can see the relations between the two groups as an ongoing challenge.

The historical sections of the book—the first two parts—are brief introductions to aspects of Christian history without pretending to be comprehensive. It is important to me that students see some of the major differences between Roman Catholic and Orthodox Christianity, and to be able to put the dynamism of the Reformation years into a reasonable perspective.

My intentions for the modern period are more complex: I want to explain why modernity itself presents challenges to Christianity and how Christians have responded to the modern world with both diversity and unity. At the contemporary level I want to show students that old lines of doctrinal difference do not always work when it comes to modern problems of practical politics. I want the students to have some sense of the complexity of Christianity in terms of the many different groups it inspires, and I want them to understand how contemporary divisions occur. Christians read Scripture differently and may have antagonistic points of emphasis, and I want to give students some indication of how different groups of Christians can come to exactly opposite conclusions on contemporary issues. Finally, rather than ending with a notion that Christians are united in terms of their goals and expressions of worship—the strategy of the first edition—I now end with a series of contemporary challenges that set the stage for Christianity at the end of this century.

My intention, above all, is for the book to be *useful*. I have not aimed at innovative scholarship, nor do I have a single dominating focus. I have tried to pose correctly, without attempting to solve, the major issues in Christianity. I hope that my approach lends *flexibility* to the text and that it places minimum restrictions on faculty subjectivity. Issues are not resolved, boxed, and tied neatly with a ribbon; rather, they are presented from a number of different perspectives so that students can wrestle with them and come to some kind of personal understanding of them. I have aimed throughout at *readability*. I have put notes and suggested further readings at the ends of chapters so that they do not interfere with the flow of the text itself. I have also included appendixes, a time line, a glossary, a list of reference works, and a highly selective bibliography at the end of the book as a series of aids for further study.

I wrote the book originally and have now revised it to be a basic framework on which one could build a variety of different structures: professors who want to be predominantly theological, or historical, or contemporary can be, all using the same structural framework. The book, therefore, is rather like the framework for a prefabricated house: it may not contain all the features one wants, may have some things in it that one does not want, and may not be quite the house one would have designed, but it is useful and it can be modified. I hope instructors will develop material to go along with the book and so have not included graphics, cartoons, readings from primary sources, or summaries of current scholarly arguments. Each teacher will have his or her own such materials and I hope the book encourages personal accents and modifications.

THE BOOK'S ORGANIZATION AND CONTENT

I have divided the book into four parts: two contain background material up to the modern period (which I have arbitrarily set at the nineteenth century) and two contain material designed to help students understand modernity and contemporary issues. Each section contains three chapters and each has a slightly different intention.

The first section—Chapters 1, 2, and 3—focuses on a biblical understanding of God, the religious experience of the Jews, the Jewish background for Jesus along with an outline of his life and work, and the emergence of the early Christian community.

Chapter 1 begins with a discussion of religious experience and explains the concept of revelation in simple terms. It is not meant to be an introduction to Israelite history or to the Old Testament, but is intended to show how the Jews came to understand their God as the powerful, transcendent creator of the world *and* as interested in their daily lives.

The second chapter is much the same as it was. It situates Jesus within his religious and historical context. Like the first, it is meant to be general and not to raise major issues: I was more concerned here to tell the Jesus story and to highlight Jewish expectation about the Messiah to point to understandable differences of opinion about Jesus among Christians and Jews.

The third chapter is also much the same, concerned with the emergence of the Christian church. I was tempted to call it the emergence of Christian churc*es*. Again, I chose what I thought were major controversies within early Christianity and then tried to move the early community out into the larger world without becoming too complex or confusing. My main purpose was to show the early community as divided over important questions. Students too often think about Christian antiquity as a time of unity, total charity, and blissful contentment, a time when no one needed to argue because they all knew what they were supposed to do. Some students long for a return to a "golden age" of early Christianity and I was constrained in this chapter to show it as an exciting time, but not at all an age of unanimity. In all three of these early chapters one could be much more complex: any of the issues I have raised—religious experience, exegesis, Jewish context for Jesus, the development of the early church—admit more than one interpretation, and my choices and explanations will please some and not others.

The second part of the book—Chapters 4, 5, and 6—is meant to give a wide-ranging and relatively brief historical overview of Christianity up to the nineteenth century. I have tried to recapitulate the central core of Christian history and have made some necessary additions to the previous edition, but I am still aware that no one book can cover all this territory adequately. I wanted to write a history of Christian *diversity* rather than a complex history of Christianity. My experience with teaching the history of Christianity at the beginning undergraduate level does not suggest that students want more historical information, and I have tried to keep their needs uppermost as I reconstructed this section.

Chapter 4 has been revised to explain the differences between Roman Catholic and Eastern Orthodox Christianity with more clarity, *and* to introduce some of the complex issues of medieval Christianity. I focused on power and politics when describing the differences between Roman Catholic and Eastern Orthodox Christianity because that is where the practical issues arise and because it gives me a simple way of differentiating Christianity in its Eastern and Western contexts. Throughout the chapter I have used an interpretive concept I call "the idea of Rome" to explain some of the goals of Christian institutional life.

Chapter 5, thanks to the suggestions of many readers, has been modified in its interpretation of Luther and Calvin, and now includes some discussion of early biblical scholarship. Otherwise, it is much the same, focusing on similarity and difference and meant to further an understanding of Christian *diversity*. It still tries to pull together major aspects of the Reformation—before and after Luther—and to show the roots of the many Christian groups that emerged from that controversy.

Chapter 6 continues the story of diversity in its European context, with some attention to the American context for Christianity in the seventeenth and eighteenth centuries. Its purpose is to bring the European divisions up to date briefly, and then to open the discussion of the new American context. I try as well to introduce the general context of modernity, but only briefly, as I will concentrate on that in some detail in the next section. One of my strategies in this revision has been to cover the same modern historical ground more than once by using different contexts and angles of vision. This preview of the Enlightenment is simply that, a beginning, a way to get myself and the students out of the eighteenth-century American context and ready for a closer look at the modern world. By the end of Chapter 6, students should have some idea of how and why so many different Christian groups formed during those times.

The third part of the book—Chapters 7, 8, and 9—constitutes the newest approach to this revised text. I have used these chapters to explain the nineteenth century from a number of different perspectives. I have written a new chapter to introduce the concept and challenges of modernity and have used it to tie up some loose ends and anticipate further growth. The middle chapter is a discussion of the massive proliferation of Christian diversity in nineteenth-century America. The final chapter of this section is new. I thought I should find yet another way to explain Christian diversity and unity and so concentrated on two nineteenth-century movements, missions and ecumenism.

Chapter 7 introduces students to the modern world by way of its contrast with the medieval world. I use this chapter to explain how and why the separation of church and state is a modern idea that challenged the churches, and I have written an extensive introduction to secularization in order to explain the new philosophy and politics of the Enlightenment.

The rest of the chapter discusses reactions to modernity. I try to explore Roman Catholic resistance to modernity in a way that I hope contextualizes the changes in Catholicism brought about by the Second Vatican Council. The responses of Protestant Christianity, as I note, are harder to contain in general descriptions, and I have tried to sort out two different kinds of responses. The section on evangelical Pietism and the Oxford Movement constitutes an introduction to conservative Christianity, while my discussion of the biblical movement and social activism allows me to show both conservative and liberal responses to modernity.

Chapter 8 is an introduction to Christianity in America in the nineteenth century. It is meant to continue the story of Christian diversity through an incredibly prolific era. As before, I have concentrated on types of Christian development, with some representative samples in each area. The students sometimes find this chapter daunting, and it is a challenge to make it accessible to them, I know. At the same time, I did not choose to eliminate particular movements simply because they tax one's ability to comprehend them.

Chapter 9, devoted to the missionary movement and ecumenism, is new. If Chapter 8 left students with the impression that Christianity, however rich, is hopelessly fractured, I thought it best to give them some introduction to the ways Christians themselves in the nineteenth century reacted to the great diversity they encountered. In discussing the missionary movement, I recapitulate a brief history of the missions and talk about Christianity in China and in the new world in the sixteenth century. I have also explained why Protestant missionary zeal did not catch fire until the nineteenth century.

I found that the best bridge between missionary enthusiasm and the beginnings of the ecumenical movement was the dedication of Christian students in the nineteenth century. Accordingly, I used some of the student movements of the time to draw the discussion to ecumenism and then explained how the World Council of Churches developed. My opinions about ecumenism—whether it is wise or possible—are foregrounded in this chapter, and I have also indicated where some groups, notably, Roman Catholics and some evangelical Christians, have not warmed to the fires of ecumenical fellowship. The discussion of the nineteenth century, therefore, constitutes what I hope will be a welcome addition to the book: the challenges of modernity, the diversity of nineteenth-century America, and the cooperative ventures of the missionary movement and ecumenism all set the context for the last part of the book.

Part Four—Chapters 10, 11, and 12—takes some of the material from the first edition's Part Three and adds other material from that earlier section. I have recast this section so that it concentrates on contemporary issues, and in response to reviewers' criticism I have eliminated the chapter on worship altogether. The chapter on Christian polity has now become an appendix. I have added a final chapter which is an extended discussion about the ways fundamentalism and liberalism continue to challenge Christianity by means of a set of complicated issues.

Chapters 10 and 11 are pretty much the same as chapters 8 and 9 in the first edition. I have written a new introduction to the section which explains the diagram more coherently, but I have kept the material intact. I still want to gather groups together and redivide them according to practical or ethical positions. The diagram I use is still not derived from H. Richard Niebuhr's *Christ and Culture*, and ought not to be judged by how well it reflects his purposes. I mean it to be a useful introduction to the ways in which Christian groups can be understood apart from their historical development. These two chapters look at the Christian groups that have been explained historically from a different perspective. These chapters are meant to flesh out the picture and to make the story of Christian diversity both more complex and more contemporary, to make the historical sections relevant, and finally, to raise some large issues within Christianity in a way that will engage students and provoke thought and discussion.

Chapter 12 is new. In the first edition I was eager to avoid extended discussion of contemporary problems because I thought they would date the book prematurely. I chose to mention some of the thorny issues of contemporary debate briefly. I have now given them a chapter of their own. For the purpose of making a connected introduction to three important issues, I have related them to specific problems within the churches. I discuss the women's movement in terms of ministry: the question of women's ordination. I discuss the nature of the church in terms of modern technology and the "electronic church," and I introduce some problems in the nature of the Christian mission in relation to Third World theologies.

In the first edition, I thought it best to leave students with a sense of peacefulness about Christianity, so I ended with a chapter on worship which showed that whatever differences separated Christians from one another, we could still find recognizable points of correspondence in their various modes of worship. I have now eliminated that chapter from the book entirely and have chosen to end the book not with peace, but with conflict. This approach may be a little unsatisfying emotionally, but it is decidedly more realistic and leaves the students with a sense that Christianity is a living movement responsive to real issues of practical politics.

The appendixes provide handy information about some of the themes mentioned in the book but not elaborated on. Appendix 1 simply shows the different ordering of books in the Hebrew Bible and the Christian Bible. Appendix 2 provides a simple, story-line synopsis of books in the Old and New Testaments and is meant to be used like a reference table. Appendix 3 is an outline of early Christian literature, an area not covered in the book but alluded to in the discussion of tradition (Chapter 4). Appendix 4, also meant to be used as a reference table, pulls together the various ecumenical councils in the history of the Christian church and shows which groups follow which councils; here the Romanness of the Roman Catholic church is visible in another way. Appendix 5, another reference table, simply delineates some of the creeds (or confessions) within Christianity in an attempt to show some of the doctrinal developments that were not treated within the text. Appendix 6 is a brief introduction to church polity that shows the structural differences among Christians. Appendix 7, a historical time line, is a study aid for students, as is the glossary, made up of terms from the text itself that are not fully explained there.

Let me say a word about various bibliographical information. In the first edition the bibliography contained every book that I mentioned throughout the text plus many books that I thought students might find useful for further research. I have changed my approach in this edition. The suggestions for further reading at the ends of chapters are chatty and, I hope, enticing. They reflect the kinds of books I have found helpful or illuminating over the years and are specific to the matters under discussion in each chapter. I have also added endnotes to the chapters to elaborate on people or controversies mentioned in the text. These notes are meant more for teachers than for students and, again, reflect my own predilections. I have usually *not* repeated these references—suggested readings or endnotes—in the new bibliography. Rather, the bibliography is now meant to be a small, useful selection of books that students might consult for further information. I have updated the old entries in the case of new editions, eliminated most periodical references, and tried to select books that students can really use. Accordingly, I have eliminated many books that, while interesting and useful to me and perhaps to other teachers, tend, when gathered together into a very long list, to have a daunting effect on the students. The list of selected reference works is pretty standard and simply lists the kinds of sources students should consult for general information.

In the course I teach I have found it helpful to build on the parts of this book by assigning four short papers on a specific Christian group chosen by the students. The first paper deals with the background of the group and its relation to Jesus. The second places the group in its appropriate historical context, especially in its American embodiment. The third relates the reactions of the group to the challenges of modernity and discusses the group's relation to missions and ecumenism. The fourth places the group on the diagram and discusses ways the group relates to some modern challenges. By investigating a particular Christian group from all these angles, students get a deeper understanding of one group and of the broader questions Christians ask themselves in the modern world. The bonus for them is the ease with which they are able to tackle assignments that ask them to write two- to three-page papers and their amazement at the end of the semester when they have a draft of a ten- to twelve-page term paper and a good grasp of either their own religious background or one completely new to them.

ACKNOWLEDGMENTS

In his classic text *American Renaissance*, F. O. Mathiessen said this:

> During the course of this long volume I have undoubtedly plagiarized from many sources—to use the ugly term that did not bother Shakespeare's age. I doubt whether any criticism or cultural history has ever been written without such plagiary, which inevitably results from assimilating the contributions of your countless fellow-workers, past and present. The true function of scholarship as of society is not to stake out claims on which others must not trespass, but to provide a community of knowledge in which others may share.[1]

Without elevating myself and my task to the stature of Mathiessen, I must acknowledge that I share his general feeling. This book was produced from my research and teaching experience, anecdotes told to me by friends, and informative arguments from colleagues. Many of those who have used the first edition have written to me over the years to suggest better ways of explaining things or to save me from ignorant judgments. I am grateful to them and realize that many of the improvements in this edition are due to their kindness. Like many of you, the older I get, the busier I get and the less inclined to take the time to write to perfect strangers about their work. I am especially thankful to Bryan J. Whitfield, and Bradley Nassif. Those who have made that effort on my behalf are, I hope, cherished by the angels. I also appreciate the numerous constructive comments of the following reviewers: Eugene V. Gallagher, Connecticut College; Philip Riley, Santa Clara University; and James C. Spalding, University of Iowa.

I am not always able to say where I have found a particular definition or distinction and in the production of this volume—in its first edition and again in the revision—I have made use of many of the standard reference works listed at the back of this book. *The Oxford Dictionary of the Christian Church* has been a welcome companion of mine for the last twenty years, and the new *Encyclopedia of American Religious Experience* has lived up to its intention to provide insightful, critical analyses of Christianity in almost all its embodiments. Some of the revisions are beholden to things I have read in this new reference work and I recommend it highly to students and teachers alike. I have not, to the best of my knowledge, quoted from these works directly, but I am aware that I have often shaped an explanation or clarified a point because of the lucidity of their definitions and the organizational genius of their articles.

In the first edition I mentioned my debts to Gershom Scholem[2] and William E. Hordern,[3] and I renew my thanks to them in this edition. I have also been enlightened by Dillenberger and Welch[4] and have been happily reintroduced to the classic old church history text of Williston Walter.[5] Some of the

---

[1] (Oxford: Oxford University Press, 1968), pbk. p. xv.
[2] "Revelation and Tradition as Religious Categories in Judaism" in *The Messianic Idea in Judaism and Other Essays on Jewish Spirituality* (New York: Schocken Books, 1971), pp. 282–303.
[3] *A Layman's Guide to Protestant Theology* (New York: Macmillan, 1968).
[4] *Protestant Theology Interpreted Through Its Development*, 2nd ed. (New York: Macmillan, 1988).
[5] *A History of the Christian Church*, 4th ed. (New York: Scribner's, 1985).

material originally appeared in an Indiana University Independent Study Division text, and I thank the trustees of the university for allowing me to use it again here. Most of the refinements, however, have been suggested to me by my colleagues and students over the years. I am grateful for their intelligence and generosity, indebted to their support and good grace as I attempted to make generalizations in areas they believed needed much more sophistication than I could bring to the task.

I asked many, many friends to read the first edition so that I could profit from a wide variety of viewpoints. I have not burdened them with this second edition, but I am still in their debt and acknowledge new sources of inspiration and information, especially from the graduate students who have assisted me in the course over the last few years. I cannot mention the hundred or so people who deserve thanks for their part in this project, but I want to remember the late Robert Kleinhans, an excellent friend and good critic. In my department, all my colleagues have been helpful, but I must single out Luke Johnson for support above and beyond the call of duty. The friends who are my support in life also deserve praise, especially Marianna Bridge and Susan Gubar—since revisions carry little of the excitement of the original project and tend to make authors, this author at least, grumpy and hard to live with. The staff at Wadsworth was wonderful during the production of both editions, and I owe particular thanks to my friend and editor, Sheryl Fullerton. None of this would be possible for me outside the atmosphere of Indiana University. My colleagues in the Department of Religious Studies have led me to see other viewpoints and to think fairly about them. I owe them many thanks and make a small gesture of gratitude by dedicating this book to them.

Mary Jo Weaver

NOTE TO STUDENTS

All religions can be looked at from either the inside or the outside. When Christianity is viewed from the inside, one gets a believer's perspective and sees Christianity as *the* religion, the only possible truth. If Christianity is viewed from the outside, one gets a nonbeliever's perspective and sees Christianity as *a* religion, one perception of the truth among many. A clear and determined choice between these two approaches leads to considerable distortion from the very outset. To avoid this distortion, this book attempts to incorporate both perspectives, though within limits. This book takes an outsider's perspective insofar as it does not attempt to proclaim Christianity or prove it to be true. At the same time, it is faithful to an insider's viewpoint as it tries to read and understand the doctrines and practices of Christians as they are understood within the believing community.

Christianity has a doctrine about God that includes a belief in the life, death, and resurrection of Jesus; and it offers a method for getting in touch with God that involves a relationship with Jesus. Christians agree that it is important to know, or to believe in, or to experience Jesus, but they disagree about how that is done. There are, accordingly, many varieties of Christian belief and practice, most of which reflect differences in biblical interpretation, historical experience, and Christian self-understanding.

An introduction to Christianity can do many things, some of them more ambitious than others. This book is modest in intention and general in scope: it intends to *introduce* Christianity from a number of perspectives so that students can have some appreciation of its richness and diversity without being overwhelmed by its differences of opinion and practice. Christians are extraordinarily diverse in their beliefs and behavior, but they also share common understandings. This book delineates the historical differences and commonalities in order to introduce the dynamism and diversity of one of the world's largest religions.

A book like this is bound to be controversial however hard the author tries to be fair-minded and judicious in choosing material, examples, and topics. I can only hope that those who see significant gaps in interpretation and historical awareness will fill those gaps with supplementary reading. Though I wrote this book with a definite audience in mind—the college freshman who has little knowledge about Christianity and perhaps a minimal understanding of religion—I have been conscious throughout that it will be read by teachers and reviewers. It has been tempting, therefore, to insert complex digressions in order to preserve a professional image. I have nonetheless tried to keep the needs of the student uppermost in mind while writing.

Accordingly, though I usually allude to the fact that most issues are more complex than they may appear to be in this general introduction, I do not raise difficult questions of scriptural exegesis (critical explanation) or sophisticated historical argumentation in the body of the text itself. The notes and suggestions at the ends of the chapters and the appendixes at the back of the book give more nuances and further explain controversial issues. My approach to the Bible is informed by historical and critical scholarship and grounded in a deep appreciation of the ways Scripture is used by believing communities of Christians. Different groups of Christians read certain texts differently and I have tried to recognize that fact without attempting to solve the issues. I have tried to raise some questions about scriptural interpretation without urging one interpretation over another. I have not taken time to explain some historical material or to identify certain personalities, but I have added a glossary of terms and names to elaborate on areas not covered in depth in the text. Use the glossary like a dictionary: when you find a word or the name of a person in the text that you want to know more about, turn to the glossary for a further explanation.

Finally, I have accepted the statements from each group about itself and have made no speculations about the possible truth or falsehood of certain claims. My intention is to give each group an impartial reading and to present its history and its positions straightforwardly. I have been more interested in practical issues than in theological ones, and more interested in presenting an explanation for Christian diversity and unity than I have been in writing a comprehensive history of Christianity. My hope is that you will find the text clear, accurate, and challenging.

✤

Introduction to Christianity

Second Edition

✤

✦ PART ONE ✦

Biblical and Historical Background for Christianity

T HE FIRST PART of this book introduces the background against which the varieties of Christianity have emerged. Christianity is a revealed religion; Christians believe that God has communicated with them and has been manifested in words and in a history of saving actions. For Christians, the most important self-communication of God is Jesus Christ, whose life, death, and resurrection form the foundation of the Christian religion.

The first three chapters focus on the work of God, the life of Jesus, and the presence of the Holy Spirit in the church. Most Christians believe that God is the creator and savior of people, that Jesus Christ is God's most important self-disclosure, and that the Holy Spirit is God's power at work in the Christian community. Christians trace their roots through Judaism to the Creation. So we will begin with some general perceptions about God as creator, as providentially interested in the world and in the history of a special people, the Jews. The second chapter situates Jesus within his historical context: the apocalyptic mood and messianic hopes of the Jews provided Christians with a way to understand Jesus and to interpret his mission. The third chapter outlines the emergence of the Christian church and the importance of the Holy Spirit within the church.

Christianity did not develop easily or smoothly. There were serious arguments among Christians and between Christians and Jews about the person and

I

mission of Jesus. Christianity is a complex religion that has been growing and changing from its beginning. The first part of this book explains the basis of the dynamic growth within Christianity, and introduces the foundations of the Christian experience.

✦

CHAPTER 1

GOD AS REVEALED
IN THE BIBLE

Western religions aim to help believers follow the will of God. And how do believers know the will of God? If you ask that question of followers in any revealed religion (Judaism, Christianity, Islam), they will tell you that God has spoken, has been made manifest, has communicated with people. That is the claim of *revelation,* a word that comes from the Latin *revelare,* which means to unveil or to disclose. When people criticize a dress or a bathing suit for being too *revealing,* they mean it unveils or uncovers too much. When the word is applied to God, it means that God unveils—not by disrobing but by disclosing the divine will and personality through words and actions. Believers, therefore, know the will of God because it has been revealed to them.

REVELATION AND RELIGIOUS EXPERIENCE

Revelation is an article of faith for believers and a complex problem for theologians.[1] Since there is no single way to explain it, students have a variety of ways to understand it. Furthermore, because revelation is linked to complicated and sometimes emotional issues like inspiration,[2] a person's religious background often suggests that one particular interpretation is better or more adequate than another. In terms of a person's private beliefs, that observation is quite true: some explanations *are* more satisfying than others. For our purposes

3

here, however, we have to see whether we can put aside personal preferences and try to understand revelation in very general terms. What do people mean when they say that they have had a direct communication from God? What do they mean when they say that their lives and beliefs are based on God's *will* for them?

Because we are considering the very beginnings of Christianity, and because Christianity traces its understanding of itself back through Judaism to the beginning of time, we have to start by trying to understand Judaism as a revealed religion. Judaism began in a conviction that God had actually appeared in some fashion, or done something; that a vision of God had been seen or that God's voice had been heard. The first clue to understanding revelation, therefore, is *experience*. Theories of revelation tell us that an experience of God is often aweful and demanding: one feels bound to respond to the event and to keep it alive for oneself and one's community.

Those whose stories form the basis of Judaism and Christianity usually believe that their experience has helped them understand the will of a *personal* God. The stories of Abraham, Moses, Jesus, and Paul do not lead to the conclusion that they had some vague encounter with "something out there." Rather, they all believed that God spoke to them directly and demanded some action on their part. They experienced God as a person who initiated a relationship with them. According to these great religious figures, and others, God revealed a desire for partnership and demanded a response.

Skeptics, of course, would dismiss such religious experiences as madness or illusion, but those whose stories we find in the Bible were *believers*, though perhaps not always immediately and not without a struggle on their part. Revelation is not a one-way street, but the beginning of a partnership. God reveals, but people must choose whether to live in accordance with that revelation, a choice that often involves whether to believe that a revelation has occurred.

If people choose to accept the revelation, they usually reflect on it, remember it ritually with feasts or celebrations, tell it as a story to later generations, write it down, refine it, edit it, and apply it to new situations. They may even receive new revelations and come to deeper understandings of God over a long period of time. In Judaism and Christianity both, there is a sense of ongoing revelation: God continues to disclose Godself and to call believers into deeper levels of understanding and partnership.

Revelation is God's self-communication and can apparently occur in a number of ways. Each time, however, the pattern recurs: direct communication from God on the one hand, the response of people on the other. Revelation, insofar as we understand it in Judaism and Christianity, is a direct communication of God *intended for a group of people*. It may have originally been experienced by a single individual, but the content applies to a whole people and invites response and belief from that entire group.

Once it is accepted by a group, revelation is interpreted. An incident of God's action may be interpreted differently by groups of believers. For example,

Jews, Christians, and Muslims all agree that Abraham is extraordinarily important as an early partner of God's self-communication, but they interpret Abraham's life and history differently. Muslims trace their connections with Abraham
through Ishmael (see Genesis 16, 17, and 21), whereas Jews trace their lineage to
Abraham through Isaac (Genesis 17–22). Jews have interpreted the story of the
sacrifice of Isaac (Genesis 22) as a test of Abraham's obedience and a strength-
ening of the covenant, whereas Christians have tended to see the same story as
a typology for the sacrifice of Jesus on the cross.

Whatever particular interpretations have shaped Judaism, Christianity, and
Islam, however, each religion bases itself on revelation: in each religion one can
find stories of God speaking to a group through the experience of special
people; what God has said and what God has done are foundational for each
group. Jews, Christians, and Muslims all believe that they have discerned God's
intentions for their lives because of the ways God has spoken and acted in history. Finally, each of these groups has preserved its understanding of God in
ritual celebration, and each has produced a sacred text which, it claims, contains
"the word of God." Because Christianity grew out of Judaism and the Israelite
experience of revelation, Christians reverence the Hebrew Bible, albeit in different form. Our understanding of Christianity must begin, therefore, with an
examination of the Bible as the primary account of God's revelation.

THE BIBLE

For Jews, the Bible is divided into three parts: the Torah, the Prophets, and
the Writings. Christians rearranged the Jewish Bible and renamed it the Old
Testament. For Christians, the Bible is made up of two parts: the Old Testament
and the New Testament. Because they used different versions of the Hebrew
Bible, Catholics and Protestants disagreed about how many books should be in
the Old Testament (see Appendix 1). The Revised Standard Version, the most
reliable scholarly edition of the Bible, has thirty-nine books in the Old Testament and twenty-seven in the New Testament (see Appendix 2).

The word *Bible* means "book." To Jews and Christians it is a holy book, set
apart from others because of its sacred content and origin. The Bible has a
central place in Jewish and Christian worship all over the world. Worshipers
believe that the use of biblical texts in liturgy puts them in touch with God's
actions in history. Since those actions are regarded as saving ones, liturgical use
of Scripture enables believers to be touched by God's saving acts. The Bible has
been translated into more languages than any other book; it exists in a variety
of versions, and is constantly studied, read, quoted from, and treasured. For all
that, however, it is rare to find many people who can understand the whole
book, especially the Old Testament. Parts of it seem obscure or peculiar, some
of it is hard to read, and some of it (for example, lists of ancient genealogies)
appears to be irrelevant to life in the present.

Jews and Christians agree that the Old Testament is inspired, though they disagree about which parts are and which are not. Whether there is inspiration and how it occurred or functions is a matter of theological dispute. Some believers are content with the idea that God dictated every word of the Bible to chosen authors; others prefer to understand inspiration as a more subtle psychological process. For the most part, however, all these people believe that God somehow directed the writing of the book; that is what inspiration means. We need not belabor the way inspiration is explained by various religious groups and theologians. A broad, working definition might see inspiration as God acting and revealing through a particular community. Within that community, authors reflect on their collective experience, treasure it, and write it down. What the author writes and the way it is written is inspired, has divine influence behind it. The issue is not simple; the debate about it and refinement of its definition continue.

Even though Jews and Christians agree that the Old Testament is inspired, that God is revealed in it, that does not mean biblical content and meaning will be immediately evident to the reader. Any reader of the Bible needs to understand the enormous range of history and literature it contains. One help in understanding a particular book or passage is discovering the intention of the author. Not all books were written to respond to the same circumstances. They may all deal with God's relationship with people, but they have been written in a number of different styles, in different contexts, with probable differences of purpose.

There is considerable disagreement among Christians about how to read the Bible. Some believe that the Bible, as God's word, need only be read and understood simply and literally; that every word and explanation is absolutely true. Others believe the Bible was written for and by a particular people and that one needs to understand this historical context before the real message can be understood. Still others approach the Bible with tools of scholarship—ancient languages, archaeology, history—in order to understand different strands of the stories and the levels of intention behind those stories.

For example, the first book, Genesis, begins by telling the story of the creation of the world and the "fall" of humankind. The biblical author wanted to explain the wonders of the universe as the actions of a powerful, generous God—in other words, to show the essential goodness of creation. At the same time, that author needed to explain the sense of frustration and alienation people sometimes suffer—in other words, to show that the bad things that happen in this world are not God's fault but are the result of human error or sin. Whether the author meant to describe actual events in historical and scientific terms is a matter of dispute among Christians, but Christians do not dispute the power and beauty of the creation account and the profound way the story of Original Sin explains the presence of evil in the world.

When one turns to the Bible, therefore, one finds a great variety of literature. The Bible contains straightforward historical information as well as poetry and prose. Law and lore are included along with prophetic and devotional books; there are books that deal with serious human problems (like suffering) and books that describe ancient battles and dynasties. But for all the differences of style and literary types, one finds some central themes. Throughout the Bible, God is revealed in history as generous, eager to save people from bondage and draw them into a relationship. God makes agreements (covenants) with human beings and wants them to respond with trust and obedience, to be a faithful people.

The great variety of literature in the Bible tells us something about the many ways in which God was experienced by biblical people and understood by biblical authors. Scholars may spend their entire lives trying to fathom one particular type of biblical literature—poetry, for example, or ancient history—and still not have a full understanding of the text. As we look at two major aspects of divine purpose as revealed in the Bible, therefore, let us realize that we are dealing in very general terms.

This introductory sketch of God's personality and purpose is meant, in the long run, to stir your interest and encourage further study; for the present, we need only form an elementary understanding of God's personality as it emerged in the life of the people of Israel. The two aspects of the divine personality that are particularly helpful are creation and providence. On the one hand, God is the powerful, transcendent creator of the world who stands, as it were, above and outside human existence. On the other hand, God is interested in history and apparently willing to enter into its unfolding in partnership with people. These two aspects of the divine personality—remote yet intimately involved—are known in theological language as *transcendence* and *immanence*. We need not get distracted by a technical discussion of terms here: suffice it to say that God's personality has been, from the beginning, disclosed in both ways. Jews and Christians need not feel forced to choose between an awesome, powerful being and an intimate partner since God's personality encompasses both possibilities.

As we look at the creative and provident aspects of God's self-disclosure, a word about the chronology of events is in order. The Bible begins with a story about the creation of the world which makes sense chronologically—all good stories begin "once upon a time"—but probably does not reflect the religious reality of the situation. Remember what I said about revelation being rooted in experience. The people whose stories fill the Bible first of all had an *experience* of God as one who yearns for a relationship (the story of Abraham), or as one who hears the cries of the oppressed and acts to liberate a captive people (the story of Moses). That experience was kept alive in ritual celebration and in the constant retelling of events. In fact, the story was circulated in a variety of forms or editions for hundreds of years before it was written down, edited, and spliced together to form what we know today as the Old Testament.

As the stories of the original religious experiences were told and retold, nuances were added, new incidents were woven into the fabric of the narrative, and the life of the community became part of the unfolding of the story of God's revelation. As later generations speculated about God's presence in the world, they brought their experience to that speculation. When they had questions they could not answer from historical documents—the details of the creation of the world, for example—they invented a story based on their experience of God as powerful, sustaining, nurturing, involved, and available. The order of events as found in the Bible, therefore, beginning with creation, is probably *not* accurate. The way the story unfolds in the Bible, however, does have a clear historical flow, and we will follow the biblical chronology because of that feature. The only other thing to keep in mind is this: our purpose here is to get a general understanding of God, not to have a full-scale recital of the history of biblical peoples.

GOD AS CREATOR

The first three chapters of Genesis give us a complex picture of God as creator. We notice that

1. *God masters chaos or creates out of nothing.* Scholars read the creation account in two ways, depending on how they translate Gen. 1:1. In one, God masters primal chaos; in the other, God creates out of nothing. God is the one who can assert creative mastery over the universe.
2. *God creates in both word and deed.* In the first chapter of Genesis, God does not conjure up a spell, but simply says the word and what is spoken happens; in the second chapter of Genesis, God fashions a man from the earth, makes a person from already-existing material.
3. *God says that creation is good.* The world is not an evil place, and the material universe is not to be disparaged. One need not have a dreary attitude toward the world or think of it as a prison; it is seen by God as a good place.
4. *Man and woman are created in God's own image.* People have been made to have dominion over creation, to act as God's representatives in this world.

All these testify to the power and goodness of God. The power of God's word recurs in the Old Testament. "By the word of the Lord the heavens were made," says the psalmist (Ps. 33:6). God's word is connected with revelation and with the law: Psalm 119 is a long meditation on the law replete with references to God's word. Psalm 19 compares the brightness of the sun to the enlightenment brought by God's word in the Torah. God's word is also bound up with prophecy: all the prophets speak God's word and are prophets precisely because "the word of the Lord" came to them and empowered them. In the New Testament, Jesus is described as the preexistent "word of God" and said to be "the word made flesh." Christians believe that Jesus is the Son of God, that he incarnates the creative power of God's word.

The biblical authors tell us about God's goodness, power, and generosity but also explain that the creative act of God was disrupted. The Christian term usually used to describe this disruption is *the Fall*, a falling away from the original intention of creation. The world began as a good thing, but it is not as good as it once was. Something must have happened to account for the fact that God created a paradise, yet people experience the world as a nonparadise. The biblical authors knew from their own experience that something happened because they did not live in a paradise. They knew that life is hard work; that people can be wicked, aggressive, and selfish; and that no matter how much people have, they want more. Biblical writers were able to incorporate these human experiences into their descriptions of the dim beginnings of world history. The experience of the community and their understanding of God shaped the way they explained the beginnings of the world. The story of creation and the Fall belongs to a period usually designated as prehistory, the time for which we have no written records. All ancient peoples had some explanation for the creation of the world and the status of people within that world. When the story of creation was finally written down by the biblical authors, it reflected the experience and beliefs of their own community.

Let's look at some of the ways the Israelites might have seen creation and the presence of evil in the world. Like other peoples of the ancient Near East, they could have reasoned that the gods are like people, both good and bad, which accounts for evil in the world. They could have said, "Life is hard and people are wicked, and that must be God's fault." Neither of these explanations is bad so far as logic goes, and both of them appear in ancient literature written around the same time as the biblical story of creation. They could have said, "Oh, life is not all that bad if you look on the sunny side," and that explanation still appeals to some people. Israel knew from its experience as a community and from God's self-communication that God was good and the created order was good; the Israelites could not, therefore, blame God for the mess of the world. They knew just as well, from experience, that the world was a mess. How could it be explained? The Genesis story accounts for both kinds of experience. In the story in Genesis, God remains good and powerful, and creates people as an act of generosity; evil gets into the world, but not through God's fault. The story tells us three things:

1. People were made in the image of God (they are like God in some way, and God longs for a relationship with them).
2. People, freely, as an act of curiosity and willfulness, chose their own will over God's will and disrupted creation.
3. God promised to restore good relations among them.

To retell the story briefly: God created a man and a woman, gave them everything they could possibly want in terms of comfort and power, and added one more gift, freedom. God wanted them to respond freely, not by force. Now, the biblical authors tell us, this gift of freedom was put to a test in a very direct way. God told them they could eat the fruit of every tree in the garden except one. It is the doctrine of conditional joy, rather like a fairy tale: "You can have the beautiful princess *if* you bring her a magic radish," or "You can have three wishes *if* you bring me the little blue light." According to the Bible, the people failed the test, and in failing it, they acted as we all act. We all know what it is to have someone say, "You can do anything but. . . ." In *The Magician's Nephew* by C. S. Lewis, two children are exploring an underground world where everyone is asleep and the whole atmosphere is mysterious. In the middle of a courtyard they find a little silver bell and a hammer and an inscription that reads:

> *Make your choice, adventurous Stranger;*
> *Strike the bell and bide the danger,*
> *Or wonder, till it drives you mad,*
> *What would have followed if you had.*[3]

Lewis's ditty clarifies the dilemma the biblical author was trying to convey, exquisitely evoking the first problem of human freedom. In religious language we say that the first man and woman were tempted, egged on to do something they were not supposed to do. In the biblical story the man and woman weakened and gave in, and the biblical author says it was because they were tempted by a clever serpent. How can we interpret this story, then? Were the man and woman outsmarted? Were they just weak and curious? Did they sin? Some believers interpret the action of the first man and woman as one of pride and self-deception, others as an expression of the desire of people to set their own limits, be their own God. Whatever the interpretation, their action, their disobedience, changed things—life was no longer lived in a beautiful garden. Painful realities entered into human life: work now included frustration and might be fruitless as well as difficult, birth occurred within a context of pain, and sickness and death became part of human existence. In Christian religious language this moment of separation and alienation is called Original Sin; it is the religious explanation for the facts of life as the biblical authors and the community experienced them.

The story says something about God as creator, that God is powerful and good, and wants people to have good relationships with each other and with the deity. We also learn about the reality of sin: people are capable of it through weakness and willfulness, and it does damage and pulls people in a direction away from God.

Many times in the Bible, sin is explained in terms of direction: people turn away from God or go astray, or follow the wrong leaders or false Gods. Repentance and conversion imply a change of direction, a move back toward God.

Repentance is an important concept throughout the Old Testament. The prophets especially call upon people to remember the covenant and turn back to God. In the New Testament, Jesus calls people to repentance and conversion, which is precisely a change of direction and a turning away from sin.

GOD AS PROVIDENT

In the creation account we learned that things began well but, because of sin, people found themselves in a muddle. God's response to this situation discloses another divine attribute. When people ruined a good situation, God (as all powerful) could have let them die and then could have started over, or could have left them to their own devices. Some explanations about God's relationship with the world argue that God created the world and then left it to itself; some explanations of human life rely on concepts of fate or determinism. The biblical account, however, says something different and extraordinary: God is willing to enter into the muddle and bring the divine creative energy to bear on it without interfering with human freedom. God recreated their good options; when people moved away from God, God was willing to help them find the road back. God moved into the history of these people. God created a world, watched people make a mess of it, and then entered into that mess creatively, fashioning out of it a people, a law, and a way. Christians call God's involvement in the world *providence,* the divine provision for humanity.

Some people have wondered how an all-powerful God relates to people without violating their freedom. God's actions in history come as calls, not demands. The Bible does not usually picture God as manipulative or overbearing, but as interested and compassionate. People are invited to be in partnership with God. The pattern of providence and continuing revelation in the Bible, therefore, can be interpreted as a pattern of call and response. God still initiates the conversation and relationship, but human freedom is intact because people may choose to reject the invitation or to accept it.

The fifth book of the Old Testament, Deuteronomy, contains a summary statement about what God has done for a particular people (26:5–10). It begins by saying, "A wandering Aramean was my father" and goes on to explain what happened to him. He became the father of a great nation. That nation or people was in the course of time welcomed into the land of Egypt, but later made slaves. The passage goes on to say, "And the Egyptians treated us harshly, and afflicted us, and laid upon us hard bondage. . . . Then we cried to the Lord the God of our ancestors, and the Lord heard our voice, saw our affliction, our toil and our oppression and the Lord brought us out of Egypt with a mighty hand and an outstretched arm, with great terror, with signs and wonders . . . and he brought us into this place and gave us this land, a land flowing with milk and honey." Something has happened in the lives of this particular people which reveals how God's providence works. The creation story was about all people, the first people of the human race; it offered an explanation for universal destiny. The summary of God's works in Deuteronomy is about a specific people, a people called by God to be special and to be the bearers of God's self-communication, and to begin the work of restoring what was lost in the Fall.

The Story of Abraham

In Genesis 9 we see that God promised to do something about the havoc people brought upon themselves through disobedience. What God would do is not clear, but there are grounds for anticipation of some action in the future. The first specific idea we get about the divine plan occurs in Genesis 12, when God called Abraham.

The Abraham story has five important elements. First, God's intervention into Abraham's life came with no explanation—it was pure gift, *gratuitous*. Second, Abraham was an old man with an old, childless wife when God told him that he would be the father of a great nation. The story tells us that Abraham found God's promise confusing, funny, and awesome, but that in spite of misgivings, he responded. In religious terms we can say that he responded *in faith*. We might note here that many of the biblical heroes respond to God in faith. Although they initially have many doubts, they finally accept the assurance of God's presence and help in what they are called to do. Third, Abraham did have a son (two of them, in fact, though the first, Ishmael, drops out of this story)[4] and named him Isaac. This child was born when Abraham's wife, Sarah, was old and barren, so a *miraculous element* was involved: God acts with power and demonstrates divine lordship. Fourth, God made a pact with Abraham, a *covenant*. Finally, God *tested* Abraham's faith and obedience by asking him to sacrifice Isaac. Faith and trust in God is not a one-time event, but part of an ongoing relationship.

The word *covenant* occurs repeatedly in the Bible. Covenants spell out the terms of God's relationship with people; they are partnership agreements, contracts. In the modern world, contracts are written down with the terms specified and penalties explained for breaking the agreement. In the ancient world there *were* written contracts, but there were also spoken agreements, which were solemn and sacred. In contracts and covenants there are witnesses to the signing and to the terms. Often covenants were enacted before the gods (who acted as witnesses); all parties bound themselves rigorously to the terms. A covenant, therefore, is a solemn form of the spoken word, a binding and sacred agreement.

The terms of God's covenant with Abraham were clear: God would see that Abraham was the father of a great nation, which God would then bless and protect, and Abraham in turn was to honor God and see that every male member of his family was circumcised as a sign that he belonged to God. A further divine promise was that through Abraham and his descendants the nations of the world would be blessed; the promise was universal as well as particular.

When Abraham agreed to the terms, responded to God's specific step toward partnership with a people, he made it possible for God to do something about the muddle.

The Story of Moses

The Moses story (Exodus) has some parallels to the Abraham story and clear links with it. Abraham was the father of Isaac and grandfather of Jacob. The biblical tradition maintains that Jacob had twelve sons who were the fathers of the twelve tribes of Israel (God changed Jacob's name to Israel). They continued to honor God and to follow the terms of the covenant and so, through them, the covenant between God and Abraham passed down through history and the God of the Hebrews came to be known as the God of Abraham, Isaac, and Jacob. One of Jacob's sons, Joseph (see Genesis 37–50), is the main character in the story of the Hebrews in Egypt, which is where we must go for the Moses story.

The covenant with Abraham occurred some time between 1850 and 1600 B.C.E. (before the common era), and the flight from Egypt under the direction of Moses probably took place between 1250 and 1200 B.C.E. The Hebrews had lived in Egypt, first as welcome guests and finally as slaves, for many generations. Moses enters the story as God's chosen liberator, sent to free the Hebrews and bring them to a new land and a new covenant. We can find some of the same elements in the Moses story that we found in the Abraham story. First of all, according to the biblical authors, God's intervention into Moses's life is *gratuitous*. His birth was no different from any other Hebrew boy's and nothing explains why a hidden providence protected him and eventually selected him as the mediator for the covenant. Second, when Moses first heard God's voice (Exodus 3) he was awestruck and impressed, but also confused and afraid. His decision to return to Egypt to lead people out was his response *in faith* and trust, made in spite of his hesitation about what God wanted him to do. Third, the great events in Egypt—the plagues, the Passover, the Red Sea event (see Exodus 7–15)—were *miraculous*. God acted with power, and the Hebrews and Egyptians saw God's power in those events. Fourth, God made a *covenant* with the whole people at Mount Sinai. Finally, these people were *tested* in the wilderness.[5]

Besides these parallels with the Abraham story, other features of the Moses story stand out. The Hebrew people in bondage in Egypt "cried out" and God "heard them" and determined to help them. Because of the covenant with Abraham, because God promised to protect this people, they had a claim on God and could cry out with reminders of the divine obligation to them. When God responded to the people and sent Moses to liberate them, God said, "I am the God of Abraham, Isaac, and Jacob," thereby showing a continuity between the Mosaic and the Abrahamic covenants.

Three months after they left Egypt, God brought the people to the wilderness at Sinai, and the high point of the Moses story is the covenant made at Sinai. God not only delivered the Israelites, but called them into a partnership agreement. At Sinai, through the giving of covenant law (including the Ten Commandments), the relationship between God and Israel took on a new dimension of particularity. While the people camped below, Moses went up the mountain, "up to God." There God told Moses to say this to the Hebrews: "You have seen what I did to the Egyptians and how I bore you on eagles' wings and brought you to myself. Now therefore, if you will obey my voice and keep my covenant you shall be my own prossession among all peoples; for all the earth is mine, and you shall be to me a kingdom of priests and a holy nation" (Exod. 19:4–5). Moses went down the mountain and gave that message to the people and they responded, "All that the Lord has spoken, we will do" (see Exod. 19 and 24:3). It is clear that the people responded on the basis of their experience of God's liberation. They heard thunder and understood it as the divine voice; they demanded a mediator to interpret God's words for them, and Moses brought them the terms of the contract; they agreed to the terms of the covenant and willingly bound themselves in a relationship with God that required that they keep the commandments.

The People of the Covenant

God entered into history to make these former slaves into a special people, and did so through the covenant. Biblical tradition sees the Law as an act of divine providence enabling Israel to maintain the covenant relationship with God. They had been set free in Egypt by an act of divine justice; the Law was given to help them maintain that freedom and justice within their new society.

The history of Israel from the covenant at Sinai onward is one of keeping and violating the covenant and of God's continued intervention to restore a proper relationship. People read the Bible for many reasons, one of which is that it discloses parts of the divine personality; the Bible also shows a deep understanding of human nature and conveys the two-steps-forward-one-step-backward kind of progress most people experience in life. Even with God as their protector and guide, the people of Israel continually went astray. Why? The story in Genesis about the first man and woman helps explain the tension people find themselves in: people are attracted to good (because they were made in the image of God, who is good) and to evil (because of their sinfulness). Israel's experience demonstrates that those attractions can be equally strong, that human beings are easily confused. Is good more attractive than wickedness? The Bible is not clear on this question, and the history of Israel bears out the ambivalence. Israel's history is not unique. All human history reveals similar patterns of fidelity and betrayal.

The rest of the history of Israel builds on the same themes. During the first two centuries in the promised land, the people of Israel led a varied existence, both politically and religiously. When they were in trouble and cried out, the Lord sent help by way of heroes and heroines (see Judges). As the small band of nomadic slaves brought out of Egypt grew into a larger people and settled into the land, they were torn between wanting to maintain their uniqueness (as God's people) and their desire to be like their neighbors. The story of Israel's move toward kingship is ambivalent. For a number of reasons, and with mixed results, Israel solidified into a kingdom that reached its zenith of organization and power under David and Solomon around the year 1000 B.C.E. David's son Solomon was the last king to rule over a united Israel. For political reasons (that had theological significance for Israel), the twelve tribes split into two separate kingdoms: ten tribes in the north (called Israel) and two in the south (called Judah). Although early Israel felt deep ambivalence about the kingship of David (as a dethroning of the divine king), the later biblical tradition generally sees it as an important part of God's plan.

The two kingdoms did not last. Why not? The prophets had claimed that unfaithfulness to the covenant would lead to destruction, and later biblical writers saw that they had been correct. Prophets were those who spoke for God in some way, especially in terms of the covenant. The word *prophet* comes from the Hebrew word *nabi,* which, perhaps, means "called by God." As people neglected their contractual obligations and ignored their God, the prophets tried, often poetically and with a sense of desperate urgency, to get people to remember their relationship with God. The kingdom of Israel lasted from about 922 to 732 B.C.E., when it fell to the Assyrians. Prophets such as Amos and Hosea had warned people in the northern kingdom that God would punish them for their infidelity, but, according to the Bible, they paid no heed and were destroyed. The kingdom of Judah lasted from about 922 to 587 B.C.E., when it was destroyed by the Babylonians and its people carried off into exile. Again, prophets, including Jeremiah and Isaiah, had warned them, urging them to return to the covenant obligations, but with no success.

The People in Exile

What is the relationship between God and an exiled people? During and after the exile, many Jews looking at the grim events of history tended to see their hardships as punishment for their sins. The exile was not, for them, a sign that God had forgotten the covenant, but a sign of God's care. The exile was a punishment for disobedience, a purification. The word of the prophets—before, during, and after the exile—helped the Jews understand their experience. We can see clearly here the interrelationship between historical experience and ways a group understood God's role in their lives. In all of Israel's history and in the Bible there is a connection between the Jews' historical experience, their self-understanding, and their perceptions about God. Even when things were at their worst—when the people were in exile in Babylon—prophets continued to speak God's word. When the people wondered what would happen to them after the exile, the prophets had visions of a renewed Israel where the original purposes of the Abrahamic covenant would be fulfilled and where Israel would become a universal blessing to all nations. Thus, around 537 B.C.E., when a small group was returned to Palestine, many Jews felt they were being brought back and given another chance, a fresh start. They would never again have a kingdom, or much political power, but they still had the covenant. Their history from their return onward is one of domination by foreign powers—Persians, Greeks, and Romans. During one brief period (143–63 B.C.E.; see Chapter 2) the Jews were in control of their political lives, but in 63 B.C.E., Pompey, a Roman general, captured Jerusalem and the Romans were in control of the country when Jesus was born.

When we look at the Hebrew Bible we can find books that tell these stories in much more elaborate detail (see Appendix 2). The books of the Torah and the Prophets tell us about Israel's history and prophetic experience. The Writings fill in another dimension of Israel's experience of God. The Psalms, a magnificent, poetic prayerbook containing hymns for almost every occasion and feeling; the so-called Wisdom literature with its philosophical reflections (for example, Job); moral maxims (for example, Proverbs); the erotic poetry of the Song of Songs (or Song of Solomon); the apocalyptic visions of Daniel—all indicate an extraordinarily rich experience of God's action and presence in their lives. All of these books and most of this experience were used later by Christians to explain Jesus. For the time being, however, it is enough to know the main outline of the story, to realize that it is inexhaustibly rich and amenable to a wide variety of interpretations, and to remember that, according to the Bible, God did not abandon the Jewish people.

CONCLUSION

This chapter has set forth the ancient context and foundation of Christianity, along with some basic concepts. We have seen what revelation means and noted that the Bible is a record of God's revelation. Since both Christians and Jews look to the Bible as the record of God's revelation, we looked there to find out some of its basic perceptions of God. We found that the God of Jews and Christians is the powerful, transcendent creator of the world. More important, however, we found that God did not leave people to their own devices but remained interested in them even when they made a mess of God's good creative work. We have focused on the Abraham and Moses stories in the history of Israel as demonstrations of divine providence: the initial promise, the covenant with Abraham, the rescue of Abraham's descendants, and the covenant at Sinai all disclose God's personality. We have seen that being in a covenant relationship with God did not mean that all went smoothly or that people were never tempted to do anything wrong. On the contrary, people, even though they were in a relationship with God, continued to go astray and follow the wrong paths.

An important insight from the Bible is that God continues to be interested in a people even when they fail to keep the covenant. God judges them and redeems them; God's self-communication is revealed in an ongoing history of invitation and response.

CHAPTER 1 NOTES

[1] Revelation is an enormous problem, one that is never solved. For a look at some of the issues, see Avery Dulles, *Models of Revelation* (New York: Doubleday, 1983). The complexity of the problem is exemplified right now by some of the questions the women's movement raises about biblical language. The Bible consistently speaks about God as "He," generally contains stories about men, and is addressed to "men" or to "brothers" and "sons." Some women have no problem with this language because they believe "man" to be a generic term, used to denote both men and women. Other women have argued that the language of the Bible is sexist and its biases patriarchal. See, for example, Rosemary Ruether, *Sexism and God-talk* (Boston: Beacon Press, 1983); see also Phyllis Trible, *God and the Rhetoric of Sexuality* (Philadelphia: Fortress Press, 1978). Here's the question: Is male God-language *revealed*? Must one understand God as masculine? Or can one change the language? Or add new insights from extrabiblical literature? As feminist theologians pose the questions, the whole theology of revelation becomes a lively and practical issue.

[2] Inspiration, like revelation, is a very complex problem both theologically and practically. Almost every Christian group has its own history of understanding and explaining it. See, for example, Kern Tobert Trembath, *Evangelical Theories of Biblical Inspiration* (New York: Oxford University Press, 1987). Care should be exercised in talking about it, and the student is urged to consult standard reference works like *The Interpreter's Dictionary of the Bible* or *The Jerome Biblical Commentary* just to get some idea of the range of the problem.

[3] (New York: Macmillan, 1955), p. 51.

[4] See p. 5 of this chapter. Muslims believe themselves to be descendants of Ishmael, the son born to Abraham and his wife's maidservant, Hagar. One of the ritual actions of the Islamic pilgrimage to Mecca (undertaken once in a Muslim's lifetime) is to visit the place in the desert where God promised to make Ishmael a great nation (Genesis 21).

[5] Almost immediately after accepting the covenant, the people who agreed to keep it broke it. Furthermore (as reported in stories in Numbers), their lack of faith finally resulted in their not being permitted to enter the promised land; instead, they were forced to wander in the desert for forty years.

SUGGESTIONS FOR FURTHER READING

1. You can do yourself a great favor by leafing through *The Illustrated Dictionary and Concordance of the Bible* (New York: Macmillan, 1986). It is an elegant, comprehensive reference book, a one-volume encyclopedia with maps, photographs (hundreds in color), and outlines. It can be used like a dictionary.

2. Form criticism, understanding of scriptural passages through an analysis of their structural forms, is a relatively new and important interpretive skill, one that cannot be ignored as we try to understand the Bible. For a clear and well-illustrated introduction to form criticism, one that has easy-to-understand examples, cartoon illustrations (by Bill Woodman), and straight language, see Gerhard Lohfink, *The Bible, Now I Get It: A Form-Criticism Handbook* (Garden City, N.Y.: Doubleday, 1979). The author argues that form criticism is not just for experts but is for everyone and that a basic understanding of it is not a luxury but a fundamental tool for understanding Scripture.

3. For some sense of the geography of the Bible, see the National Geographic Book Service, *Everyday Life in Bible Times* (Washington, D.C.: National Geographic Society, 1967), or *The Harper Atlas of the Bible* (New York: Harper & Row, 1987).

4. For a clear, readable treatment of the whole of the Old Testament, see Bernhard W. Anderson, *Understanding the Old Testament*, 4th ed. (Englewood Cliffs, N.J.: Prentice-Hall, 1986).

♦

CHAPTER 2

THE CONTEXT FOR
AND LIFE OF JESUS

Jesus was born into a volatile political situation and a complex religious milieu. The Jews had been exiled to Babylon in 587 B.C.E. after the Babylonians
destroyed the southern kingdom (Judah); they remained in exile until 537 B.C.E.
When the Jews returned from Babylon to Palestine, they were faced with problems of survival and of interpreting the meaning of the exile. Their attempts to
resolve those problems had a bearing on how they perceived Jesus's life and
teaching. Their interpretations of the exile and their reactions to hellenization
were bound up with renewed seriousness about the Law, so Jesus's relationship
to the Law was also very important to them. Jewish ideas about the kingdom of
God along with the divided political situation within Judaism itself made gaining acceptance difficult for any powerful preacher: no matter what the preacher
said, there was always a different but equally valid interpretation. Jesus's life and
teaching, therefore, must be understood against this complicated background.
Similarly, writings about Jesus (and early Christians) have to be read in light of
the religious and political situation of the times. One of the important questions
for early Christian interpreters was where Jesus fit with regard to Jewish expectations. In this chapter we will see what those expectations were, where they
came from, and how they were reinterpreted by early Christian writers to fit the
life and message of Jesus.

JEWISH INTERPRETATION OF THE EXILE

The covenant at Sinai was the major event that shaped the lives and understanding of the Jewish people. It not only provided them with their specific identity as God's people, but gave them a perspective from which to interpret their history. Whatever happened to them, they could look back to the covenant, to the basis of their relationship with God, and find a way to explain it. What did the Jews think about the exile? And what do you think their captors thought of the Jews and their religion? How do you think the belief that they worshiped the one true God and were God's people looked in light of their defeat and exile? It is not hard to imagine that many people wondered just what had happened: Had God deserted them? Was God no longer interested in the Jews? Psalm 137 tells us how the Jews themselves felt: "By the waters of Babylon, there we sat down and wept when we remembered Zion" (137:1).

It must have been tempting, even for the Jews, to think that God had lost interest in them. Because of the covenant, however, and because of their long experience of God's faithfulness and mercy, the Jews did *not* interpret the exile as a sign of divine abandonment. In fact, they interpreted it in just the opposite way. When they reflected on their dislocation and their return to Palestine, they saw a sign of God's continuing interest in the covenant relationship. God was, indeed, bound up with them, repeatedly warning them and reminding them of the terms of the covenant. God continually sent messengers, the prophets, to call the people back to observance of the Law and to a better relationship. Only because they would not listen and because there was no other way, God was constrained to punish them, to uproot and replant them. Their sinfulness, their "going astray," meant that they had to be redirected. The exile was seen as the means God used to cleanse the people, forcing them to develop a clearer vision of the relationship between God and Israel. When they were brought back from Babylon (in 537 B.C.E.), it was with a renewed sense of obligation to be loyal and obedient to the commandments.

How did they intend to be God's faithful people in the future? How would they be true to the one God in their belief, worship, and everyday life? The answer—present in the terms of the covenant—lay in keeping the Law. Since they were no longer one people in one land with one ruler, the Law provided internal coherence for them. They had learned that keeping the Law was sometimes difficult when they were surrounded and tempted by a foreign culture. Their renewed efforts to keep the Law, therefore, were coupled with an intense effort to keep themselves apart from influences that might seduce them or force them away from the Law. This meant, in effect, that the Jews had a strong interest in keeping themselves separate from other people. They might be forced to live under foreign political domination, but they could resist any attempts at religious domination; by obedience to the Law they could refuse to intermarry and become part of another culture.

When the Jews were restored to Palestine in 537 B.C.E. they were subject to a number of different foreign powers. The most serious threat to their resolution to remain faithful observers of the Law, however, occurred during the Hellenistic period.[1]

HELLENIZATION AND THE JEWS

The conquests of Alexander the Great spread Greek ideas and culture to the Near East and well into Asia. Greek influence continued to spread after Alexander's death (in 323 B.C.E.), and the Hellenistic era is usually thought to have ended politically with the conquest of Alexandria by the Romans in the first century B.C.E. During the Hellenistic era the descendants of Alexander's generals hoped to consolidate their empire, unifying it in language, customs, law, and philosophy. They hoped to do this by insinuating their culture and practices into the lands they conquered, and by pursuing a policy of intermarriage with the peoples they ruled. Their policies were thus in direct conflict with the Jewish resolve to keep themselves separate.

One can imagine that some of the Greek ideas and philosophy must have seemed appealing to some of the Jews. The impulse of Hellenism was felt in Israel as everywhere else. The Jews continued to keep themselves apart from some of its demands, but at the same time they began to disagree about how far they *could* go in accommodating themselves to this new cultural influence. Could a Jew be true to the Law and study Greek philosophy? Could a young Jewish boy participate in the athletic games at the local Greek-styled gymnasium? Could Jews allow *some* statues of Greek gods in their towns? Issues like these divided the Jews not only in theory but in practice. Some Jews felt that they could enter into the spirit of the Greek culture and maintain their Jewish identity; others believed that any participation in Hellenistic civilization violated the covenant and displeased God. A strong opposition party, the predecessors of the Pharisees, arose against hellenization and those Jews who favored it. The party argued that Greek customs were foreign and idolatrous and that no Jew could legitimately participate in them.

Once aversion to hellenization took the form of a party, the arguments against Greek ways had a more political character. The opposition to hellenization grew stronger and more vocal; in the minds of Greek officials, at least, it began to appear that things could not be resolved without a test of power. In 168 B.C.E., Antiochus IV, whose rule extended over Jerusalem, from Palestine to Syria and eastward to the Euphrates, and who had already offended the Jews by selling the office of high priest (in direct violation of Jewish practice and law), began a campaign to destroy the religion of the Jews. He issued an edict that forbade Jews to practice circumcision, to celebrate any festivals, or to keep the Sabbath. All copies of the Torah were to be destroyed and the Jewish temple turned into a Greek temple. A statue of the Greek god Zeus was put up in the Jerusalem temple and Jews were forced to worship the pagan gods.

Even the Jews who had favored hellenization found the policies of Antiochus IV abominable. Opposition to Antiochus solidified behind the leadership of Judas Maccabeas and his four brothers, who revolted against Syrian domination. The revolt and their victory, which is recorded in the first book of Maccabees, is celebrated each year in the Jewish feast of Hanukkah. The struggle for religious freedom turned into a battle for political freedom. From 143 to 63 B.C.E. the Jews retained political control of Israel. But in 63 B.C.E., the Roman general Pompey captured Jerusalem and began Roman domination of the Jews.

At the time of Jesus, Herod was the regional governor of the Jews, picked by the Romans. He collaborated with the Romans and was despised by the Jews. The Romans had always allowed the Jews religious freedom, but were beginning to find them a political nuisance. It was possible, the Romans thought, that the Jews might be secret political allies of the Syrians, an alliance that would constitute a serious threat to the Romans, while either the Syrians or the Jews alone would not. Remember that the Jews had a stake in maintaining their own identity, in refusing to intermarry and to take on customs of the conquering power. Since they had maintained their own identity, they had not been absorbed into the empire. Such political autonomy, therefore, made them appear dangerous to the Romans. It was into this Jewish world ruled by Romans that Jesus was born.

JEWISH HOPES FOR A KINGDOM OF GOD

To understand fully the religious context into which Jesus was born, you must understand that faithfulness to the Law was bound up with popular Jewish expectation that God would somehow and some time act decisively in their behalf.[2] God had rescued them from the land of Egypt and had restored them to Israel after the exile. Thus they had reason to expect that God would continue to act for them. Whereas most Jews searched the Law for guidance about everyday behavior, some searched in other parts of Scripture for what God might do in the future. A strong vocal minority centered their hopes on the concept of a *kingdom of God,* perhaps because it recaptured the old ideal of a chosen people in a promised land under a divinely sanctioned king. However it was understood, the kingdom of God became a slogan for what would happen in a new age. The coming of the kingdom would mark the establishment of God's rule forever, everywhere.

Within this general understanding of divine victory, however, there were differences of opinion. Some Jews believed the Messiah would be a wise and ideal king who would establish justice all over the world. Some thought a Messiah-king would surely be of the Davidic line, since David had been the greatest of the ancient kings. Some believed that the establishment of the kingdom of God would mean Jewish political prestige throughout the world: Israel would be the most powerful nation on earth, ruling over everyone.

As the Jews became more threatened by events, especially in the second and first centuries before the common era, popular beliefs about the kingdom of God began to take on more militant aspects. During this time a literature and outlook called *apocalyptic* began to flourish. Since Jews were involved in crucial political and military struggles, their ideas about the Messiah and the kingdom of God incorporated more political and military expectations. Some people began to see the kingdom of God not so much as an ideal kingdom of righteousness but as some kind of powerful event. The kingdom of God began to be tied up with the expectation that God would perform some great act. Since the world was in such a mess, God would have to bring about a complete transformation of people and of the world.

The second and first centuries before the common era were times in which the influence of religious dualism began to be felt and an apocalyptic tone heard: people began to look at the world as a place under the influence of evil powers that could not be defeated by human powers alone. To defeat these evil powers, God would have to intervene and conquer them with divine power. People saw the world as a battleground between the forces of good and evil; they believed the universe was divided between the kingdom of God (whom they hoped was coming to the rescue) and the kingdom of Satan (whom they believed was now in power). The day was surely coming, they thought, when God would destroy the power of Satan and master the evil that abounded.

During the two centuries before the birth of Jesus, an enormous body of literature developed about the coming of the kingdom and the overthrow of the demonic powers. There was a popular concept of what would happen. The world, dominated by evil powers, would be a place of great suffering and hardship until God rose up and overthrew the kingdom of Satan. In this mood, many ideas about the Messiah focused on military conquest. The Messiah might be wise, but most of all he would be a powerful warrior-king who could conquer evil and begin the age of bliss.

THE JEWS DIVIDED

Judaism at the time of Jesus's birth was not monolithic, but varied, especially in attitudes toward Roman domination and in expectations about the Messiah. There were probably about 500,000 Jews in Palestine at the time of Jesus, divided into many different groups. Descriptions of four of them will give you some idea of the situation.[3]

The Sadducees

The Sadducees were the small aristocratic ruling class. In modern terms they might be called the Establishment. They were wealthy conservatives who kept the Torah strictly, allowed no doctrinal innovations, and were strongly associated with the temple. They controlled the office of high priest and held a domi-nant position in the Jewish governing body, the Sanhedrin. Because of their political power over the Jewish community, they were the Jews the Roman pol-iticians dealt with. Because the Sadducees were wealthy and established, they tended to deal with the Romans in a polite way. They were political collabora-tionists who were willing to adapt to Roman rule because the status quo worked in their favor. In terms of their religious beliefs, the Sadducees thought the Torah (the Law, the first five books of the Bible) the single most important religious text and were not, therefore, interested in apocalyptic literature or Jew-ish tradition. It is not altogether clear what they expected in a Messiah, but it is safe to assume that they did *not* expect a Palestinian peasant from Nazareth.

The Pharisees

The Pharisees (approximately 6,000) were made up of artisans and mer-chants, descended from the party that opposed Greek ideas at the time of Anti-ochus. In order to keep the Jews faithful to the Law and away from any foreign influence, they were inclined to extend the Law to every phase of life and insist on perfect observance. They were liberal in that they constantly applied the Torah to new situations and built up a whole new tradition of interpretation. The Pharisees associated not so much with priests but with lay people, with scholars and teachers. They believed that every decision in life could be governed by the Torah, and they developed a system of elaborate interpretation (which later became the Mishnah and Talmud). They did not approve of political col-laboration with the Romans and desired separatism. They accepted as authori-tative the prophetic and other writings of the Bible, which the Sadducees did not accept, and incorporated some of the apocalyptic notions of the time into their religious understanding. Since they were not as interested in political mat-ters and were not established economically like the Sadducees, they had differ-ent expectations of a Messiah. The Pharisees were more religious than political, and their opinion of the future of Israel was a religious one. The Messiah, for them, would probably be a religious leader and teacher who perfectly observed the Law and who could lead people to repentance and the power of the Torah.

The Essenes

The Essenes (approximately 4,000) were disenchanted ascetics and apoca-lyptic visionaries who withdrew from general society to form communes in the desert where they waited for the Messiah and the destruction of the Romans. We know something about this group because of the discovery of the Dead Sea Scrolls, documents of the ancient Essene desert community of Qumran. Like the Pharisees, the Essenes had been part of the revolt against Greek customs, and their protest finally took the form of complete withdrawal from society.

They lived by themselves in the wilderness, preparing for the coming of the kingdom of God. Their expectation was apocalyptic. They believed that the end of the world was near and that their lives should be lived in perfect obedience to God in the short time remaining. They believed that God was about to begin the messianic kingdom on earth and would form a new covenant with them. The new covenant and the Messiah would be bound up with the defeat of the Romans and with the promise of eternal life. They believed they had been called by God into the desert to be recipients of the new covenant. Thus they called themselves the community of the new covenant and thought they were the true Israel.

The Zealots

The Zealots were a small band of underground activists who expected another armed uprising against the Romans in Israel. In modern terms they were potential guerrilla warriors, collecting arms and soldiers for an impending struggle. They looked on the Romans as enemies to be overthrown and expected the Messiah to be a warrior-king who would lead them into battle against the Romans.

The common people, who were the bulk of the Jewish population, were variously influenced by these and other groups, and by apocalyptic literature. These people probably had a number of different ideas of what a Messiah should be, and biblical authors had drawn *some* ordinary people into messianic expectation in a special way by emphasizing God's concern for the *anawim*, the lowly and downtrodden people to whom the Messiah would eventually appear (Amos 2:7, Isa. 61:1). Most Jews in Palestine at the time of Jesus were not associated with any particular group. As one interpreter concludes, the "majority of Jews were the ordinary peasants of Israel, who were in general lukewarm about religion."[4]

SUMMARY OF THE CONTEXT

The Jews saw the covenant as the central event of their lives; it provided the central motif for their interpretation of history. The most important part of the covenant was the keeping of the commandments. In order to avoid foreign corruption of their practices and beliefs, the Jews held themselves apart and maintained religious and ethnic purity. The Jews were looking for God to enter into history in a radical and transforming way, for a Messiah who would defeat the powers of evil, and for the establishment of a new kingdom. Finally, the Jews had differing expectations about the Messiah. Some thought he should be a warrior-king, others a strict observer of the Torah, others that he should be a man of the temple, and still others expected a revolutionary or the one who would usher in the end of the age. When Jesus came, those who became Christians perceived that he was none of these, that he did not at all fit into the expectations of the time, but they claimed that he was the Messiah nevertheless.

THE LIFE OF JESUS

Jesus was born into the situation described above. Scholars generally agree that he was born in 4 B.C.E., but they disagree about the date of his death; some say he died in 30 C.E. and others in 33 C.E. He is not mentioned in non-Christian literature until the end of the first century C.E.,[5] and when he is mentioned, references to him are vague. Most of what we know about Jesus was written down by Christians, and most of the New Testament material was not written until at least thirty-five years after his death. The earliest Gospel, Mark, was probably not written until about 70 C.E.; Matthew and Luke were both composed about 85 C.E.; and John was probably not written until sometime between 80 and 100 C.E.

There is no one story of Jesus; each of the Gospels has a different idea about him. We could, however, piece together a story based on reading all four Gospels. Jesus was born in Bethlehem during the reign of Herod the Great, probably around 4 B.C.E. He was born into obscurity, and some traditions assert that he was conceived through the Holy Spirit (that his mother's pregnancy was a direct act of God and a miracle), and that he was born of a virgin named Mary (who had not had intercourse with her husband Joseph before her pregnancy).

Jesus grew up in a small town, Nazareth, where he was the son of a carpenter. Whether or not he had any education or was ever part of a particular religious group within Judaism, we do not know. A few years before his death, perhaps somewhere between 27 and 29 C.E., Jesus was drawn to the preaching of John the Baptist, a Jewish preacher calling people to repent and believe that the kingdom of God was at hand. John the Baptist embodied some of the apocalyptic and messianic hopes of the time and was, according to Luke, a cousin of Jesus. The writers of the Gospels understood John as one sent to prepare the way for Jesus, to attract those with messianic hopes and then point them to Jesus.

John baptized Jesus in the Jordan River, an event of great significance for the gospel writers. They interpreted Jesus's baptism as the time when Jesus was anointed as Messiah: according to them, the heavens opened, the Holy Spirit descended on Jesus, and God said, "This is my beloved Son." In the Old Testament, the Spirit's presence indicated a special calling or mission. It is clear from the Gospels that Jesus spent some time in a special ministry around Galilee and northern Palestine, where he was renowned for his teaching and powers of healing. Pharisees and Sadducees sought him out to ask questions and were astonished at the depth of his answers. He was, apparently, a threat to both groups and a disappointment to the Zealots. We know nothing about his relationship to the Essenes. Like John, he preached the coming of the kingdom of God and called people to repent. The significance of his words and actions was not always clear. Even his close friends and disciples did not always understand his mission. Still, he attracted crowds and had many followers.

For reasons clear only to himself, he was determined to go up to Jerusalem and preach there. His friends warned him against this because he was not in favor with the authorities there, but he believed that his mission called him to Jerusalem. We might note the similarity between Jesus, Abraham, and Moses: All had intense religious experiences and felt called by God to radical action. The people of Jerusalem welcomed him, and some of them may even have been drawn to him as the Messiah, but within a week he was arrested, accused of blasphemy and sedition, tried, and executed. He celebrated the Passover with his disciples one night and the next day was flogged, mocked, and sent back and forth between Pontius Pilate and Herod as a strange and interesting prisoner; he was then crucified by the Roman officers stationed in Jerusalem.

After he died his body was sealed in a tomb with a great stone in front of it. His followers were stunned and afraid. The Gospels affirm that three days after his death, however, the tomb was empty. Some people said that his disciples stole the body and were going to claim that Jesus had risen from the dead. His followers, however, said that they did not steal the body, but that Jesus in fact had risen from the dead and appeared to some of them. The resurrection of Jesus was the sign to his followers that he was the chosen one of God, the Messiah. The early preaching about Jesus was simple: Jesus, who was crucified, has been raised from the dead; repent and believe that he is Lord and Messiah.

THE ACCOUNT OF JESUS IN THE NEW TESTAMENT

The New Testament is the Christian holy book. It contains twenty-seven books, some about the life of Jesus, others about practical problems within the young Christian community; it ends with an apocalyptic vision, a Christian version of the end of the world. Taken together, these books are the canonical literature of Christianity: they are considered to be inspired by God. Most of what we know about Jesus comes to us from the Gospels; much of what we know about the early Christians comes to us from the Epistles. The Book of Revelation is in a class by itself; it is representative of an apocalyptic consciousness and was probably written during a severe persecution of the Christian churches.

The Gospels

The Gospels (the first four books of the New Testament) are not biographical materials in any sense of the word. They are, rather, specific reflections on the life, death, and resurrection of Jesus written by people who were mainly interested in the last few years (or even months) of his life. They all reflect the perspective of faith: the gospel writers believed that Jesus was the Messiah, and that he had been crucified in Jerusalem and had risen from the dead. They based their perspective of Jesus on their belief in his resurrection, and they shaped the material available to them about his life according to that belief and to the needs of their audience.

No one gospel contains a complete, objective account of the life, death, and resurrection of Jesus. Each gospel was written from a specific perspective and used the material about Jesus to emphasize particular things about him. The first three gospels—Mark, Matthew, and Luke—are similar in content and tell many of the same stories about Jesus. If you put these gospels in parallel columns you can see how similar they are. Because they can be seen together, they are called *synoptic* (from the Greek for "seeing together"). The style and content of the synoptic Gospels is different from that of the fourth gospel, John.

The Gospel of Mark is the shortest and probably the earliest gospel. It presents Jesus as the Son of God tragically misunderstood by his followers, and its picture of Jesus has an apocalyptic edge: he expects the end of the age to come soon. In the Gospel of Mark, Jesus is pictured as *a Messiah who must suffer.* Jesus is clearly the Messiah, but he does not conform to any of the expectations of some groups; he is not a warrior-king or a revolutionary, but a man with power to work miracles, the Son of God, who must suffer and die. The Resurrection is a sign of his power over death. In Mark the powers of evil (demons being exorcised) recognize Jesus before people do. People expected God to establish his kingdom by overthrowing the powers of evil. Jesus, in Mark, has the power to do that and the demons see that their reign is about to end.

The Gospel of Matthew sees Jesus as *the new Moses,* the giver of the new law. Jesus, for Matthew, is the fulfillment of the biblical prophecies; for many of Jesus's sayings and actions Matthew finds a parallel in the Old Testament. All the expectations about where the Messiah would be born, how he would enter Jerusalem, and what he would do are used by Matthew to explain Jesus. The parallels between Jesus and Moses are strong in this Gospel: Moses gave the people the old law from Mount Sinai, Jesus delivers the new law in the Sermon on the Mount. The main emphasis in Matthew is on God's generosity to people manifested in Jesus and the kingdom. Human beings are to respond to that generosity by loving one another joyfully.

The Gospel of Luke and the Book of Acts should be read together as the first conscious history of the Christian movement. Scholars agree that the same author wrote both books. Jesus, for Luke, is a merciful savior who grants forgiveness to those who repent. There is a special focus on Jesus's compassion and tenderness. Luke emphasizes *universality*—Jesus came for everyone, not just for the Jews—in his account of Jesus's work and message; Luke traces the geneaology of Jesus back to Adam (the father of the human race) rather than back to Abraham (the father of the Jewish people) as Matthew does. Luke has many stories about the poor and downcast; in his view Jesus relates positively to the Samaritans (a despised people) and gives women a place of importance.[6] The great parable of forgiveness, the parable of the prodigal son, is found only in Luke. In the Resurrection, God reveals Jesus as the one who brings mercy for all. The message of Jesus is to be taken to the ends of the earth. The Book of Acts takes up the theme of the universal mission of the Christians and will be discussed in the next chapter.

The Gospel of John differs from the synoptics in organization, style, and content. John presents the *mystery* of Jesus, who is like other people but above them in some way. John focuses on the eternal origin and divine nature of Jesus. The gospel begins with Jesus as the preexistent word of God—an important concept when you remember that the world was created through God's *word*. John says the word through whom the world was made had now been made flesh. Jesus was more powerful than death even before his resurrection: the story about Jesus raising Lazarus from the dead is found only in John. Remember that many Jews believed that in order to establish the kingdom, God would have to enter the world in some radical, transforming way. The Gospel of John says Jesus is God become a man, God entering the world in a radical, transforming way. John also structures his gospel differently. Some interpreters say the Gospel of John contains two books, a book of *signs* (John 1–12; see, for example, the miracle at Cana, 2:1–12) and a book of *glory* (John 12–21; see, for example, the farewell discourse, 17:1–26).

The Epistles

The other literature found in the New Testament is in the form of a series of letters. There are twenty-one letters in the New Testament; at least nine of the major ones were written by the apostle Paul. The Epistles are not about the life of Jesus as the Gospels are. They reflect the life, questions, and conflicts of the early community, and they show a developing theology or reflection about Jesus and his mission. The Resurrection is central to them as it is to the Christian message as a whole, as a sign of God's action and a vindication of Jesus's life and work. It was the Resurrection that enabled Jesus's followers to understand him as the Messiah and Lord, and the Resurrection provided the key to his authority—his teachings and his miracles all pointed to his power over death and his divinity. Death and the Resurrection make Jesus the Savior. His power to forgive sins and to restore the created order are tied up with his victory over death. And the Resurrection shows people that God does not mean for death to be the end of things, but indicates that God calls people to fellowship even beyond death. Paul said that nothing can separate the believer from the love of God, not even death.

The Book of Revelation

Revelation, the last book of the New Testament, pictures the end of the world and is written in highly symbolic language. Its author had visions of God's merciful government of all creation, and wrote this book to sustain Christian hope during severe persecution. It has functioned to sustain Christian hope ever since. It is not an easy book to read because it is full of symbols, numerical calculations, strange beasts, and other apocalyptic figures. Many contemporary Christians use it to predict the end of the world, to speculate about what Jesus will do when he comes back to judge people, though its probable purpose, like the rest of the New Testament, is to reveal the gospel and to inspire Christians to check their lives and see whether they are living according to the gospel.[7]

JESUS AND JEWISH EXPECTATION

Some Christians think that Jesus was so clearly the Messiah that no one could fail to recognize him as such. People who believe this often see Jews as stubborn, blind, or deprived of their chance for salvation. This hostile interpretation of Judaism, which has been present in Christianity from the beginning, has led to a long and painful history of atrocities against the Jewish people. Since the time of Jesus, Christian history has been marred by serious crimes against the Jews, often perpetrated in the name of religion.[8] A necessary step in the understanding of Christianity is a better appreciation of Judaism.

Christians who see Jews as a "problem" might be surprised to learn that Jesus has been a continual puzzle for Jews. Medieval Jews tended to picture Jesus as an apostate Jew, a man who had lost his faith; nineteenth-century Jewish scholars had an image of Jesus as a great ethical teacher. They could not agree whether he claimed to be the Messiah or not, though modern scholars agree that Jesus did *not* make that claim for himself. Today, some Jewish scholars study the Gospels as sources for studying Jewish life in the first century and find parallels between the life and work of Jesus and that of other charismatic Jewish leaders at the time. The issue of whether or not Jesus was the Messiah, therefore, is not the only point of discussion between Jews and Christians, though it is still an important one.

When Jesus lived and died, some people were expecting a Messiah. Christians believed that Jesus had been raised from the dead and was the promised Messiah. Belief in the Resurrection was not a matter of evidence, it was a matter of faith: if one did not first accept the Resurrection, the messianic claims made no sense. Jews who did not accept Jesus as the Messiah had good reasons for not doing so. Not everyone, after all, was expecting a Messiah. Jesus's life and teaching, therefore, were of no interest to some, and unconvincing to others. Insofar as Jewish history was full of God's action on their behalf and also full of hope for a *decisive act of God*, there were, in some quarters, hopes for a Messiah. Whether Jesus lived up to those hopes is precisely the dividing issue. The earliest Christians were also rooted in Jewish history. Jesus was a Jew. His apostles were Jewish—they knew the biblical stories about Abraham, Isaac, and Jacob; they understood deeply the meaning of the covenant and the experience of the exile. Their belief in the resurrection of Jesus enabled them to believe that he was the

Messiah. When they preached about Jesus they said that with Jesus a *new history*—built upon the old, but also different from it—began.

It is important to see what this means. The Jews believe that history has a purpose, that God has acted and will continue to act in it. Christians claim that history has a purpose, that God has acted in it so decisively in Jesus that a *new* history has begun. Jews are still waiting for the messianic age to begin because they do not accept the Christian claim that Jesus was the promised one of God. For Jews, many of the messianic promises were *not* fulfilled in Jesus: in Isaiah (11:6–7), for example, it says that people will live together in peace when the Messiah comes, that the lion will lie down with the lamb; those events did not happen with Jesus. In that way, Jesus was a *scandal* to messianic expectations. After his death nothing changed: the Jews were *not* restored to political power; Jesus did *not* meet the personal qualifications of messianic hope because he was not righteous (according to the Pharisees); and Jesus's death on a cross made him unacceptable to Jews because the Torah says that a man hanged upon a tree is cursed by God (Deut. 21:23).

Christians and Jews interpret the Bible differently. For Christians, Jesus shakes up the old order of things and makes it possible to see everything that went before him as pointing essentially toward *him*. For Jews, the events of the Bible do not point toward Jesus at all, but beyond him to a future Messiah. The differences in interpretation are profound: for the Jews the Hebrew Bible points toward something still to come, but for Christians it sets the stage and provides an explanation for someone who has already arrived.

Look, for example, at Jeremiah 31:31–33: "'Behold the days are coming,' says the Lord, 'when I will make a new covenant with Israel . . . not like the covenant which I made with their ancestors when I took them by the hand to bring them out of the land of Egypt . . . but I will put my law within them, and I will write it upon their hearts; and I will be their God, and they shall be my people.'" For Jews, this new covenant is yet to come, but Christians have, from earliest times, applied these words to Jesus. The early eucharistic formulas (in 1 Corinthians, for example) relate that Jesus, on the night before he died, blessed the cup and said, "This cup is the new covenant in my blood" (11:25). Later, in Hebrews (8:8–12), the author quotes from Jeremiah explicitly to draw theological conclusions from it: if there is a new covenant found in the New Testament, it is based on an experience of Jesus and is not understandable apart from that experience. One cannot expect non-Christians, therefore, to read those texts in the same way.

Early Christian authors used the Hebrew Bible as a typological gold mine: events in Israelite history were interpreted as "types" or symbols for what would happen to Jesus. The Hebrews passed through the Red Sea during the Exodus. This event was taken as a symbol that Jesus would pass through death. Similarly, the sacrifice of Isaac might symbolize the Crucifixion. Again, these events become types only in a specifically Christian interpretation.

The new perspective of the Christians is most evident in what they did to the Hebrew Bible (see Appendix 1). They adopted it as their own book, but renamed it the Old Testament (old covenant), a name that implies the existence of a new one. And they changed the order of the books. The Jewish Bible ends with the exile, with the expectation that God will act in the future. The Christian Old Testament ends with the books of the so-called minor prophets (those whose books are shorter compared to those of the "major" prophets), which are full of references Christians apply to Jesus. Micah, for example, says, "But you, O Bethlehem . . . who are little . . . from you shall come forth for me one who is to be ruler in Israel" (5:2). Where does the New Testament say Jesus was born? In Bethlehem. The Book of Habakkuk is about the sovereignty of God and contains the phrase that appears later in the Epistle to the Romans: "The righteous shall live by faith" (Hab. 2:4; Rom. 1:17). The Book of Haggai records God's promise "I am about to shake the heavens and the earth" (2:21), interpreted in Hebrews (12:26) as accomplished in Jesus.

All these books have an edge of expectation. The Book of Zechariah pictures the Messiah as prince of peace and a good shepherd and contains the quotation "Lo, your king comes to you, triumphant and victorious is he, humble and riding on an ass, on a colt the foal of an ass" (9:9). The New Testament authors used that quotation to describe Jesus's entry into Jerusalem. The Book of Malachi is about the impending coming of the Lord and about a forerunner. All these books were written in the sixth or fifth centuries B.C.E., and were therefore full of meaning for the Jews quite apart from any link with messianic hopes, but Christians saw them as an immediate foreshadowing of the coming of Jesus. It is a big step from the end of the Jewish Bible to the New Testament, from the exile to Jesus, but when a Christian reads the Old Testament minor prophets, he or she expects something to happen. To Christians, Jesus appears as the proper and natural end of these prophecies. That was the Christian intention in reordering the books. But one can see how both the Jewish and the Christian interpretation of the life of Jesus could have grown out of the same Scripture.

CONCLUSION

The Jewish context of the life of Jesus was, of course, a great deal more complex than I have indicated here: Judaism at the time of Jesus was enormously varied politically, religiously, and sociologically. The groups described here, for example, were composed of relatively few Jews and the purpose in presenting them was to give you some indication of the variety within Judaism at the time. It is tempting to think that there was a normative Judaism, very neat and tidy, and that Jesus offered a clear alternative to it. Such thinking indulges in fantasy, though. There was no single Judaism at the time of Jesus, people were incredibly divided on all sorts of issues, and whatever alternative Jesus offered, it was probably no more clear than anything else at the time.

In major matters, Jewish opinion was divided. Most Jews were moved by Israel's institutions and were loyal to the temple, the Law, feasts, Jerusalem itself, and the idea of a holy land, but differed over theological concepts and methods of interpretation. It is not clear, for example, how many Jews were waiting for a Messiah. Christian interpretation is most congenial to a view that many were, but it is likely that very many Jews scarcely gave it a thought. You might compare it to a contemporary Christian interest in the end of the world. Do most Christians think often about the end of the world? Would you say that most of them are eagerly or even consciously waiting for it? Some are, of course, but are most of them? Probably not, even though, as a concept, it is part of their tradition. The same thing was probably true of the Jews and messianic expectation. At the same time, since the goal of this chapter was to situate Jesus in a clear and relatively simple context, messianic expectations were emphasized here.

There were certainly major differences of opinion within Judaism about the appropriateness of an apocalyptic edge in scriptural interpretation, just as there are major differences within Christianity on the same issue. The apocalyptic vision was the focus here because the intertestamental period (one hundred years before Jesus to one hundred years after) *was* a time when hundreds of apocalyptic books were written and when it did seem to be "in the air."

Finally, a word about the Torah. The Torah as such—the first five books of the Bible—was being edited, refined, and written down about the same time the Jews were returning to Palestine from the exile. When I talk about their hope to be more faithful to the Torah, therefore, I am speaking in a general way about fidelity to the covenant and the commandments. Even on this crucial issue of the Law, Jews were of different minds—Sadducees (conservatives) kept to the letter of the Torah *as it was written* and did not allow for refinements or interpretations or extensions, while Pharisees (liberals) extended applications of the Torah to every phase of life and generated a body of interpretation that, in time, became as binding as the Torah itself.

I have simplified the life of Jesus in order to present a fairly coherent view of him and his work. On the level of pure story, this is quite possible: I have woven strands together to come up with a composite picture which is, itself, an interpretation. I think it is appropriate at this level to look at the life of Jesus in this way, but one should also do so with certain cautions. Scholars argue about almost everything—which gospel was earliest, where the gospel writers got their material, how accurate they were, who their audiences were—and I have tried to spare you those arguments here. At the same time, I have to say that it is very hard to really reconstruct the life of Jesus. The Gospels are not biographies; they are theological interpretations that tell us more about what Jesus meant than what he actually did. How many of the words attributed to Jesus are actually his is disputed not only by scholars but by Christians in general. Even the *geographical* details cannot be taken without further investigation: for example, did Jesus have a mission in Galilee and then "go up to Jerusalem"?

Most scholars are not quite sure about this. Luke's journey motif is brilliant and rich, but that does not make it historically precise.

This chapter, therefore, has given you a simplified version of the context for and life of Jesus, what I hope is a good beginning for your understanding. As you read more widely you will discover some of the nuances I have tried to allude to here.

CHAPTER 2 NOTES

[1] The Hellenistic period began with the death of Alexander the Great (323 B.C.E.) and was a time when Greek ideas, culture, philosophy, manners, language, and art were extremely influential in the ancient world. The Jews were touched by Hellenistic civilization, as evidenced in the Bible by the so-called Wisdom literature (Proverbs and Ecclesiastes, for example).

[2] Some groups of Jews did not believe this since it was not written in the Torah itself, and it is not altogether clear just how many Jews *did* believe that God would act in this way.

[3] David Rhoads, *Israel in Revolution, 6–74 C.E.: A Political History Based on the Writings of Josephus* (Philadelphia: Fortress Press, 1976), pp. 32–46 discusses these groups within their political context.

[4] Rhoads, p. 33.

[5] See Cornelius Tacitus, *The Annals of Tacitus, Books One to Six,* edited with a commentary by R. R. D. Goodyear (Cambridge: Cambridge University Press, 1972), 15.44. For a look at "Jesus in Extrabiblical Sources," see Howard Kee, *Jesus in History: An Approach to the Study of the Gospels,* 2nd ed. (New York: Harcourt Brace Jovanovich, 1977), pp. 40–75.

[6] Jesus's conduct toward women was simply extraordinary, especially when read against the background of Jewish practice and the place of women at the time. See Joachim Jeremias, *Jerusalem in the Time of Jesus* (Philadelphia: Fortress Press, 1969), pp. 359–76.

[7] One statement of this view can be found in Vernard Eller, *The Most Revealing Book of the Bible: Making Sense out of Revelation* (Grand Rapids: Eerdmans, 1974). Look in the subject catalog of your library for some sense of the enormous range of interpretation.

[8] Jews have been persecuted in Christian countries in many ways: anti-Semitic sermons and absurd charges have been circulated; Jews have been forced to wear distinctive clothing, live in ghettos, and pay special taxes; they have not been permitted to socialize with non-Jews, engage in some forms of business, vote or hold office; sometimes Christians have forced Jews to convert to Christianity or to flee from their homes to new lands. Christians have a long history of physical abuse of Jews that includes attacks on Jewish communities, arson, vandalism, mob murder, judicial murder, and genocide. Life for Jews in Christian lands did not improve with time, but grew considerably worse, culminating in Hitler's "final solution" in the death camps of the Nazis. A good book on this tragic history is still Edward H. Flannery, *The Anguish of the Jews* (New York: Macmillan, 1965). Two brief articles on aspects of the Jewish-Christian dialogue are: Edward

J. Fisher, "The Holocaust and Christian Responsibility," *America* 144 (14 February 1981), 118–21; and Leonard Swidler, "The Dialogue Decalogue," *Journal of Ecumenical Studies* 20 (Winter 1983), 1–4. For a clear exposition of some points of interfaith discussion, see Leonard Klenicki and Geoffrey Wigoder, editors, *A Dictionary of the Jewish-Christian Dialogue* (New York: Paulist Press, 1984).

SUGGESTIONS FOR FURTHER READING

1. For more on the context and Jewish background of Jesus, consult Joachim Jeremias, *Jerusalem in the Time of Jesus* (Philadelphia: Fortress Press, 1969), and Marcel Simon, *Jewish Sects at the Time of Jesus* (Philadelphia: Fortress Press, 1967). Simon provides a good bibliography as well, pp. 163–68. See also Howard Kee, *The New Testament in Context* (Englewood Cliffs, N.J.: Prentice-Hall, 1984).

2. It is hard to choose any one book as a New Testament introduction, but Norman Perrin, *The New Testament, An Introduction: Proclamation and Parenesis, Myth and History,* 2nd ed. (New York: Harcourt Brace Jovanovich, 1982), is a good beginning. It is a textbook and therefore geared for students, clearly written and illustrated. See also Howard Kee et al., *Understanding the New Testament,* 4th ed. (Englewood Cliffs, N.J.: Prentice-Hall, 1983). For an interpretive introduction that is both straightforward and erudite, see Luke Timothy Johnson, *The Writings of the New Testament* (Philadelphia: Fortress Press, 1986).

3. Jesus has been interpreted in many ways over the last two thousand years. For an introduction to some of the different pictures of Jesus we can find in history, see Hugh Anderson, editor, *Jesus* (Englewood Cliffs, N.J.: Prentice-Hall, 1967). It contains essays on Jesus, nineteenth-century liberal views, existential understandings, scholarly reconstructions, and other essays.

4. For a condensed introduction to New Testament writings, one that provides a good introduction without oversimplifying things, see Günther Bornkamm, *The New Testament: A Guide to Its Writings* (Philadelphia: Fortress Press, 1973).

5. For a different viewpoint on Jewish-Christian dialogue, see Stuart E. Rosenberg, *The Christian Problem: A Jewish View* (New York: Hippocrene Books, 1986). According to Rosenberg, Christians have to become "more Jewish" to avoid their own idolatrous tendencies and mistakes about Judaism.

✦

CHAPTER 3

THE EMERGENCE OF THE CHRISTIAN CHURCH

Christians interpreted the Bible as they did because they believed that Jesus was the Messiah, a belief supported by their experience of Jesus as risen from the dead. Christians today sometimes think the apostles saw the risen Jesus, obtained a blueprint from him, and proceeded in happy agreement to construct the Christian church. The truth is that members of the early Christian community disagreed with and misunderstood each other. They were no more compatible than any other group, no less immune to argument, no more peaceful.

The early Christian community began with the energizing belief that God's spirit had been sent to them in Jesus, and the first believers were enthusiastic, eager to share their good news. Although they were unified in their belief in Jesus, they were divided over other issues. This chapter discusses some of those issues and also introduces some of the complex questions Christians had to face as they encountered other religions, incredulous reactions, and persecution.

THE EXPERIENCE OF THE APOSTLES

According to the Acts of the Apostles, Jesus, after he was raised from the dead, stayed on earth for forty days and then ascended into the heavens (1:1–12). We can speculate that the apostles were overjoyed about the Resurrection but, at the same time, were mystified about what it really meant. They were convinced that Jesus had risen from the dead—they had heard about it, seen him, eaten with him, touched him—but they were not sure what the implications of that experience were. What did the Resurrection mean, for example, for their behavior? What were they now to *do?* Relate this for a minute to some biblical stories. Abraham believed that God had spoken to him, but he wasn't initially sure what that meant; God led him to understand it step by step. Moses believed he had had an encounter with the "God of Abraham, Isaac, and Jacob," but was appalled to find out that God wanted him to go back to Egypt and confront the powerful pharaoh there. The prophets, too, were sure about their encounters with God, but mystified or reluctant about what those meant for their mission. So it was with the experience of the risen Lord. The apostles believed it, experienced it as a miracle of prodigious proportions, but were also stunned by it. Even after the Resurrection, there was not such clarity that there were no questions, and not such charity that there were no arguments.

The experience of the Resurrection empowered human beings by God's spirit (life) so that their lives were changed. Not all New Testament writings agree on exactly what that meant. The Acts of the Apostles talks about the role of the Holy Spirit a great deal, by means of a narrative recounting of the church's beginnings. It is clear that things are idealized considerably. We suspect, for example, that the first believers were not so completely united as Luke suggests (see Acts 5:1–5). But the story does help us see how the history of the Christian movement was perceived as a continuation of the story of Israel, precisely because the same Holy Spirit was at work in both.

The Old Testament tells us that the Spirit was sent to people who had a special mission (prophets and judges, for example), but was to be shared with all people in the final age. The prophet Joel states an especially clear prophecy about the Spirit: "And it shall come to pass, afterward, that I will pour out my spirit on all flesh; your sons and your daughters shall prophesy, your old men shall dream dreams, and your young men shall see visions" (Joel 2:28). The coming of the Spirit to the apostles, therefore, is set within the context of God's promises about the last days. Throughout Acts one can see how the power of the Spirit is interpreted. The Spirit is the driving force behind the proclamation of the gospel, the agent who brings about conversion and faith in Jesus as the Christ; the Spirit strengthens people and helps them endure persecution, guides the early missionary efforts—especially those of Paul—and inspires the Gentile mission. Through the Spirit's work the loose group of early believers begins to form the Christian church.

The story of the coming of the Spirit to the apostles is found in Acts 2. Just looking at the story, we are struck by certain things. Notice that the Spirit came to the apostles on the Jewish festival of Weeks, Shebu'ot, also known as *Pentecost.* This feast commemorates and celebrates the giving of the Law at Sinai. The New Testament account is written to stress this parallel. It conveys the sense of something new happening, something that can replace or go beyond the old way (the old covenant).

The outline of the story is this: The apostles were gathered together in one place and were confused and frightened. All of a sudden they heard a sound like a mighty wind (in Greek the word *pneuma* means both spirit and wind) which filled the house, and tongues of fire hovered over the head of each of them. God's appearances in the Bible are often accompanied by wind and fire; the New Testament account, therefore, is surely meant to convey that the apostles experienced the presence of God in wind and fire. The apostles were filled with the Holy Spirit and began to speak not according to their own designs, but as the Spirit directed them. They spoke in languages they did not know, and visitors to Jerusalem from all over the Middle East heard them speaking about the mighty works of God.

After they received the Spirit, the apostles spoke to the crowd. The most famous speech was delivered by Peter, who quoted Joel's words about the pouring out of the Spirit and ended by saying, "And it shall be that whoever calls on the name of the Lord shall be saved" (Acts 2:21). Notice the word *whoever*: not just Jews, but all who call upon the name of the Lord will be saved. This is a radically new idea and one, the author suggests, that the Spirit gave to Peter. The apostles are supposed to go beyond the terms of the covenant at Sinai and extend the saving message of Jesus to everyone. The Acts of the Apostles is a partisan record of this extension.

After that startling statement, Peter told his audience the story of Jesus, especially how he was crucified but had been raised up from the dead. Imagine the impact of a statement like this! Some listeners thought the apostles were drunk or crazy; others were moved and asked what they should do. Peter told them to repent (to change their direction, to turn toward God by following Jesus) and to be baptized. According to the Pentecost story in Acts, three thousand people were baptized that day.

Acts 2 summarizes the enthusiasm characteristic of the early Christian community, but it also gives the impression that it was united in mind and heart from the beginning. The account in Acts implies that the coming of the Holy Spirit clarified the meaning of Jesus's words and life. It is historically naive to think this was the case. The New Testament says the apostles were enlightened, had an experience of the risen Lord, received the Holy Spirit, and were filled with a desire to carry the saving message of Jesus to others. Acts presents Pentecost as the inauguration of a truly universal preaching about Jesus that ultimately transcended all boundaries of nationality, speech, and religion. That universalist understanding about Jesus, however, was not something clearly evident at the outset. The argument about who should hear the gospel was the most serious controversy in the young community.

INTERNAL CONFLICTS IN THE EARLY CHURCH

A popular picture of earliest Christianity is that it began in perfect uniformity and split into groups. A better picture is that it began with *variety,* and only in the course of generations came to an explicit sense of *unity*. Some deep issues caused conflict among the first believers, and only time and the accidents of history brought them to a shared view.

Four general questions arose within the early community:

1. Who can hear the gospel? (universality)
2. Who is in charge? (authority and doctrine)
3. What does it mean to be free? (law and freedom)
4. Where can the authentic words of and stories about Jesus be found? (formation of the New Testament)

Because these questions caused conflicts, a principle emerged that came to be used as a norm against which to measure everything. That principle was *apostolicity:* when people wanted to know whether a writing was reliable, whether the right person was in authority, and so on, they asked whether it was apostolic, clearly connected with the work and intentions of the apostles. Understanding the conflicts is essential to understanding the principle, which developed along with the community.

Universality of the Gospel

For whom was the gospel intended? Did Jesus offer his message for everyone or just for Jews? There is no single answer to this question in the Gospels themselves because the Gospels reflect, in part, the life of the early community, which was divided on this question. So in some parts of the Gospels it seems as if Jesus has come only to preach to the Jews (Matt. 10:5–7), and in others his words seem intended for all who believe (Matt. 28:19). Jesus, remember, was Jewish and so were his apostles; his life and mission were interpreted in the light of Jewish prophecies and expectations. It was logical to assume—as some did—that the message of Jesus was intended only for the Jews. Yet the account of Pentecost in Acts includes "all who call upon the name of the Lord." That statement represents a position adopted by the early community only after a severe struggle.

A particularly vivid account of this argument is found in the Epistle to the Galatians (chapters 1 and 2), where Paul recounts his own growth in understanding. He began, he tells his readers, hating Christians and persecuting them precisely because he was "so extremely zealous for the traditions of my fathers" (1:14). God called him, converted him, and made it clear that he was to "preach among the Gentiles" (1:16). He was asked by God to do an extremely difficult task, namely to abandon his background, training, and beliefs to set out on a daring new path. He did not do so without approval from the rest of the community, and Galatians tells the story of his approval by the Jerusalem community, especially by Peter (who was preaching to the Jews). Peter himself, however, was not free from ambivalent feelings on this issue. He welcomed Paul's approach in Jerusalem, but on a visit to Antioch he reverted to an anti-Gentile position (Gal. 2:11–17) and was confronted by Paul. The early community made no attempt to hide the fact that they argued over this issue, and we should remember the arguments as we read those stories that make the concept of a universal mission seem much smoother.

In Acts, for example, one finds the story of Philip going to Samaria and bringing about a remarkable conversion there (chapter 6). Most Jews regarded the Samaritans as heretics and enemies,[1] yet, according to the story, the Samaritans received the word of the Lord eagerly and were converted. The author's point is that the power of God's word and the Spirit are not put off by heresy: this Spirit can work in any situation. Later in Acts there is an even more dramatic story. Peter was preaching, for the most part, to Jews, but one day received a message from a Roman soldier, Cornelius, inviting him to dinner. It is hard for us, perhaps, to grasp the impact of the invitation. Jewish dietary regulations were considered to be part of God's will. The terms of the covenant forbade Jews to eat certain foods and to eat with non-Jews. A Jew could not eat dinner in a Roman house, therefore, without being in serious violation of divine law. What was Peter to do? In Acts (chapter 10) the author takes the question out of Peter's hands and says that the Spirit instructed Peter to go, that he did go, ate, preached to Cornelius, and saw that "God shows no partiality . . . the Spirit has been poured out even on the Gentiles" (11:34 and 11:44).

The stories in Acts make the decision to pursue a universal mission look much easier than it was because Acts was written after the fact and from a perspective that favored universality. The climax to this question occurs in Acts 15, when some members of the Jerusalem community said, "Unless you are circumcised according to Moses, you cannot be saved" (15:1). In other words, the message of Jesus could be extended, but only through Judaism. In order to be a Christian, one had first to be Jewish, to be circumcised, and to follow the Law of Moses. This position of the so-called Judaizers precipitated a clash, and an important meeting was held in Jerusalem to resolve the issue. When all sides had been heard, they deliberated and decided that the gospel was to be extended freely to all and that one did not have to become Jewish in order to become a Christian. In the letter written to different Christian communities about this meeting, the leaders assembled in Jerusalem used a very telling phrase. Describing the process of decision making they said, "It seemed good to the Holy Spirit and to us. . . ." The implications of that statement are large: the young community considered itself to be in *partnership* with the Spirit. They decided this important matter together and would decide future matters together.

This assertion about the presence and guidance of the Holy Spirit is a fundamental principle within Christianity. God is continually present to Christians by way of the Holy Spirit, who resides in the church. The continual presence of the Spirit keeps the church alive and faithful to God's commands and leads it to deeper understandings. Christians agree about the importance of the Spirit in the church but, as we shall see, they disagree intensely about where the Spirit resides, how it is experienced, and what its powers are. For now, it is enough to see that the early church resolved the issue of a universal mission and, in the process, established the principle of the abiding and guiding presence of the Spirit in the church.

Authority and Doctrine

The Christian church, as you can imagine, grew increasingly complex as it grew in numbers and extended itself to a wide range of cultures and peoples. All religions are, to some extent, shaped by the cultural milieu in which they thrive; Christianity in Syria was different from Christianity in Rome and from Christianity in Egypt or Palestine. Questions arose about behavior and practice. How should the Lord's Supper be observed? Who may participate? Must one practice perpetual virginity after baptism? How is the forgiveness of sins to be enacted? How is discipline to be maintained? What prayer forms are appropriate? Which stories about Jesus are trustworthy? To complicate the situation, Christianity arose at a time when many different religions were practiced and in an environment where interchange and cross-fertilization were inevitable.[2]

Should the Christian community be seen as an organization needing officers, or as a community of believers trusting the guidance of the Spirit and willing to attempt consensual decision making? Both views were present in the early church and continue to be present in the modern Christian church. Some think Christians should form themselves into small, manageable groups of believers who are "of one heart and soul" (Acts 4:32). Others believe that the church needs an organizational model with certain people in charge and streamlined, hierarchical methods of decision making.

Structures of authority grew along with the church: they were not there from the beginning, nor was it immediately clear that such structures were needed.[3] Paul's first letter to the Thessalonians makes no mention of church leaders. Yet in the Acts of the Apostles, we find not only leaders, but several kinds with different functions—elders and deacons, for example. Paul's farewell address to the elders at Ephesus (as reported in Acts) is a handing on of his authority, and pictures Paul as an authority figure. By the time the pastoral Epistles were written (two letters to Timothy and one to Titus), we find a strong, directive interest in church administration. These letters were not written by Paul—scholars are nearly unanimous in their agreement about this point—and so do not show a development in Paul himself, but they do show a development within the early community. The first letter to Timothy not only mentions bishops, but also lays down qualifications for them (3:1–7) and suggests some regulations for worship (2:1–15); the letter to Titus also specifies qualifications for bishops and elders. Christian literature not included in the New Testament—the Didache, for example, or the Apostolic Constitutions—is primarily devoted to administrative matters and questions of true teaching and practice.

As the church developed, a certain organizational model eventually emerged as the dominant one. Officers (bishops) were elected by congregations to teach and to supervise. You can imagine that as long as a particular community remained fairly homogeneous, few problems arose. Once the Christian church began to attract large numbers of new members from all classes and occupations, however, controversies and questions arose on every conceivable issue. We can see already in Paul's letter to the Corinthians that Christians had to *learn* how to celebrate the Lord's Supper properly (chapter 11), and that is an early letter. Imagine the complex problems that would arise in a church that had communities throughout the ancient world, and members who were from all social and economic classes, with different educational and religious backgrounds.

Questions arose at all levels. Within the structure of the church there were questions of discipline (what to do if someone violated a commandment), of jurisdiction (whether priests from one place could work in another without the permission of the local bishop), membership (whether a soldier could be a Christian without resigning from the army), and doctrine (whether Jesus was truly the son of God), to name a few. Sometimes questions were handled locally within the church or within the district, but as time went on and as questions grew more complex, church leaders from a large region met to discuss them. In later centuries (beginning in 325 C.E. at Nicaea), worldwide meetings (or councils) were held to decide important matters of doctrine and practice.[4]

Little by little the ancient equivalent of a corporate flow chart emerged within the Christian church. In terms of regional organization, the church owed some debts to Roman imperial structures which, after all, had enhanced the smooth administration of a massive empire. In terms of teaching and moral authority, the bishops, individually or collectively, came to decide things. In matters that involved the entire Christian world—especially matters of doctrine—all the bishops of the world gathered to debate, reflect, and decide. In their decision-making process they were conscious of the partnership they had with the Spirit, so their decisions were considered to be extensions and refinements of divine will.

Law and Freedom in the Spirit

The apostle Paul preached a gospel of freedom and believed that God had given him the authority to do so. "It is no longer I who live," he said, "but Christ who lives in me" (Gal. 2:20). As a serious young Jew, Paul knew the Law and upheld it; as a Christian, converted by God to preach to the Gentiles (Acts 9), he was constrained to explain, from many different perspectives, the relation between the Law and the gospel. One gets some sense of the brilliance with which he held these two concepts together in his Epistle to the Romans: in chapter 7 he discusses the Law and its place in Christian life, and in chapter 8 he discusses life in the Spirit.

Paul's claim that his authority was God-given rested on two things: his vision of the risen Christ and his style of servant leadership (following Jesus's model). On his missionary journeys he founded churches and he thought of himself as a nurturing parent (1 Thess. 2:7, "like a nurse"; 2:11, "like a father") to those congregations. He was loath to build a superstructure of rules or legal authority but not at all afraid to give his opinions about specific questions. Some groups in Christian history point to their reading of the early Pauline model precisely to argue for Christian freedom. Some Christians see Pauline congregations as congregations in which the chief presiding officer was Christ and his Spirit, not priests or bishops or even Paul. He told communities they were called to freedom (Gal. 5:13), but a freedom that did not lie in doing whatever one pleases. The freedom of the gospel is the freedom to love one another, to be servants, to be solicitous for each other's needs. Care for one another does not mean slavery; rather, people are called to "freedom in the Spirit," freedom from the old law, freedom from attempts to domineer over other people's faith, freedom to support one another.[5]

Paul did not create a new norm, but saw Christ as a new standard. He exhorted people to live in communities of freedom and to be faithful, to "be imitators of me as I am of Christ" (1 Cor. 11:1). The ancient moral commandments are not up for discussion—they hold; yet, in Romans 10:4 he says that Christ is the end of the Law. The new law of Christ is Paul's gospel of freedom.

Formation of the New Testament

One problem the early community faced, especially as it expanded into the Hellenistic world, concerned the place of the writings that were later to be known as the New Testament. During the first two centuries of the Christian movement, the preaching of Jesus and stories about him were recorded and circulated to Christian congregations, accepted in these congregations in some forms and not in others, regarded first as an interpretive key to the Hebrew Bible, regarded later as a book with religious authority of its own, and eventually regarded as inspired and as the word of God.

The New Testament was written down and its form fixed because people had serious questions about doctrine, practice, and worship and needed a consistent, universal guidance. The books of the New Testament came to be regarded as norms in these matters. The problem was complex because many books were written about Jesus within the Christian movement:[6] there were stories of what Jesus was like as a little boy, what his mother was like, how he grew up, what Joseph thought about Jesus. Some books demanded rigorous asceticism for all Christians, arguing that all should abstain from sex, alcohol, and dancing; some writers claimed that because Christians were free, they could not sin and could therefore live licentiously. There were treatises on the Second Coming of the Lord with all the signs of the times; some books dealt with points of doctrine, arguing that Jesus was or was not God, was or was not a man, did or did not die, rise, ascend to heaven, and so forth. How was it possible to make a selection from all this literature? By what criterion could some books be selected as inspired and some rejected? Why does the New Testament contain the Gospel of Matthew and not the Gospel of Thomas?

In the early church the norm that developed and prevailed from the selection of New Testament books was *apostolicity,* as mentioned earlier. Had a particular book been handed down from the apostolic church, and was it attributed to an apostle or a disciple? Did it reflect the mind and practice of the apostolic church and did it have the capacity for continuing this mind and practice? This last question is an interpretive one: What *was* the "mind and practice of the apostolic church"? Was there just one? Who determined whether a book was a reflection of the apostolic church? These questions are not only ancient ones. Scholars today ask the same questions from contemporary perspectives and use developments like the formation of the New Testament to argue that the so-called apostolic tradition (as it has come down to Christians today) is *not* the authentic tradition of Jesus.[7]

These four conflicts were by no means the only ones to trouble early Christians, but they reflect some of the major arguments not only within the young Christian community but within Christian churches yet today. Christians do not wonder whether or not to extend the gospel to the Gentiles, but they do wonder how much they can adopt from non-Christian religions; they continue to differ about authority and doctrine, about the meaning and function of apostolicity,[8] and about the limits of Christian freedom. No one wants to add or subtract books from the New Testament canon—it took nearly four centuries to fix it—but there is some argument about the books that *were* left out at the time and an increasing interest in the variety of literature written during the early Christian period.[9]

EXTERNAL CONFLICTS OF THE EARLY COMMUNITY

The church in its first three centuries, from New Testament times to the reign of the first Christian emperor, Constantine (d. 337), grew from a small group of dedicated believers with no uniform structure to a worldwide movement with organized hierarchies of management and established norms of behavior. As we have seen, early believers differed, sometimes radically, about practice and doctrine, and one can understand their differences from two perspectives: from looking at some of the early conflicts (as we have just done) or from looking at the context in which these and other conflicts were worked out.

The world of early Christianity was geographically large, religiously diverse, and culturally heterogeneous. In a variety of ways, Christians had to learn to answer for themselves. How were they different from Jews? What did Christianity have in common with Judaism? How could their beliefs be reconciled with Hellenistic philosophy: how could they explain Jesus to someone who read and loved Plato? How were they going to define their beliefs? And what relationship was there between doctrinal and practical matters: what kind of structure or teaching authority would work best? Why were Christians rigidly monotheistic? Why did they refuse to worship any other gods? How would they adapt to the rich and enticing variety of Roman religions?

No matter what cultural context they found themselves in, they had to address these and other questions. This section will discuss three different cultural contexts and three specific facets of Christian identity. Like all simplifying generalizations, this one is imperfect, since much more was going on in each of these contexts than I can discuss here, but it is also useful to give a general sense of developing Christian identity. Christians developed their religious, philosophical, and political identity as they grew and interacted in the complex ancient world. Let us focus on their *religious* identity within the Jewish context, their *philosophical* identity within the Greek context, and their *political* identity within the Roman context.

The Jewish Context and Religious Identity

Christianity was born into a Jewish context and emerged from it with a separate religious identity. Early Christians did not think of themselves as separable from Judaism, but as a Jewish sect distinguished by their belief that Jesus was the Messiah. Their worship was modeled on Jewish services and their understanding of the mission of Jesus was derived from the Hebrew Bible. Christians believed Jesus had come to gather the Jews together in preparation for the final days; they voted to extend his saving act beyond the Jewish community.

What do you think a universalist position meant to Jewish Christians? Their position was determined to some extent by the political and religious situation, especially growing Roman antipathy and their own apocalyptic expectations. Because of political and religious tensions, Christianity's relationship to Judaism was precarious from the outset. The early Christian community in Jerusalem perceived itself as a temporary community living in the interim between the coming of the Messiah and the final coming of the kingdom of God, the end of the age. It is not clear that Jewish Christians welcomed the mission to the Gentiles, or saw much reason to set up enduring structures or policies.

The Jews were in a volatile political situation punctuated by periodic outbreaks of insurrection. Any rebellion could give the Romans the excuse they wanted for crushing the Jews, and from 66 to 70 C.E. an unprecedented revolt of the Jews against the Romans took place. It was one of the most savage wars in history: more than a million Jews were killed or sold into slavery. Since a large part of the early Christian community was Jewish, this war of national liberation presented a serious problem to the early church. Jewish Christians were caught between the demands of national identity and the words of the gospel. Full of apocalyptic expectation and reminded of the words of Jesus about the last days (Matt. 24 : 15–21), Jewish Christians felt obliged to flee the city, an action that made them traitors in the eyes of the Jews.

The fall of Jerusalem in 70 C.E. marked the end of any Jewish Christian hope to convert the Jews. In the minds of Gentile Christians it vindicated the decision for universality. Gentile Christians pointed to the fall of Jerusalem to argue that Jewish Christian apocalyptic hopes were false; later they claimed that the Jewish aspects of Christianity were unnecessary. Jewish Christians were homeless: they were not welcome in Judaism and not comfortable with a universalist Christianity. Accordingly, the Jewish Christian discussion of early Christianity diminished and the way was paved for a separate Christian church.

When the Sanhedrin was restored in Jerusalem (90 C.E.), many Jews wanted to condemn any Jew who had accepted Jesus and to rid Judaism of any trace of Christianity. Liturgical practices that had been in any way contaminated by Christian usage were changed; a formal curse against Christians was added to Jewish morning prayer. Christians were no longer able to associate with Jews.

The de facto and de jure segregation of the Jews from Christians gave the Christians a profound cultural shock. Christians regarded their faith as the extension of the covenant between God and Abraham; they believed they were part of the Jewish heritage even if they did not agree with Jewish cultural exclusivity. When the Jews severed connection with *them,* Christians were forced to rethink their position.

Christians made a variety of responses to their dilemma, as reflected in early Christian writings (see Appendix 3). In the heat of the controversy, some writers disparaged Judaism, arguing that it was worthless and unnecessary to Christianity. Christians made changes in the practical order to complete the severance: they celebrated the Lord's Day (the Sabbath) on Sunday instead of Saturday, and celebrated their main ritual meal, the Lord's Supper (Eucharist), every week instead of once a year (at Passover).

Christianity therefore developed an identity separate from Judaism, but it could never leave Judaism totally behind. Christians were indebted to Jews for liturgical consciousness and forms of worship, for a sense of roots, and for the Bible. Like Jews, Christians believe in one God, the Creator and Judge of the universe; like Jews, Christians accept providence, free will, and a history of salvation. Without the Hebrew Bible, Christians would have been unable to make sense of the life, death, and resurrection of Jesus.

The Greek Context and Philosophical Identity

Christianity matured in the Hellenistic world, the world of pagan philosophy and ideas. Since the Greek world respected philosophical sophistication, members of the early Christian community began to adapt themselves to the task of making Christian faith philosophically respectable.[10] In their encounters with Greek philosophy, early Christian writers and scholars laid the philosophical foundations for what would later become an elaborate Christian theology.

The task was a difficult one because of internal and external opposition. Externally, Christian philosophers had to learn to talk to people who had just freed their understanding of the divine from a mythological tradition: when Christians arrived on the scene talking about the Son of God, Greek philosophers thought they were dealing with a backward people. Internally, there were problems of definition and interpretation: What did it mean to be free from the Law, or to be free in the Lord? Some people thought they were bound by no laws and could, in effect, be a law unto themselves; others felt free to pick and choose parts of the Bible or parts of Jesus's teaching to suit their own particular philosophical interpretation. Some people thought they were saved by faith; Gnostics thought they were saved by *knowledge* (from the Greek *gnosis*) and developed elaborate systems of secret knowledge, passwords, and esoteric doctrine.

In an effort to define orthodox Christian views *and* to make their beliefs understandable to a philosophically sophisticated audience, early Christian writers borrowed some of the philosophical ideas of the time and attempted to present a systematic Christianity. Justin Martyr (100–165 C.E.) arranged the sayings of the gospel under the headings of "self-control," "universal love," and "being blameless." Theophilus of Antioch (late second century) did much the same thing, adding insights from the Ten Commandments. Once they had a set of Christian maxims, writers could combine them with Greek philosophical ideas about spiritual perfection through the cultivation of the soul. Clement of Alexandria (d. 215 C.E.) and Origen (185–254 C.E.) interpreted the Christian life as one beginning in faith and ending with a real likeness to God; they tried to synthesize philosophical Christianity and Neoplatonic philosophy.[11]

Christian philosophers were relating to the outside world effectively, but there were other pressing matters; internal problems plagued the Christian church. Early Christian writers wrote philosophical works; they also wrote treatises on behavior, decorum, and Christian practice. Originally, members of a local church handled problems of belief and discipline in that congregation. In the second and third centuries, however, bishops began to exercise their power and authority more strongly. The Christian church became larger and more complex; the bishops believed that the church needed centralized authority, which rested in the office and administrative power of the bishop. With authority to judge doctrinal matters, bishops believed they could protect people from dangerous doctrines and practices. Accordingly, the early church moved slowly but surely toward a monarchical episcopacy: the bishop was like a king, a man with high authority who could decide (by himself or in consultation with other bishops) whether a certain position was right or wrong.

In the context of the Hellenistic world, then, Christianity developed a structure for handling problems. The office of the bishop and the authority of the bishops culminated in a series of meetings called councils (see Appendix 4), where Christian doctrine was defined and Christian practice regulated. Philosophically, the church adopted new vocabulary and ideas. Christian philosophy and apologetics (explaining Christianity to a potentially hostile audience) was the work of theologians and was central to the church's development in both East and West.

The Roman Context and Political Identity

Christianity was born into a Jewish religious context and learned how to negotiate in a Hellenistic philosophical environment, but the real rulers of the world into which Christianity emerged were the Romans. At the beginning of the second century, the Roman Empire stretched from Mesopotamia to Scotland, from the Danube to the Sahara Desert. Within this area lived many peoples with different cultures and world views. The Roman Empire was one of the most highly organized, well-ruled, sophisticated civilizations the world has ever seen. Two languages dominated: Latin in the West and Greek in the East. The emperor, an absolute ruler with pretensions to divinity, stood at the top of this large edifice.

The ideals of human decency (called *philanthropeia* in Greek, *humanitas* in Latin) and universal brotherhood were supported by the power and uniformity of Roman law. The empire was not without problems: huge slave populations, horrible slums, and terrible poverty existed side by side with Roman elegance. In addition to social ills there were serious political problems. Lack of a peaceful way to choose a successor to the emperor caused periodic anarchy and instability; a nonindustrial base caused gold drainage and severe inflation; a farm crisis and decimating plagues undermined the empire; and the army was mercenary rather than composed of Roman citizens. The political reforms of Diocletian in the third century helped to ease some of these situations, but the real reform came in the fourth century with the emperor Constantine, who chose to favor Christianity over all the other religions in the empire.

Roman religion, an amalgam of various cults throughout the empire, was often more concerned with form and rite than with spiritual teaching; in some ways it focused more on devotional practices than on inner experience. As the empire expanded, the mystery religions of the Mediterranean peoples gained influence precisely because they emphasized internal aspects of religion: a savior-God, mysterious rites (sacraments—*sacramentum* is the Latin translation of the Greek word *mysterion*), intimacy, and emotional response. The spiritual side of Roman religion was shaped by outside influences, by the beliefs and practices of conquered peoples. The most important outside influences were Stoicism, Epicureanism, Mithraism, the mystery religions, and Christianity.

Stoicism and Epicureanism, philosophical systems developed in the Greek world, both rested on a theory of human perfectibility. Epicureans thought that everything hung on *fate,* and since there was no given order in the universe, they advocated the freedom to pick and choose the very best things in life. Stoics, on the other hand, believed in an ordered universe, a cosmic intelligence or world soul that permeated the universe and made it possible for people to attain perfect freedom by living in total harmony with reason. Stoics are sometimes pictured in our minds as withstanding pain and refusing to admit their feelings or fears. They *did* attempt to control their passions by living fully in accord with reason, but a more accurate picture of them would show them trying to get in touch with the universe, feel its vibrations, resonate with its harmonies. Both these attitudes continue to appeal to people today (though not, perhaps, in their pure philosophical form), and you can imagine that they appealed to the Romans as well.

The mystery cults were an entirely different matter and appealed on a more experiential level. Through their mysterious rites they not only offered a way to an emotional religious experience, they offered immortality: if one believed in the savior-God and followed the mysteries, one could live forever. The fertility cult of Cybele celebrated its feasts orgiastically; the Egyptian cult of Isis had magical initial rites including a ceremony of death and rebirth. The most important mystery religion for the Romans was probably Mithraism, a dualistic system that may have developed in Persia. Dualism divides the world into two parts, good and evil, and the followers of Mithraism believed that there were powers of light and powers of darkness at work in the universe. What one hoped to do, through religious rites, was to get in touch with the powers of light and withstand the powers of darkness.

Christianity developed in the Roman Empire on the heels of these other religions and philosophical systems and learned to adapt some of the best parts of them to its own belief system. In some ways of looking at it, Christianity did not have to prepare its own ground, but was able to grow in the soil prepared by others. Hellenized Judaism in Alexandria brought a consciousness of monotheism to the empire and provided it with a Greek translation of the Bible. Stoicism, with its concept of universal brotherhood, prepared the Romans for a universalism unknown in other religious circles. Neoplatonism, with its quest for ultimate perfection and mystical awareness of the divine, introduced an aspect of spiritual exaltation. The mystery religions were especially important: they had emotional appeal, a concept that everyone could be saved, a savior-God who died and was reborn, and a sacramental rite that brought believers immortality by association with the sufferings and eventual triumph of God.

Christianity knew how to adapt itself, where to borrow, and how to shape its message into the atmosphere of the times. It was universalist and aimed (in some quarters) at ultimate perfection through mystical union. Baptism and the Lord's Supper developed into sacramental rites, with ceremony and emotional appeal. Christianity was ancient because it was rooted in the Hebrew Bible: it could trace itself back to the creation of the world and the first inklings of a divine-human partnership. Most of all, however, Christians offered a savior-God who was historically concrete. According to Christians, Jesus was not a mythic savior but a real person, a man who had lived and died on earth and in history (*not* "once upon a time"), one who talked and suffered in the sight of others, who died publicly and rose again where people could see and touch him. Christianity endured longer than these other religions and was eventually declared the official religion of the empire. In the second and third centuries few people could have predicted the *survival* of the Christian religion, let alone its rise to a position of favoritism. In order to understand how phenomenal the rise of Christianity was, we must look back at the first three hundred years of its life when the Christian church was persecuted.

The Romans were essentially tolerant of different religions, yet their policy toward Christians in various parts of the empire was one of periodic but severe persecution. Christians were strict monotheists who refused to recognize the Roman gods; in times when *everyone* in the empire was supposed to make some sacrifice to the gods—to insure victory or forestall harm—Christians refused to offer sacrifice. Christians also refused to worship the emperor. Instead they held their own unauthorized gatherings on the Lord's Day, and were regarded with suspicion both by the Roman populace and the authorities. Christians were sometimes killed or tortured by officers of the state. Why? Some Romans believed that Christians subverted good order and that the Romans ought to attempt to eliminate Christianity by killing its bishops and burning its books.

Christians responded in different ways to persecution. Some witnessed to the truth of their beliefs by suffering and dying and are remembered as martyrs (the Greek word *martus* means witness); others endured torture and were honored as confessors (they confessed their Christian faith and were tortured but not killed for doing so). Another group escaped persecution either by denying their beliefs or finding some loophole in the law that allowed them to avoid a confrontation. When these people are remembered at all—many people believe the persecutions produced only heroes—they are recalled as the *lapsi*, people who lapsed from their religion. Because of the martyrs the Christian church developed a cult and theology of martyrdom: their deaths were interpreted as heroic imitations of the passion and death of Jesus; the martyr was the true disciple who followed Jesus even into death at the hands of the state. Because of the *lapsi* the Christian church was challenged to a more systematic administration of the sacrament of reconciliation or penance.

In the Roman context, therefore, Christians had sufficient freedom to adapt a variety of religious ideas and practices to their own beliefs, but they also suffered persecution because their religious stance put them at odds with the empire. Their survival convinced them even more of their special mission to the world.

CONCLUSION

The early Christian community was small, adapted to new situations, was courageous in the face of death, and was agile in adopting new solutions to problems. Despite differences, a catholic consensus about doctrine and discipline was growing. Ancient ecclesiastical functions and early models of church structure—a bishop, a board of elders, and a college of deacons—eventually gave way to a monarchical episcopacy. By the beginning of the fourth century the small group of believers had become a large body with members in all parts of the Roman Empire and beyond its bounds; it was universal in outlook, well organized, and theologically complex. Christians developed methods of discipline, a growing philosophical literature, and political autonomy. Early in the fourth century Christians were probably less than 10 percent of the Latin-speaking population of the West and not more than 35 percent of the Greek-speaking East. But with the support of the state, Christianity's ascendancy as the dominant religion of the Roman Empire was assured, and Christianity became the universal religion of the Mediterranean.

As Christianity moved into a more complex world and spread, the challenges and problems presented to it by new cultures and religions increased. Christians in New Testament times thought the world would end soon; after that, many had a negative view of the world, regarding it as presenting a strong temptation to sin. By the end of the third century, Christians had a more positive response to the world; they had learned to live with it, to adapt to it, and, to a great extent, were ready to conquer it.

CHAPTER 3 NOTES

[1] According to Joachim Jeremias, *Jerusalem in the Time of Jesus* (Philadelphia: Fortress Press, 1969), p. 352, Samaritans were considered "the lowest degree of the scale" and a group with whom the Jews had a particularly embittered relationship during the time of Jesus.

[2] For a readable and informative essay about the effect of a cultural milieu, read Stephen Benko and John J. O'Rourke, editors, *The Catacombs and the Colosseum: The Roman Empire as the Setting of Primitive Christianity* (Valley Forge, Pa.: Judson Press, 1971).

[3] Roman Catholics argue that not only were the structures needed, Jesus instituted them by making Peter the first among the apostles. For an ecumenical and contemporary discussion of the place of Peter and the claims for a papal church, see Raymond Brown et al., *Peter in the New Testament: A Collaborative Assessment by Protestant and Roman Catholic Scholars* (Minneapolis: Augsburg Press, 1973).

[4] See Appendix 4 on councils, and look at Jaroslav Pelikan, *The Christian Tradition: A History of the Development of Doctrine—The Emergence of the Catholic Tradition (100–600)* (Chicago: University of Chicago Press, 1971). This book is hard to read, but you might leaf through it to get some sense of the complexities involved.

[5] For a theological approach to Paul, see Joseph A. Fitzmyer, *Pauline Theology: A Brief Sketch* (Englewood Cliffs, N.J.: Prentice-Hall, 1967). This is a short, compact book that you may need some introduction to, but that outlines an interpretation of Pauline theology in a fairly accessible way.

[6] Look through some apocryphal books in Edgar Hennecke and Wilhelm Schneemelcher, editors, *New Testament Apocrypha,* two volumes (Philadelphia: Westminster Press, 1963).

[7] See, for example, Elisabeth Schüssler-Fiorenza, *In Memory of Her: A Feminist Theological Reconstruction of Christian Origins* (New York: Crossroad, 1983). For a shorter, simpler version of her argument, see her "Breaking the Silence—Becoming Visible" in *Women: Invisible in Church and Theology,* an issue of *Concilium* (Edinburgh: T. & T. Clark, 1985), edited by Elisabeth Schüssler-Fiorenza and Mary Collins, pp. 3–17.

[8] Roman Catholics use *apostolic* to describe something identified with the church of the apostles by succession and continuity of doctrine; Protestants use it to mean primitive in contrast with real or supposed corruptions from postapostolic times. For both groups the notion of apostolicity is a key concept in defining authority and in defining authentic ministry within the church. The phrase *apostolic succession* provides a foundation for

Christian ministry and refers to the derivation of Christian ministry from the apostles by way of continuous succession. Bishops, in this perspective, are held to be the successors of the apostles; that is, they perform the function of the apostles and can trace their ministry back to that of the apostles. The fact of continuity has been disputed within Christianity, and the necessity of physical continuity has been denied by most of Protestant Christianity. Roman Catholics believe they can trace the office of the bishop of Rome—the pope—back to Peter in an unbroken line, and that such a continuity of succession confirms their claim to be the true church. This understanding of Roman Catholicism has been modified somewhat since the Second Vatican Council (1962–65), but not so much in official documents. For a more subtle understanding of the Catholic position, see Richard McBrien, *Catholicism* (Minneapolis: Winston Press, 1980), pp. 657–729.

[9] See, for instance, Elaine Pagels, *The Gnostic Gospels* (New York: Random House, 1979), for a survey of some of the more interesting issues raised by Gnostic literature of the period.

[10] We can see some attempts at this kind of adaptation already in the Acts of the Apostles, in Paul's speech to the Athenians (17:16–34).

[11] It is worth looking up Neoplatonism in an encyclopedia and following some of the leads it gives you—the whole tradition of divinization (human beings becoming divine) has its roots there. For a modern interpretation of a medieval expression of this doctrine, see Matthew Fox, *Breakthrough: Meister Eckhart's Creation Spirituality in a New Translation* (New York: Doubleday, 1980).

SUGGESTIONS FOR FURTHER READING

1. For more on the development of early Christian literature, see Henry Bettenson, editor, *The Early Christian Fathers* (Oxford: Oxford University Press, 1969) and *The Later Christian Fathers* (Oxford: Oxford University Press, 1970), which together contain textual excerpts from the earliest times (Clement of Rome) to the sixth century. For a sketchy introduction to the "Fathers," see Patrick J. Hammell, *Handbook of Patrology* (New York: Alba House, 1968). For a clear and readable introduction to major issues and figures, see G. L. Prestige, *Fathers and Heretics: Six Studies in Dogmatic Faith with Prologue and Epilogue* (London: SPCK, 1940).

2. For a deeper understanding of Christianity as it developed from earliest times, see (for a *general* history) Edward Lohse, *The First Christians: Their Beginnings, Writings, and Beliefs* (Philadelphia: Fortress Press, 1982); (for a *sociology* of early Christianity) Abraham J. Malherbe, *Social Aspects of Early Christianity*, 2nd ed. (Philadelphia: Fortress Press, 1983); and (for a critical evaluation arguing that there was never a golden age and that Jesus was a radical), Robert L. Wilken, *The Myth of Christian Beginnings: History's Impact on Belief* (New York: Doubleday, 1971).

3. For an introduction to Gnosticism, see Robert M. Grant, *Gnosticism and Early Christianity* (New York: Harper & Row, 1966). Also, Kurt Rudolph, *Gnosis: The Nature and History of Gnosticism* (San Francisco: Harper & Row, 1983).

4. For a clear and detailed analysis of martyrdom, see W. H. C. Frend, *Martyrdom and Persecution in the Early Church: A Study of a Conflict from the Maccabees to Donatus* (New York: Doubleday, 1967).

5. For the intersection of Christianity and the classical tradition, see Henry Chadwick, *Early Christian Thought and the Classical Tradition: Studies in Justin, Clement and Origen* (Oxford: Clarendon Press, 1966), which contains clear, witty lectures on Alexandrian Christianity. A classic that explains the impact and attraction of Christianity in the classical world is A. D. Nock, *Conversion: The Old and the New in Religion from Alexander the Great to Augustine of Hippo* (Oxford: Oxford University Press, 1969).

6. For more on the relationship between Christianity and the Roman world, see Robert M. Grant, *Augustus to Constantine: The Thrust of the Christian Movement into the Roman World* (New York: Harper & Row, 1970), an extremely readable and clear history of the issue. For a discussion of Christianity as a small sect that eventually triumphed in the West, one that is straightforward and contains pictures and maps, see R. A. Markus, *Christianity in the Roman Empire* (London: Thames & Hudson Ltd., 1974).

7. Some recent works take seriously the *urban* character of many early Christian communities. See for example Wayne A. Meeks and Robert Wilken, *Jews and Christians in Antioch in the First Four Centuries of the Common Era* (Missoula, Mont.: Scholars Press, 1978) or Gerd Theissen, *The Sociology of Early Palestinian Christianity* (Philadelphia: Fortress Press, 1979). For a reconstruction of the social milieu of the Greek-speaking Christians in the provinces, see Wayne A. Meeks, *The First Urban Christians* (New Haven: Yale University Press, 1983).

❖ PART TWO ❖

Historical Roots of Christian Diversity: From Constantine to Modern Times

T HE SECOND PART of this book introduces the variety of Christian belief and expression by focusing on the roots of Christian diversity. It is not meant to be a comprehensive history of Christianity, but a general explanation for the major divisions among the various expressions of Christian belief that have grown up since the fourth century. Christians differ substantially in doctrine, practice, and ecclesiastical structures, and those differences all arose within specific historical contexts. The more serious arguments among Christians led to major divisions within Christianity itself and the formation of separate churches and denominations. These chapters explain those differences.

The first major rift in Christianity occurred between what are now called the Roman Catholic church and the Eastern Orthodox church. These groups grew up in different parts of the vast Roman Empire and, from the early fourth century especially, confronted radically different problems: Western Christians battled to survive, while Eastern Christianity, protected by the state, hammered out the foundations for Christian doctrine (see Appendix 4). They developed different liturgical practices and patterns of ecclesiastical authority, and eventually separated into two distinct forms of Christianity.

The second major division occurred in the West during the Reformation. Reform attempts within and outside the church led to the development of several new forms of Christianity distinguishable from one another in polity, belief, and practice. We will follow the Reformation itself and then watch the reforming spirit of the sixteenth century move through the seventeenth and eighteenth centuries. By the beginning of the nineteenth century there were many new varieties of Christianity.

These chapters cover an enormous range of history and development and have been written specifically to explain how and why there are so many different kinds of Christianity. Part Two should therefore be read not as a history of Christianity but as an attempt to look historically at Christian controversy over fifteen centuries and to explain how some of those controversies led to the formation of separate denominations.

One important principle to keep in mind is this one: conflict and controversy characterize any living religion. We have already seen that the young Christian community was shaped by many different questions and defined itself in various contexts. The fact that the early Christians had to figure things out rather than follow some predisposed plan of action is not a negative judgment but is a testament to the complicated realities of community life. As we will see in this section, conflict and controversy sometimes became so acute that new denominations were formed. Some people see this proliferation of denominations as tragic, as a betrayal of the essential unity of Christianity. One can wonder, however, whether there ever was the kind of unity that some people project into the distant past. Christians have always argued heatedly over important issues and have often treated one another with hostility, suspicion, and anger. The point of this section is to explain how and why there came to be so many different kinds of Christianity and to present each new group sympathetically enough to identify its special understanding of the Christian life.

CHAPTER 4

ORTHODOX CHRISTIANITY
AND ROMAN CATHOLICISM:
FROM THE FOURTH TO THE
FOURTEENTH CENTURIES

T wo distinct forms of Christianity grew up in the eastern and western parts of the Roman Empire: Roman Catholicism in the West and Orthodox Christianity in the East. Orthodox Christians and Roman Catholics are the largest and most ancient Christian groups. They share central assumptions, but because they developed in radically different religious and political climates, they also have significant differences and represent conflicting orientations. Roman Catholic Christianity tends to be more legalistic in the structures of church life and in its approach to the sacraments; Orthodox Christianity is more mystical in its liturgical preoccupations, more concerned with inner spiritual content. Differences in perspective have shaped the way each group articulates doctrine and celebrates liturgy. One general example may make this difference more clear. Western Christianity explains that the word of God became flesh in order to save people from their sins; thus Western Christians stress salvation. Eastern Christianity explains that the word of God became flesh so that people could become like God; thus Eastern Orthodox Christians stress deification.

My approach to the material in this chapter is somewhat different from my approach in later chapters and perhaps deserves some word of explanation. Because we will not *specifically* follow later developments in Orthodox Christianity, especially in relation to Roman Catholicism, and because Roman Catholicism and Orthodoxy, in contrast to Protestantism, put a premium on the development and canonization of tradition and on the model of sanctity represented by the monastic tradition, my discussion of these two groups is meant to give you some idea of the deep unity of ancient Christianity. At the same time, because these two groups developed in very different geographical and political situations, they became, for all their shared heritage, two quite distinct expressions of Christianity. Those differences are most evident in their patterns of authority and in terms of worship. This chapter, therefore, does not simply describe a profound historical breach; it attempts to show some of the consequences of that break in terms of different structural and liturgical expressions.

POINTS OF CORRESPONDENCE

Belief in the authority of tradition distinguishes Roman Catholics and Orthodox Christians from most other Christian groups. Both Roman Catholics and Orthodox Christians posit the need for a religious authority alongside the Bible based on postbiblical experience and practice. They share an ancient doctrinal system and have liturgical preoccupations that are accepted only in part (if at all) by other Christian denominations. Both also place a high value on monasticism and avowed religious life, institutions that have not been important in other Christian groups. We explore these points of similarity between the two churches first.

Tradition as a Religious Authority

In some Christian groups the Bible is the most important source of religious authority, but not the only one. Why? The Old and New Testaments were written in a particular place and time and their messages respond to the spiritual and psychological needs of the people to whom they were addressed. Since the written sources of Christianity were intended for a people in a historical situation that no longer wholly obtains, some groups believe the written words need to be continually studied and applied to new problems. This reinterpretation then forms a parallel source of religious authority: tradition.

The Bible and tradition are not opposed to one another. Tradition is the way the Bible is read and applied in the church, and almost all Christians see the need for it. A debate arises, however, over how much authority different groups invest in tradition. Not all Christians accept the dogmatic decrees of the early councils (see Appendix 4) as authentic interpretations of the gospel, and none but Roman Catholics accept the councils after the ninth century as an authentic expression of Christian tradition. As we shall see, Protestant reformers were especially critical of the Roman Catholic acceptance of traditions (like the claims of the papacy, or innovative theological explanations about the Lord's Supper) that (as they perceived it) had no roots in the New Testament at all.

Tradition is a specific interpretation of Scripture as elaborated within the Christian community and affirmed by the church. It is meant to be fluid, not fixed, and tension can result when a group shows a tendency to absolutize or canonize tradition. Originally tradition was meant to allow for new interpretations, but at certain points tradition itself appeared to be fixed and unmovable. The development of tradition is not meant to lead to an ecclesiastical rigidity, but to recognize the dynamic interplay between the concrete, fixed authority of Scripture and the fluid, developing authority of daily practice.

Tradition adds something new: it enlarges upon and gradually builds up the written words. Human ingenuity is a factor in the development of tradition because people often expand a concrete communication beyond its original scope. Tradition is built up slowly, almost imperceptibly, until it becomes authoritative and sometimes even supersedes the authority of Scripture. In Judaism the original revelation was contained in the Torah; the Prophets and the Writings were considered "only tradition." Much later, however, when the canon of the Hebrew Bible was established, these traditions had come to be considered inspired, worthy to be called Scripture. In Christianity the original message of Jesus was contained in the early preaching—Jesus who was crucified has risen from the dead—and then written down in the synoptic Gospels. The stories recounting the words and deeds of Jesus were considered superior to the writings of Paul (written before the synoptics) and John (written after the synoptics); their writings were regarded as interpretations or commentaries, only part of the tradition. Yet when the canon of the New Testament was finally drawn up, many of these writings were accepted as the word of God and were placed in the New Testament.

The tradition included in Scripture is not the same as the tradition that has developed since then, the postbiblical collection of opinions, practices, and dogmatic definitions. Roman Catholics and Orthodox Christians disagree about some parts of the tradition—especially the authority of the pope—but they agree on the principle of tradition; both see a need for an extrabiblical religious authority. For them, Scripture without tradition lacks vitality, tradition without Scripture lacks foundation, and either one of them without observance and practice lacks credibility.

Models of Sanctity

One model of the Christian life portrayed in the New Testament is life in common: people shared work, prayer, and food, lived simply, and grew in fellowship. Another New Testament concept is the life of perfection. Jesus once said, "You, therefore, must be perfect, as your heavenly Father is perfect" (Matt. 5:48). Christian monasticism derives from these two concepts as they developed in a world where an ascetic ideal already existed. Greek philosophers used the word *asceticism* to describe a system of discipline intended to combat vice and enhance virtue. The word comes from the Greek word for training or exercise; ascetics are people who train themselves for virtue. In Christianity the words of Jesus about denying oneself, taking up one's cross, and following him (Mark

8:34) provide inspiration for Christian ascetic life: negative self-denial on the one hand and positive following of Jesus on the other. But what does it mean to deny self and follow Jesus? For some early Christians it meant living in anticipation of martyrdom, to others it meant living an ascetic life: being alert and watchful, praying and fasting, giving up earthly possessions, and turning away from pleasures of the flesh (food, drink, and sex). Those who chose asceticism were monks.

The life of perfection sought by monks cannot be lived "in the world." They usually retire to faraway places removed from the cares and stresses of worldly life. The first people to withdraw from the world went to the desert; the Greek word for desert is the root of the word *hermit*. By the middle of the third century many hermits lived in deserts and caves in remote areas of Egypt and Syria. Monks differ from hermits in that they live not in isolation but in community, and follow a common rule; the first monastic communities formed when groups of hermits came together for safety or fellowship and then built a fence or wall around all of their hermitages. Later communities lived in monastic houses where monks slept, ate, and prayed under the same roof. Monastic life was open to both men (monks) and women (nuns). They spent their days in prayer and work, and lived under vows (solemn promises) of *poverty* (without private possessions or money), *chastity* (no sex), and *obedience* (to the will of the local superior). These vows are sometimes called the counsels of perfection, a phrase that indicates that those who follow them desire to live a life of religious perfection, in line with the command of Jesus (Matt. 5:48).

As the ascetic life flourished, some of the early Christian writers undergirded it with theoretical and theological support. In the third century, Clement of Alexandria and Origen both extolled asceticism and encouraged Christians to live pure and perfect lives. Because Clement and Origen lived and wrote in a Neoplatonic environment, they combined their interest in asceticism with the Neoplatonic concept of contemplation. Monasticism combined a desire for perfection (the ascetic life) with mystical ascent (the contemplative life). In the Eastern Church, contemplation and mysticism were always the central preoccupations of monastic life, and Eastern monasticism has remained contemplative. Monastic life in the West was similar, but also developed a more active concept of religious community life: Western Christianity supported religious congregations and orders of friars and canons who lived under a semimonastic rule (life in common and specific vows) but followed specific active vocations in the church like preaching or teaching.

The church both East and West contained some extremists in the monastic life. In the West were Irish monks who put themselves out to sea in open boats with few provisions and no oars so they could see where God would send them. They manifested an ascetic ideal—an individual pilgrimage to God embodied in a life of wandering—that was not commonly practiced. In the East were extravagant ascetics who spent many years on top of high pillars in one position in order to discipline the flesh and draw closer to God in attitudes of eternal prayer. In both East and West were some who thought the ascetic life required extreme penances: long fasts, the wearing of spiked chains close to the flesh, and so on. For the most part, however, monastic life was not extreme; it was community life lived under a sensible rule.

Furthermore, monastic life in both East and West, however much it stressed avoidance of worldly temptations, placed a corollary emphasis on hospitality to the faithful. All monks and nuns, whether they lived in community or alone, were supposed to be ready to share their material and spiritual goods with those in need of them. If monks or nuns found the demands of the faithful to be interfering with their spiritual quests, their only recourse was to move further into the desert and limit accessibility to themselves. Refusing hospitality to those in need was never an option in monastic life.

Monasticism in Orthodox Christianity has been based, essentially, on the writings of Basil the Great (330–79 C.E.). Some people refer to the "Rule" of St. Basil, but his writings really constitute letters of spiritual advice to those trying to find a deeper union with God through prayer and ascetic practices. Although there have always been—and still are—hermits in the Orthodox tradition, Basil stressed communal life and encouraged monks to practice manual labor and obedience, prayer and work. Since Orthodox monasteries were protected and often financed by the government, and since Orthodox Christianity grew in a relatively peaceful environment, Orthodox monks have been free to pursue the mystical life to the exclusion of other concerns. Orthodox monasteries are usually not great centers of learning or scholarship; they are places where people can dedicate themselves totally to prayer and contemplation. Eastern monasticism is much the same today as in its origins: monks still follow the wisdom of St. Basil, wear the same clothing, and live simply. Their lives combine asceticism, mysticism, and discipline in search of a direct experience of God. The chief mystical experience is the vision of divine light, and the main preoccupation of the monk is the desire for union with God.

In contrast to Orthodox monasticism, Western monasticism is based on a clear rule devised by Benedict of Nursia (480–550 C.E.). Benedict stressed work and prayer, and monks were required to bind themselves to a single monastery for life. According to the Benedictine Rule, the first piece of Western monastic legislation developed for monks living in politically unstable Europe, monks were supposed to lead a traditional monastic life. In fact, however, monks in the West often lived unconventional monastic lives because their situation demanded it. Western monks, however much they may have wanted to devote their entire lives to union with God, often were called upon to act as teachers, political advisers, and missionaries. Monks were the great librarians of the West, primarily responsible for the preservation of learning during the Dark Ages and entrusted with copying and preserving ancient manuscripts.

Furthermore, since the politically unstable situation of the Western church created an environment for change and creative adaptation, monasticism in the West inspired a variety of experiments in religious life. Some of these new groups devoted most of their energy to teaching or begging, to crusading or spiritual knighthood, to religious or political reform. According to some interpreters, the role of monks and religious communities in the civilization of the West after the fall of Rome was of utmost importance.[1]

THE POWER OF ROME AS AN IDEA: TWO CHRISTIAN MODELS

Jesus was born into a Mediterranean world ruled by Rome at a time when the Roman mystique was at its apex. The world had never experienced an empire so vast or so efficient, and when people thought of "Rome" they envisioned a set of associated ideas. Rome was vast, peaceful, beautifully organized, and ruled by a great legal system; it was religiously complex, with impressive shrines and monuments celebrating its own glory and providing inspirational spaces for its people; it was distinguished by a highly developed intellectual and cultural life where playwrights, poets, and philosophers spoke classical Latin and wrote essays and histories that were so good we still read them today. Rome was presided over by Caesar, a central ruling authority who stood close to divinity and who symbolized in his person the glory of Rome. As that glory dimmed—Marcus Aurelius, the "last good emperor," died in 180 and so began a period of decline and political anarchy—and then appeared to be restored to some degree by Constantine, it was natural to wonder whether the old Rome might, indeed, reclaim the attention of the world.

If we can see Rome more as an idea than a place, perhaps we can imagine that it was very powerful and attractive. Rome was a goal, an ideal to shape policy. It is not surprising that it attracted Constantine, and it probably should not be disconcerting that it attracted Christians in general. As we begin to look at political arrangements, East and West, it might help to keep the "idea of Rome" in the back of our minds as a kind of explanation for events. If we ask who could have revived Roman dreams or restored Roman glory in the context of the fourth century, we will find several answers. As the Roman emperor, Constantine clearly had the best claim on the project, but when he moved his capital from the city of Rome to a new site in the Eastern part of the Roman Empire, he left a political vacuum in the West and invited rival claimants. In the West several groups were inspired to restore Roman glory: old senatorial families, new barbarian families, and, most of all, the bishops of Rome, later known as popes.

For all their shared heritage in tradition and monasticism, therefore, the two ancient forms of Christianity grew into distinct churches mostly because of widely differing political experiences. The Orthodox church organized itself in two ways: at the local level, ecclesiastical organization was based on the local community with the bishop as its head. In an ideal form, local churches are united by a community of love rather than by an institutional bond. At the same time, the broader version of the Orthodox church organized itself along the administrative lines of the Roman Empire, wherein the chief administrative officer was the emperor, thought to be God's agent on earth. The patriarch of Constantinople, the highest-ranking church official in the Eastern church, understood that his standing was tied to the emperor, who could approve patriarchal elections, call councils, and pass ecclesiastical laws. In matters of faith, however, Christ was understood to be the head of the church, and Christ's will for the church was stated and defended by the patriarchs.

The Roman church organized itself according to the claims of apostolicity, especially the claims that Peter was *the* most important apostle and that his territory (Rome) was *the* seat of religious authority. The patriarch of Rome, the highest-ranking church official in the Western church, understood that his standing was greater than the emperor's and that he (the bishop of Rome, later called the pope) was the head of the church. Both pope and patriarch thought of themselves as Roman and as heirs of the greatest political empire in the history of the world. We look next in greater detail at each of the two systems of church-state relations, as they developed in their historical contexts. We can see how this led to a great schism between the two churches that has endured until the present day.

Constantinople as the New Rome: The Greek Orthodox System

When Constantine reunited the fragments of the Roman Empire in the early part of the fourth century, he did so under the sign of the cross.[2] The claim made by Constantine's biographer, Eusebius, was that Constantine—like Paul in the New Testament—was called directly by God to embrace Christianity. The political results of this claim were momentous for the church: it meant that Constantine ruled by divine right, that he considered himself appointed by God, and that his government was a theocracy (that is, the people believed that God, through a mediator, the emperor, ruled Byzantium). Neither Constantine nor the emperors after him ever claimed to be divine, but they did see themselves as God's representatives on earth, ranking just below Christ in the administration of earthly justice. The office of the emperor was, in a sense, the visible manifestation of God on earth. The emperor was like God because God's business was to bring the heavens into a peaceful unity and harmony and the emperor's business was to create a state in which all people coexisted in unity and harmony. God ruled the cosmos and the emperor ruled the earth.

Through a series of victories and treaties, Constantine became the sole master of the western half of the empire by 313 C.E., and master of the entire Roman Empire—East and West—by 324. The decisive battle in which Constantine won control of the West was the Battle of the Milvian Bridge (outside Rome). Before this battle Constantine had a dream or vision which he later understood as a revelation: he saw a cross superimposed on the sun and heard the words "In this sign conquer." Constantine took control of the West under the Christian sign of the cross, and from that time was more sympathetic to Christianity than to any other religion. It was Constantine who passed the Edict of Milan, which granted religious freedom to all and ended the persecution of Christians; it was Constantine who began the process of making the empire Christian. He began gradually to transfer all the religious revenues of the ancient world to the Christian church, and by 324 began a massive church-building program so the most impressive buildings in the empire were Christian places of worship.

Constantine called the first ecumenical council at Nicaea in 325 (see Appendix 4). Politically astute, he saw that the Roman Empire needed a unifying ideology, that a geographically massive empire with a variety of philosophical schools and cultures needed some common belief to bind people together. Constantine saw Christianity as the perfect unifying force. Universal in scope, it was beginning to take hold of people's religious imaginations. It combined some rituals and beliefs of the mystery religions with belief in a historically concrete savior-God, and it had developed a sophisticated philosophical and political framework that enabled discussion of issues and evaluation of positions. And it was *organized*. Besides, Constantine believed he had been called by God, blessed with a revelation experience, appointed to build a Christian empire.

The religious symbols associated with the Christian empire solidified his claims. Constantine's mother, Helena, made a pilgrimage to Jerusalem and found there some of the implements of Jesus's death—the cross, the nails, and the sign of the cross that identified Jesus as king of the Jews—which became the great religious talismans of the empire and tokens of divine favor.[3] The people of Byzantium—renamed Constantinople when Constantine moved the capital of the empire there in 333—considered themselves both Romans and the chosen people of God. Coins were stamped with pictures of Jesus and the motto Jesus Christ, King of Rulers. The actions of the emperor took on a sacred and symbolic character; military expeditions were sacred and the ceremonies of war were holy. People believed the real ruler of the empire was Christ: the cross was carried into battle as a standard and laws were passed in the name of the Lord Jesus Christ, Our Master.

Constantinople, the capital of the eastern part of the Roman Empire, was called the new Rome. All the weight and civilizing importance of Roman history was adopted by Byzantium. The new Rome differed from the old in that the new one was Christian; the task was no longer just to civilize, but to bring all people to salvation in Christ. Constantine perceived himself as an apostle sent by Christ to bring the gospel to the world; one of his titles, carved on his tomb when he died, was Equal of the Apostles. When Constantinople fell to the Turks in 1453 the title and the claims to be the new Rome—the third Rome—fell to Moscow and the Russian Orthodox church. In the fifteenth century Russia was the only politically independent power remaining in the Orthodox world. The czar called himself Beloved of Christ, as the emperor of Constantinople had done. The claims and tasks of the Orthodox system fell to the czar and the

Russian Orthodox church, and in Russia religious and political destinies were intertwined as in old Byzantium. The idea of an Orthodox Christian state lasted until July 16, 1918, when the last Russian czar, Nicholas II, was executed.

Where was the church in this theocratic system? It was bound up with the state, supporting and reinforcing the state's power. The head of the church, the patriarch of Constantinople, seldom had occasion to exercise direct *political* power because the East always had a strong emperor. When Constantine moved the capital to the East, a political vacuum was created in the West. Rome and the West lacked a strong political system, and the result was political chaos. The head of the church in the West, the bishop of Rome, finally managed to rise to power, to make order of the political disorder. The patriarch of Constantinople seldom had that opportunity; as head of the church he had full spiritual power, but what political influence he had he exercised in support of the emperor in the East. No independent religious authority in conflict with the emperor's political authority emerged in the East.

In the Eastern system the church was protected and established by the state: it was supported by state-collected taxes, met with no persecutions, feared no attack from outside. But sometimes the state became overprotective, and the church had to deal with emperors who wanted to take on spiritual functions and make spiritual decisions. It was not the patriarch of Constantinople or the bishop of Rome who called the first ecumenical council; it was the emperor.[4] When Constantine entered the hall where the bishops were meeting in Nicaea to open the council, Eusebius described him as "an angel of God descended from heaven, radiant in the fiery glow of the purple and adorned with gold and precious gems—such was his outward appearance. But his soul was visibly ornamented with the fear and adoration of God."[5] This description is both political and spiritual, and emphasizes the enormous power of the emperor in both realms.

The patriarch of Constantinople was the chief celebrant of the sacraments and the one who presided over the synod of bishops; he was the leader of the church, but it was the emperor who bore the title Vicar of God on Earth. The power of the patriarch of Constantinople was to be exercised in the spiritual realm; he was not to interfere with political decisions. Even his spiritual functions were to be exercised in cooperation with the emperor, who was—by virtue of his titles and power—permitted to operate within the spiritual realm. At its best, the cooperation between patriarch and emperor on the spiritual front was what the Greeks called a *symphonia*, a harmony of spirits.

Things were not always at their best, however, and the patriarch often had to struggle against the emperor and to safeguard the spiritual freedom of the church. By definition the patriarch was to be spiritually free, but sometimes that freedom was encroached upon by the powers of the state. When the Orthodox system moved to Russia in the fifteenth century, the harmony between patriarch and emperor (czar) was destroyed; the czars took full control of the church. In the eighteenth century, Czar Peter the Great abolished the patriarchate and established the internal life of the church along lines he thought were better suited to it and to an enlightened view of church structure.

In summary, then, the Orthodox system conformed to the model of the Roman Empire; Constantinople was the new Rome and Constantine was appointed by and beloved of God. The old Roman emperors sometimes proclaimed themselves gods; Constantine and his successors did not need to make such a claim because even without it they held an enormous amount of power and prestige in an essentially theocratic state. As the Vicar of God on Earth the emperor also held a central position in the church. He protected and subsidized the church, called and presided over the ecumenical councils, and promulgated all the conciliar dogmas. In this situation the church could not compete for political power and sometimes had to fight even to maintain its own spiritual power, defending matters of doctrine from imperial interference. A much different situation obtained in the West.

The West as Roman Catholic: The Rise of the Papacy

Constantine sought to establish a new Rome in Constantinople and to be the earthly ruler of a theocratic state. He wanted to replace the old (pagan) Roman Empire with a new (Christian) one, and he succeeded in the eastern half of the empire. The situation in the West, however, did not support the same kind of result. Constantine left a politically chaotic situation in the West. In that situation the bishop of Rome tried desperately to bring the various barbarian chieftains[6] and their peoples into the Christian communion so that religious and political unity would flourish in the West as they had in the East. In order to establish his claim to moral authority in the Western world, the bishop of Rome began to interpret Jesus's words in Matthew 16—"You are Peter, and on this rock I will build my church"—to justify his attempt to control and supervise the Latin church and the peoples in the western part of the empire. Constantine claimed to rule by divine appointment, citing his revelation experience before the Battle of the Milvian Bridge; the bishops of Rome also claimed to rule by divine appointment, citing the words of Jesus about Peter. The principle of apostolic succession and the power of the keys given by Jesus to Peter provided the theoretical foundation for the power of the bishops of Rome.

In the East the emperor's political power was so strong that it sometimes spilled over into the spiritual realm; in the West the bishop of Rome's power inevitably embraced the political realm. In both parts of the empire spiritual and political power overlapped; at best there was a *symphonia,* a harmonious cooperation of interests, but at worst—in the chaotic Dark Ages—confusion and a battle for power resulted. The political situation in the West was precarious; the collapse of the Roman Empire, the devastating effect of the barbarian invasions, an unstable economy, and other serious problems created a need for a strong leader located in the West. The leader who emerged was the bishop of Rome, a spiritual leader who found it possible to become politically powerful as well. The first task in the West was not unity (as in the East) but survival; beyond that the church in the West set itself the task of making the gospel known to various tribes and unsophisticated peoples. The bishop of Rome began to insinuate himself into the political vacuum and to suggest that the most natural place to look for moral leadership was to the old capital of the empire, Rome. By the fourth century the bishop of Rome began to call himself the pope, the president of the whole Western Christian church.

From the Council of Nicaea on, Christians clearly recognized that the bishop of Rome had a *primacy of honor*. Rome had been the capital of the empire, it was renowned for its orthodoxy, and people believed its church was founded by Peter and Paul. Peter was believed to be the apostle of Rome. His bones and those of Paul were buried there and it was, after Jerusalem, the most popular place to go on pilgrimage. The bishops of Rome said that Peter was the first bishop of Rome and that they were his successors. Peter, they reasoned, was first among the apostles and his successor should be first among the successors of the apostles, the bishops. The bishop of Rome did not want to be first among equals, but wanted simply to be first.

The hierarchical system of authority that developed in the Christian church and that was legislated at the Council of Chalcedon rested in the five patriarchs: the leaders of the church in Rome, Constantinople, Alexandria, Antioch, and Jerusalem. The bishop of Rome was the undisputed patriarch of the Western church and was accorded a primacy of *honor* among his fellow patriarchs; he wanted the other patriarchs to recognize that the bishop of Rome had a *juridical* primacy over them, but they never did. The *papal* claim is the assertion by the bishop of Rome of his authority over the entire universal church, a claim rejected by Orthodox Christians and Protestants. The *patriarchal* claim is the assertion that the bishop of Rome is the undisputed head of the Western church, a claim that was accepted by Orthodox Christians and rejected later by Protestants. Friction between East and West usually involved the papal claim.

The history of the papacy is primarily one of attempts on the part of the bishops of Rome to exercise their authority over the church in the West. In establishing their authority in the West, however, they also asserted their authority over the entire church. The papal and patriarchal claims have, therefore, been confused in the minds of the popes themselves and in the minds of most Christians. Popes began to press their claims over the entire church in the fourth century. By the end of the sixth century the theological claims for papal power had been worked out and supported with the reforming and evangelistic initiatives of the popes.

The strongest papal assertion of political power did not come until the year 800, when the pope made a political alliance with a particular Frankish tribe and sealed that alliance by crowning the Frankish king, Charlemagne, emperor. This was a politically momentous move that proved disastrous for the papacy on some counts. An emperor (actually an empress, Irene) reigned in Constantinople when the pope conferred that title upon a barbarian king. Now there was a genuine political rival in the West who adopted many of the titles and functions of the emperor in the East: he protected and subsidized the church and also sometimes interfered in its life.

Once the pope introduced the idea that he had the power to name and crown the emperor, the office of the papacy was elevated to a political importance it had never known before. With the collapse of the Carolingian empire[7] and the onset of the so-called Dark Ages, the papacy became a pawn in a dirty game of Italian politics. The first reform attempts were made in the tenth century by Otto I, an emperor who wanted a holy papacy. The reformed papacy—culminating in the reign of Gregory VII (1073–85)—then wanted to establish autonomy and reform the empire. That desire led to the medieval church-state controversies. The history of church-state relations in the West up to and beyond the Reformation was a history of conflict: sometimes the pope was strong enough to control the secular ruler and sometimes the emperor or king was strong enough to control the pope. The controversies usually involved a clarification of roles.

The ever-present danger in the Eastern Orthodox system was that the emperor would use his power to interfere in spiritual matters; in the West the danger was both that the pope would use his spiritual power to interfere unduly in politics *and* that the emperor (or king) would use political power to interfere with the life of the church. Neither the popes nor the kings would relinquish their powers in the name of peace, for roughly the same reasons that the leaders of the modern world insist they cannot disarm unilaterally. In the West neither pope nor king ever had a total victory, just as in the East the patriarch never had an opportunity to develop political independence. Whether the popes should have been involved in the political order to the extent that they were is a matter of dispute among Christians. Some argue that the church had no business wielding political power, and some argue that without papal involvement the state would have controlled the church in the West as it had in the East. Whatever the merits of each side of the argument, the history of the papacy is an integral part of Western political *and* spiritual history.

The East-West Schism and Contemporary Relations

To review the preceding two sections: the types of church government in Eastern and Western Christianity were remarkably similar but were distinguished from one another by their relationship to the emperor. In the East the emperor often acted as if he were the head of the church and as if the patriarchs were no more than liturgical leaders; in the West the pope was clearly the head of the church, though he sometimes had to defend himself from imperial interference. Both churches tended to think of themselves as the kingdom of God on earth.

Given the role of the pope in the West and the claims he made for jurisdiction over the universal church, it is not surprising that a schism arose between

East and West. Orthodox Christians never acknowledged the theological claims of the papacy, yet the church in the West grew up assuming those claims were true. The church in the West thus became less recognizable to Christians in the East. The situation was exacerbated by a growing cultural division: Greeks ceased to speak Latin and Western Christians could not speak Greek. Thus when they met they could not understand one another's language and did not recognize one another's system of church authority. They argued as heatedly about relatively peripheral matters—the kind of bread to use for the Eucharist, whether to allow priests to have beards—as they did about more substantial things like the *filioque*[8] clause in the Nicene Creed (see Appendix 5) and clerical celibacy.

When the old Roman Empire collapsed, the new Rome interpreted that fall as God's vengeance, as a sign that the Orthodox church was to carry forth God's plan in the world. When the popes, through a series of shrewd political moves and some luck, emerged from the ruins of the old empire as the leaders of the West, they interpreted their recovery as a sign that God intended the power of Peter to be passed down through the line of the bishops of Rome. Orthodox Christians developed a legend of St. Andrew to counter the claims about Peter: they argued that Andrew was called to be an apostle before Peter and that Andrew had come to Constantinople. The popes responded with a systematic exploitation of the texts of Matthew 16, which say that the church was built upon Peter. Both were at pains to deny the claims of the other.

The addition to the Nicene Creed of the *filioque* clause was partly a doctrinal wedge between the two churches, but more than that it was a symbolic manifestation of the differences between them on the issue of spiritual authority. Orthodox Christians could simply not understand how anyone could add something to the doctrines or words of a council. There were jurisdictional disputes between East and West about new Christian territories, especially Bulgaria, Moravia, and Byzantine provinces in southern Italy; some old ethnic rivalries—between Serbians and Croatians, for example—date back to religious arguments. The frequent clashes between East and West over religious matters led to a formal schism between Rome and Constantinople in 1054.

The great rift between Orthodox Christianity and Roman Catholicism occurred during the Crusades. In 1204 Constantinople was captured by crusaders from the West; monasteries, churches, palaces, and libraries were robbed and fire destroyed many of the Byzantine art treasures. The crushing blow was the establishment of a Latin patriarch and emperor in the city. When the Turks threatened to capture Constantinople in the early part of the fifteenth century, an attempt was made to reunite the two churches, but it did not last. The rift between them was too old and too deep. The Turks captured Constantinople in 1453. Thus ended the Byzantine Empire, but the "third Rome," Moscow, took over the Byzantine tradition and the principles of the Orthodox church and gave them soil in which to survive and flourish.

Besides some real theological differences, the main stumbling block between Roman Catholic and Orthodox reunion today is church authority. The

Orthodox churches do not accept the office and universal authority of the pope. Some Greek churches do accept the authority of the pope, but are otherwise quasi-autonomous. Roman Catholics call them *Uniate* churches. In discipline (clergy may marry) and liturgical practice they resemble the Orthodox church. A variety of Orthodox churches exist: Russian, Greek, Rumanian, and so forth, each with its own system of authority. Although these groups share educational resources and a rich liturgical heritage, they have been unable to achieve *structural* unity; attempts to form an American Orthodox church have failed. Orthodox Christians remain identified as Greek, Rumanian, and so on, a description that refers *not* to ethnicity but to old ecclesiastical territorial divisions. Greek Orthodox Christians, for example, were not all Greek, but all lived in a territory headed by the patriarch of Constantinople.

Roman Catholics have been more open to dialogue with all other religious bodies since the Second Vatican Council (1962–65). Members of the Orthodox church attended the council and (with the exception of the Greek church) agreed to begin dialogue with Rome on equal terms. Recent popes have been eager for reunion, visiting Orthodox patriarchs and welcoming them to Rome. Still, the stumbling blocks to reunion are many: authority is only the easiest one to see.

LITURGY AND DOCTRINE IN THE TWO CHURCHES

Roman Catholicism and the Orthodox church both have distinctive patterns of worship and ancient systems of doctrine. They display some crucial differences in liturgical art and practice as well as in doctrinal issues. Some of these differences are culturally explainable, but many derive from orientations established in the early Christian church. We look at these differences next.

Icons and Divinization: The Orthodox Perspective

One of the most beautiful manifestations of Orthodox piety is the icon.[9] The artistic style and place of icons in Orthodox life and worship grew out of the mosaic tradition of early Byzantine art. Used to decorate Orthodox churches, they are images of Christ, the Virgin Mary, and the saints painted in a highly stylized way. There were not always icons. Christianity, growing as it did from Judaism, was very much against idolatry and the veneration of pictures of holy persons. For a number of reasons, however, pictures of Jesus and Mary began to be prevalent from the fifth century onward.

According to pious Orthodox belief, icons are not made by human hands. Theologically, icons are an expression of a central Christian belief, the union of the divine and human natures in Christ. As it says in the Gospel of John, "the Word became flesh" (1:14); God became visible in Christ. Icons, therefore, are thought to be manifestations of heavenly archetypes. They are always painted on a gold background (to represent a heavenly atmosphere) and they are re-copied as they are, not embellished or made subject to new artistic styles. They are consecrated, sacred images, not art objects. In Orthodox belief, heaven comes down to earth, especially in the celebration of the Eucharist where the earthly congregation meets and eats with the heavenly congregation. The icons represent this coming to earth of God and the angels and saints.

Orthodox believers venerate icons (bowing in front of them, kissing them, lighting candles before them) both at home and in church. In an Orthodox home, the eastern corner of the living room and/or bedroom is the so-called beautiful corner, with a series of icons and candles, often decorated with flowers. An Orthodox church has an *iconostasis,* originally a low barrier, currently a high wall completely separating the sanctuary from the rest of the church. Icons are arranged on the iconostasis in a fixed order. On the center door of the icono-stasis are icons of the angels Michael and Gabriel, to the right of the door is an icon of Christ, and to the right of that is an icon of John the Baptist. On the left side of the door is an icon of the Mother of God and to the left of that, an icon of the saint to whom the church is dedicated. Above these major icons are rows of smaller icons representing the story of redemption and presenting a visible image of eucharistic piety and belief.

Icons are an integral part of Orthodox dogma. Genesis records the words that people are made "in the image of God." The Orthodox interpretation of this is that people carry an image (or icon) of God within themselves. This idea has interesting doctrinal consequences: sin is understood as a distortion or taint-ing of the image of God within oneself. The doctrine of the Trinity and expla-nations of Christology and the role of the church are all defined in terms of images.

Though for political reasons Constantinople was considered the new Rome, for liturgical reasons it was more of a new Jerusalem, a holy city. There were many different churches, all of which were filled with tangible reminders of the saints (relics) and decorated with icons. Religion was a way of life for people: religious controversies were not so much abstract arguments as they were mat-ters of great popular interest. The notion that the divine energy was present in everything fostered a piety that tended to revere the whole created order. The bond between the Resurrection and the sacred meal celebrated in the Eucharist made the liturgy essentially a joyful event. The endless reenactment of the Chris-tian mysteries in the liturgy was the way the corporate life of the people found its religious expression.

Orthodox liturgy is elaborate, rich in gestures, vestments, and hymns. Many forms developed in the context of certain historical preferences and prohibi-tions. A ban on instrumental music in Orthodox churches led to a highly devel-oped tradition of choral singing and chanting that uses the human voice as an instrument of praise; a preference for certain types of art led to an elaborate range of art in murals, mosaics, and icons. A ban against the theater and drama encouraged people to use their dramatic energies and talents in the celebration of the liturgy. In both East and West came rich, dramatic developments of liturgical prayer and style, and a proliferation of different liturgies. In both cases the liturgy was finally standardized and celebrated in the same way everywhere. Both Orthodox and Roman Catholic liturgies are substantially different from most Protestant worship.

The doctrinal complexion of the Orthodox church is mystical: the great dogmatic preoccupations are deification, sanctification, rebirth, resurrection, and transfiguration. The emphasis is not so much on truth and justice as on beauty and love. The Orthodox believer's aim is to become a new creation, to be transfigured by grace. God did not become human in order to satisfy divine justice, but to enable people to become like God. Sin is not so much a violation of a law as a diminishment of the original image of God in a person; redemption is, therefore, bound up with renewal and transfiguration. Orthodox Christians lack a concept of predestination and do not emphasize eternal punishment of sinners. They expect the final judgment to be a time of grace and love more than separation and judgment. This doctrinal view is very much at odds with that of Roman Catholicism.

Survival and Salvation: The Roman Perspective

Recall that the circumstances in which Roman Catholic Christianity developed differed greatly from those of Orthodox Christianity. Where Orthodox Christianity interacted with Hellenistic philosophy and mystery religions, the Roman church faced barbarian tribes. Where Orthodox Christianity developed within a stable government system, the Roman church built upon the old Roman legal system to prevent the total collapse of civilization in the West. Where religious life in the East was confined to monasticism, it developed into monasticism plus a variety of functional religious orders in the West. The liturgical preoccupations of Orthodox Christianity were essentially mystical; the church in the West developed a fascination with practical understandings of doctrine and worship.

One can find both mystical and practical aspects in the New Testament; Roman Catholicism was more moved by definitions and ordinary Christian life, though it was not without a mystical tradition. Roman pagan religion had been a very legalistic affair: the priest knew the correct forms of prayers and sacrifice, how to please the gods. Pagan piety was not concerned with dogma and ethics, but with proper cultic acts scrupulously performed, with precise rules and rigorous exactitude in religion. Influenced somewhat by old Roman religious concerns, Western Catholicism was preoccupied with sin and justification. In Orthodox Christianity, the church is the place where one can become transfigured by meeting with the heavenly community. In Roman Catholicism, the church is a place of justice; God has laws, people break them, and justice demands that people make reparation. The church is the place where reparation is made possible: the bishop—or his agent, the priest—determines the degree of sin and the kind of reparation necessary. Penance (which in Orthodox Christianity is more pedagogical than punitive) developed into a system very much like juris-prudence: sins, like crimes, were weighed, and punishments (penances) deter-mined for them. The priest was the legitimate agent of divine law.

Western Christianity also rallied its resources to define doctrines as precisely as possible. In the Orthodox tradition after the great councils, the elements of the Nicene Creed have never been rigorously rationalized and defined; in Ro-man Catholicism, the need to explain doctrines to new and primitive peoples and the fascination with logic and Scholasticism tended to foster doctrinal defi-nitions and systems of theology. Doctrines of sin, grace, eschatology, and pre-destination as well as explanations of sacramental power and papal primacy were all based, to some extent, on a legal interpretation of the relationship between God and people. Anselm of Canterbury (1033–1109) made the legal understand-ing of this relationship the key to his theological explanation of the Incarnation. For Anselm, the Word of God became flesh in order to satisfy the demands of divine justice: when people sinned and upset God's original plan (the Original Sin story in Genesis), they so offended divine justice that only a perfect sacrifice could satisfy its demands. Christ, therefore, is the perfect victim, the one who died in order to satisfy divine justice and save people from their sins.

The practical perspective is evident in Roman liturgy and in the more gen-eral life of the church. Whereas the observance of the Eucharist in the Orthodox church was a joyous celebration of Christ's presence and the Resurrection, in the Roman church it emphasized the sacrifice of Christ on the cross. Both the Orthodox and Roman churches hold that the bread and wine are transformed into the body and blood of Christ, but only the Roman church developed a precise theory of how and when this transformation occurs, the doctrine of transubstantiation.[10]

The doctrinal complexion of the Catholic church was shaped by the practi-cal realities of survival. Whereas Orthodox Christians tended to emphasize the divinity of Christ and to imagine Christianity as a means of divinization, Roman Catholics tended to focus on the humanity of Jesus, and to experience Christi-anity as a comfort in a life of sorrow. Western Christians found consolation in the fact that Jesus was like them in some ways, a human being who suffered and died, but who triumphed over death and was even now waiting to reward their patience. Sin was a transgression against the laws of God which, at the very least, could diminish one's chances for an afterlife in heaven and at the worst might lead straight to the eternal punishment of hell. Catholics learned to obey the laws of God and the laws of the church in order to avoid damnation.

MEDIEVAL CHRISTIANITY IN THE WEST

For practical reasons, we will now leave the world of Orthodox Christianity to concentrate on Roman Catholicism in the centuries preceding the Reforma-tion. The differences between these two ancient forms of Christianity are fasci-nating ones: the perception of deification as opposed to salvation, and the Orthodox tendency to value knowledge gained through prayer and fasting as opposed to the Catholic preference for rational reflection or ecclesiastical pronouncement are only two examples of the many ways that Orthodoxy and Catholicism represent two conflicting orientations that would probably find reunion very difficult. At this point, however, we need not speculate about the future, but should turn our attention to the dim past of medieval Christianity.

We have seen how Constantine attempted to rebuild Rome in his new city of Constantinople. How did the bishops of Rome attempt to restore Roman glory in the West? They had a much harder problem for several reasons: they were not primarily political leaders and so had no armies and no clear mandate; they lived in a situation that was politically unstable (remember that the Roman Empire in the West fell in 476 after nearly three hundred years of turmoil and chaos) and dangerous; they were besieged by barbarian tribes looking for new land and for a share of old Roman glory; and they were faced with a massive missionary problem in their hope to convert the West to Christianity.

At the same time, the religious leaders of the West, the bishops in general and the pope in particular, had some strong support: they presided over a church that was, on the whole, well organized, philosophically sophisticated, and liturgically attractive; Christians had a history of survival and expansion, and they had the support of the emperor, wherever he was located. In addition, Catholicism, through its monastic system, had a large, relatively well educated group of functionaries to help with the expansion of the Christian mission. Finally, the popes and bishops were often men with political savvy and high reputation: they were able to press their claims for Rome as the holiest city in Christendom (after Jerusalem) and strengthen their position as the supreme leaders of all Christians based on Jesus's words to Peter in Matthew 16.

Up to the Reformation, the Roman Catholic church was involved first in survival and then in consolidating church authority. Since no comprehensive vision of church history can be given in a limited space, we need to focus on an idea that can help organize our understanding. Recall the aspects associated with the idea of Rome: vastness, peace, organization, jurisprudence, religious sensibility, glory, beauty, intellectual life, a common language, and Caesar. At some level, this set of characteristics is what the popes attempted to achieve for the Roman Catholic church. I will deal with them individually in order to say something about the various ways different parts of the church cooperated in the great adventure of the Middle Ages.

The Catholic church was *vast*. We have seen how Christianity spread and adapted itself to a variety of different cultural situations. The missionary impulse was part of Christianity from the beginning: Constantine supported missionaries throughout the Eastern part of the empire, and the popes and bishops sent their ablest priests to the remote regions of the West. You might know something about St. Patrick (d. c. 461), who was one of the most famous early missionaries, but there were others just as important, like St. Boniface (d. c. 755), who worked in Germany, and St. Augustine of Canterbury (d. c. 605), who was sent to England by Pope Gregory I. Because of their work, thousands of people became Christians and whole countries were eventually "won" for Christianity. By the time of the Reformation the entire Western world, as it was then known, along with great stretches of the "new world" discovered at the end of the fifteenth century belonged to the Catholic church.

Catholicism was, in theory at least, *peaceful*. The impressive strength of the Roman military made the old Roman Empire so relatively free from war that the term *pax Romana*, meaning "the Roman peace," was part of the description of the empire. *Pax vobiscum*, meaning "peace be with you," was a phrase in the Catholic liturgy. All those in monasteries and convents were forbidden to engage in warfare and encouraged to avoid even the feelings of hostility. Those who were dedicated to fighting were urged to engage in "holy wars" or crusades, which were fought far away from European soil. The church itself, through a series of pronouncements, forbade any fighting during Lent (six weeks in the spring), Advent (four weeks before Christmas), on all Sundays, Fridays, and other notable feast days.

This system of peacekeeping worked remarkably well for a long time, partly because the church had a weapon of its own: excommunication. Those who disobeyed the laws of the church could be expelled from the communion of the church. Anyone who died in a state of excommunication, so it was believed, went to hell forever. Besides the threat of excommunication, the church had the power of its popes, who had learned over the years to become skilled negotiators and shrewd political operators. After some early setbacks—the compromise with Charlemagne and the ensuing horror of the Dark Ages—popes emerged in the eleventh century as strong men able to keep the peace in the West precisely because they refused to be dominated by secular rulers.

The Catholic church was splendidly *organized* along old Roman imperial lines. The local churches in the vast territory of Christendom were organized into dioceses presided over by bishops. The bishops themselves were organized into districts or along national lines and reported directly to the pope, the chief bishop and supreme ruler of Christendom. As you can imagine, the church as an institution needed bureaucrats: little by little, an organized body of men dedicated to running the internal affairs of the church developed into the Curia, a complex entity with a variety of offices, concerns, procedures, and personnel intent on keeping the machinery of ecclesiastical life running smoothly. Some critics find the very idea of church bureaucracies scandalous, as if a religious institution has no need of such offices, but it is safe to say that every church organization, even at the local level, has some kind of governing body. Furthermore, from the eleventh century onward, the Catholic church developed a system to insure the peaceful election of popes: the College of Cardinals (established by Nicholas II in 1059) was not always perfect, but it did function often in an orderly way to insure peaceful succession of papal authority.

Christianity in the West administered its own *legal system*, eventually known as Canon Law. The development of legal structures in the West was long and arduous. The church as it converted and interacted with various new peoples adopted some of their legal procedures and also inserted some of its own into new law codes as they developed. The theoretical principle for church-state interaction was the one attributed to Jesus in Matthew 22:21, "Render to Caesar the things that are Caesar's, and to God the things that are God's."

The problem, of course, lay in the application of the principle. Were the laws governing marriage civil or religious ones? What part of the taxes collected by a secular ruler had to be turned over to the church? If the church in a particular place needed the protection of the local baron, and if he had to raise an army for that protection, who paid for the army? If the archbishop of Milan was *also*, by historical precedent, the chancellor of the empire, to whom did his loyalty belong in case of conflict? Was it appropriate for the pope to collect taxes from the churches in France? If so, was it also appropriate for the pope to lend that money to the king of England so that he could wage war against France? A list of such questions could fill volumes. Eventually the church in the West worked out a system of ecclesiastical law that was meant to make justice available to everyone. Peasants who were treated badly or paid so poorly that they nearly starved could bring suit against wealthy landowners in ecclesiastical courts. Needless to say, questions about divorce, the legitimacy of children—often important in matters of imperial succession—and other matters of religious interest were a major concern of this legal system. Ameliorations of social life—laws about the ways landowners had to treat serfs, or the ways husbands were to treat their wives—were also concerns of ecclesiastical law.

The Catholic church was characterized by great *religious sensibility* and creativity. In the early years it had been difficult to make the liturgy and the sacraments available to all Christians in the West. Furthermore, the years of the barbarian invasions and the Dark Ages tended to destabilize religious life along with political life. By the tenth century, at the end of the Dark Ages, monastic life was often lived in unconventional if not clearly corrupt terms: the rules of chastity, poverty, and obedience were not fully practiced.

Common liturgical life for ordinary people was also in a poor state: priests were few; many were ill prepared and so did not preach effectively or celebrate the sacraments properly. In the tenth and eleventh centuries, however, a great surge of religious reformation took place: a small band of reform-minded monks emerged from the Black Forest to found the influential monastery at Cluny in France, various towns began to plan for and build impressive cathedrals,[11] and a new series of popes—Leo IX, Nicholas II, and Gregory VII—encouraged the growth of a reforming spirit throughout Europe. With the Cluniac reform of monasteries, the great building projects, and the attention of the popes, religious life in the West flourished.

New religious orders appealed to those who wanted to devote their lives to God by devoting them to some vexing problem in the world, like poverty, care of orphans, teaching, or preaching. New forms of prayer and devotional life attracted Western Christians: some went on pilgrimages to the shrines of powerful saints, or to Jerusalem to walk on the ground that Jesus had walked during his lifetime.[12] Churches were decorated with paintings and statues depicting events in the life of Jesus and making popular saints "visible" and available for prayer or petition.

At a different level of sensibility, many churches collected and housed *relics* of sanctity, pieces of clothing or hair or bones associated with some holy person and sometimes reputed to have almost magical powers. It is easy to laugh at the medieval devotion to relics and to use stories of extreme credulity to dismiss this particular kind of piety. At the same time, if you know someone who has gone to Graceland or Shea Stadium to get a blade of grass, or if you know someone who has tried to get close enough to a rock star to touch him or her, perhaps you understand a little bit of what people felt in the thirteenth century when someone told them that the local church had a relic of the very cross on which Jesus was crucified.

Catholicism was full of *glory* and *beauty*. The pomp and ceremony increasingly associated with the papacy and with the various church functions testified to lavish wealth. Did the church go too far in promoting splendor in itself? Who paid for all the glory? Were church taxes too high? One medieval king is reported to have written to the pope and said, "You are supposed to feed the sheep, not fleece them." At the same time, the buildings in Rome—especially St. Peter's, the Vatican museum, and the cathedrals—are monuments to an era in which religion was thought to be the most important activity on earth. Kings and queens endowed churches specifically so that they would be richly adorned and thus would glorify God. Because of royal money and the tithes of the people, the liturgy was impressive: the cups and plates used for communion were made of pure gold, the vestments of the priest were fashioned from rare silk and embroidered with pearls and golden threads. Music was written especially for church services and sung by highly trained choirs. The overall effect was splendid, which is precisely the mood most church leaders wanted to convey.

Catholicism had a rich *intellectual life* from the earliest days of the Church Fathers (see Appendix 3) through the founding of the great European university system. The official language of the church was Latin—as it was in the Roman Empire—and the scholarly language of the university was Latin. Charlemagne had been a great patron of education. He invited a famous monk and scholar, Alcuin of York (d. 804), to his court in Aachen. Alcuin set up a new form of elementary education and a plan of higher education based on the study of the seven liberal arts. His system, which was divided into two parts, the *trivium* and *quadrivium*, became the basis of medieval intellectual life. The first part of the curriculum gave a student certain tools—language, logic, disputation, and clarity of expression—and the second required mastery of certain subjects, usually practical ones like arithmetic and geometry.

Little by little, Alcuin's system was applied to religious and philosophical questions and a new way of doing theology was born. Whereas mystics attempted to understand God through direct experience, and monks spent their lives in dedicated work and prayerful reflection on the Bible in order to achieve union with God, university life produced something new: theologians engaged in rational argument about God's personality and about the ways the divine design offered certain opportunities to the human race.

Scholasticism was the *method* used by medieval scholars to arrive at logical conclusions about the deepest mysteries of Christian faith. The great universities of Europe were devoted to the study of many subjects, but the most respected was theology. The greatest theologians were those who were able to combine the tools of logic and disputation—aided from the twelfth century onward by the use of the philosophical works of Aristotle and Plato—with their insights about God as revealed in the Bible and in the classical writings of the Church Fathers. Peter Abelard (d. 1142) was one pioneer of scholastic theology and one of its most romantic and tragic figures.[13] Thomas Aquinas (d. 1274) was the most prominent of all medieval theologians, so influential and brilliant that in the nineteenth century when the Roman Catholic church was looking for a way to answer the modern critics of religion, Leo XIII (d. 1904) called for a revival of the study of Thomas Aquinas as the best and most effective way Catholic theology might cope with the modern world.[14]

The influence of the church on intellectual life and vice versa is one of the great stories of the medieval period. Here as in other quarters of the Western world, differing opinions sometimes led to conflict and condemnation. New theories were subject to ecclesiastical approval—strange as that may seem to us today—and those who attempted to apply their new understandings without the permission of the church were sometimes condemned to death. Medieval intellectual life, therefore, should not be confused with the modern concept of intellectual freedom. At the same time, the idea behind the church's involvement—that the church, guided by the Holy Spirit, was a divinely guaranteed teaching authority which could guard against mistakes in any quarter—made perfect sense at the time and was supposed to lead to an atmosphere of intellectual play and discovery.

For many years, this concept of university life worked very well: scholars were able to debate one another with zest and to submit the most important of life's questions—God's purpose, human nature, the meaning of love and will—to rational scrutiny and public argument. As we will see in the next chapter, scholars began to ask serious questions not only about intellectual matters—nature and grace, for example—but also about practical issues like ecclesiastical authority and the papacy. The university system, therefore, however much it may have upheld the "the church's truth" in some ways, also carried within it the potential to disrupt that status quo in times that seemed to cry for reform.

Finally, the Catholic church had its *Caesar*, in the person of the pope. From the early writings of Pope Leo I (d. 461), who laid the theoretical foundations for the medieval papacy, through the work of Pope Gregory I (d. 604), who strengthened the secular or temporal power of the papacy, to Gregory VII (d. 1085), who asserted his authority by excommunicating the Holy Roman Emperor, Henry IV, and forcing Henry to stand barefoot in the snow begging papal forgiveness, the power of the papacy had been strong. In these early years, however, the popes had no major political rivals and their moral authority in the West was enough to insure their political success. Pope Urban II (d. 1099) called the first Crusade, which was an enormous event. By urging princes and soldiers from all over Europe to liberate Jerusalem from the Turks, he basically proclaimed himself to be the personal leader of Christendom.

Secular rulers sometimes fought with the popes, and it was clear that the church could be attacked and resisted, but it could not be ignored as a political power. Pope Innocent III (d. 1216), perhaps the most powerful of the medieval popes, was constantly involved in important political questions and presided over a church that was at its religious and theological apex. After Innocent III, papal power held its own for a while, but from the thirteenth century on, strong national rulers were increasingly in a position to challenge papal authority in political matters. As we shall see in the next chapter, religious reformers from the fourteenth to the sixteenth century were also increasingly in the position to challenge the pope's spiritual authority as well.

CONCLUSION

The break between the Greek Orthodox church and the Roman Catholic church in 1204 was the first major split in the Christian church, which continues down to the present day. The church in the East developed under the protection of the emperor and had no chance to assert its independence from the empire; the church in the West was able to become more politically independent. In the course of its history, the Roman church asserted the primacy of the pope as the supreme leader of the entire Christian church, a claim that Orthodox Christians could not—and still cannot—accept. In addition to the issue of church authority, concepts and traditions crucial to both churches developed differently East and West: monasticism and liturgy are ancient and central in both churches, but they have become quite different in ethos and practice.

The difference in general perspective between East and West reflects the history and early environment of each church. The tasks of the Christian church were different for both groups, and they developed different outlooks. At the same time, however, they are remarkably similar: both are committed to certain doctrinal positions though they have different emphases; both observe an ancient, fixed liturgy; both recognize the importance of tradition; and both believe the church includes the communion of saints (dead and alive). The Christian groups that derived from the Reformation disagreed with the Roman church on nearly all of these issues. It is important, therefore, to see the points of correspondence between the Orthodox and the Roman Catholic churches as well as to know where their differences lie.

Medieval Catholic Christianity, as it has been sketched here in brief form, was an elaborate system that involved everyone in a cosmic scheme of salvation. The church emcompassed life in every quarter and was involved in intellectual development, political action, religious practice, and cultural expression. As the foundation and patron of all aspects of life, the Catholic church exercised enormous influence and wielded great power. As we shall see in the next chapter, great power led to great corruption and eventual reform. It is important to remember, however, that at its best, medieval Catholicism encouraged most of the activities and qualities associated with Western civilization.

CHAPTER 4 NOTES

[1] Christopher Dawson, *Religion and the Rise of Western Culture* (New York: Doubleday, 1958), pp. 44–67. From a different perspective, but one still laudatory about the role of monks in civilization, see Kenneth Clark, *Civilization* (New York: Harper & Row, 1969), pp. 1–60. Clark is an art historian and focuses on the emergence of civilization by way of its art.

[2] One clear account of Constantine's life and rise to power can be found in Hermann Doerries, *Constantine the Great* (New York: Harper & Row, 1972).

[3] According to Roman Catholic tradition, Helena is a saint. She made her famous pilgrimage to Jerusalem in 326. You can imagine the sense of power attached to Constantine's claim to be in possession of the very cross on which Jesus died.

[4] Let me suggest a way to begin to understand the human side of the Council of Nicaea. Dorothy L. Sayers's *The Emperor Constantine* (Grand Rapids: Eerdmans, 1976) is fictional, but created from historical sources. Sayers (you may know her through the Peter Wimsey detective novels) wrote this play for the Colchester Drama Festival in 1951. In it she shows you how Constantine understood his church-state arrangements, what his role in the council was, and how he made his own inner pilgrimage to Christianity. Sayers does an amazing (if imaginative) job of getting inside this man's mentality.

[5] Eusebius of Caesarea, *The Life of Constantine*. See *A Select Library of Nicene and Post-Nicene Fathers of the Christian Church,* second series (Grand Rapids: Eerdmans, 1952), pp. 481–560, quotation from p. 522.

[6] The Roman Empire in the West fell in the fifth century for a number of reasons, one of which was plunder by various barbarian tribes. The interaction between the leaders of some of these tribes and the leaders of the Roman Catholic church helped set the stage for a new kind of civilization. When we talked about the universal mission of Christianity (in Chapter 3) we talked about Christian adaptation to different but fairly civilized societies (Hellenistic and Roman). In the West, however, the Christian message had to be made accessible to tribal peoples whose gods were understood not so much in terms of reason but in terms of power. For an unusual and striking interpretation of this interaction and the rise of "miracle cults," see Albert Mirgeler, *Mutations of Western Christianity* (Notre Dame, Ind.: University of Notre Dame Press, 1968), pp. 44–66.

[7] Charlemagne began a movement to solidify, educate, and reform, and his empire was one of the high points of civilization before the eleventh century, but (for complicated reasons based on patterns of feudal succession) it did not last. For a readable and detailed account of the history of this period, see Norman F. Cantor, *Medieval History: The Life and Death of a Civilization,* 2nd ed. (New York: Macmillan, 1969).

⁸*Filioque* means "and the Son." In the creed adopted by the Council of Nicaea (325 C.E.) there is a statement about the Holy Spirit that says, "The Holy Spirit proceeds from the Father." This is a complicated bit of theology about the Trinity and you need not pursue it, just notice that it says "from the Father," period. Later, especially in the West (and to strengthen the arguments for the divinity of Jesus Christ), many people began to add the word *filioque,* so that the phrase now said, "The Holy Spirit proceeds from the Father *and the Son.*" The theological point was never much in dispute, since everyone believed in the divinity of the Son. The question at issue was whether or not one could add (or subtract) words from a sacred council document. The Eastern Christians said no, and when the West adopted the *filioque* as part of the creed, they invited a fierce and hostile argument. For a clear explanation of this complicated problem, see R. G. Heath, "The Western Schism of the Franks and the *Filioque,*" *Journal of Ecclesiastical History* 23 (1972), 97–115.

⁹For a short introduction to icons, see Ernst Benz, *The Eastern Orthodox Church—Its Thought and Life* (New York: Doubleday, 1963), pp. 1–20. You cannot really appreciate icons until you see them in color, so check the subject catalog in your library and see what art books you can find with icons in them. In ancient churches where few could read, the stories about Jesus had to be told and pictured. Icons and the great mosaics of Orthodox churches give you a good indication of how beautiful the Christian story was for those people.

¹⁰The doctrine of transubstantiation was based on a distinction between the substance of a thing (its essence) and its accidents (how it looks, feels, tastes, and so on). In trying to explain the unexplainable, philosophers argued that the accidents of the Eucharist remain the same (it still tastes like, looks like, smells like bread), but its substance changes (*trans* = change; *transubstantiation* = change in substance): its essence is the body and blood of Christ.

¹¹The construction of a cathedral required the dedicated efforts of everyone living at the site plus the impressive work of thousands of artisans. For a picture of this process, see David Macaulay, *Cathedral: The Story of Its Construction* (Boston: Houghton Mifflin, 1973). This book is full of sketches and takes you through the process of cathedral building from the time it is a hope in the hearts of the townspeople until it is finished.

¹²Pilgrimage is a modern reality as well as a medieval activity, but that does not make it altogether understandable. Two books are helpful here. For a scholarly look at this phenomenon, see Jonathan Sumption, *Pilgrimage: An Image of Medieval Religion* (Totowa, N.J.: Rowman and Littlefield, 1975). For a rollicking good *story* about pilgrimage, read the historical novel by H. F. M. Prescott, *Friar Felix at Large* (New Haven: Yale University Press, 1950). Prescott tells us the story of a historical figure, Felix Fabri, a German monk who went on a pilgrimage to Jerusalem in 1480 in a skeptical frame of mind. The experience changed his life and he returned for a second time. The book is full of his own notes from diaries and the gaps are filled in by Prescott's intelligent imagination.

¹³Peter Abelard is more than a medieval theologian, he is a tragic figure who has captured the imagination of novelists and scholars for centuries. His famous love affair with Heloise is legendary, and you will find many books about him by contemporary authors. My favorite is an old one: Helen Waddell, *Peter Abelard* (New York: Holt, Rinehart & Winston, 1933).

¹⁴The influence of Thomas Aquinas on the history of Roman Catholic thought cannot be underestimated, and I urge you to get an introduction to him by simply looking him up in a variety of encyclopedias. It is also worthwhile to go to the library and hold

a copy of his famous *Summa Theologica* in your hands and to get some idea of the ways medieval theologians operated.

SUGGESTIONS FOR FURTHER READING

1. For a good general introduction to Eastern Orthodoxy, see Ignace Dick, *What Is the Christian Orient?* (Westminster, Md.: Newman Press, 1967). Dick explains the patriarchates, Orthodox doctrine, liturgical families, and languages, and shows how Orthodoxy developed in various parts of the world. One also gets a sense from this book about the linguistic complexity of Orthodoxy. Whereas Christianity in the West developed mostly in Latin for the first thousand years or so, Eastern Christianity took root in cultures that spoke Greek, Syriac, Coptic, Armenian, Georgian, Arabic, and Slavonic (to name a few).

Another good introduction to Orthodox Christianity is John Meyendorf, *The Orthodox Church: Its Past and Its Role in the World Today*, 3rd rev. ed. (Crestwood, N.Y.: St. Vladimir's Seminary Press, 1981). This book originally appeared in 1960 and has been revised to be more informative about contemporary issues and present-day ecumenical relations. It contains a useful bibliography.

Two other useful books are Sergius Bulgakov, *The Orthodox Church* (New York: Morehouse, n.d.), an introduction from an insider's perspective, and Demetrios J. Constantelos, *Understanding the Greek Orthodox Church* (New York: Seabury Press, 1982), a multidisciplinary approach to faith, history, worship, and ethos.

2. For a clear account of the differences between Eastern and Western patterns of religious authority, one that untangles things, see Francis Dvornik, *Byzantium and the Roman Primacy* (New York: Fordham University Press, 1966). See also John Meyendorf, *The Primacy of Peter*, 2nd ed. (Leighton Buzzard, Bedfordshire: Faith Press, 1973).

3. For a look at some primary sources chosen especially for students to give them an introduction to the events of this period, see Marianka S. Fousek, *The Church in a Changing World: Events and Trends from 250–600* (St. Louis: Concordia, 1971).

4. The following books are general introductions to a variety of areas that I have not tried to cover in the text. We talked about hermits in the desert: for an engaging account of their lives, mostly by way of quotation from them and their stories, see Helen Waddell, *The Desert Fathers* (Ann Arbor: University of Michigan Press, 1966). I mentioned people who believed God wanted them to wander, who set out with no goal: they were not a large group, but an unusual one. See Eleanor Duckett, *The Wandering Saints of the Early Middle Ages* (New York: W. W. Norton, 1964). Finally, I mentioned early Christian writers and referred to Appendix 3, which gives a very brief sketch of their tasks. In many ways there is no substitute for reading to get some idea of who they were and what they wrote about, and then reading what they said. One biography of perhaps *the* major writer in the Latin West is worth citing because of its sympathy, lucidity, and general excellence: Peter Brown, *Augustine of Hippo: A Biography* (London: Faber & Faber, 1967). Brown makes Augustine not just a major religious figure and philosophical/theological thinker, but a human being I think you can relate to; read pp. 1–181 for the story of his search for himself and for God.

❖

CHAPTER 5

ASPECTS OF THE REFORMATION

The Reformation was not so much an isolated incident of protest as a series of reform attempts and movements between the fourteenth and seventeenth centuries. During that time the political and cultural climate changed substantially; old connections between church and state broke down in the face of emerging nationalism, and the issue of religious authority finally divided Christianity into a variety of factions that persist to this day.

I have chosen to highlight only a few of the factors that made these times so intensely creative and chaotic. We left the medieval world with an impression of stability, but with a few hints that maybe everything was not as settled as it looked. As we enter the fourteenth century, we find a much more volatile situation. The rise of strong national rulers led to a variety of political problems between nations and within the church. New sources of money and employment gave people more mobility, and the invention of printing contributed to a higher rate of literacy: people were more inclined to ask questions and to demand answers. Intellectual life was vibrant and scholars began to challenge old methods like Scholasticism and to encourage new reliance on biblical scholarship. Finally, preachers and religious figures added new dimensions to their understanding of spirituality and so fed an increasing interest in the means of salvation. All of these changes, and others, led to two centuries of religious reformation.

This chapter focuses on the historical context for these great reform movements, and on aspects of each of the reform movements themselves. The protests of Wycliffe and Hus, the reforming efforts of the conciliar movement, and the atmosphere of humanism and the Renaissance all provided support for some creative reforms within Christianity. Unfortunately and inevitably, those reforms also led to a severe break within Christendom, and from the sixteenth century on there would no longer be just two branches of Christianity (Roman Catholic and Eastern Orthodox) divided geographically; the Protestant Reformation resulted in new churches and distinct denominations. We will look briefly here at the four major strands of the Protestant Reformation, and at the reformation of the Catholic church from within.

THE HISTORICAL SITUATION

From the fourth to eleventh centuries, the church in the West had been challenged to survive, to withstand political pressure from outside, and to convert barbarian tribes to Christianity. To some ways of thinking, the church had been a remarkable success: most Europeans were Christians, a system of international church law tried to insure justice and fairness, liturgical life and ecclesiastical discipline were being made uniform, religious life flourished in a variety of forms, and the church had managed to secure autonomy by becoming a powerful political entity as well as the highest spiritual authority in the West. To other ways of thinking, the church had assumed too much power, meddled in the wrong issues, and devoted insufficient attention to spiritual matters. This perception, prominent from the late eleventh century on, increased markedly throughout the Reformation.

From the eleventh to fourteenth centuries, the Western Catholic church was in a process of consolidating its power. Because the political world was changing so dramatically, the church found itself involved in intense political struggles.[1] The image of an international church presided over by a wise pope was being challenged by the emergence of a new kind of *national* ruler. Kings, in England and France particularly, resented what they considered papal intrusion in their own political affairs. There was no longer a political vacuum in the West for the pope to fill, as had been the case earlier, and there was no longer a predictable political struggle between the *one* secular ruler (the Holy Roman Emperor) and the pope, as had been initiated with the crowning of Charlemagne. Some people, especially scholars in universities, believed that the pope ought to give up all political power, leave politics to kings, and become a strictly spiritual ruler.[2] They argued this position on both political and religious grounds. The response on the part of the official church was to exaggerate the papal claims: popes declared they had power over the entire world (as vicars of Christ), or that they could step into any situation in which sin had been committed—into any situation, in other words.[3]

At the beginning of the fourteenth century, a startling response to papal claims was made by Philip IV, king of France. Pope Boniface VIII and the king had been involved in a series of moves and countermoves against each other for some time, and animosity was growing on both sides. The conflict was over power and money and had long since passed the point where polite conversation or arbitration could resolve it. The pope, counting on power that had worked in centuries past (power he no longer had), threatened to depose the king. In 1302 the pope issued a document, *Unam Sanctam,* which ended thus: "We therefore declare, say and affirm that submission on the part of every human creature to the bishop of Rome is altogether necessary for his salvation."[4] In earlier times the king might have capitulated; this time the king began a plan to depose the pope. Boniface VIII was arrested and died on his way to Paris to stand trial. The new pope was not Italian but French, and the papacy moved from Rome to Avignon, a small town in France. The papacy was now under the control of the French monarchy; the popes became in effect agents of the king.

King Philip's defiance of the papacy was the dramatic end to the powers of the medieval popes. If you will remember that Pope Gregory VII forced the Holy Roman Emperor to stand barefoot in the snow begging papal forgiveness (1077), you can appreciate the power that popes were able to exercise over secular rulers. If you can imagine Boniface VIII being forcibly taken to Paris to stand trial for his crimes (1302), you can see how much things had changed in two hundred years.

The Avignon papacy is remembered as one of the great scandals of Christendom. It lasted from 1304 to 1377, when Catherine of Siena, among others, persuaded the pope to return to Rome and restore some sort of normalcy to a church that was increasingly divided. Within fourteen months, the pope died in Rome and a new election was called: the College of Cardinals, under some pressure from the Romans, elected an Italian, Urban VI. For a number of reasons—Urban's plans for reform, his general lack of tact, rivalries between Italian and French cardinals—this same College of Cardinals returned to Avignon and elected a second Pope, Clement VII. From 1378 until 1415 the Roman Catholic church was ruled by two men both claiming to be the duly elected pope.

This further scandal, known as the Great Western Schism, tended to divide Europe along religious and political lines: England, the traditional enemy of France, backed the Roman pope, for example, while Scotland, the traditional enemy of England, backed the French pope. Unless you have read widely in the history of the period, you cannot begin to imagine the turmoil. Suffice it to say that the church was clearly in need of *institutional* reform.

The situation in the fourteenth century was unusual, to say the least. In addition to political and institutional turmoil, Europe was just recovering from an outbreak of bubonic plague that had struck in the 1340s. The Black Death, as it was called, was quick and fatal: it killed nearly one-half of the European population in a short time. Not surprisingly, this period was characterized by great religious anxiety: many people believed that the plague had been a divine punishment and so were terrified about their own survival and chances for salvation. Others called for massive repentance and joined movements of extremists who went from town to town whipping themselves (literally) into a frenzy and frightening people with visions of the end of the world.

In the Rhineland and in England mystical experience and writing increased dramatically, while in other parts of Europe new forms of religious life emerged that encouraged profound consciousness of a deep personal relationship with God. Some of those who were influenced by popular religious movements became anti-institutional and so were condemned as heretics. Many of those following the new devotionalism, however, were simply looking for a different kind of piety, one with an inward dimension that could not be shaken by external institutional abuses. The book that best exemplifies the kind of religious life many people were yearning for is *The Imitation of Christ* by Thomas à Kempis (d. 1471).

Finally, the fourteenth century was characterized by deep social unrest and intellectual upheaval. During this time a series of peasant revolts and uprisings took place as people attempted to gain more power or protection in a changing political situation. Intellectually, the fourteenth century was a time of birth: some focus on the rebirth (renaissance) of classical learning, and others on the new birth of biblical scholarship. The invention of the printing press, the availability of books, the tremendous influx of Greek manuscripts after the fall of Constantinople (1453) all gave scholars new things to discuss and new ways to discuss them. It is within this general context that we must understand a series of religious reform movements that began in the fourteenth century. These were not the *only* such movements, but they are perhaps most characteristic.

RELIGIOUS REFORM BEFORE LUTHER

The two most important reform movements that began in the fourteenth and extended into the fifteenth century were those of John Wycliffe and John Hus, on the one hand, and the conciliarist movement on the other. Wycliffe and Hus wished to free the church from control of the ecclesiastical officials, from specified forms of liturgy, and from complex creeds and dogmatic tests. The conciliarist movement aimed to reform the institutional church and to restructure it. One of the central questions concerned religious authority: Where did one turn for the truth? Some of the answers to that question included the pope, ecumenical councils, the Bible, classical antiquity, tradition, mystical experience, and one's own conscience. These answers are not unlike the options available in the modern Christian church, nor are they peculiar to the fourteenth century; some of them had been present within Christianity from the beginning. In the climate of the Reformation years, however, the variety of answers divided Christians from one another and split apart what had once been a united Christendom.

Reforms of Wycliffe and Hus

One of the most significant protest movements before Luther was that associated with two university professors, John Wycliffe (c. 1330–84) in England and John Hus (c. 1372–1415) in Bohemia (present-day Czechoslovakia). Wycliffe was a philosopher at Oxford who gained support and fame by arguing that religious authority ought to be reserved for the righteous and that unworthy, immoral people (like the Avignon pope and wayward priests) had no legitimate right to exercise religious authority over people. Since he believed that religion had become too much a matter of clerical authority and esoteric doctrines, he attacked the authority of the pope and extolled the authority of the Bible. He argued that the office and claims of the pope had no support from Scripture and that the only way one could judge holiness was by whether or not one's behavior accorded with the gospel, not by whether one possessed a certain ecclesiastical title.

One of the most daring reforms associated with Wycliffe was a translation of the Bible into the language of the people (in this case, English). The Catholic church had for centuries used the Latin translation of the Bible, known as the *Vulgate*, and had for some time discouraged translations into the vernacular. They held that Scripture was to be read and interpreted by the church; that is, by designated authorities within the church. Wycliffe thought all Christians should be free to read the Bible for themselves, and that to do so they needed to read it in their own languages. In arguing that Scripture is the highest authority for every Christian, Wycliffe was not anticipating Luther's appeal to *sola Scriptura* (Scripture alone). Wycliffe accepted the interpretive authority of the Church Fathers (see Appendix 3), and he respected many of the church's theologians. His criticism was directed against those parts of the church that were, in his view, *unscriptural*. The papacy was not to be found in Scripture, and the greed and corruption of the papacy in Wycliffe's day convinced him that a pope who grasps for power and wealth is an anti-Christ.

Wycliffe's followers were called Lollards (mumblers, a word of derision with a Dutch origin). The Lollard movement is remembered as one of ecclesiastical reform. Their chief authority in religious matters was the Bible as they read and interpreted it. Based on their reading of the Bible they attacked unscriptural *doctrines* (like transubstantiation and clerical celibacy) and unscriptural *practices* (like indulgences and pilgrimages). They extolled evangelical poverty and contrasted the poverty of early Christians (and many contemporary Christians) with the wealth of church officials. The Lollard movement was at first one of academic criticism (which was denounced by the church and persecuted) and later a more popular religious reform movement. People from the poorer classes were drawn to it and, for a while, it looked as if it might lead to an active revolt against the institutional church. By the middle of the fifteenth century, however, the movement had dwindled and effectively ended. But not before it had influenced John Hus.

Hus was a reforming priest in Bohemia who had been deeply moved by the teachings of Wycliffe. His life coincided with the Great Western Schism and the political divisions caused by that schism, so his reform attempts were, to some extent, linked with political issues. He denounced the hierarchical organization of the church and preached against an immoral clergy. In the middle of a stormy religious controversy, he was invited to the Council of Constance (see Appendix 4), where his safety was guaranteed by the emperor. Constance was a dangerous place for reformers and reforming ideas like those of Hus. The council condemned Wycliffe posthumously and demanded that his remains be dug up, burned, and thrown into a river. Hus was brought to trial for heresy but refused to recant unless the council fathers could prove to him, from Scripture, that he was wrong. He was burned at the stake in 1415.

While Hus was in prison, his followers in Prague took the daring step of administering the cup of wine to the laity during Communion services. For hundreds of years lay people in the Catholic church received only the eucharistic bread. Hus and his followers found this practice unscriptural and so returned to receiving Communion in both forms. The council forbade lay people to receive the cup, a move that only fueled the fires of rebellion. What followed were a series of Hussite wars in which the Communion cup (or chalice) became an emblem of resistance. The Hussite wars lasted throughout the Reformation period and were the first consistent armed attack on feudal politics and the Roman Catholic church. People claimed the right to make religious decisions for themselves rather than accept the practices decreed to them by a hierarchical church. As such, the Hussite movement helped pave the way for the Protestant Reformation.

Conciliarism

Conciliarism was the most notable internal reform movement to arise out of the chaotic situation of the Great Western Schism. Wycliffe and Hus were not so much interested in reforming the existing church as in denouncing it as unreformable: their message, in general, encouraged people to leave the corrupt church, read the Scriptures, and live a decent Christian life. The conciliarist movement, on the other hand, believed that the institutional church was necessary but that it needed a basic constitutional reform, one that would limit papal power and restore a more ancient—collegial—type of church government.

Gregory VII (pope from 1073 to 1085) had set the tone of the medieval papacy by arguing that the pope was the supreme authority within the church.[5] Gregory VII had said that no council could be called without papal permission, that papal decrees could be annulled by no one, and that the pope could be judged by no one. The conciliarists opposed this position. Armed with a growing body of reform literature and opinion, they set out to argue that an ecumenical council is superior to the pope as a religious authority.

The first council called to heal the schism and restore the church under the leadership of one pope was the Council of Pisa (1409). People loyal to both popes came to Pisa, deposed both popes, and elected a new one, who, unfortunately, died within months. Most people attending the council had already gone home, and those who were left at Pisa elected another man, a powerful leader who, they thought, could heal the schism by force if not by persuasion. He took the name John XXIII. His election and the Council of Pisa did not heal the schism but made it worse; after Pisa *three* men claimed to be the pope—John XXIII, the French pope, and the Roman pope. Pisa was, at best, a step toward the Council of Constance, called by John XXIII in 1414 at the urging of the emperor Sigismund.

The Council of Constance deposed all three popes and elected a new one, who ratified his election by pronouncing the council a valid ecumenical council. Two important conciliar documents were passed at the Council of Constance: the first, *Haec Sancta* (1415), asserted the supremacy of the council over the pope as a religious authority; the second, *Frequens* (1416), declared that ecumenical councils should be held at least every ten years. Finally, the council drew up a list of abuses and called for significant reform in the church. It looked, for a while, as if the Council of Constance would lead to a major reformation in church structure and policy. As it turned out, however, the council did *not* reform the church, a failure that some interpreters argue led directly to the Protestant Reformation.[6]

HUMANISM AND THE RENAISSANCE

Lord Acton, a famous nineteenth-century historian, said, "Power tends to corrupt and absolute power corrupts absolutely." Perhaps that explains why popes did not reform the church along lines that limited their power. It may also explain why national leaders developed into national despots when they assumed broad political power. Whatever the reasons, the battles between church and state in the fifteenth and sixteenth centuries were mostly fought over political power. The old prerogatives from the medieval papacy were at odds with the spiritual and intellectual uneasiness of an awakening world. The agent of that awakening was a loosely defined movement known as humanism and, later, as the Renaissance. Humanists responded to the religious and political chaos around them by remembering ancient conceptions of humanity, culture, ideals, and destiny. Their goal was to rediscover the sources of and to delight in the type of life portrayed in classical Greek and Roman documents. Their efforts led to a rebirth of classical learning, the Renaissance.[7]

To get a sense of the importance of the Renaissance, we need to look at two settings and several characters. The excitement about the recovery of classical literature first blossomed in Italy, under the genius of Francesco Petrarch

(1304–74). His love of Latin antiquity led to a scorn for medieval methods and attitudes. In religious terms, he was more interested in the mystery of humanity than in the study of divinity, intent more on the ways human beings adapted to life on earth than on the ways they worried about heaven and hell. Petrarch's friend Giovanni Boccaccio (1313–75) brought the same enthusiasm to the revival of Greek classics that Petrarch held for Latin ones. Finally, Lorenzo Valla (1407–57), an enthusiastic student of Greek culture, revived an interest in the *Christian* literature of Greece. He was an avid reader of the Fathers (see Appendix 3) and an accomplished grammarian. Valla is of major interest to us because he was one of the first scholars to study New Testament texts with historical, critical methods. He compared the Vulgate with ancient Greek versions of the New Testament to show the major differences between them. Perhaps most shocking of all, Valla undermined the power of the papacy by exposing the Donation of Constantine as a forgery.[8]

None of these Renaissance scholars was attempting to overthrow Christianity or to encourage a return to paganism. On the contrary, they thought that the study of ancient classics could only strengthen their Christian beliefs. They tended to reject medieval methods like Scholasticism, but they did not reject basic Christian doctrines.

The second setting for the Renaissance was a northern one, nourished in the great universities of Germany and England. German humanists were also interested in the revival of Latin and Greek classics, but their primary interests were religious: unlike their Italian counterparts, whose literary works were usually *not* religious in nature, German Renaissance scholars used their interests in classical antiquity to study the Bible and to focus on religious topics. This ability to combine theological interest with humanist scholarship led to passion for reform: German scholars especially were interested in a reform of church and society.

Johannes Reuchlin (1455–1522) was one of the first Christian scholars to study Hebrew in order to better understand the Old Testament. His Hebrew grammar and dictionary opened up a whole new vista of historical and critical scholarship for biblical studies.

Desiderius Erasmus (c. 1466–1536), born in Rotterdam, was the greatest of the northern humanists. On a trip to England in 1499, Erasmus met the great English humanists John Colet (c. 1467–1519), who was teaching Greek at Oxford, and Thomas More (1478–1535), a lawyer and writer who was later made chancellor of England under Henry VIII and then beheaded by that king for "treason." Erasmus became an avid student of Greek and eventually published a Greek edition of the New Testament. More important for us, he was a reformer at heart: he longed for a church that was not riddled with superstition, corruption, and error. As a Renaissance man, he hoped that a return to the pure sources of Christian antiquity would lead to significant changes for the better.

None of these northern humanists sought to overthrow the Catholic church: on the contrary, they were passionately devoted to it and hoped only to use their new scholarship to make it stronger, less vulnerable to charges of corruption, and better able to acquit itself honorably in intellectual discussions.

How did the Catholic church react to the Renaissance? Many scholars, as we have just seen, were enthusiastic about it. Ordinary people, so far as we can tell, were often moved by new currents of popular piety grounded, to some extent, on a return to earlier embodiments of Christianity. Because of the printing press, many more people were aware of these new currents than they had ever been before. Scholastic theologians, we can suppose, might have been threatened by it. The Renaissance popes reacted to the Renaissance in an unusual way. Popes began to believe that they need no longer confine themselves to religion and politics: the Renaissance provided them with an opportunity to become great patrons of the arts.

Remember the "idea of Rome" as we discussed it in Chapter 4? Rome was the great ideal of ancient civilization, and the medieval church was fashioned to be its religious successor. During the Renaissance the popes believed that Rome should be the spiritual and cultural capital of the universe. They set out to rebuild the city, to endow museums, build magnificent buildings, and patronize artists.

In order to accomplish this goal, popes believed they had to oppose two major threats to their power, rising nationalism (an external threat) and growing conciliarism (an internal threat). Accordingly, the popes created a competitive national power of their own in Italy and systematically "forgot" to implement the decrees of the Council of Constance. The popes in this period became Renaissance princes who wielded power and maintained an army. During this time we can find a series of popes whose interests were political and financial rather than spiritual. The rationale behind their policies was the protection of the church. They believed that the only way to insure the future of Catholicism was to keep the papacy (and, by extension, the church) free from secular control.

Recall that the Catholic church understood itself to be based on papal power; according to its position, Jesus had given a mandate to Peter that needed to be carried out if the church was to remain free and able to pursue its spiritual functions. Popes believed—and rightly so—that the strength of the church had been the agent of unification and civilization in centuries past. Could it still be so? Reformers thought not and argued that the medieval conception of the papacy had simply outlived its usefulness; others believed it needed simply to be refortified. That disagreement, in some ways, was at the heart of the Protestant Reformation. And the humanist/Renaissance movement supported that reformation by providing an alternate reading of the sources of papal power. Martin Luther's position was not fundamentally new—Wycliffe and Hus had said many of the same things before—but he backed up his protest with the fruit of humanist/Renaissance labor. He was able to supply some of the critical scholarship from which real reform and (to some ways of thinking) revolution would come.

THE PROTESTANT REFORMATION

The reform movements before Luther did not lead to separate and distinct groups within Christianity; Luther himself did not intend to found a different church, but hoped to reform the existing one. Because the reform movements of the sixteenth century led to a major break in Western Christianity, because they were protests with more severe consequences than earlier movements, we mark them with a distinctive title and call those who departed from prevailing Christian beliefs Protestants.

The Protestant Reformation drew the arguments in the church back to *religious* issues, always with an impact on political arrangements. There were four main channels of the Reformation: Lutheran, Reformed (associated with Zwingli and then Calvin), Tudor (or Anglican), and Radical (or Anabaptist). All of these movements were interested in the same basic issues, but their approaches differed. They were united in their opposition to traditional Roman Catholic notions of the nature of salvation, the church, and religious authority. We look at each of these four movements in greater detail next.

The Lutheran Reformation

As we have seen, humanist scholars rediscovered the Greek New Testament and began to see what it means to understand a text in its historical setting. Furthermore, beginning in the middle of the fifteenth century, there was more general interest in the Bible: many more copies than ever before were available, and the Bible was circulated both in its Latin version (the Vulgate) and in vernacular translations. Scholars began to wonder what it might mean to the church if doctrinal teachings were based on the Greek original rather than on a Latin translation. Increasingly, young reformist scholars began to use the Bible to question the church's teaching authority, to wonder whether the church's teaching tradition was consistent with the Scriptures.

Martin Luther (1483–1546), a young German monk and professor of Scripture at the University of Wittenberg, was one of those young scholars influenced by German humanists. His Scripture studies and the humanist atmosphere of the German universities helped him articulate a strong new position, *sola Scriptura*. Earlier humanist scholars like Erasmus deplored abuses, studied the Greek New Testament, and argued that some of the conclusions of scholastic theologians were false, but they did not deny the authority of church tradition. Luther, however, went further: he concluded that the entire teaching tradition of the church might be wrong, that judged against the teaching authority of Scripture alone, tradition was often erroneous.

Luther did not arrive at his position all at once or alone. By the time he was ready to engage in debate about a specific issue, he was nearly thirty-four and his university was clearly supportive of his conclusions and goals. The first target of Luther's public protest was not an esoteric point of scriptural interpretation, but an abuse of an old system related to salvation and popular piety. Luther's immediate protest was raised against Johann Tetzel (1470–1519), a Dominican monk and a high-powered ecclesiastical peddler of *indulgences* in a town near Wittenberg.

Over a long period of time and for a variety of philosophical and historical reasons, the Roman Catholic church had developed the doctrine of purgatory, a place where the punishment due for sins could be worked off after death.[9] The reasoning was that God's *justice* demands that sinners pay a penalty (in this life or the next) for sins, while God's *mercy* will not allow a repentant (but not fully paid up) sinner to spend eternity in hell. Therefore, it was speculated, there must be a state en route to heaven where sinners can stop for a while and pay their penalties in full. This speculation seemed logical at a time when the task of theology was rational inquiry about God and the divine relationship to humanity, and when scholars worked to formulate systematic, all-encompassing explanations. The idea of purgatory was one such logical speculation. When it was coordinated with ideas about the church's power, the rationale for indulgences was developed.

The church believed that the obedient sacrificial death of Jesus and the good works of Mary and the saints had built up a treasury of merit, like a bank account that the church could draw on to pay the debts of sinners. Indulgences were a draft on the account. Sinners could earn indulgences by doing what the church suggested: good works, prayers, and devotions. People who went on pilgrimages received indulgences, as did those who did good works, bore their sufferings patiently, or said certain prayers. During the Avignon papacy the popes, in need of money for a variety of projects, began to *sell* indulgences; one wit noted that the popes had discovered the fiscal possibilities of purgatory. The practice of selling indulgences went from bad to worse and was in a scandalous state when Luther began his public protest against the church's corruption in 1517.

Luther's protest against indulgences was inspired partly by his disgust with a greedy practice, but also by his new understanding about the Christian life. The sixteenth century was a time of deep and paradoxical religious energy: many people were attracted to a new devotional life that stressed a personal relationship to God and a kind of inner fervor, yet they experienced great anxiety about their own salvation. The Catholic church taught that one was saved through a faith that activated itself in good works. Christians did not save themselves by doing good works, but their pious deeds, their prayers, their devotions all were indications that their faith was genuine. One can see how many people were confused about the relationship between faith and works in an atmosphere full of the paraphernalia of religious practice—relics, indulgences, pilgrimages. Anxious people could ask themselves whether they had "done enough" to merit heaven. Indulgence peddlers like Tetzel gave Christians the impression that they could bargain with God about their salvation, somehow appease divine anger with certificates. Indulgences made it look as if one could buy peace of mind, and Luther's experience contradicted that implication radically.

Luther originally intended to be a lawyer, but in a profound spiritual crisis he gave up the study of law and entered a monastery (in 1505) and was ordained a priest (1507). Anxious about his own salvation, Luther thought that monastic life was the best way to overcome doubts about his relationship with God. He was an exemplary young monk, scrupulous about his devotions and duties, obedient, and thoughtful. Yet he did not gain any confidence about his relationship with God and was often in a mood of despair and pessimism about his own salvation. In this melancholy context he finished his doctorate in theology and began to teach Scripture at Wittenberg.

Slowly, as he worked as an exegete and teacher, he had a breakthrough experience. Scholars differ about what actually happened to him, when it happened, and how it can be explained in terms of scriptural exegesis. Classically stated, Luther came to see that one is saved by faith alone. Good works—including the whole theological foundation for the theory of indulgences—were, as he saw it, absolutely useless for one's salvation. Indulgences harm Christian belief in two ways: they give Christians a false sense about their salvation, and they pervert a right understanding of God.

If medieval Catholics sometimes saw God as an avenging judge who needed to be appeased, Luther finally experienced God as a loving father who forgives freely. Luther understood salvation as a relationship in which the individual sinners have "faith" (trusting absolutely in God's mercy) and God "justifies" them (forgives them even though they do not cease to be sinners). The scriptural passage often cited as Luther's key to this understanding is Romans 1:17: "For in [the gospel] the righteousness of God is revealed through faith for faith; as it is written, 'He who through faith is righteous shall live.'" Faith is not a "work," not something that one can "do," but is, rather, a gift from God.

The freedom and sense of release Luther felt in the wake of his insight were phenomenal. His experience obviously touched a chord in the hearts of many Christians at the time, since it was a message of religious consolation. Add to the sense of relief a zeal for reforming some of the abuses in the church, and you have an idea of why Luther's protest generated a whole new movement within Christianity.

Luther believed that Roman Catholic doctrine and practice put up walls around religion, that the church operated as a power structure that so controlled the means of religious experience it was virtually impossible for people to have an assurance of God's love and their own salvation. The church, as he perceived it, controlled *Scripture* by insisting that it be read only in Latin and not translated into the vernacular, and that the church was the sole authorized interpreter; it controlled *doctrine* by means of theological complexity and clerical formulations; and it controlled *grace* by binding grace to reception of the sacraments and the practice of acts that would secure merit. All of this control was tied up with the power of the priesthood, a power that extended up and down a hierarchical ladder from pope to bishops and from bishops to priests.

Luther set out to free the gospel from the control exercised over it by the Roman church; he wanted to extend the freedom and assurance of faith-alone salvation to others. He translated the Bible into German and made it available to the people. For Luther, hearing Scripture was a kind of sacrament; he believed that if people could just hear the word of God in Scripture, in language they understood, it would have a powerful effect on them. Scripture, he argued, creates its own unity; people do not need to be confined to the official interpretations of the church, nor do they need to have their own interpretations of the gospel regulated in some way. He shared his own insights and told people what the best interpretations were; those interpretations, he believed, could be discovered and bear fruit in a more scriptural model of the church. He insisted that the church was not a hierarchy, but a "priesthood of all believers," and a fellowship. Finally, he insisted that salvation was granted to believers on the basis of faith alone. People did not need to rely on complex doctrines, or on a system of sacraments and indulgences dispensed by priests; they had only to trust that God would regard them as righteous.

Luther did not intend to form a new church, but to reform the existing one. By 1519, however, it was clear that his positions were radically at odds with Roman Catholic doctrines and a break from Rome seemed inevitable. In 1520 he wrote three famous treatises—*Address to the Christian Nobility of the German Nation, The Babylonian Captivity of the Church,* and *The Freedom of a Christian Man*—which spelled out his political and religious positions. Luther argued for German (*not* Roman) control of the German churches; he denied the power of the pope as the final interpreter of Scripture; he denied the power of priests to mediate between the believer and God; and he rejected all sacraments except baptism and the Eucharist. He was excommunicated from the Roman church in 1521.

Luther spent most of the rest of his life alternately supporting and curbing his reform movement, translating the Scriptures into German, and writing catechisms and hymns. His reading of Scripture and his experiences led him to support certain theological conclusions, and fortified his conviction of the uselessness of human effort and reason in matters of salvation. His religious experience convinced him that God is gracious and looks upon people as if they were righteous, if only they have faith and confidence in God's goodness and Christ's atonement. Righteousness was granted to people freely through the grace of Christ. Luther drew religion away from its political entanglements in the Roman church and insisted that it was based on Scripture and faith alone; religion, therefore, was a personal matter between God and the individual believer. At the same time, however, he did not free it from political involvement: he allowed the church to be subordinate to the political power of the state and appealed to the political power of the German princes to suppress quasi-religious revolts like the Peasants' Revolt (1524).

Luther's reform movement led to the formation of a separate church and inspired similar revolutions by other reformers. Lutheranism was systematically defined in various Lutheran creeds (see Appendix 5), all of which were combined in the Book of Concord (1580). Justification by faith alone and the primacy of Scripture as a religious authority are major tenets of Lutheranism. Luther was essentially conservative within his own movement; he did not support those who argued for extreme spiritualization. He was also cautious in relation to other reform movements; he did not support what he considered to be the extreme reforms of Zwingli, our next topic.

The Reformed Tradition

The man who initiated the movement that later became associated with the Reformed church was a contemporary of Luther's, Ulrich Zwingli (1484–1531), a Swiss reformer. Zwingli had been influenced by the humanists, especially by Erasmus, and was drawn to the reform movement through his studies of Scripture. Based on these studies, he argued against clerical celibacy, monasticism, and indulgences. In 1519 he gave a series of lectures on Scripture using Erasmus's edition of the Greek New Testament. Zwingli's position was simple: The word alone is enough, and one does not need the accumulated interpretations of the church and the commentaries of scholars. Zwingli, like Luther, argued that churches should be freed from Roman control. In 1523 the city council of Zurich approved Zwingli's positions about restoring the practice of the primitive church and ordered all priests to comply with them: organs were destroyed and images and statues removed from churches, priests were encouraged to marry, the liturgy was simplified and monasticism abolished.

Whereas Luther's protest was inspired by his own questions of personal salvation, Zwingli's desire for reform was motivated by his conviction that Christians could be bound only by what they found in the Bible. Accordingly, their views about the Christian life differed: Luther emphasized reconciliation and freedom, while Zwingli put more stress on the obligation of the Christian to conform to God's will as found in the Bible. Even though they agreed about many things—the need for reform, the scandal of indulgences, the centrality of the Bible—they disagreed profoundly about others, and their theological arguments led to the first rift within Protestantism, the break between the Lutheran and the Reformed traditions.

A central point of disagreement between Luther and Zwingli was the presence of Christ in the Eucharist. Roman Catholics believed the actual body and blood of Christ were present in the bread and wine consecrated in the Divine Liturgy. Catholics even had a philosophical explanation for *how* that happened. Luther rejected the metaphysical explanation but not the belief: for him the body and blood of Christ were really present in the bread and wine and received by the faithful. Zwingli located the presence of Christ in the hearts of the believers rather than in the elements of bread and wine. For him the Eucharist was a *memorial* meal that unites the faithful by means of a common bond with the Lord.[10]

These different interpretations led to a severe break between Luther and Zwingli: as Luther perceived it, Zwingli had simply gone too far. Those who would later be called Anabaptists believed that Zwingli had not gone far enough, and they, too, broke away from his movement to form a fellowship of their own. When Zwingli was killed in a religious war in 1531, the Swiss wing of the Reformation—Zwingli's ideas and points of emphasis—was adopted, modified, and developed by a second-generation reformer, John Calvin.

Calvin (1509–64) was a French Protestant theologian and the person most closely associated with the Reformed tradition. He originally intended to be a Roman Catholic priest, but apparently had some doubts about his vocation and about the Roman Catholic church. He studied to be a lawyer even though he was more attracted to Hebrew and classical studies; as a student he was influenced by the humanists. His active role in the Reformation was precipitated by a religious experience in 1533 in which he felt himself called to join the movement to restore the Christian church to its original purity. When he turned his energies to the Reformation he used them to systematize Protestant theology—his *Institutes of the Christian Religion,* 1536–59, were revised several times during his lifetime—and to develop his doctrinal system in the context of a theocratic state, the Geneva experiment, 1541–64.

Calvin continued the disagreement with Luther about the Eucharist. That argument led to the separation of the Protestant church in Germany into the Lutheran church on the one hand and the Reformed church (Calvinist) on the other. A more serious disagreement between Luther and Calvin, however, involved politics and the relation of the state to the church. Calvin restored the political power of the church and organized a church-dominated society. For Calvin it was not enough to define the church as a "priesthood of all believers"; the church, he believed, needed power as well as fellowship.

Calvin was invited to Geneva, Switzerland, as a reformer; there he hoped to create a refuge for French Protestants (who were being persecuted by the Catholic government of France) and to design a city government based on early Christian polity. An initial attempt (1536–38) failed, but from 1541 until his death, Calvin governed Geneva and was able to develop a theocratic government there: God was the supreme authority and God's laws were clear; Calvin interpreted them and utilized the secular powers to enforce them. He organized a constitutional government based on New Testament offices and hoped that the state would be subordinated to the church. Calvin had far-reaching powers not only in religious matters but over the private lives of all the citizens of Geneva. He established disciplines for everything, religious and secular; his laws were based on the Bible and enforced by civil magistrates. Any deviation from the law was punished, and opposition was punished severely. Geneva was a haven for religious refugees, a place for a new beginning. In a chaotic time full of injustice, persecution, and religious confusion, it promised a visible and godly order and a chance for a well-regulated Christian life under the providence and sovereignty of God.

In Calvin's theology, God's providence governs everything, and the fate of everything and everyone in the world is in God's hands; the believer should strive to have his or her own will taken up into the sovereign will of God. But how does one know God's will? Calvin proceeded from the premise that the Bible contained God's will and divine laws for every facet of human life: everything necessary for salvation has been revealed in Scripture in a clear and certain way. The Bible is read and understood in the church, which is a community under the sovereignty and grace of God. The church, therefore, is essential for salvation: it is the locus of God's covenant of grace because it is supported by the person and work of Christ. People are freed from anxiety about their salvation because it lies in God's hands.

To people who look at it from the outside, one of the striking features of Calvin's theology—a logical extension of his beliefs about the absolute sovereignty of God—is the theory of divine election and predestination. Since God knows everything and is absolutely powerful, it follows that God knows who will be saved and who will be damned. In fact, Calvin argued, God elected those to be saved and predestined those to be damned, and then God saw to it that those on the road to damnation were sinners and those on the road to salvation were saints. God's people—the elect—have been put on earth to work out the divine plan; election, therefore, is a calling and the Christian life a serious vocation.

Both Luther and Calvin had a gloomy view of human nature: both of them believed that people were sinful by nature and unable to do any good of their own accord; both perceived the Roman Catholic doctrine of intrinsic justification[11] as unbiblical and hopelessly wrong. According to Luther, salvation was accomplished by Christ and was granted freely to people on the basis of faith. Calvin agreed, but emphasized that faith and salvation depended on election. The teaching about predestination has borne most of the anti-Calvinist criticism, but ought not to be taken out of context or given disproportionate attention: it was meant to release people from anxiety about their salvation, to give them a sense of sinfulness and a profound sense of God's forgiveness, an experience that resulted in feelings of thankfulness and joy. The doctrine was also meant to divert their attention from worries about personal worthiness, and to focus it on Christian life as a calling and on God's sovereign role in the salvation of a person.

One of the followers of Calvin, Jacob Arminius (1560–1609), changed his mind about the doctrine of predestination even while he was trying to defend it. He and his followers in the Dutch Reformed church argued for conditional predestination and a more liberal theology. Arminianism is usually associated with honoring the role of free will (as opposed to Calvinistic determinism) and the concept of unlimited atonement. Arminius's followers were condemned at the Synod of Dort (1618–19) in Holland.

From this Reformed synod one can find a clear expression, in brief form, of Calvinist doctrine. There are five major points, which can be remembered as TULIP:

1. *Total depravity of humankind:* Since the Fall, people can only sin; they are incapable of sinless acts.
2. *Unconditional election:* Once a person is saved (by faith), that person is always saved.
3. *Limited atonement:* Christ died to save the elect, not to save everyone.
4. *Irresistible grace:* There is no freedom to resist God's grace.
5. *Perseverance of the saints:* The elect must lead saintly lives and persevere to the end; they cannot assume they are saved, nor can they rest in an assurance of salvation.

Once one accepts the sovereignty of God and the certainty that Scripture is the supreme rule of faith, one is to accept the world as created by God and is challenged to maintain its order. If the Bible is normative for every facet of human life, following the Bible allows one to uphold and glory in God's sovereignty and world order. The Calvinist system blended well with the demands of emerging capitalism: Calvin extolled thrift, hard work, sobriety, responsibility, and self-reliance, the very virtues that were crucial for those who wished to make substantial progress in modern mercantile society.

Calvin wrote a systematic theology of major Reformation positions and laid the groundwork for a theocratic society. Calvinism has been defined in various creeds (see Appendix 5), the most famous of which is probably the Westminster Confession. The form of church government Calvin proposed—Presbyterianism—and his religious ideas had a major impact on the religious future of English Protestants in the sixteenth and seventeenth centuries. The principles of the Synod of Dort and some of the ideas associated with the Geneva experiment—new beginnings, a refuge from religious persecution, and a visible, godly society under divine sovereignty—were the predominant influence in the minds and intentions of the Puritan founders of the American colonies.

The Tudor Reformation

The reformations of Luther and Calvin were doctrinal, liturgical, and disciplinary as well as structural, and they were pursued for predominantly religious reasons. Both Luther and Calvin set out to change the situation in the church. Luther hoped to reform the Catholic church by calling it back to its religious roles and informing it with more scriptural understanding; Calvin set out to purify Christianity and to organize Protestant Christianity into a theocratic system. The Tudor (Anglican) Reformation was not like either of its European cousins. It took place in England, and when it was over, much of what was Roman remained in liturgy, doctrine, and practice, despite its break with the papacy. Like Catholics, Anglicans continued to accept the episcopal structure of the church whereby authority moved from the top down; the liturgy was not substantially altered and there were, at first, no great doctrinal changes as in Lutheranism and the Reformed tradition.

The Roman Catholic church in England had been a rich and powerful institution dating back to the sixth century. One of the first missions of Pope Gregory I had been to organize the English church on the model of papal primacy.[12] At the same time, England was the first country to have a strong monarchy (able to oppose the pope on some issues) and a strong parliamentary government (able to oppose the monarch on some issues). England was a religiously vibrant country: the first significant reform movements occurred there (with Wycliffe and the Lollards), and an impressive array of mystics flourished in fourteenth-century England (Julian of Norwich, Richard Rolle, Walter Hilton, and the author of *The Cloud of Unknowing*).

The precipitating cause of the Tudor Reformation was a conflict between King Henry VIII (1491–1547) and the pope about divorce. Henry wanted to divorce his wife, Catherine of Aragon, to marry another woman, Anne Boleyn. The breakdown in negotiations between the king and the pope led to an administrative and judicial change in the structure of church government in England. Henry asserted the royal primacy over the church, declaring that the king (or queen), *not* the pope, was to be head of the church in England. Theologically, Anglicans attempted to find a middle way between Roman Catholicism and continental Protestantism. Accordingly, they kept much of the Roman Catholic doctrine and liturgical celebration, adopted a significant structural change, and allowed changes in some disciplinary matters like clerical celibacy.

When Henry VIII died, his son Edward VI (only a child) was king, and England was ruled by regents. The regents were substantially more sympathetic to European Protestants—especially to the Reformed tradition—than Henry VIII had been. At this time some changes were introduced into the Anglican Book of Common Prayer and it looked as if the Anglican church might become more thoroughly reformed. Edward VI died in 1553 and Mary Tudor, Henry's oldest daughter, granddaughter of the king of Catholic Spain, and a strong Roman Catholic supporter, became queen. With her ascension to the throne the stage was set for a confrontation between Anglicans (who had accepted the Reformation and the changes in the Church of England) and Roman Catholics (who had not accepted Henry's changes but had remained loyal to Rome). Mary at first simply forbade the practice of the Protestant religion, but within a year she established ecclesiastical courts to find and sentence heretics. She is remembered as Bloody Mary because of the severe persecutions during her reign. John Foxe's *Book of Martyrs* (1563) was written to chronicle the stories of many Protestants who were cruelly tortured and executed for their religious beliefs.

Mary was succeeded by her half-sister Elizabeth I, daughter of Anne Boleyn. Elizabeth (queen from 1558 to 1603) was suspicious both of Catholics (who judged that she was not the legitimate monarch) and of Protestants (who would have destroyed some of the protection offered to her by the episcopal polity of the Anglican church). In 1570 Pope Pius V issued a formal condemnation and excommunication of Elizabeth and released all English people from allegiance to her. Catholics were forced to choose between their citizenship (loyalty to the queen) and their religion (loyalty to the pope), and Queen Elizabeth had no choice but to see Roman Catholics as traitors. Up to this time English Protestantism and Roman Catholicism existed side by side; after the condemnation, Roman liturgy (the Mass) was forbidden and Catholics met increased persecution. By the end of Elizabeth's reign, England was the foremost Protestant country in Europe.

The Radical Reformation

The word *radical* comes from a Latin word meaning root. Radical reformers separated from other reform movements because they did not believe those reform movements really returned to the root of primitive Christian faith. Some radical reformers were called Anabaptists, a derogatory name from a Greek word meaning to *re*baptize. Anabaptists did not believe that it was scriptural to baptize babies and so *re*baptized one another and from then on baptized only adults. They wanted more than a structural and doctrinal reform: they wanted to restore apostolic Christianity, to live in conformity with Scripture and the faith of the first Christians. In order to do this, they saw the New Testament as the sole norm for Christian life and understood their relationship to Jesus as one of discipleship. For the Anabaptists, the life, death, and resurrection of Jesus were important not merely as elements in a doctrine of justification, but as norms for Christian behavior: the Christian was one who lived as Jesus had lived.

Several disparate groups of Anabaptists formed in the early part of the sixteenth century, some of which were not typical of later Anabaptist practice. The Zwickau Prophets, for example, joined the Peasants' Revolt, and a group of Münster Anabaptists under the leadership of John Leyden established a theocracy and practiced polygamy. Two important early groups were the Mennonites and the Hutterites. Mennonites were named for Menno Simons (c. 1496–1561), a Dutch reformer. Their views were similar to those of the Swiss Brethren, a group that split from the state church in Zurich (Zwingli's church) because the Reformation there hadn't been radical enough and because they regarded the whole notion of having church affairs subordinate to state control as unscriptural. The Hutterites took their name from Jacob Hutter (d. 1536) and were distinguished from other Anabaptist groups by their adoption of common ownership of property.

Anabaptists differed radically from other reform groups in practice and behavior. Their reading of the New Testament led them to some ethical conclusions about their life in the church that were at odds with the practices of both Catholics and Protestants. Thus the Anabaptist vision was threatening to other

Christians, and Anabaptists were persecuted by both Catholics and Protestants. Five Anabaptist beliefs were particularly radical:

1. *Separation from the world:* The world was perceived as a place controlled by evil and Anabaptists believed they should separate themselves from it; that is be disinterested in politics or the affairs of the state.
2. *Refusal to swear oaths:* Taking Jesus's words "Do not swear at all. . . . Let what you say be simply 'Yes' or 'No'" (Matt. 5:34, 37) literally, they refused to swear oaths; since the oath was the basis of the juridical feudal system, it looked as if they stood against the basic organization of society.
3. *Nonresistance:* Doing as Jesus did and refusing to fight evil with evil, they refused to do anything violent; that is, they refused to fight in wars for any reason.
4. *Adult baptism:* They regarded baptism and responsible faith as matters of adult conviction, not the province of children, who were regarded as innocent until they reached an age of accountability.
5. *Community of goods:* They believed in sharing one's goods with everyone, friend and foe alike; in its extreme form, everything was owned in common, as with the Hutterites.

Anabaptists were a small but important strand of the Reformation. Their beliefs and their radical discipleship distinguished them from other groups and had the effect of keeping their numbers small. As we shall see in later chapters, Mennonites and Amish (a later Anabaptist group) continue the traditions of the Radical Reformation not only in terms of belief and religious practice, but sometimes in the very old-fashioned way they live in the contemporary world.

These four major strands of the Protestant Reformation all grew into separate denominations which, as we shall see, inspired the growth of other churches. The creative protests of Wycliffe and Hus, the reforming decisions of the conciliar movement, and the supportive atmosphere of the Renaissance all worked together to energize the reforming impulses of Christianity. The Protestant Reformation was the beginning of a rich period of religious growth which, for Protestant denominations, was especially vibrant in nineteenth-century America. Catholicism was also urged to reform during this time, and it is to that group that we now turn.

THE CATHOLIC REFORMATION

The Catholic Reformation is sometimes called the Counter-Reformation, a term that implies little more than a reaction to Protestant reform movements. It would be more accurate to say that reform movements had been going on within and outside Catholicism for some time, and that some of the early Protestant reform movements were originally attempts to reform the Catholic church. Still, there *was* a significant Roman Catholic response to the Protestant Reformation.

The charter of the Roman response was contained in the decrees of the Council of Trent (1545–63), a reforming council that met on and off for nearly twenty years. Roman Catholics refused to meet Protestant reformers halfway on any issue and used Trent instead to reassert church authority, to clarify traditional doctrine, and to establish a solid basis for the renewal of discipline and spiritual life within Catholicism. After Trent, the Roman Catholic church emerged with a clear system of doctrine and discipline, and some significant moral and administrative reforms. Among the doctrines and practices affirmed by the Council of Trent were the following (notice that they respond to Protestant questions or positions by denying them):

1. A creed is important, and the official creed is the Nicene Creed.
2. Scripture is *not* the only source of divine revelation; *tradition* is on an equal footing with Scripture as a source of religious authority.
3. Individuals may *not* interpret the Bible for themselves: the church is the sole interpreter of the Bible, and the official Bible is the Vulgate.
4. The Protestant doctrine of sin and justification is false; people have free will, and justification is intrinsic and related to grace.
5. There are *seven* sacraments instituted by Jesus Christ, and sacraments are necessary for salvation.
6. The doctrine of transubstantiation is the official explanation for the real presence of Christ in the Eucharist.
7. The eucharistic doctrines of Luther, Calvin, and Zwingli were condemned.
8. The chalice (wine) was denied to the laity.
9. The value and importance of the liturgy (the Mass) were reaffirmed.
10. Reforming moves aimed at bishops, seminaries, and diocesan synods were established.
11. The doctrines that supported purgatory and the use of relics and indulgences, all of which were severely criticized by Protestant reformers, were upheld.

To insure the success of the Catholic Reformation two offices were established (or reestablished under different rules): the *Inquisition* (a final court of appeals for heresy cases, not to be confused with the Spanish Inquisition, which was instituted in the late fifteenth century by the Spanish crown as a means of using state power against Muslims and Jews) and the *Index* (an official list of books that members of the Roman church were forbidden to read).

Protestant reformers had protested that religious orders and monastic institutions in Catholicism were corrupt. In the sixteenth century a number of new reformed religious orders were established; a particular one, the Jesuits, was established for the energetic support of the church.[13] In all of these religious groups, members had a reputation for piety and austerity as well as great preaching and teaching ability. On a popular level, as a tangible example of reform in the church, they were effective.

The Catholic church made no significant overtures to Protestants or to members of the Orthodox church until the Second Vatican Council (1962–65). At that council, efforts were made to talk with and understand Protestants, and much of what has been characterized as the "siege mentality" of Trent began to disappear. The primary importance of Scripture was affirmed, the importance and role of lay people in the church was stated, Protestants were recognized as true Christians, it was declared permissible to celebrate the liturgy in the vernacular, more congregational participation in worship was encouraged, and the Index was abolished. The changes of the Second Vatican Council were sweeping, and the effects of those changes as well as the development of some of them into significantly different practices and attitudes continue to be felt.

CONCLUSION

Throughout his public life, people asked Jesus, "By whose *authority* do you do these things?" Questions of religious authority have marked the Christian church from the beginning and have contributed to the variety in its life. During the Reformation, questions of religious authority were bound up with questions of doctrine and practice and led to a full-scale division of the Christian church into Protestant and Catholic in the West. Orthodox Christians were interested in the reformers' protests against papal power, but not much inspired to make doctrinal and liturgical changes; the Reformation, therefore, did not significantly influence them.

By the middle of the sixteenth century, Protestants and Catholics had begun wars against one another; each group understood itself as the instrument of God's will and wrath, commissioned to bring the other group to its knees. Both Catholics and Protestants persecuted Anabaptists whenever they could, and otherwise killed and tortured each other in the name of religion. The wars of religion (involved with political issues as well) formally ended with the Peace of Westphalia in 1648. The wars ended, but not the controversy, and not the proliferation of Christian churches.

CHAPTER 5 NOTES

[1] See Brian Tierney, *The Crisis of Church and State 1050–1300* (Englewood Cliffs, N.J.: Prentice-Hall, 1964), or Bennett D. Hill, editor, *Church and State in the Middle Ages* (New York: John Wiley, 1970). Political conflicts were not the whole story at this time.

There were struggles, changes, and growth in every sector of life and in religion; the political emphasis I give helps to focus more clearly the beginnings of protest. For a look at how church-state politics continues to influence religious life, see Charles Villa-Vicencio, *Between Christ and Caesar: Classic and Contemporary Texts on Church and State* (Grand Rapids: Eerdmans, 1986). Villa-Vicencio supplies significant texts throughout Christian history, ending with contemporary South Africa.

[2]The spiritual road for the pope was suggested periodically throughout history, but never willingly taken. The first pope to rule without power over the so-called papal states (a large and significant slice of present-day Italy, right across the middle) was Pius IX (1846–78), and then only because they were taken away by force. Why didn't the popes give up their political power? No one can answer for sure, but read what a Renaissance pope himself had to say about the matter: "These are not times in which virtue is regarded. It is of all importance whether it resides in the strong or in the weak. A helpless virtue is despised by the princes. I have often felt inclined to agree with those who think that the temporal power ought to be separated from the spiritual; for I thought that the priests would be better enabled to perform their functions and that the princes would be more obedient to them. But now I have learned that virtue without power is scorned, and that the pope without the patrimony of Peter [the papal states] is but a servant of Kings." These are the words of Pope Pius II, from *De Concilio Basil.*

[3]These positions can be found in the writings of Pope Innocent III (1198–1216) who, perhaps more than any other pope, embodied the extremes of ecclesiastical-political doctrine.

[4]For a translation of excerpts from this document, see Anne Freemantle, editor, *The Papal Encyclicals in Their Historical Context* (New York: New American Library, 1963), pp. 71–77.

[5]There are, as you can imagine, countless books on the rise of the papacy, and few of them are as objective as one would like. One clear introduction to the issues and personalities from the beginning to the fifteenth century is Geoffrey Barraclough, *The Medieval Papacy* (New York: Harcourt, Brace & World, 1972). The book is beautifully illustrated and Barraclough gives you a sense of the controversy and flavor of the times.

[6]The conciliarist movement has an interesting historical footnote. In 1516 the pope issued a decree that condemned conciliarism. The first words of that degree—the words that should have set it apart from all other papal documents, past and future, because no two papal documents ever begin with the same words—were *Pastor aeternus.* Yet in 1871, when papal infallibility was declared by the First Vatican Council, the first words of their degree were *Pastor aeternus.* Coincidence, or symbol of a return to papal absolutism? Let me add something to it. The great conciliarist council (Constance—which held, among other things, that councils were superior to popes) was called by Pope John XXIII. Since he was deposed right after the council, his name and number were forgotten until 1958, when Angelo Roncalli was elected pope and took the name of John XXIII. Coincidence, or symbol of a return to conciliarism? The modern John XXIII called the Second Vatican Council (1962–65), the most sweeping reform council in modern Roman Catholic history and one that again extolled a collegial kind of church government.

[7]For some sense of the scope of the Renaissance, see Donald Weinstein, editor, *The Renaissance and the Reformation 1300–1600* (New York: Free Press, 1965). Weinstein's introduction to this collection of documents is brief and clear.

[8]The Donation of Constantine, which we now know to be a forgery, was the document used by the popes to claim their ownership over the papal states (sometimes known as the patrimony of St. Peter), a vast territory in central Italy. According to the docu-

ment, Constantine, in gratitude to Pope Sylvester I (314–35), gave him primacy over all the patriarchates (Antioch, Constantinople, Alexandria, and Jerusalem), along with dominion over all of Italy, including Rome and the cities and lands of the Western empire. The boundaries of the papal states changed somewhat throughout history, but the claim to the territory was consistently pressed by the popes, even after Valla and others demonstrated that its documentary support was false. One of the reasons Italy did not become a united country until 1870 was the resistance of the popes and their claim to own the papal states. The great revolutions in Italy during the nineteenth century placed Pope Pius IX squarely in the middle of a prolonged political battle, and when the papal states were taken from him by force, he still refused to relinquish them in theory. The final settlement of the matter did not come until 1929, when Pope Pius XI signed the Lateran Treaty with Benito Mussolini.

[9]Purgatory is one of those doctrines that make sense to believers and appear utterly incomprehensible to nonbelievers. One way to get to the medieval understanding of salvation (including concepts of heaven, hell, and purgatory) is through Dante's *Divine Comedy*. Written at the beginning of the fourteenth century, it gathers the doctrines, corruptions, personalities, and questions of the times into a cosmic vision, and, as one of the first and most important pieces of Italian national literature, is a pleasure to read. For a clear explanation of purgatory, see the introduction to the second part of the *Divine Comedy,* the *Purgatory,* in the translation by Dorothy L. Sayers (London: Penguin, 1955), pp. 1–71.

[10]The word *memorial* is a tricky one. Zwingli meant that at the Lord's Supper one simply shared bread and wine with the community and remembered what Jesus did. For an analysis of the word with its Jewish roots and Christian understandings through history, see Louis Bouyer, *The Eucharist* (Notre Dame, Ind.: University of Notre Dame Press, 1968), pp. 103–6.

[11]A general way to distinguish between Roman Catholic and early Protestant doctrines of justification is through the terms *intrinsic* (Roman Catholic) and *extrinsic* (Protestant). The key question is whether or not something really happens to human nature through grace. Let's start with the premise that human nature is sinful to begin with (a dungheap): extrinsic justification says that if you have faith, then even though you remain a dungheap, you smell like a bed of roses to God; nothing really happens, but by virtue of the grace of Christ, God treats you like a garden. Intrinsic justification says that if you do those things that give grace (say your prayers, live virtuously, and so on), you will be changed into a rose garden; something really happens, or, to put it in the religious language of the times, "grace transforms nature." Luther did not believe this.

[12]See for example Bede, *A History of the English Church and People* (London: Penguin, 1955). This book was written in the eighth century by Bede, a Benedictine monk. In it one can see how the English church was set up along the lines of Roman primacy, and one can see how power was passed along.

[13]The Jesuits (the Society of Jesus) were founded by Ignatius Loyola (1491–1556) to be a missionary order, but they became the great religious force of the Catholic Reformation.

SUGGESTIONS FOR FURTHER READING

1. For two general background books, see R. W. Southern, *Western Society and the Church in the Middle Ages* (London: Penguin, 1970), and Roland H. Bainton, *Early and Medieval Christianity* (Boston: Beacon Press, 1962). Southern is more dense with infor-

mation and gives an excellent general introduction to the divisions in the religious world in the Middle Ages, the proliferation of religious orders, the various fringe groups, and the papacy. Bainton is straightforward and eminently readable and deals with the patristic period, medieval theology, and its transformation before and during the Renaissance.

2. For a documentary introduction to the Reformation, see Hans J. Hillenbrand, editor, *The Reformation: A Narrative History Related by Contemporary Observers and Participants* (Grand Rapids: Baker Book House, 1964). This is full of pictures and documents linked together by a simple narrative style.

3. For good histories that were written for students and are full of pictures and illustrations, see A. G. Dickens, *Reformation and Society in Sixteenth-Century Europe,* and *The Counter Reformation* (New York: Harcourt, Brace & World, 1966 and 1969).

4. For an insider's history of the Radical Reformation, see Donald F. Durnbaugh, *The Believers' Church: The History and Character of Radical Protestantism* (New York: Macmillan, 1968). Also, J. Denny Weaver, *Becoming an Anabaptist: The Origin and Significance of Sixteenth-Century Anabaptism* (Scottdale, Pa.: Herald Press, 1987).

5. For a book that shows the link between popular spirituality and Protestantism, see Frank C. Senn, editor, *Protestant Spiritual Traditions* (New York: Paulist Press, 1986).

❖

CHAPTER 6

THE REFORMATION CONTINUES: CHRISTIANITY IN THE SIXTEENTH, SEVENTEENTH, AND EIGHTEENTH CENTURIES

T he Reformation responded to and encouraged religious ferment. The main groups of the Reformation were relatively clear-cut and confined to a small geographical area, new offshoots of a unified Christianity within a fairly uniform cultural context. As Christianity moved into the seventeenth and eighteenth centuries, the social and religious situation became much more complex. Religious reform continued, but not in such a way that it could easily be classified as Lutheran or Calvinist. New religious groups formed, sometimes within a particular Reformation church and sometimes as a more generalized response to some secular attitude. In the eighteenth century especially—when the Enlightenment and new scientific discoveries threatened all religions—new Christian groups were formed on the basis of widespread religious response to a particular cultural development.[1]

This chapter summarizes some significant developments within Christianity in the sixteenth, seventeenth, and eighteenth centuries. We review the European situation in the first two of these centuries briefly and then focus on Christian diversity in England. The English situation merits closer attention for two reasons: it was extraordinarily rich in new forms of Christianity, and it is the parent of the American religious experience. After a brief description of the struggle between science and religion in the eighteenth century (which provides a context for the birth of Deism and Pietism and the growth of Methodism), we move to the American context, where we will concentrate throughout most of the rest of this book.

SIXTEENTH- AND SEVENTEENTH-CENTURY CHRISTIANITY: INCREASING DIVERSITY

The Reformation raised issues of polity, doctrine, and practice so profound that its reverberations continued for centuries. We can often identify and define issues in the sixteenth and seventeenth centuries as one specifically religious view in competition with another. It is even possible, with only slight modifications, to continue to differentiate religious groups as further divisions of the major strands of the Reformation. For our purposes, the developments within Lutheranism, Catholicism, and the Radical Reformation can be described simply and briefly. I will discuss the Reformed tradition within the context of English Puritanism at some length so that you can begin to understand the roots of the American religious experience. It is within the English context that I will mention—only briefly—developments within the Tudor Reformation.

Roman Catholicism

The reverberations of reform were felt in the Roman Catholic church in a proliferation of new religious orders but not in new liturgical or doctrinal forms. Church-state issues—the political power of the pope, the role of the church in the conquest of the new world, and relations between European nations and the Vatican—continued to play an important role in the history of Roman Catholicism. The Council of Trent strengthened the Roman Catholic church against the demands of the reformers and inspired a real reformation within the church. Roman Catholicism was defined by the teachings of the Council of Trent up until the middle of the twentieth century. Because of its strong centralized model of ecclesiastical authority, Roman Catholicism did not foster or accept divisions within itself: one was either a loyal Roman Catholic or one left the church (by choice or through excommunication). By definition, a loyal Roman Catholic was one who followed the teachings of the church, accepted the hierarchical structure with the pope at its head, and participated in the specified liturgical and sacramental life of the church.

In many ways, Catholicism flourished after the Reformation by reaffirming some of the things Protestants denied, and by attending to their legitimate complaints about corruption. Many of the abuses were eradicated. For example, training for the priesthood was regularized, which meant that the clergy was increasingly well educated and that men entering the priesthood were often more dedicated to the spiritual welfare of their people than they had been in the past. If Protestants were seeking a simplified Christianity, stripped of splendor and mystery, Catholics responded by emphasizing those very things: churches were lavishly decorated, especially in Rome, where artists gave Roman Catholicism a glorious baroque flavor; liturgy was celebrated with pomp and ceremony, often accompanied by elaborate orchestrations of the Mass; and new devotional forms were added to attract people to the everyday mystery of Catholic practice.

Lutheranism

Lutheranism spread throughout Germany and the Scandinavian countries without division. The Lutheran church was strongly congregational; issues of polity and practice were left up to the local congregation.[2] Accordingly, Lutheranism developed in different but not divisive ways: in some places one could find a liturgy that looked vaguely Roman Catholic—structured, formal celebration of the Eucharist—and in other places services were more clearly Protestant—worship consisting mainly of hymns and Bible study. The primacy of the gospel was the most important Lutheran principle; it was solidified in creeds like the Augsburg Confession, part of the Book of Concord (see Appendix 5).

Radical Reformation

The polity of Radical Reformation groups was strongly congregational and was therefore able to support a variety of practical forms within the general framework of Anabaptist vision. Anabaptists were often victims of brutal persecution by both Catholics and Protestants and by both religious and secular authorities. Their strategy during this time was one of survival. The two main groups—Mennonites and Hutterites—continued to exist and to move from place to place to be free from harassment. One new Anabaptist group emerged at this time, the Amish. They were the conservative followers of Jacob Amman, about whom little is known. The Amish split from the Mennonites because they wished to see a strict enforcement of *Meidung,* the practice of shunning the excommunicated. They became a separate group at the end of the seventeenth century and migrated to America in the eighteenth century.

The Reformed Tradition in the Context of the Puritan Reformation

The most fertile soil for religious proliferation was England, and the most productive Protestantism to flourish there was the Reformed tradition. The specific nature of the Tudor Reformation made England a place where some of the fundamental arguments of the Reformation could continue. The religious situation on the Continent stabilized with the Peace of Westphalia (1648):[3] France and much of southern Europe were Catholic, northern Europe was Protestant (either Lutheran or Reformed and not at war with one another), and Germany was a patchwork quilt of Catholicism and Protestantism depending on the religion of the regional ruler. England was a Protestant country, but not in the sense that some of the European countries were. The rationale for the Tudor Reformation had been *political;* the key document, the Act of Supremacy (1534), stated that the monarch was the legitimate head of the church in England. The argument focused on the rights of the monarch versus the rights of the pope in religious matters. The issues of the continental Reformation—polity, liturgical practice, and doctrine—were not as important in England as the question of supremacy. Thus the Church of England continued to operate within a hierarchical structure (versus the congregationalism of Luther or the presbyterianism of Calvin), continued to celebrate the eucharistic liturgy (versus the more simplified worship services found in many Protestant churches), and continued to support ancient doctrinal formulations (not the new doctrinal positions of the continental reformers). In some senses, therefore, the Church of England under Henry VIII had not been reformed; it had simply been cut loose from Roman supremacy.

Let's review the English situation briefly. After Henry's death England was ruled by regents and the Church of England grew a little more Protestant, but when Mary I (Henry's daughter) came to the throne, Protestant measures were reversed, Roman Catholicism restored, and severe anti-Protestant persecution began. During these persecutions many religious reformers fled to the continent, where they imbibed a pure Calvinism and nurtured a strong desire to reform the Church of England. Their chance would come, they hoped, with Mary's death.

Mary's successor, her half-sister Elizabeth I (1558–1603), wanted religious and political stability and found that she had to negotiate her way through three different sets of religious complications: Catholic, Anglican, and Puritan. Roman Catholics, favored by her sister Mary, were still a significant part of the English population. When Elizabeth came to the throne, she was willing to live and let live, and so allowed Catholics to practice their religion openly. When the pope condemned Elizabeth, arguing that she was not the legitimate successor to the throne, English Catholics were forced into a completely untenable position: if they professed their loyal Catholicism, they were, in fact, in treasonous opposition to the crown, and if they identified themselves as loyal subjects of the queen, they were bound to recognize her as head of the church, thereby breaking their allegiance to Roman Catholicism.

Anglicans were the officially recognized church. Elizabeth was indebted to them because they upheld her legitimacy and so insured her right to rule. In addition, the Church of England was a compromise group, one that attempted to find a *via media* (a middle way) between Roman Catholicism on the one hand and the thoroughgoing reformation of continental Protestantism. Elizabeth, like her father, asserted the independence of the Anglican church. Under her supervision the church adopted the 1552 version of the Book of Common Prayer and revised and reduced the Forty-two Articles to the Thirty-nine Articles (see Appendix 5).

The third group, one with wide-ranging possibilities in both religious and political terms, was the Puritans. Those religious reformers who had fled during the reign of Mary I happily returned to England during Elizabeth's reign. They hoped to find her sympathetic to their desires to institute a more comprehensive reformation in England. Their movement for religious reform was inspired by continental Calvinists and urged a purification of the church. They wanted a Christianity purged of anything Roman in practice, liturgy, or doctrine. All their talk about purity earned them the nickname Puritans.

There were two main groups of Puritan reformers: Presbyterians and Congregationalists. One of the fundamental issues of the continental Reformation was church polity; the reformers protested against the unscriptural basis of a hierarchical church. The Puritans were united in their protest against the hierarchical structure of the Anglican church, but they were divided about which continental model to adopt. Both Luther's congregationalism and Calvin's presbyterianism derived from the New Testament. Since both models had a biblical base there was no agreement about which one to choose, and no authoritative way to decide between them.

Congregationalists. Congregationalism is a form of church government that rests on the autonomy and freedom of the local congregation, and defines a church as a group of believers bound together under the headship of Jesus Christ (see Appendix 6). In Congregationalism, each local church is truly and fully the church. Those people holding congregational views who found themselves unable to remain within the Church of England separated from it and are sometimes referred to as Separatists.

Presbyterians. Presbyterianism is a form of church government that combines some congregational insights (the importance of the local church) with some advantages of the hierarchical model (more centralized authority) (see Appendix 6). This model was adopted by two major groups: the Reformed church (in Europe) and the Presbyterian church (in England and Scotland). The Presbyterian church is the English and Scottish branch of the Reformed church founded by John Knox (c. 1513–72).

Presbyterians were the dominant Puritan group in England in the sixteenth and seventeenth centuries. Elizabeth did not cooperate with them and neither did her immediate successors, because there had been an old and mutually advantageous relationship between the monarchy and the episcopal form of church government. When the cry for religious reform (from the Puritans) was combined with the cry for political reform (from the Parliamentarians), the result was the English Civil War (1642–48). When the monarchy was defeated, so was the episcopacy, at least for a while. In 1646 presbyterianism was substituted for the episcopal polity of the Church of England. During the interregnum (the period in which there was no monarch: 1649–60), it was a crime to use the Book of Common Prayer. When the monarchy was restored in 1660, it was not merely a political victory; it was a victory for the Church of England over the

Puritans. In 1662 the Act of Uniformity required episcopal ordination of all ministers (restoring power and control to the bishops) and decreed that the Book of Common Prayer was the only legal worship book in England. In reaction to the Act of Uniformity more than two thousand clergymen resigned from the Church of England to celebrate their own worship in Nonconformist *chapels*.[4]

Thus by the end of the seventeenth century the Reformation in England had resulted in the establishment of the Anglican church as the official Church of England. It had an episcopal structure, was protected by the monarchy, affirmed the Thirty-nine Articles, and used the Book of Common Prayer as its sole liturgical source. Not all Christians in England belonged to the Anglican church. Roman Catholics, still suspected of disloyalty to the crown, maintained a low profile and did not take a prominent place in English life until the end of the nineteenth century. Nonconformist groups—both Presbyterian and Congregational—existed along with Anglicanism and continued to attract new members. Two new religious groups were formed within this Nonconformist context: Baptists and Quakers.

Baptists. The Baptist church was a new denomination that had Congregationalist roots. It shared the church polity views of the English Congregationalists, but developed a distinctive teaching about baptism. Since 1644 the name Baptist has been applied to those who believe two things about baptism: that it must be done by immersion (not by pouring water over the head or sprinkling), and that it can be administered only to convinced believers; that is, to adults and not to babies. The first group of Baptists formed in Holland at the beginning of the seventeenth century. A group of Separatist Congregationalists led by John Smyth (1554–1612) migrated to Holland to live in an atmosphere of religious freedom; there, influenced by some Mennonites, they repudiated infant baptism and formed the first English Baptist congregation.

Quakers. The Religious Society of Friends, or Quakers, was a new religious group founded by George Fox (1624–91) that attracted many unattached Nonconformists.[5] Fox, disillusioned with the ferocious wars fought for Christian truth and frustrated with the disparate claims of the churches, sought a new religious understanding. In 1646 he had a religious experience that caused him to find peace within himself, an experience that led him to the doctrine of the Inner Light. According to Fox, all people have the voice of God within them; the Inner Light is the fundamental source of religious certainty and deep spiritual assurance. The Quakers presented a new religious alternative for people by opposing traditional Calvinist doctrines of human depravity and the preeminence of biblical revelation. A person with the Inner Light is not depraved, but possesses the voice of God within; if God speaks directly to the heart, biblical revelation is less central. Since the Inner Light is so important, Fox believed, all outward forms of religion should be rejected: church institutions, sacraments, ritual, ministers, hymn singing, all outward signs of established institutional church life were dropped. Like the Anabaptists, Quakers refused to swear oaths or to participate in wars and were persecuted physically and legally.

Summary of Sixteenth- and Seventeenth-Century Christianity

By the end of the seventeenth century there were many more religious groups than there had been at the beginning of the Reformation.[6] Roman Catholics did not divide into separate churches, but did continue to be touched by the reforming spirit of the times. Lutherans moved into Scandinavia, forming new congregations without any significant division, though the Pietist movement (see next section) was very important in Lutheranism at this time and beyond. The Anabaptists struggled to survive and the main groups—Mennonites and Hutterites—continued to baptize members into their fellowship. The only significant division was the formation of the Amish church at the end of the seventeenth century. In England the Reformed tradition inspired the Puritan movement, which eventually split into several different groups: Congregationalists, Presbyterians, Baptists, and Quakers. Ultimately, the Anglicans were the established Church of England, though non-Anglican chapels were permitted to exist in England and continued to attract new members throughout the country. Representatives from all these different religious groups emigrated to America and played an important role in American religious history.

THE EIGHTEENTH CENTURY: RESETTLEMENT AND REFORMATION

In the eighteenth century, religious arguments did not occur as frequently between one church and another, but most churches had members who began to challenge some of the fundamental assumptions of Christianity. New religious alternatives such as Deism and Pietism were generated in response to some of these challenges. My purpose here is to summarize the eighteenth-century context briefly in order to describe Christianity in Europe and then in America. The next section of the book will deal with Christianity in the modern world, and will review the impact of science and the Enlightenment as we expand on the challenges of modernity for Christianity in general. At this point, however, we are going to take only a quick look at the context so that we can have some appreciation of the patterns of resettlement—Christianity in the new world—and continuing reformation up to the nineteenth century.

The Scientific Revolution

The church in the Middle Ages was the single most powerful institution in the West and claimed (as we have seen) to have jurisdiction over virtually everything. Conflicts arose when someone disputed that claim (as, for example, when political leaders challenged the church's political power). As scientists began to learn more about the world and its wonders, they began to disprove some long-held and religiously supported views. The Protestant Reformation gave an implicit impetus to the scientific revolution by questioning religious authority and thereby making it easier for scientists to question established patterns.

The discoveries of Copernicus (1473–1543) and Galileo (1564–1642) upset old notions of the order of the universe and undermined what some people believed to be an immutable view of the cosmos and our centrality therein. One of the most famous cases in which the church condemned a scientific view (one we all know today to be true) was the condemnation of Galileo. His support for the Copernican view that the sun is the central body in the universe and that the earth moves around *it* was not the officially sanctioned view. In 1633 he was called to Rome by the Inquisition and forced to retract his scientific findings.

René Descartes (1596–1650) and Francis Bacon (1561–1626) established the importance of the scientific method based on empirical observation and systematic doubt; Isaac Newton (1642–1727) brought the world to the threshold of modernity with his physical and mathematical discoveries. Very few people believed that science could really endanger religious beliefs, yet as the world was transformed by new discoveries, a great change came over the way educated people looked at the heavens and the earth. The discoveries of the scientific revolution suggested that the whole universe might be subject to the control and domination of human ingenuity.

The Enlightenment and the Beginnings of Deism

The Enlightenment followed on the heels of the scientific revolution. People were called out of the darkness of religion (perceived as mystery or superstition) and into the "enlightened" world of reason: they were given light to see the world around them and encouraged to believe in an orderly universe. "Dare to know," the Enlightenment philosophers challenged, and their followers stretched toward a new individualism and a theory of human perfectibility. Immanuel Kant (1724–1802), perhaps the greatest of the Enlightenment philosophers, wrote *Religion Within the Limits of Reason Alone* to argue for the need for moral consciousness without miracles. Old Christian doctrines like divine providence were seen as needless interference in the orderly lives of people.

The combination of scientific discoveries about the universe and Enlightenment philosophy challenged old and cherished Christian assumptions. During the next hundred years, Christians reacted in various ways to this challenge, as they still do today. Some grew defensive, spending their energy denying the legitimacy of the challenge; others tried to defend Christianity by using the skills and tools of post-Enlightenment scholarship. Still others, in the eighteenth century at least, tried to combine Enlightenment insights with religious impulses and so developed a new religion, Deism.

The old religion was criticized for being ponderous and superstitious, for crippling rather than enhancing human freedom. Deism was extolled for its simplicity and reasonableness and for its insistence on religious toleration and freedom. Deism is a religion of logic that believes God is sufficiently revealed in the natural world. There is, accordingly, no need for supernatural revelation. According to Deist belief, God created the world and filled it with reasonable people and discernible natural laws; one's task is to discover the laws of nature and to live according to one's reason. John Locke (1632–1704) wrote his essay "The Reasonableness of Christianity" to prove that the ethical injunctions of Christianity were in conformity with the dictates of reason: the excellence of Christianity lay precisely in its reasonableness.

The rationalism of the Enlightenment and Deism was a philosophical response to some of the confusion and distress present in Christianity in the sixteenth and seventeenth centuries. Wars fought in the name of Christianity and the systematic use of torture by one group against another caused many people to abandon organized religion altogether or to be less than enthusiastic in their religious devotion. A religious response to the rationalism of the Enlightenment and Deism and to a growing sense of moral laxity and confusion was evangelical Pietism. It not only regenerated some churches, it inspired new ones.

Pietism and the Emergence of New Christian Churches

The original impetus for Pietism arose during the seventeenth century in a new reformation within German Lutheranism. Associated with the teachings of Philipp Jakob Spener (1635–1705) and August Hermann Franke (1663–1727), this movement was a reaction to moral laxity, formalism, secularism, and religious indifference. Spener longed for a rebirth of religious seriousness within the Lutheran church. He organized Bible study groups in his home, which were known as the *collegia pietatis,* later the Pietists. Spener was more interested in a right feeling in the heart than he was in pure doctrinal formulation and his teachings were ultimately condemned by the Lutherans, though they continued to have an effect on the Lutheran church. Franke, a professor at the University of Halle, built Pietism into the ministerial curriculum of the university. More than two hundred Lutheran ministers graduated from the university every year, each with some exposure to Pietistic doctrines. Pietism has some dominant characteristics: a Bible-centered faith, a keen sense of guilt and forgiveness felt in the heart, personal conversion, practical holiness in simple Christian living, and a concern for the needs of other people. All of these characteristics were thought to be manifested and supported by an emotional outpouring of one's feelings and aspirations. Pietism influenced members of many different churches and inspired the formation of new religious groups, including the Brethren and the Methodists.

Brethren churches. The Brethren were an Anabaptist group formed in Germany by Alexander Mack (1679–1735). Mack had been a member of the Reformed church, but separated from it, along with some others, in order to find a more biblical expression of Christianity. His group was composed mostly of Pietists and Anabaptists; in 1708 they formed a new fellowship and elected Mack as their leader. Because of persecution, they migrated first to the Netherlands and then to Germantown, Pennsylvania; they had all come to America by 1735. They were sometimes called Dunkers or Dunkards, though their official name was the Fraternity of German Baptists. Brethren are distinguished in practice by a threefold immersion at baptism and a threefold Holy Communion service: footwashing, the Lord's Supper, and an *agape* or fellowship meal, sometimes called a love feast.

Methodists. Methodism was a revivalist movement within the Anglican church influenced by Moravian Pietists.[7] John Wesley (1703–91), his brother Charles (1707–88), and their friend George Whitefield (1714–70) were at Oxford University together when they experienced a religious awakening. They and a few other students were interested in a more heartfelt religious experience than they found among people in the Church of England, and they spent much time in prayer and spiritual discipline in search of it. Other students ridiculed them for trying to devise a method for religious experience and the name Methodist stuck to Wesley and his work. John Wesley was influenced by Moravians in the American colony of Georgia (where he went as a missionary in 1735) and in England (where he returned dejected a year later). On a visit to a Moravian settlement at Aldersgate in 1738, Wesley had a religious experience in which he felt his heart "strangely warmed," when he knew that God took away all his sins. From that warm assurance, his acquaintance with Pietist doctrine through the Moravians, and his own early preoccupations wih religious experience, Wesley built a significant religious movement.

Wesley called the world his parish: he rode more than 250,000 miles on horseback and delivered in excess of forty thousand outdoor sermons; he preached in slums and prisons, anywhere people would listen to his message of religious regeneration. The emphasis on personal conversion, warm fellowship, and fervent preaching made Methodism attractive to thousands of people inside and outside the Anglican church. One important factor in the spread of Methodism was the hymnody; the Methodist hymnal, said Wesley, was a "distinct and full account of scriptural Christianity." The hymns were comforting and easy to sing; they reassured people about God's love for them.

Methodism, as a revivalist movement within the Church of England, was never intended to become a separate religious group; Methodists were members of the Anglican church and Methodism was their style of fellowship and religious revival. It was a means of regeneration within the church, as Methodists desired inner holiness and wanted to live lives of prayer, discipline, and fellowship. In order to maintain a disciplined prayer life for converts, Wesley established Methodist societies and classes, and specified weekly prayer meetings and other means of communication and fellowship. All these disciplinary innovations made Methodists *feel* separate from the Church of England. They were not separate, however, so long as they were dependent on the Anglican church for sacraments and ordination. The English Methodists did not become a separate body until 1897.

While the scientific revolution and the Enlightenment inspired Deism and a reaction to it, the migration of various religious groups to America caused further religious changes in the seventeenth and eighteenth centuries. We look next at the American context and the changes it engendered.

THE AMERICAN CONTEXT

We have to step back for a moment to the seventeenth century in order to understand the American experience in the eighteenth century. Puritan Congregationalists and Presbyterians who did not stay in England fled to America in the early part of the seventeenth century; the Pilgrim colony at Plymouth was founded in 1620 by the first of such groups. In 1648 representatives of the Congregational churches of New England met in Cambridge, Massachusetts, where they adopted *A Platform of Church Discipline*. The statement, which quickly became known as the Cambridge Platform, was not a creed, but a plan of action based on Congregational principles. One of the points stressed in the Cambridge Platform was *covenant theology*. Puritan New England was founded not on principles of religious toleration, but on federal or covenant theology. The Puritans believed that God operated in history through covenants and was now forming a new covenant with them in this new land; interpretations of covenant theology had an important influence on the political and religious order in New England. Because the community was a covenanted one, each member of the community was to follow God's law as it was found in the Bible and enforced by local religious and civil magistrates. Puritanism in America in its early years was a powerful religious force, a thriving community.

Nevertheless, by the middle of the seventeenth century religion became less important in many people's lives, and the Puritan ideal was crumbling. Although preachers accused people of infidelity and called them to return to the principles of the covenant, they did not respond to the challenges of the Puritan ideal, perhaps because they were occupied with settling the new land. Puritanism lost much of its persuasive power. By the middle of the seventeenth century, survival was no longer the primary issue in people's lives; Puritan exhortations about fear of the Lord did not strike responsive chords in them. Ideas from the Enlightenment—a reasonable God and the advantages of religious toleration—undermined the Puritan system, which was built on a sovereign (not always reasonable or understandable) God and intolerance of other forms of religious expression. The lures of the modern world—mercantilism and commercialism—affected Americans as it had Europeans: they were often more interested in the adventure of making money than they were in the drama of salvation. Within this context, two different movements are worthy of attention: the revivalist impulse of the Great Awakening and the rationalist religion of Deism in its American form.

The Great Awakening

The eighteenth century began with a total religious decline. It is not clear how many of the American colonists were church members: probably only a few. Religious indifference was as much a part of the American scene as it was in Europe. One of the revivifying factors for European Christianity was Pietism; American Christianity was regenerated by revivalism in a movement known as the Great Awakening, a series of revivals that spread throughout the American colonies from 1725 until the 1760s. The Great Awakening cut across denominational lines and engendered a spirit of religious cooperation based on shared religious feeling.

The revivalist movement began in specific churches through the efforts of charismatic preachers. Theodorus Frelinghuysen (1692–1747), a member of the German Reformed church, was influenced by Pietism. He came to America in 1720 to preach personal repentance and a more emotional expression of religion to people of several Dutch Reformed churches. Gilbert Tennent (1703–64), a Presbyterian minister influenced by Frelinghuysen, brought the revivalist message to Presbyterians and to Christians of the middle colonies. The most famous figure of the period was Jonathan Edwards (1703–58), a Congregationalist theologian and preacher responsible for the New England phase of the Great Awakening. By the 1740s these evangelical preachers had high hopes for a religious revival in America; there was, after all, a religious revival occurring in England under the impulse of Methodism, and American Christians were quite enthusiastic about a new awakening of religious fervor. About this time George Whitefield, Wesley's friend and a phenomenally successful preacher, came to America. Whitefield was a strong Calvinist-Methodist who took the country by storm. In his zealous preaching, tireless travel, and contagious religious excitement, he set the pattern for roving revivalist preaching in the colonies for years to come.

American Evangelicalism was born in the Great Awakening: it emerged from the Reformed tradition and the Puritan experience, but it also stressed new forms and some new content in the Christian message. The religious strategy of Evangelicalism is designed to elicit a response: it stresses *new birth,* which is sudden and which determines whether one is or is not a Christian; the importance of the *emotions* to demonstrate that the conversion is of the heart and not just of the head; and the *sufficiency of God,* underlining the Calvinist preoccupations of the message. This last point underwent some rather profound changes in subsequent revivalist movements, but during the Great Awakening, God's sovereignty was a fundamental tenet; evangelists recognized that God glories in a person's absolute dependence, that God alone grants the conversion experience.

The Great Awakening regenerated American Christianity, but also caused

further divisions within it. Tennent's preaching about the dangers of an uncon-
verted ministry caused a division within the Presbyterian church: New Side
Presbyterians welcomed the revivalist message, Old Side Presbyterians repudiated it. The Congregational church split into New Lights and Old Lights.
Charles Chauncy (1705–87) was the outspoken opponent of revivalism within
the Congregational church and the leader of the Old Lights. He was a spokes-
man for the rationalism of the Enlightenment and a forerunner of the Unitarian
schism in the Congregational church in the nineteenth century. Even those who
favored the message and tactics of the Great Awakening argued about the place
of the emotions: radicals said that the heart alone accounted for conversion,
moderates recognized the importance of the heart but did not want to deny the
importance of an intellectual understanding of Christianity as well.

Deism in America

Many of the founding fathers of America were Deists: Benjamin Franklin
(1706–90) and Thomas Jefferson (1743–1826) were both deeply affected by the
rationalism of the Enlightenment; both believed that religion could be reduced
to ethical consciousness and good moral conduct. Deism, remember, was a reasonable religion; doctrines not understandable through reason—miracles or the
doctrine of the Trinity—were denied. Many of the accents of Deism are echoed
in the Declaration of Independence: reason, religious toleration, optimism
about the pursuit of happiness, and a trust in a reasonable God. Deism was able
to attract people because it stood in judgment of many of the troublesome religious trends of the time: it was against dogmatism, sectarian infighting, enthusiasm, and clericalism. On those grounds it appealed to many people who were
formally connected with churches.

Growing Denominationalism

By the end of the eighteenth century, America was an independent nation
with a highly diverse religious population. During the early years of settlement
there was reason to predict regional churches in America—different religious
groups tended to settle together in different regions—but by the end of the
eighteenth century, *denominationalism* was a fact of American religious life.[8]
Many different churches were allowed to coexist peacefully within the same region. As a consequence of the Enlightenment, the Constitution of the United
States supported the "great experiment" of religious freedom and toleration. No
church was supported by the state, nor did the state interfere with the internal
life of the churches. The separation of church and state supported a relatively
new religious idea—voluntarism—whereby church membership was understood to be purely a matter of personal choice.

The census of 1790 showed the following numbers of Protestant churches
in America: Congregational, 749; Presbyterian, 495; Baptist, 457; Anglican,
406; Lutheran, 240; German Reformed (Calvinist), 201; Quaker, 200; and

Dutch Reformed, 127. There were no figures in that census for Roman Catholics because Catholics were still not welcome in the English colonies: they were not allowed to live in some places, not permitted to hold public office or own land in others. In 1785 there were fewer than 25,000 Roman Catholics in a population of 4 million; there were 56 churches.

Roman Catholics. Though scarce in the English colonies, Roman Catholics were the dominant religious group in the Mississippi basin by the end of the century. Catholics had come to the new world with the Spanish and French explorers and settled peacefully into French and Spanish territories. The city of New Orleans and the southern Louisiana territory were predominantly Catholic.

Quakers, Mennonites, and Amish. The religious climate of Pennsylvania was unique in the American colonies and made it a haven for a variety of religious groups that were unwelcome or actively persecuted in other colonies. William Penn (1644–1718) was a convinced Quaker whose interest in founding an American colony was motivated by principles of religious freedom and liberty of conscience. The federal theology of the Puritan colonies did not allow religious toleration, and many of the other colonies had legislated restrictions against one religious group or another (usually Roman Catholics, Quakers, and Anabaptists). Penn founded his colony as a "holy experiment," and established it upon a constitution that permitted all forms of worship compatible with monotheism. Mennonites and Amish settled there and moved west from there in the nineteenth and twentieth centuries. The Quakers also settled in Pennsylvania. Their positions, especially their pacifism, made them victims of persecution. Their history in eighteenth-century America is a relatively quiet one; they separated themselves from the rest of the society by their plain dress, their obscure biblical forms of speech, and their avoidance of worldly ways.

Brethren. The Brethren originally settled in Germantown, Pennsylvania. But they were persecuted during the Revolutionary War for their refusal to participate in it, and the geographical scattering of the Brethren occurred at this time. They experienced one minor schism, but not over pacifist principles: the Ephrata Community advocated celibacy and mystical religious experience and formed as a separate group in 1728, but lasted as a society less than one hundred years.

Lutherans. The Lutherans settled into the colonies with no major divisions.

Puritans (Presbyterians and Congregationalists). The Puritans divided denominationally into Congregationalists and Presbyterians, the major religious groups within the colonies. Both groups were regenerated during the Great Awakening, and both groups experienced some division because of the revivalist nature of that regeneration, as we have noted earlier.

Baptists. The Baptists, led by Roger Williams (1603–83), had originally grown out of the Congregational church in England, and continued to grow and to attract members of that church. During the Great Awakening hundreds of people separated from the Congregational church in order to become Baptists. The decline of the Baptist religion during the first half of the eighteenth century was totally reversed during the Great Awakening; by the end of the eighteenth century the Baptists were the largest single Christian denomination in the United States, with their greatest strength in the South.

Anglicans. The Anglican church in America was supported by the British crown and suffered many of the vicissitudes of seventeenth-century English history. The early Anglican communities reflected the variety of opinion within the Church of England. The most pressing problem for the American Anglican church was the lack of native bishops; for complex political reasons bishops were not sent to the American colonies. With the support of the English government, Anglicans established missionary societies, colleges, and influential churches. These gains, however, were outweighed by their liabilities: Anglicans were politically suspect during the Revolution, their ministers were forced to go back to England for ordination (by a bishop), they tended to attract mostly aristocratic people and had little common appeal, and they refused to participate in the Great Awakening. In 1789 the Anglican church in America re-formed itself as a separate entity within the Church of England: it was in communion with the Church of England, but established its own episcopacy and called itself by a new name, the Protestant Episcopal church.

Methodists. The situation for Methodist societies in America changed the course of Methodist history. Once Anglican priests (who could administer the sacraments) began to return to England during the Revolution, American Methodists were left without access to the sacraments. In response to this situation John Wesley ordained two lay leaders as deacons and elders, and appointed a superintendent for the American group. Wesley was a minister in the Church of England and knew that ordinations could be valid only when performed by a bishop. By the end of the eighteenth century, however, he had become convinced that bishops and priests differed from each other in terms of function but not in terms of power. His ordination of the two lay leaders, therefore, was done in good faith and with no intention of forming a separate denomination. Thomas Coke (1747–1814) was the man appointed by Wesley to be the superintendent of American Methodists; he in turn ordained Francis Asbury (1745–1816) as a general superintendent at the Christmas conference of Methodist preachers held in Baltimore in 1784. At that conference the American Methodists established themselves as a separate denominational group with the name Methodist Episcopal church. Asbury assumed the title of bishop and, despite severe remonstrances from Wesley, would not relinquish it. When Asbury first came to America in 1771 there were 1,200 Methodists in various Methodist societies and prayer groups; when he died, there were more than 214,000 members of the Methodist Episcopal church.

Summary. By the end of the eighteenth century, a wonderful and somewhat surprising arrangement had taken root in America: almost every conceivable variety of Christianity was practiced in relatively peaceful coexistence with other groups and even with professed Deists. The struggle for religious freedom was more complicated than I have indicated here. The Baptists, especially under the leadership of Roger Williams and John Leland, worked very hard to secure freedom of worship for all, including Jews. Still, some groups continued to feel the sting of religious persecution; sectarians and Roman Catholics encountered prejudicial laws and bigoted behavior from some of their neighbors well into the nineteenth century. For the most part, however, Christians in America were free to practice their religion without interference from the government and without hostility from other groups.

CONCLUSION

The Reformation continued in Europe, stimulated in part by a growing antagonism between science and religion. Although significant religious growth occurred throughout Europe, we have focused mainly on England, where the arguments between Anglicans and Puritans (and later, the influence of Pietism) produced a rich variety of religious responses. Representatives of nearly all Christian groups moved to America in the seventeenth and eighteenth centuries and settled in specific regions of the country. The Great Awakening regenerated much of Protestant Christianity in America and stimulated new growth in many churches. The American experience engendered two new denominations that had formerly been part of the Church of England: the Protestant Episcopal church remained in communion with the Church of England but acquired its own separate hierarchy; the Methodist Episcopal church separated from the Church of England—against Wesley's intentions and desires—to form a new religious body. By the end of the eighteenth century the American religious climate was ready to foster the phenomenal growth that characterized nineteenth-century Christianity.

CHAPTER 6 NOTES

[1] For a clear introduction to these issues, see Gerald R. Cragg, *The Church and the Age of Reason 1648–1789* (London: Penguin, 1960).

[2] I do not mean to suggest here that one cannot also find episcopal polities in some Lutheran churches—in fact, there are Lutheran bishops. For a more complete discussion of church structures and differences, see Appendix 6.

[3]This was the general treaty that ended the Thirty Years' War (1618–48—a complicated struggle involving many political and religious issues) and also ended religious warfare.

[4]The word *chapel* here does not denote a small church (as in a little country chapel) nor does it mean an alcove or secondary place of worship within a big church. The distinction between *church* and *chapel* in England is based on establishment: the *Church of England* is supported by the state and is the official religion of the English people. Those who do not worship in the Church of England do not, therefore, belong to the church (so designated) but are said to worship in *chapels*. That distinction is not so alive today as it was in the seventeenth century, but one still finds it in literature sometimes.

[5]Not everyone who was disenchanted with the Church of England was attracted to one of the new groups that developed into a major denomination. In England at this time there were many small religious sects: Familists (the Family of Love), for example, or Ranters, or Seekers (waiting for the emergence of the true church, convinced that it did not exist in any group). Many of these people were attracted to the Society of Friends (Quakers).

[6]I have not covered here all the religious groups that sprang up because I thought it would be more confusing than helpful. There was, for example, a minor schism within Roman Catholicism in the Jansenist movement. It was mostly a movement of French intellectuals and did not lead to a separate religious group, but it did leave an attitude of moral pessimism and religious rigorism in parts of the Roman Catholic church. There was a minor schism within the Lutheran church as well, a kind of sixteenth-century version of born-again Christianity—the Schwenkfelders. They were named for their founder, Kaspar Schwenkfeld (1489–1561), whose doctrines were condemned by the Lutheran church. He preached a spiritualized Christianity where justification was not merely external but a continuous inner experience, and where one's worship focused on hearing the inner word of Jesus spoken in the heart. The Schwenkfelders moved to America in 1734 with about 2,500 members.

[7]Moravians trace their heritage to the reforms of John Hus in the fourteenth century, a movement re-formed under the impetus of Pietism. Through the help of a wealthy Pietist, Count Zinzendorf (1700–60), the Moravian church was able to solidify and become ongoing. They settled in Pennsylvania—both Nazareth and Bethlehem are Moravian colonies—and were pioneers as missionaries and leaders in American Christian education.

[8]For more on the emergence of denominationalism, see Sidney Mead, *The Lively Experiment: The Shaping of Christianity in America* (New York: Harper & Row, 1963), pp. 16–38 and 103–34.

SUGGESTIONS FOR FURTHER READING

1. For further reading on specific denominations, consult the bibliography at the end of the book.

2. For an excellent introduction to the Puritan ethic and a feel for Puritanism in the young American colonies, read Edmund S. Morgan, *The Puritan Dilemma: The Story of John Winthrop* (New York: Little, Brown, 1958).

3. For a documentary introduction to the Catholic experience in America, see John Tracy Ellis, editor, *Documents of American Catholic History* (Milwaukee: Bruce Publish-

ing, 1956). Ellis begins with the document "dividing the new world between Spain and Portugal" (a line drawn by Pope Alexander VI) and goes up to the 1950s. Just looking at the table of contents of this book will give you some indication of where Catholics were in America at this time and what their main issues were. See also John Cogley, *Catholic America*, rev. ed., updated by Roger Van Allen (Kansas City, Mo.: Sheed & Ward, 1986).

4. For an engaging and informative history of Protestantism in America, see Martin E. Marty, *Righteous Empire: The Protestant Experience in America* (New York: Dial Press, 1970). Marty draws from a vast number of stories and documents.

5. For an extremely useful and clear look at American religious history through documents and commentary, see George C. Bedell, Leo Sandon, Jr., and Charles T. Wellborn, editors, *Religion in America*, 2nd ed. (New York: Macmillan, 1982). This book was written as an introductory text and tries to deal equitably with Protestants, Jews, and Catholics. The documents the authors include are interesting and their introductions good. See especially pp. 131–88 on revivalism in America.

PART THREE

Christianity in the Modern World: Context and Creativity in the Nineteenth and Twentieth Centuries

T HE THIRD PART of this book situates Christianity within the modern world so that the growth and diversity in the nineteenth and twentieth centuries make contextual sense. Concentrating on the nineteenth and twentieth centuries forms a bridge to the last part of the book, which looks at contemporary problems and challenges. We need to remember that our goal is not a comprehensive understanding of Christian history, but a general sense of how and why so many different forms of Christianity developed. The purpose of this section is to sketch the problems offered to Christianity in the modern context.

The most perplexing question one faces when attempting to discuss the "modern world" is finding a date for its beginning. What constitutes modernity? Is it scientific discovery and the unsettling of the old notion that the earth is the center of the universe? Or is it geographical exploration which opened up new frontiers for Christianity in the Far East and eventually in a whole "new world"? Is it new philosophical challenges which raised vexing questions about the relationship between reason and revelation? Or is it the new political arrangements, national rulers in the seventeenth century giving way to various forms of republican and democratic governments throughout the eighteenth and nineteenth centuries?

In some ways all of these things constitute the fabric of modernity and must act as a backdrop against which we can understand the major developments of Christianity during the nineteenth and twentieth centuries. But what is at the bottom of all the newness? What caused Christians to continue to search for new expressions of their religion? What, in other words, is the modern challenge?

There is no simple explanation. Beginning with the attention to human achievement during the Renaissance and continuing through the scientific revolution and the Enlightenment, the entire focus of human life shifted from the supernatural to the natural realm. If you were to walk through an art gallery historically arranged, you would notice that medieval art featured religious themes—paintings of events in the life of Jesus, for example—and mythological figures, but Renaissance artists began to concentrate on human subjects and objects in the natural world. In the nineteenth and twentieth centuries, religious subjects are only a small part of the artistic repertoire.

The medieval worldview divided reality into two realms, heaven and earth. The qualities of heaven were similar to the qualities of God: heaven was the realm of grace, eternity, absolute truth, and revelation; it was God's place and the "true home" of all creatures. The qualities of earth were quite different: earth was the created order, the realm of nature, time, change, and human reason; it was a temporary home, a testing place from which one hoped to escape. In this model, the church was the bridge between the two worlds, the institution that offered human beings the means to get from this world to the next.

Because God had intervened in human history—in the Bible and in the life and mission of Jesus—the church had its mission, its laws, and its authority. The church, in other words, was the place where God's work on earth was done: its dogmas, symbols, and authority were, like God, changeless, eternal, and absolute. The church—Catholic, Orthodox, and Protestant—functioned on earth as Christ had during his lifetime, with utter authority. As such, the church could demand obedience and understood itself to be in an unassailable position. Modernity challenged this understanding by posing a series of difficult questions and developing a set of new structures over a 200- or 300-hundred year period. The Christian attempt to answer these challenges in the last two centuries has led to some remarkable new religious forms and ideas that we will investigate in this section.

Chapter 7 deals with the challenges of modernity, an attempt to concentrate on the kinds of issues raised since the eighteenth century that many Christians have found threatening. I will talk in general terms about ways various forms of Christianity reacted to those challenges. Chapter 8 focuses on the proliferation of new Christian movements in the new world in the nineteenth and early twentieth centuries. Because the American context was so rich in new religious experiments, we will concentrate our energies there. Finally, in Chapter 9 we will look at the beginnings of two phenomena that are both old and new—the missionary movement and the ecumenical movement—in order to get a general understanding of the state of Christian cooperation in the world. All of these chapters are meant to lead logically to the final section of the book, which deals with some contemporary issues as a set of different angles from which to appreciate the diversity of Christianity.

Again, it is important to remember that Christianity has survived partly because of its genius for both accommodation and resistance to trends in the world surrounding it. The early Christians adapted themselves to the realities of Greek and Roman culture even as they resisted some of the claims of those cultures. Medieval Christianity shaped itself in relation to the political realities of the time and imposed its own order on the world in ways that were both beautiful and dangerous. Christians during the Reformation looked back to the ancient church for models of interpretation and authority and also made realistic adaptations to the newly emerging modern world. Since the Reformation, Christianity in its many forms has had to define and redefine itself in relation to momentous new intellectual, political, and cultural movements. This section explains the general terms of some of those movements and shows some of the ways Christians learned to cope with them in order to survive.

❖

CHAPTER 7

CHRISTIANITY AND MODERNITY

We take the modern world for granted. Most of us have no experience of a world in which, as in medieval times, church and state were united in a single task. Most of us cannot fathom a world in which the church was "established"—that is to say, supported and sometimes governed by the state—nor can we imagine government leaders arguing with church authorities over political questions.

We have to begin, therefore, by remembering the experience of the very early church. Christianity was born into a Roman world where church and state were separate entities. Christianity was one religion among many, in no way favored by the empire and not thought to be any more true or worthy than any other religion. The Constantinian turning point changed this system dramatically because, as we have seen, Constantine perceived the power and usefulness of Christianity and sought to merge his political ambitions—the re-creation of the Roman Empire—with the missionary enthusiasm and enormous attractiveness of early Christianity. The Christian empire, as Constantine understood it, was a felicitous blend of political power and religious energy. We have seen that this model led to centuries of controversy and to ingenious attempts to define the ultimate source of authority, and we have seen the emergence and triumph of medieval Christianity.

The Reformation did not challenge the basic model. The political assumptions of Luther, Calvin, Zwingli, the English monarchs, and the Puritans were similar to those of the Catholics: the state and church were linked in common cause and cooperated with one another for the general good of society. The only dissenting voice to this understanding of church-state relations was that of the radical reformers: Anabaptists were considered dangerous by both Catholics and Protestants precisely because they conceived of religion as a separate reality. Mennonites, Hutterites, Brethren, Amish, and Quakers understood their allegiances to be entirely defined by the Bible and used their interpretations of discipleship to resist the demands of the state to pay taxes, to swear oaths, and to fight in wars.[1] Anabaptists were, therefore, troublesome to other Christians, but they were a small movement and their ideas did not reconstitute society.

The separation of church and state, which characterizes the modern world, was indebted to a series of political philosophies and revolutionary movements in the seventeenth and eighteenth centuries. The American Revolution and the French Revolution in particular—and later, the Russian Revolution—led to the disestablishment of the church and forced Christians to ask themselves what it meant to be a Christian in the modern world.

SECULARIZATION: THE NEW PHILOSOPHY AND POLITICS

From the seventeenth to the nineteenth century, people in general were faced with a new set of intellectual and social problems. Secularization, the shift from a theological to a humanistic worldview, was a slow, subtle, and pervasive process that occurred in an enormously complicated context. Scientific discoveries focused attention on the natural world and suggested that men and women could figure out the problems of their lives for themselves without recourse to the "mysterious" and intervening aspects of revealed religion.

Before the Enlightenment, people asked themselves difficult questions about life. What can I know? What must I do? What may I hope for? Christianity provided answers to those questions: Protestants and Catholics differed on the sources of authority for the answers, but they agreed that the questions had certain religious answers. Enlightenment thinkers and scientists, however, argued that the questions needed to be asked again and that there were probably no certain answers. Early modern philosophers did not so much question the *sources* of religious authority as they questioned the whole *idea* of religious authority. To their way of thinking, religious authority, with its reliance on revelation, providence, miracles, and other supernatural phenomena, was a kind of backward mentality that preferred superstition and ignorance to scientific inquiry and demonstration.

Enlightenment philosophers and scientists wanted people to use their reason and to think for themselves. They attempted to involve religious people in an adventure—some would say a crisis—of freedom. They themselves experienced the terror and delight of uncertainty: they were free from the fetters of faith and so had the exhilarating experience of figuring things out for themselves, but they were also hostile to faith and so could reap none of its rewards and assurances.

The spiritual odyssey of one of the eighteenth-century French philosophers, Denis Diderot (1713–84), may help explain the general mood of the times. He was born a Catholic but found the superstition and unverifiability of some of the church's claims to be troublesome, so he became a theist; that is, he still believed in a personal God, but without the institutional support and, to his mind, superstitious nonsense of the church.

As he explored the conclusions of the new science, he was led to questions and speculations about the place of religion in human life. If the universe was a realm in which the laws of cause and effect were operative, he reasoned, then divine providence was not necessary. Humanity did not need a God who breaks into the world in order to make things happen, Newton had said; events occur according to scientific laws and human beings ought to question authority and to demand that "truth" have the certainty of mathematics. It was therefore reasonable to conclude that failure to prove something meant that it was not true.

You can see where this position leads: the Holy Spirit, inspiration, providence, and miracles—the mainstays of religious belief—could not be proven with mathematical certainty and so must be rejected. Still, the created order had a logic within it, and one could show that some cosmic intelligence must have made the world. There must be some kind of supreme being, Diderot reasoned, and so he became a Deist. He believed in an impersonal God who created the world and established a set of scientific laws to govern its events.

As a Deist, Diderot tried to live in harmony with the laws of the universe and to be reverent in his feelings for the Supreme Being, but he was not personally involved with God and found the God of the Bible to be a childish belief. Eventually, as Diderot continued to ask questions, he was led to skepticism and wondered what, if anything, could ever really be proved. Finally, he said, he was forced by the processes of his own quest to become an atheist, to believe formally that God did not exist at all. He found atheism unsatisfying but true, whereas he experienced Catholicism as emotionally attractive but false.

I have introduced Diderot here not to make a slippery-slope argument for religious belief, but simply to suggest that the kinds of questions the early modern philosophers asked were not intended to provide *comfort*. Diderot was a pioneer. He looked backward in time and saw a medieval world that was dangerous and violent, where men and women were forced by circumstances to submit to things they could not understand, where nature dominated the human spirit. Diderot looked forward to a time when humanity could dominate nature, learn its secrets, and change the world. He imagined a future in which people could be safe, free, and in command of their own destinies. To his way of thinking, such a shift in the balance of power required a real revolution of spirit, a heroic resistance to fate. The Enlightenment, therefore, was not simply a quest for knowledge, it was an attempt to impose one's rational will on the environment and it required self-reliance, daring, and a sense of adventure.

The political results of much of this new thinking led to the great revolutions of the eighteenth century. In an age of turmoil, new political leaders forged concepts of democracy and talked about rights and progress. By 1800, after the American and French revolutions, the notion of equality had become a profound new political value. It is not easy to understand the momentous shifts that the revolutionary period brought to government unless we contrast them with the ideas of absolute monarchy that were advanced in the medieval world by the church and in the seventeenth century by monarchs like Louis XIV. Even without having much sense of political history, we can still understand these new political ideas when we compare them with what we already know about religion.

Let us remember for a moment what religion looked like in the period following the Reformation. Wars of religion occupied thousands of people from the mid-sixteenth to the mid-seventeenth century. The Peace of Westphalia (1648) was the treaty that ended the last set of wars fought for purely religious reasons and marked a change in that future wars would be fought for reasons of state.

Besides igniting religious wars, the Protestant and Catholic reformations extended medieval notions of religious intolerance to new levels. Religious persecution and torture of Catholics by Protestants and of Protestants by Catholics—not to mention the persistent persecution of Jews by Christians—was a scandal that endured into the twentieth century. The frenzy of persecution against witches that began in the latter part of the fifteenth century lasted almost until the beginning of the nineteenth and found most of its support in the treatises and fears of religious writers. And the resistance to new scientific discoveries, like those of Galileo, came from religious authorities and appeared, by scientific standards, to be arbitrary and unreasonable. All of these characteristics provided the immediate context for those Enlightenment thinkers who urged skepticism about religious authority, tolerance for different viewpoints, and a general sense of human equality.

Enlightenment thinkers and new politicians looked at the world around them and saw how old models of church and state had led to persecution and inequality. The Anglican church was established in England and barely tolerated dissenters. Colonial powers in the new world attempted to govern and tax the residents without their consent. Upper classes in France asserted their authority over commoners and gloried in their nobility. City folk felt superior to their country cousins, believers fought with unbelievers, Christians with Jews, Catholics with Protestants. European immigrants to the new world exploited the Amerindians and imported black people as slaves. The idea that "all men were created equal," while it did less for women and minority races than it did for white, Anglo-Saxon, Protestant men, still introduced a new idea into the new world. The constitutional guarantee for freedom of religion and the insistence on separation of church and state would have profound consequences for religion.

CHALLENGES TO SECULARIZATION

Secularization did not occur without resistance on the part of religious institutions and individuals. By 1800, religion was only one interest among many and had to compete with science, industry, and new ideas. In the sixteenth century, Protestant and Catholic reformers relied on creeds and religious authority, but Christianity had suffered a general decline in the seventeenth century because the authority of reason offered an attractive alternative to many people. The idea of a world based on tolerance, reason, logic, and an ability to control one's destiny was a persuasive one.

The political independence of the new world and the notion that human beings were perfectible rather than naturally depraved gave a sense of adventure to emigration to and new life in a democratic new world. When millions of people migrated to the American colonies they found that they had to rely on themselves, and they gloried in self-reliance. Old religious notions of predestination seemed to be obsolete in a land where, it was said, anyone could find work, prosper, and rise to undreamed levels of power and respect.

By 1800, the arts were removed from their primarily religious concerns: music, painting, and sculpture focused on human models, and thinkers talked more about ethical ideals than about religious mysteries. The age of reason challenged religion and set the stage for the battles that religious believers would carry into the twentieth century.

At the beginning of the nineteenth century an attempt was made in Europe to restore the old regime, to reassert the claims of monarchy. By mid-century, however, a new series of revolutions had unsettled most monarchical governments, and powerful new ideas threatened to shake the world at its foundations. Karl Marx (1818–83) interpreted world history in terms of class warfare and delineated a theory of modern socialism. Charles Darwin (1809–82) postulated his theory of organic evolution and argued that evolution proceeds by the basic rule of the survival of the fittest. In religious philosophy, Ludwig Feuerbach (1804–72) argued that Christianity is not the decisive force in modern life and stated that his goals included what he called the humanization of religion. Toward the end of the century, Africa was "discovered" and divided among the world's great powers. Finally, the world inhabited by Christians had undergone a profound industrial revolution that changed the nature of the family and the economic value of certain kinds of work.

Throughout the century all realms of life underwent progressive secularization, and religion was forced to reconstitute itself and determine new ways to attract believers. In this tumultuous period, religious institutions and thinkers set new boundaries in which to conduct religious inquiry. The Catholic church, for the most part, adopted a posture of resistance to the modern world. The internal battle within the Roman Catholic church was defined by papal opposition to modernity and by a series of movements that pitted "modernists" (those who hoped for accommodation to the modern world, its theories and methods) against "ultramontanists" (those who supported strong papal authority). Protestants, because they were already divided on a number of issues, cannot be so easily labeled, but in general the Protestant churches were also defined by their reactions to modernity, with liberals forging links with the modern world while conservatives resisted any such attempts to accept the terms of modernity.

We will see some of the creative responses to the modern world in the next chapter, in the context of American Christianity. In this chapter, however, we need only understand some general characteristics and attitudes as well as some specific movements in the European context.

ROMAN CATHOLICISM AND MODERNITY

The Roman Catholic church reformed itself at the Council of Trent and in many ways was not prepared for the Enlightenment and the scientific and industrial revolutions. The French Revolution was a profound shock to Catholicism, and one place to begin our examination of modern Catholicism is with reactions to that revolution. Try to imagine a country where hierarchy and religious order had been fundamental characteristics of society. Remember the alliances between the early Frankish tribes and the papacy, the power of the pope during the medieval period in France, and then the power of the monarch from the Avignon papacy through the reign of Louis XIV. Then picture a revolution that culminated in the beheading of the king by the people, and a general overthrow of the notion of privilege on any terms.

For some, the French Revolution was a great step forward: liberty, equality, and fraternity were meant to be slogans for a whole new order. Royalists and nobles fled or were killed, the church became a department of state without power of its own, and the new government claimed to reflect the power of the people. For others, however, the French Revolution was a tragedy, an end to any semblance of law and order, a descent to mob rule and a rejection of religion.

In November 1789 the National Assembly seized all the property of the Roman Catholic church, approximately one-fifth of the country! You can imagine that the church did not welcome the revolution, and perhaps you can understand why the church tended to greet Napoleon Bonaparte (1769–1821) as a kind of savior. At first it appeared as if Napoleon's empire would restore order and return Catholicism to its former position of power in France. The Catholic church was soon to find out that Napoleon was not its champion: he wanted to restore some semblance of religious order for his own aims, not for the sake of the church.[2] When Napoleon, for a series of complicated political reasons, imprisoned the pope, Pius VII, for five years, he did not weaken the power of Roman Catholicism. On the contrary, the pope emerged from imprisonment with the respect of the world and had the sympathy of all Catholics and many Protestants.

The experience of the Roman Catholic church during the revolutionary and Napoleonic years set the stage for Catholicism's battles with the modern world. In the beginning of the nineteenth century, great waves of support enveloped the papacy. As people tried to imagine a world that was free from the disruptions of revolution, some began to look "over the mountains" (hence the name ultramontanists) to Rome for a renewed sense of leadership and moral power. To their way of thinking, Enlightenment philosophy, with its rejection of revelation in favor of the power of human reason, had led to tragedy and anarchy. What was needed, they believed, was a strong reassertion of religious authority. Ultramontanism was, in part, an attempt to reclaim the authority of revelation by upholding the power of the papacy to define the terms and limits of religious truth.

Although some of the early nineteenth-century popes were unable to assert their power rigorously—because they were occupied with complicated political problems involving the so-called papal states and various revolutionary moves in Italy—Pope Pius IX (1846–78), the first of the modern popes, claimed his spiritual authority in no uncertain terms.[3] He began his reign with some liberal reforms, but he quickly retreated to a conservative position in relation to the modern world.

In 1864 Pius IX issued the *Syllabus of Errors*, which summarized eighty modern errors and enjoined Catholics to avoid naturalism, socialism, communism, the conclusions of modern biblical scholarship, modern political arrangements like the separation of church and state, freedom of religion, ethical theories, and even the idea that the Roman Catholic church should reconcile itself with the modern world. In 1870 this pope called the First Vatican Council, which defined papal infallibility and appeared to make future councils unnecessary.[4]

His successor, Pope Leo XIII (1878–1903), was somewhat more accepting of the inevitabilities of the modern world and attempted to define the ways that Catholics could be good citizens in modern liberal states, but he was essentially conservative and unbending about accommodations to modern thought. Leo XIII is remembered for his encyclicals about the narrow limits in which Catholics could pursue some of the conclusions of modern biblical criticism, and for his letters about the relationship between the church and the working classes.[5]

Pope Pius X (1903–14) presided over the Catholic church during the modernist controversy, the most difficult crisis to face late nineteenth- and early twentieth-century Catholicism. The modernist controversy involved two uncongenial groups: a loosely connected collection of European scholars who hoped that the Catholic church could make some profound intellectual adjustments to modern biblical scholarship, and a tightly organized group of religious authorities who refused to accept any such accommodations. That controversy is too complicated to describe here. Suffice it to say that the pope condemned "modernism" in terms that made it impossible for future Roman Catholic scholars to be anything but defensive in relation to the modern world and laid to rest any hope that Roman Catholicism would be in any way defined by the conclusions of modern scholarship.

Roman Catholics who hoped for modernization had to wait for the Second Vatican Council (1962–65). That council was called to bring Catholicism up to date, but an institution as enormous as the Catholic church, with a history of resistance to the modern world, is not easily changed. Today many Catholics are energetically involved in serious conflicts about the extent to which the documents of Vatican II can really be understood to be an acceptance of modernity.

PROTESTANTISM AND MODERNITY

Protestantism, as we have seen, experienced phenomenal growth and development from the sixteenth to the nineteenth century. New expressions of Protestant Christianity were formulated especially in England and in America and became the soil out of which newer understandings of the Christian life would grow. Protestant Christians, like their Catholic counterparts, had to respond to the challenges of modernity. And just as one can find liberal Catholics in the nineteenth century, one can find liberal Protestants as well.

The main difference between the two groups lay in the ways internal church controversies were settled. In the Roman Catholic church, liberals were condemned and those who sought accommodation to the modern world were silenced or forced out of the church. The strong hierarchical model buttressed by clear assertions of papal infallibility in the nineteenth century insured that Catholicism would have one particular profile, a conservative one that resisted the claims of modernity. In the Protestant churches there was no such appeal to a single authority. Protestant liberals tended to take up the Enlightenment challenge in a quest for new values, whereas conservative Protestants reacted to modern questions with attempts to reassert traditional orthodoxy or to reclaim traditional values. We will see some of the ways these two groups emerged in the context of nineteenth-century America in the next chapter. Here we need only get a general understanding of differing religious climates and attitudes.

Protestants had to figure out what it meant to be a Christian in the modern world. How could they relate the claims of Christianity to the new conclusions of science? How could they understand the authority of the Bible in relation to new historical studies of biblical literature that threatened some of the traditional beliefs of Christianity? What could they say about divine authority, grace, and the will of God when confronted with theories of personal freedom and human perfectibility? And how could they relate the goals of the church to the goals of society?

We will look at four areas of concern as they affected different kinds of Protestant Christianity: Evangelical Pietism and the Oxford movement were two conservative attempts to respond to modernity, whereas the emergence of biblical criticism and the relation of the gospel to the social conditions of the world were two liberal responses to the modern world. Because Protestantism is a fluid concept, these four areas have some natural overflow from one group to another and are not intended to be hard and fast categories. For example, the attempt to relate the gospel to the real needs of people in depressed social conditions was a concern of both liberal and conservative Protestants. Still, these four areas can give us a preliminary understanding of some of the background and attitudes that shaped Protestantism throughout the nineteenth century.

Evangelical Pietism

As we saw in Chapter 6, Pietism arose in the context of the seventeenth century as a reformation of Lutheranism. Reacting against creeds and formalism in religion, and in an effort to stimulate renewed interest in Christianity, Pietism placed its stress on feelings rather than on arguments and dogmas.[6] The Enlightenment claim that everything had to be proved with mathematical certainty led some people to the logical conclusion that religious truths had to be abandoned. For Diderot, as we have seen, atheism was cold comfort but necessary given the presuppositions of rational philosophy. Diderot is interesting for us precisely because he kept an emotional longing for traditional religion even as he believed he had to reject its unprovable claims.

Pietism was, in part, a response to that kind of longing. It reasserted the power of Christianity to change the lives of men and women. Whether the claims of Christianity can be proved with mathematical certainty was, for Pietists, beside the point: a fervent emotional response can touch the human heart, lead to deeply held convictions, and stir religious sensibility.

Furthermore, Pietism could attract Christians on an international level: Francke and Spener in Holland, Wesley in England, Count Zinzendorf and the Moravians in Bohemia, Jonathan Edwards and other early American revivalists in the new world were all drawn to the notion that religion is based on feelings of absolute dependence on God. Christianity was not limited anymore to geographical arrangements and treaties, nor was it reduced to ineffectiveness by the hostile claims of the Enlightenment. On the contrary, the claims of Evangelical Pietism proved that religion was an intensely rich *experience* that could revivify Christianity in a variety of places and in a variety of forms. As such, Pietism rejected the demands of the Enlightenment to force religious belief into certain kinds of proofs. Christians may have suffered a momentary letdown during the seventeenth and eighteenth centuries, but the evangelical contribution to a worldwide revival of religious interest and religious life proved to Pietists that religion was stronger than rational philosophy and still as compelling as it had been in the early days of the Christian movement when people experienced the power of Jesus and the attraction of his calls for repentance and new life.

The Oxford Movement

The Oxford movement occurred in England in the early part of the nineteenth century as a reassertion of traditional orthodoxy in the face of what appeared to be a general decline of religious interest. In many ways it was a return to certainty by way of acceptance of some traditional Roman Catholic doctrines coupled with a new experience of religious fervor on the part of a small group of young Anglican divines at Oxford University.

The same horrified reactions experienced by the Catholic church in the face of the French Revolution also stirred many Christians who were not Catholic: they, too, felt that the revolution threatened the order of the world, and they cried out for a reassertion of religious authority. In addition to revulsion at the French Revolution, the leaders of the Oxford movement shared the perception that the Church of England had grown lax in its religious commitment and that the very belief in God—theism—was threatened by modern industrial life. In July 1833, John Keble (1792–1866), a professor of poetry at Oxford, preached a sermon on "national apostasy," in which he accused the nation of moral laxity and insisted that the only road to salvation lay in a renewed devotion to sacramental Christianity.

The leaders of the Oxford movement—John Henry Newman (1801–90), William George Ward (1812–82), Edward B. Pusey (1800–82)—were not Roman Catholic, nor did they intend to become Roman Catholic, but their appeal to tradition led them to accept and argue for positions that were both Catholic and classically Anglican. They called believers back to the Anglican Book of Common Prayer and extolled the importance of apostolic succession for the proper reception of the sacraments (a traditional Roman Catholic belief).

As the group veered closer to Roman Catholic belief, Newman attempted to restate the beauty of traditional Anglicanism with his book *Via Media* (showing how Anglicanism forged a middle way between Catholicism and traditional Protestantism). Finally, however, many of the Oxford movement thinkers were led to the conclusion that the Roman Catholic church was the true expression of Christianity, and many of them converted to Catholicism. Their actions led to their dismissal from Oxford and the rescinding of their academic degrees, but they also stimulated a renewal of interest in Christianity and in religious argument and practice in England.

The response of the Oxford thinkers to the modern world was similar to that of Catholics, a reassertion of traditional religious authority based on belief in the rightness of ancient Christian tradition and the office of the papacy. The effect of the Oxford movement, however, was to force a renewal of Christianity in England both in the revival of Roman Catholicism and in the restimulation of Anglicanism.

The Biblical Movement

We have seen that Enlightenment thinkers rejected traditional concepts like inspiration, providence, and miracles which were standard expressions of biblical faith, and we will see in the next chapter how the battle between American fundamentalists and liberals was shaped by their different understandings of the possibility of error in the sacred text. In addition to Enlightenment critics, Christians had to deal with the theories of evolutionists like Darwin, whose scientific conclusions directly contradicted the information in the Bible about the creation of the world and the creation of humankind.

In response to threats to biblical authority, and in relation to new methods of historical scholarship, a movement of biblical criticism began in the nineteenth century. A critic, remember, is an expert, not one who finds fault, and a biblical critic is one who applies linguistic, archaeological, or historical expertise to biblical texts.

Protestant Christians had long accepted one kind of biblical criticism: the search for the best *textual* edition of the Bible had motivated scholars during the Reformation period and led to a rejection of the Vulgate as the most acceptable Bible for Christians. We have seen how humanist scholars like Erasmus applied themselves to the problems of finding the best edition of the Greek New Testament, and we have noted that Luther's theological insights were indebted, in part, to his interpretation of the Greek text.

This search for the best text is sometimes called "lower criticism" to distinguish it from the biblical movement in the nineteenth century, "higher criticism." Nineteenth-century scholars were interested in a set of problems different from those relating to the text itself: they were interested in historical and literary matters and so asked questions about authorship, date of composition, relationship of biblical materials to other ancient texts, and intention. Though this kind of questioning was not invented in the nineteenth century—recall the critical work of Valla, Reuchlin, Erasmus, and others (Chapter 5)—it made major strides in the nineteenth century and caused significant religious turmoil.

Many of the conclusions of nineteenth-century biblical scholars are accepted today by Christians, but they were often resisted at the time and perceived to threaten the very foundations of biblical faith. For example, the traditional view of the Pentateuch (the first five books of the Old Testament) was relatively simple: Moses was the author and recorded what God inspired him to write. Julius Wellhausen (1844–1918) showed how the Pentateuch developed historically by applying the science of textual comparison to those first five books. His work, along with that of other scholars, led to the conclusion that the Pentateuch was a composite work (not written by one author) which developed over a long period of time (not written at one time). In New Testament scholarship, critics looked at the synoptic Gospels in relation to the Gospel of John and concluded that John was not historically reliable, and that the synoptics themselves were all written from particular, sometimes antagonistic, points of view.

These conclusions and others led to some serious conflicts as Christian scholars questioned the credibility of the biblical history and the reliability of the Gospels for an accurate picture of the life and words of Jesus.[7] The anxiety early biblical criticism produced led conservative Protestants and Catholics to reject its conclusions. The modernist controversy in the Catholic church was precipitated by the work of Alfred Loisy (1857–1940), a Catholic biblical critic whose work was condemned by the Vatican. The rise of Protestant fundamentalism can be directly traced to its inflexible resistance to biblical criticism and its insistence on biblical inerrancy and inspiration.

At the same time, the biblical movement played a significant role in the development of liberal Protestantism by engendering a respect for scientific method and a general spirit of open-mindedness and optimism about the future of Christianity. One of the most influential liberal Protestant thinkers of the nineteenth century, Anglican clergyman Frederick D. Maurice (1805–72), argued that the real danger to Christianity was not biblical criticism—which allowed the Bible to continue to speak powerfully in a modern context—but *resistance* to criticism, which implied that the Bible is feeble and in need of protection.

Christianity and Social Concern

One of the insights of the Renaissance that won strong acceptance during the Enlightenment was the focus on this world. We have seen the emergence of monasticism in early Christianity and noted that medieval conceptions of the Christian life placed perfection in a rejection of "the world" in favor of a life totally dedicated to one's relationship with God. One of the insights of the reformers was that a life dedicated to God could be lived anywhere: one did not have to enter a monastery or become a priest to be a perfect Christian. On the contrary, Christians were called to serve God in the world wherever they worked. Calvin's doctrine of election—that God chooses certain people for salvation before they are even born—carried with it the demand that Christians glorify God in their daily lives by their honesty, hard work, sobriety, and thrift. This general openness to life in the world characterized Protestantism from the beginning and made it clear that one could be a good Christian entrepreneur so long as one used wealth wisely and shared one's bounty with the less fortunate.

The nineteenth century offered a new challenge to Christian social responsibility which was responded to in various ways. The industrial revolution tended to be better for the owners of industry than for the workers, and sectors of massive poverty in the nineteenth century led social critics like Karl Marx to interpret history as a continual struggle of the workers against social elites. Protestant and Catholic Christians had to strive to respond to issues of poverty and social welfare, and that effort continues to this day, as we shall see in the last section of this book.

The problem was a complicated one. On the one hand, Catholics and Protestants both had ways to accept the status quo: Catholics focused on this world as a preparation for eternal life and so did not tend to take positions that would define the mission of the church in terms of the restructuring of society. Protestants, with their sense of vocation and sharing, were able to interpret their duties to impoverished peoples in ways that did not threaten social structures. As the list of social ills grew more pressing during the nineteenth century, Christians began to reexamine the relationship of the gospel to life in the world. Some looked for ways to change things, to use the gospel as a blueprint for a more enlightened society, while others looked for ways to maintain the status quo. We will examine some modern interpretations of this conflict in the last section of the book. For now we need simply to understand some of the general positions that moved Christians to action on these issues in the nineteenth century.

Evangelical Christians, especially during the Second Great Awakening—as we shall see in the next chapter—believed that conversion to Christianity required a personal relationship with Jesus expressed in social awareness and concern. The Evangelical Alliance, formed in 1846 (which we will consider in Chapter 9), was a powerful advocate for a wide range of social causes from antislavery activism to Prohibition. Catholics began to take positions in support of the rights of workers in the late nineteenth century and have continued to struggle with social questions in a variety of forms to the present time. Let us focus here on the responses of English liberal Protestantism to the grave social ills of the nineteenth century.

The same Frederick D. Maurice who championed biblical criticism was also a pioneer in a movement known as Christian socialism. As he looked around in mid-century he concluded that the churches were not responsive to the social realities of the times. Old Calvinist ideas about poverty as God's judgment or curse coupled with new evolutionist notions about the survival of the fittest were leading some preachers to conclude that Christians ought not help the poor (understood as morally unfit) and ought surely to pursue wealth as a sign of God's favor. Maurice along with religious reformers like William Booth (1829–1912), founder of the Salvation Army, looked at the human suffering caused by the industrial revolution and indicted the churches for not being more responsible to those whose lives were ruined by industrial "progress." Poverty, they said, was not a curse but was the result of exploitation, and the church's proper role in society was to make such exploitation impossible. Maurice hoped to make the gospel relevant to social conditions, while Booth attacked the ravages of poverty with a series of practical solutions and attempted to prod the conscience of Christians so that they would be aroused to the pain of hidden human suffering.

We will look at American expressions of social concern later. For now, it is important only to perceive the emergence of a new Christian principle: the gospel ought to be made relevant to human life in such a way that it can be used as a plan to restructure society and eliminate social ills. If Christianity had adopted some of the Renaissance and Enlightenment ideals about individual happiness, readings of the Social Gospel reminded Christians that sin and salvation could also be conceptualized in social terms. Contemporary Christians are still faced with these questions and have extended them to apply to arguments about the relation of Christianity to the political order (as we shall see in the last section of this book). In that way, the question of Christian social concern in the nineteenth century has been one of the major contributions to the continuing diversity and unity of Christianity.

CONCLUSION

We have examined the Christian response to modernity in a variety of ways in order to make contextual sense of the remaining chapters of this book. No attempt has been made here to provide a comprehensive history of the nineteenth century or to outline the great theological and philosophical debates that characterize nineteenth-century Christianity. Rather, we have tried to get an appreciation for the modern spirit and the kinds of questions it raises. We have looked more closely at some of the ideas we take for granted in the modern world—separation of church and state and the secularization of society, for example. We have tried to understand the impact of the Enlightenment on political and religious life and have seen that there were various levels of resistance and acceptance of the modern spirit on the part of Catholics and Protestants. This chapter has been designed to make it easier to understand some of the movements described earlier (Pietism and revivalism, for example) and some of the controversies that will occupy the last section of the book. This chapter should also serve to contextualize some of the highly creative responses of nineteenth-century American Christianity to the thrill and challenge of the new world.

CHAPTER 7 NOTES

[1] John Howard Yoder, *The Politics of Jesus* (Grand Rapids: Eerdmans, 1972), argues that the teachings of Jesus represent a coherent approach to the issues of Christian behavior in the world. His studies argue for pacifism as an application of Christian politics to situations in the modern world.

[2] An old but still valuable book on the revolutionary period and the papacy is E. E. Y. Hales, *Revolution and the Papacy* (Notre Dame, Ind.: University of Notre Dame Press, 1966). It is also often useful to look at some of the primary documents from the period; in this case, see "The Civil Constitution of the Clergy, 12 July 1790" and "Concordat Between the Holy See and the Republic of France, 15 July 1801" in Colman Barry, editor, *Readings in Church History III* (Westminster, Md: Newman Press, 1965).

[3] See Chapter 5, note 8, for a description of the papal states, and note 2 for more on Pius IX. The best introductory book on Pius IX is still E. E. Y. Hales, *Pio Nono* (New York: Doubleday Image, 1962).

[4] See Chapter 5, note 6.

[5]The major encyclical on the church and the working classes was *Rerum Novarum* (1891), and Leo XIII's encyclical, *Providentissimus Deus* (1893), narrowly set the limits of Catholic biblical scholarship, but with a cautious allowance for scholars to begin to study the Bible in historical terms. Leo also attempted to develop a Christian doctrine of the state, based on a reading of Thomas Aquinas in *Immortale Dei* (1885). His devotion to Aquinas was profound, and his encyclical, *Aeterni Patris* (1879), had far-reaching consequences because it recommended a revival of Thomistic philosophy as the best way Catholics could enter into solid philosophical discussion in the modern world.

[6]The Protestant thinker usually credited with being the father of modern liberal theology is Friedrich Schleiermacher (1768–1834). His roots were in Pietism, specifically in the Moravian tradition, and he was influenced by the Romantic movement, the reaction of artists and thinkers in the early nineteenth century against dry intellectualism and in favor of a stress on mystery and feelings. For him religion was not a way of thinking but a way of feeling, a sense of and taste for the Infinite. Schleiermacher and the Pietists both understood Christianity in terms of religious experience, but he differed from the Pietists in his stress on the social character of Christianity. Whereas Pietists tended to interpret religion in individual terms, Schleiermacher understood humanity as bound together in an organic unity.

[7]One development in Protestant thinking to emerge from early biblical questions was the search for the "historical Jesus," which led to debates about the differences between the Jesus of history and the Christ of faith. See Harvey K. McArthur, *In Search of the Historical Jesus* (New York: Scribner's, 1969).

SUGGESTIONS FOR FURTHER READING

1. For more on the Enlightenment, begin with articles in encyclopedias and follow their leads. A good basic introduction to some of the issues and personalities is Frank E. Manuel, editor, *The Enlightenment* (Englewood Cliffs, N.J.: Prentice-Hall, 1966). A scholar of the Enlightenment whose books are all elegant is Peter Gay; see, for example, *The Enlightenment: A Comprehensive Anthology* (New York: Simon & Schuster, 1975).

2. Understanding the complex nature of modern theological development requires wide reading. Two general texts that are useful, if a little difficult sometimes, are James C. Livingston, *Modern Christian Thought: From the Enlightenment to Vatican II* (New York: Macmillan, 1978), and John Dillenberger and Claude Welch, *Protestant Thought Interpreted Through Its Development*, 2nd ed. (New York: Macmillan, 1988).

3. For more on the Second Vatican Council, see Hans Küng, *The Council, Reform and Reunion* (New York: Doubleday Image, 1965) and any good collection of the documents of Vatican II.

CHAPTER 8

MODERN AMERICAN CHRISTIANITY

T he American atmosphere in the nineteenth and early twentieth centuries
was exuberant and expansive; American Christianity reflected that atmosphere. The nineteenth century gave rise to extraordinary religious diversity that
continued into the twentieth century. Many of the complex issues of worship,
interfaith cooperation, varieties in church structure, and Christian attitudes toward the world versus American cultural values will be explored in subsequent
chapters. In this chapter we explore the proliferation of religious groups in
America. A section on the twentieth century at the end of this chapter is a
general summary of the results of some of the religious hopes stirred in the
nineteenth century, and the continuation of some of the arguments begun after
the Civil War.

THE NINETEENTH CENTURY: AMERICAN
RELIGIOUS DIVERSITY

The nineteenth century, like the eighteenth, began with a general religious
decline in America. The enthusiasm of the Great Awakening had subsided, religion had become a purely voluntary matter, and people were moving away from
the cities to settle the new frontier. The population of the United States, which
was about 2.5 million in 1776, grew to 20 million by 1845. The population boom

reinvigorated religion so much that in the nineteenth century, "American Christianity became a mass enterprise."[1] A new wave of revivalism, sometimes called the Second Great Awakening, began in the nineteenth century and added new accents to American Evangelicalism. Enlightenment philosophy continued to be felt in what came to be known as Liberal Protestantism. In the climate of religious freedom at the turn of the new century, several communitarian groups and some new churches formed in expectation of the Second Coming of Christ. Two new American religions were founded in the nineteenth century: Mormonism and Christian Science. Churches that had settled in America still faced problems: those from non-English-speaking countries sometimes disagreed about adopting the customs and language of the new country; those with more conservative intellectual traditions were pressed to respond to the fervor of revivalism in the churches. The Civil War divided almost every church over the issue of slavery and spawned specifically black churches within the established denominations. Not surprisingly, divisions continued within the churches over internal matters; some new groups formed because of disagreements about church discipline and doctrine.

For purposes of convenience and internal unity, this section on the nineteenth century covers some new religious movements and denominations up to the outbreak of the First World War in 1914. Many churches that were divided over a number of issues in the nineteenth century then attempted to reunite or to join with other churches to form a new denomination. We cover the continuation of these efforts into the twentieth century so that we can have a coherent idea of the general history of the group.

American Evangelicalism

The nineteenth century began with a new wave of revivalism that differed significantly from the First Great Awakening. The central figure of this new wave was Charles Grandison Finney (1792–1875), a lawyer whose religious experience transformed him into a preacher. Finney, inspired by methods used by politicians, understood revival as the controlled manipulation of religious phenomena. During the First Great Awakening, preachers tried to elicit a response and commended emotional conversions, but they did not pretend to understand the mysterious inner working of conversion itself; the work of conversion was God's. Nineteenth-century revivalism, conducted in camp meetings[2] and on the frontier, proceeded from the notion that holiness is voluntary and conversion a matter of personal choice more than divine action.

According to Nathan Hatch (see note 1), revivalism coupled with the revolutionary spirit of the new American republic led to a new religious phenomenon: common people became significant actors in religious matters, and religion became dramatically more democratic. Distinctions between a learned clergy and an ignorant laity began to break down as virtue came to be associated with popular piety, and untutored preaching (from the *heart*, not the head) came to be preferred to erudite sermons. Furthermore, new religious movements, including Evangelicalism, put a premium on the spiritual impulses of ordinary people who were encouraged to define faith for themselves and to be enthusiastic about it.

After the Civil War, Dwight L. Moody (1837–1899) applied business and advertising techniques to religious revivalism and developed large interdenominational urban meetings similar to the large camp meetings of the first part of the century. He founded Moody Bible College to train evangelical ministers. The revivalist message was simple and often anti-intellectual: it centered on the redemptive love of God in Jesus Christ and contained a strong call to repentance. Revivalism was designed to be an emotional experience leading the sinner to rebirth and to a healing experience of God's love. Many evangelicals expected conversion to be accompanied by a manifestation they called exercises, which might include crying, running, or some kind of physical tremors.

American Evangelicalism often promised and produced social as well as moral improvement, readying people for a life of action. The Evangelical Alliance was formed in 1846 to concentrate evangelical energy in the service of scriptural Christianity and against what were considered to be unscriptural religions (for example, Roman Catholicism). Societies were formed throughout the nineteenth century to spread the evangelical message (the American Bible Society and the American Tract Society) and to inspire moral improvement (the American Temperance Union).

Evangelicalism has often been used to describe an emotional approach to religion: Methodist revivals in England, for example, ridiculed by some as too emotional, were known as evangelical. For the most part, however, it describes those who stress religious experience and the importance of making a clear, definite decision for Jesus Christ. Evangelicals emphasize biblical authority and human sinfulness; they insist on the need for a new birth and a life of holiness and personal witness.

In addition to specifically evangelical denominations,[3] evangelical groups exist within mainline Protestant denominations: one can find Evangelical Mennonites, Evangelical Presbyterians, Evangelical Methodists, Evangelical Lutherans, and so on. It cannot be assumed that these churches are always characterized by American evangelical beliefs or practices. The word *evangelical* is sometimes used (in Europe especially) to distinguish Protestants from Roman Catholics; it sometimes refers to Christians influenced by Methodist revivalism; in American religious history, it has often meant personal religious experience and new birth in Christ often combined with Christian fundamentalism.[4]

Liberal Protestantism

Inspired by the rationalist philosophy of the Enlightenment and Deism, and often in reaction to the emotionalism of revivalism, some groups of Christians became more liberal in their interpretation of Scripture. The clearest example of a new denomination with these characteristics is Unitarianism. Formed within

American Congregationalism and associated with the work of William Ellery Channing (1780–1842), Unitarianism rejects the mysterious doctrine of the Trinity in favor of a belief in the unity of God. Unitarians base their positions on the Bible and refuse to accept some theological tenets of the Reformation, especially the Calvinist doctrine of total human depravity.

Liberalism sometimes means freedom from prejudice and a readiness to welcome new ideas and progress in religion. By these criteria one can find liberals in all churches: Catholic, traditional Protestant, and Evangelical. *Liberal Protestantism* usually refers to an understanding of Christianity that emphasizes its humanitarian impulses rather than dogmatic propositions or emotional conversion. It is, accordingly, an often misunderstood term and frequently used to criticize people for being insufficiently religious in a traditional sense.

Communitarian Groups

A variety of religious experiments flourished in the climate of religious freedom of nineteenth-century America. The communitarian impulse derived from the early Christian tradition of members sharing their goods and living a common life (see Acts 4:32–37).[5] The monastic tradition (as we have seen in Chapter 4) sprang from the desire to live a life of perfection and to do it in a community. Throughout history communitarian groups have drawn together for these general reasons: for example, the Waldensians were a twelfth-century group that gathered around Peter Waldo (c. 1176) in order to live in apostolic poverty.

We have already seen that groups can break off from a major Christian denomination to form a separate religious entity (the Amish splitting from the Mennonites, for example). Communitarian groups sometimes split from a parent group and sometimes were an entirely new creation. In America, many of them were drawn together by their belief in the Second Coming of Christ. Whatever their beliefs, they were usually founded by a strong leader, and lived together in separate villages or communes, often with some distinguishing practice or belief. There were groups inspired by perfectionism and made up almost entirely of intellectuals and literary people (like the Brook Farm movement), and groups inspired by German Pietism who practiced celibacy and waited for the world to be restored to harmony (like the Rappites, also known as the Harmony Society). Some of the products we use today (or brand names we know) were originally associated with nineteenth-century communitarian groups, like Amana appliances, connected to Amana Church Society in Iowa, and Oneida silver, connected to the Oneida Community founded in New York by John Humphrey Noyes (1816–86). Let us look more closely at two of these groups.

The Hopedale community. This group was founded in Massachusetts in 1842 by Adin Ballou (1803–90), an American Universalist preacher. Universalism is the doctrine that affirms the salvation of all people; God's love for everyone and desire for the salvation of all souls accomplishes this universal saving action.[6] Hopedale was a nonviolent utopian community that required no common beliefs, but did require members to refrain from violence, taking oaths, and intoxicating drinks. It disintegrated as a community in 1857, but the Universalist movement—of which Adin and Hosea Ballou (1771–1852) were among its most important leaders—continued, became the Universalist Church of America, and merged with the American Unitarian Association in 1961 to form the Unitarian Universalist Association.

The Shakers. The United Society of Believers in Christ's Second Appearing is the official name of the Shakers, a group of "Shaking Quakers" led to New York by Mother Ann Lee in (1736–84) in 1774. Shakers believed that God was manifested in male form in the person of Jesus Christ and in female form in the person of Mother Ann Lee. In New York, they established a community of celibacy, pacifism, and cooperative living. Membership depended on conversion and tended to fluctuate dramatically. Because of long-lived members and modern conversions, some Shaker communities still exist—in Canterbury, New Hampshire, and in Sabbath Day Lake, Maine—though most have disappeared. They were the largest of the communitarian groups and are remembered historically for their ritualized ecstatic dancing, their distinctive architecture and furniture, and their theological innovations, specifically for their belief in a female manifestation of God.

Most of these communitarian groups have ceased to exist, but many of their settlements are preserved as historical sites and they continue to be remembered for their experiments in community living.

Millennialist Groups

From the New Testament we can see that Christians have, from the beginning, thought about the Second Coming of Christ. If we think about the return of Christ, certain questions occur to us: *When* will he return? *What will happen* when he does? Some Christians, reading Revelation 20:1–10, believe that Christ will establish a thousand-year period of bliss, and so wait joyfully for the millennium (millennium means a thousand-year period). Most Christians believe that Christ will return to judge the living and the dead, but they do not all attempt to predict the time of the Second Coming. Millennialist groups in the nineteenth century were preoccupied with questions about the Second Coming and very much involved with interpreting the signs of the times so as to maintain a high level of expectation about the imminence of Christ's return. The three most significant groups of millennialist Christians formed in the nineteenth century are the Adventists (represented here by the Seventh-Day Adventists, though there are other adventist groups),[7] the Jehovah's Witnesses, and the Dispensationalists.

Seventh-Day Adventists. Adventism, as a movement, originated with the prophecies of William Miller (1782–1849) about the end of the world. Miller, a lay preacher in the Baptist church, concentrated on the books of Daniel and

Revelation and devised a way to tell when the end of the world was coming. In 1831 he began to preach that Christ's Second Coming was to be expected in 1843. His preaching was apparently convincing, since more than seven hundred ministers of various denominations welcomed him to their pulpits and helped him spread the word. When Christ did not return in 1843, Miller recalculated and predicted two dates in 1844, by which time between fifty thousand and one million people had left their congregations to wait for the coming (advent) of Christ. When Christ did not return on the second set of dates, some of these people left their churches altogether, some returned to their own congregations, and still others formed splinter adventist groups.

In general, Adventism is the belief that Christ's Second Coming is at hand, that the wicked are soon to be punished and the good rewarded. The largest and most famous of the adventist groups is the Seventh-Day Adventist Church founded by Joseph Bates, James White, and his wife, Ellen Gould White (1827–1915), who is considered the prophetess of the Seventh-Day Adventist Church. The first conference of the new church was held in Battle Creek, Michigan, in 1863; Ellen White's numerous visions were crucial in resolving early questions of doctrine and practice. Seventh-Day Adventists observe Saturday (not Sunday) as the proper day of Christian worship; they accept the Bible as the only authoritative rule of faith and interpret it literally. They also affirm the prophecies of Ellen White and believe that the spirit of prophecy is present in their church. They are strict sabbatarians and follow many Old Testament dietary laws; they wait for the Second Coming of Christ, but do not attempt to predict an exact time for it. They believe Christ *began* his judgment in 1844 (the date Miller set for the Second Coming), and will finish it in his own time.

Jehovah's Witnesses. The Jehovah's Witnesses were founded by Charles Taze Russell (1852–1916), who studied the Bible and became convinced by 1872 that Christ would return secretly in 1874 and that the world would end in 1914. His published opinions secured a large following, and from 1879 he established himself as pastor of an independent church in Pittsburgh, where he published *The Watchtower.* His followers were known by different names, including the Watchtower People. They were named Jehovah's Witnesses by their second leader, Joseph Franklin Rutherford (1869–1942). The sect grew from a few thousand to 106,000 during Rutherford's lifetime and today claims more than a million members in various countries.

Jehovah's Witnesses believe that only the elect of Jehovah (a form of the Hebrew name for God) will get into the kingdom of God. The present world, according to them, is ruled by Satan, and all government, business, and organized religion is in league with the devil and in conflict with the will of Jehovah. They consider themselves part of a theocratic kingdom and, accordingly, will not serve in the armed forces, salute any flag, or hold political office. They avoid the ways of the world and traditional religious feasts, refusing to celebrate Christmas or Easter. Based on the books of Daniel and Revelation they believe that only Christ and 144,000 elect have immortal souls and that everyone else has a mortal one, but will be given a second chance during the millennium. The present world will end and be replaced by a new world. At that time the just will reign and the wicked will perish, the 144,000 will go to heaven and the rest will live forever on earth.

Dispensationalists. Dispensationalism is a system of biblical interpretation that divides all time from the creation of the world into units called dispensations. In each dispensation God is revealed in a new way and treats people differently. The first five dispensations refer to periods in the Old Testament, the sixth is the time of the Christian church, and the seventh is the coming of the kingdom. If Christians are now living within the sixth dispensation they are, in a sense, living at the edge of the kingdom and should expect the return of Christ soon. Dispensationalists read the Bible from this perspective and interpret its prophecies to support their beliefs. Twentieth-century American Dispensationalists use the Scofield Reference Bible, edited by Cyrus I. Scofield (1841–1923), which offers a dispensationalist key to the interpretation of Scripture. Scofield's notes on the King James Version of the Bible gave people a way to understand the Bible for themselves, to find in it all the answers to their concerns.

New American Religions

Most "new" religious groups were formed from a particular established church, or established on the basis of a generalized belief—such as nineteenth-century Adventism—that swept through all churches. Two religious groups founded in the nineteenth century, however, were *really* new: they did not spring from established churches or movements, and they were specifically American, with distinct aspects growing out of the American context. These were the Mormons and the Christian Scientists.

Mormons. The Church of Jesus Christ of Latter-Day Saints (the Mormons) was founded in New York by Joseph Smith (1805–44) in 1830. Smith had a revelation experience: he was led by an angel to discover the Golden Plates, which contained "the fullness of the everlasting Gospel." According to Mormons, the Book of Mormon was translated by Smith from the Golden Plates; it is approximately five hundred pages long and is divided into books like the Bible. The Book of Mormon describes the lives of the "lost tribes of Israel" who migrated to America; it covers the years 600 B.C.E. to 421 C.E. According to the Book of Mormon, Jesus appeared to these people after the Resurrection and established a church among them; it is this church that Smith claimed to revive. According to Smith, no other churches have divine authority; his authority came directly from God and he was ordained by John the Baptist.

Smith and his followers moved to Kirtland, Ohio, where an entire congregation joined them. From there they moved to Missouri, then to Illinois, where they prospered but aroused their neighbors' animosity. Smith was killed by a mob in Illinois in 1844. When he died, the church divided into several groups, two of which are particularly important. The largest group followed Brigham Young (1801–77) to Salt Lake City, Utah. There they established a theocracy and openly practiced polygamy, one of the doctrines of their faith, from 1852 to 1890. According to Smith, marriage was important for salvation—singlehood and celibacy were considered to be against God's will—and plural marriage a revealed doctrine.

In Mormon theology God was once a man, who later achieved divinity, as can any man. Mormons say, "What man is now, God once was; what God is now, man may become."[8] A man becomes a god by successfully living through the testing period of mortality on earth; if he does well he can become a god presiding over his own world; there are many worlds and many gods. In Mormon belief God is the literal father of human souls; God is a polygamist who mates with female deities to produce an abundance of spirits or souls. In order for those souls to have an opportunity to become divine, they must become embodied, be born as human beings. Thus Mormons regard it as a duty to have as many children as possible, to embody as many souls as possible. The practice of polygamy enabled more souls to become embodied.

The other significantly large group of Mormons is the Reorganized Church of the Latter Day Saints (1852). It considers itself the legitimate successor of Smith's church and repudiates some of the later doctrines, especially polygamy and polytheism. Theologically this body resembles traditional Protestantism. It is headquartered in Independence, Missouri. Joseph Smith Jr. (1832–1914) was the original president, and this group owns the original church in Kirtland, Ohio, and the original manuscript of the Book of Mormon. Millennialism is an important part of all Mormon belief.

Christian Scientists. The Church of Christ, Scientist was founded by Mary Baker Eddy (1821–1910) in 1875. Most of her life she had been unhappily married and critically ill, but her life changed radically in the 1860s when she met Phineas Parkhurst Quimby (1802–66), a mental healer. After a healing experience with him she developed her own system; in 1866 when she was seriously ill, she read the account of Jesus raising the daughter of Jairus (Luke 8:40–56) and was cured. This was a decisive experience for her. She had discovered the real meaning of the Gospels: that Christ healed by spiritual influence.

According to Eddy, Jesus taught people the power of the mind to eliminate the illusions of sin, sickness, and death. All people, she taught, can be loving, confident, and well instead of hateful, fearful, and sick if they simply understand the spiritual nature of all reality: God is a spirit or *idea* and God is everything. Human beings, as a reflection of God, are also spiritual and good. The role of Christ is to bring people to this understanding. Eddy wrote *Science and Health* in 1875 and added to it "A Key to the Interpretation of Scripture"; this book, according to Christian Scientists, presents the *only* way to read the Bible. In following it, people find that the only reality is *ideas* and that matter does not exist; God is all good and there is no room for sickness; the cure comes when one can perceive this fact. In 1877 Eddy opened the Massachusetts Metaphysical College, where she trained healers. By 1886 these healers were so successful that the National Christian Science Association was founded. By 1900 there were over 100,000 Christian Scientists.

Christian Science was one part of a larger intellectual and emotional movement known as New Thought. Mental healing was popular and influential in the late nineteenth century, and its teachings appealed to members of many different Christian denominations. According to the followers of New Thought, God is a life principle; salvation is happiness here and now; the absence of sin makes repentance unnecessary; and Jesus Christ is the symbol of the divine spark of goodness in everyone. New Thought promises secret inner power and a "real" understanding of Christianity to its followers. While there are certain common beliefs in New Thought—spiritual healing and the creative power of thought, for example—it was never an organized denomination. At the same time, as a healing movement, it influenced people like Mary Baker Eddy who did found organized churches.

Americanization and the Churches

English-speaking denominations in some ways set a pattern for American religious development. Non-English-speaking groups—especially German Lutherans and European Catholics—had some trouble determining how American to become. Catholics had the added difficulty of being perceived as a church dominated by a foreign power.

Lutheranism. Lutherans from Germany, Austria, and the Netherlands began to immigrate to America in the seventeenth century, but never were well organized as a confessional group. In the eighteenth century a German missionary, Henry Melchior Mühlenberg (1711–87), came to America to minister to and organize American Lutherans. He organized the first synod (group of Lutheran congregations), and by 1770 eighty-one Lutheran congregations existed in Pennsylvania alone. By the nineteenth century many more Lutherans had come and were spread out over a wider territory. Many of them were German. One question that arose in the minds of many of these people concerned the relationship between their ethnic and their religious identity. They wondered whether to maintain their German heritage or to become more thoroughly American in language and custom; they wondered how much being Lutheran had to do with being German.

The dilemma of Americanization gave rise to three general solutions. The wholeheartedly pro-American option was defined by Samuel Simon Schmucker (1799–1873). He urged Lutherans to band together into one American Lutheran church and to dissociate themselves from ethnically defined churches; he hoped to build a church without ethnic barriers. Schmucker had been touched by American Evangelicalism and his plan was based on some doctrinal compromise; he was willing to abandon some traditional Lutheran positions in order to become more American. The conservative reaction to Schmucker's position was led by Carl F. W. Walther (1811–87), who supported strict confessional Lutheranism (giving nothing to American Evangelicalism) and German ethnic heritage. Walther's group formed a German Lutheran Synod in the 1840s, which eventually became the Lutheran Church–Missouri Synod. The middle-of-the-road alternative was defined by Charles Porterfield Krauth (1823–83) and became the basis for the Lutheran Church of America. Krauth supported the traditional Lutheran confessionalism of the conservatives, but also advocated an American Lutheran identity as urged by Schmucker; his group maintained its Lutheran doctrines and also abandoned Old World ways. As more Germans entered the country, these arguments continued; the three main branches of the Lutheran church in the United States reflected the divisions and arguments.

In 1974 there was a major schism within the Missouri Synod, which resulted in the Association of Evangelical Lutheran Churches. The dividing issue was the interpretation of Scripture; the new group adopted methods and positions often associated with more liberal viewpoints. In 1982 the Lutheran Church of America, the American Lutheran Church, and the Association of Evangelical Lutheran Churches voted to merge into a single new church. This merger, which was completed in 1987, marks an important step not only in Lutheranism (making it the third-largest Protestant denomination in the country, after Baptists and Methodists) but in American religious history.

Roman Catholicism. Roman Catholics encountered two problems related to their Americanization. Internally there was a division between the more liberal Irish bishops who pushed for Americanization and the more conservative German bishops who wished to avoid Americanization in favor of preserving their ethnic identity.[9] Externally, hostility from a variety of anti-Catholic nativist movements followed Catholics up to the second half of the twentieth century. The English colonies had never welcomed Roman Catholics nor made them very comfortable; Catholics suffered from a variety of social and legal restrictions and a lack of religious freedom. During the colonial period few Catholics came to the colonies, but from the 1820s to the 1870s the Catholic population increased from 195,000 to 4,504,000; most of them were immigrants. The rapid increase in the Catholic population and their foreign connections (by birth or church affiliation) inspired the rise of nativist movements.

Nativism is intense suspicion and dislike of any foreigner, especially a Roman Catholic. Revivalist preachers and nativist publications warned Americans against the "international conspiracy" of the Roman Catholic church. Catholics, they said, were under the domination of a foreign monarch (the pope) and were by definition (as members of a hierarchical, non-democratic church) unable to support American freedoms. In the early part of the nineteenth century, people were easily convinced that Catholics were a menace, that convents were dens of iniquity, and that there was a Roman conspiracy led by the pope and managed by the Jesuits. In some anti-Catholic riots people were killed and convents burned.

From the 1850s to the present there have been nativist movements. The Know Nothing movement (so called because members always claimed to know nothing about their secret activities) was founded in the 1850s as a secret political society. In 1854 they formed the American Party to combat foreign influence, popery, Jesuitism, and Catholicism. Their political aim was to exclude all Roman Catholics from public office and in 1856 they gained 25 percent of the popular vote. The Know Nothings disappeared after the Civil War partly because of their alliance with the proslavery movement, but nativism did not disappear. In the 1880s new waves of eastern and southern Europeans, predominantly Catholic, immigrated, and the American Protective Association was formed in 1887 to limit the Catholic population with a stringent immigration quota system. By 1896 the American Protective Association had a million members; it lingered as an association until 1911. In the 1920s the Ku Klux Klan was revived against blacks, Jews, and Roman Catholics; Klan policies against foreigners were supported by a systematic use of terrorism.[10] The Klan gained political power and was able to support legislation that restricted immigration of eastern and southern Europeans. The revival of the Klan in the 1970s is a modern example of nativism as directed against foreigners.

Catholics responded to nativism with withdrawal and patriotism. On the one hand they pulled back from the mainstream of American life, founded a separate, extensive private school system, and organized Catholic neighborhoods and social units. When necessary, however, they exhibited intense patriotism—as if to prove that Catholics were especially good Americans. The most significant response to nativism, however, led to the most divisive argument within the American Catholic church in the nineteenth century.

The two predominant groups of Roman Catholics in nineteenth-century America were Irish and German, with church leadership in predominantly Irish hands. German Catholics settled into the so-called German Triangle defined by Milwaukee, Cincinnati, and St. Louis, where they hoped to live quietly and continue to retain their ethnic identity and the German language and customs they believed to be so superior to American or Irish Catholicism. A group of liberal bishops—John Ireland (c. 1838–1918), John J. Keane (1839–1918), and John Lancaster Spalding (1840–1916)—who were enthusiastic about American pluralism urged an American Catholicism without ethnic divisions. Through a series of conflicts and misunderstandings centered more in Europe than in the United States, the pope condemned Americanism in 1899. The papal condemnation was based on an inaccurate understanding of the American situation, but tended to dampen all efforts toward liberalization within the American Catholic church. The American Catholic experience in the 1890s set the tone for the conservative, isolated Catholicism of the first 60 years of the twentieth century.

Catholics deplored the tactics and theological positions of American Evangelicalism; they stressed the importance of the organized church and the sacraments as opposed to emotional conversions and reliance on subjective religious experience. Still, revivalism did influence the Roman Catholic church's concept of missions.[11] Specially trained priests moved from parish to parish, preaching missions that were intended to strengthen Catholic identity and renew religious experience. Their style was not that of revivalist preaching in the American evangelical churches, but the desired goal was similar. Revivalist preachers aimed at conversion as manifested in response to an altar call; Catholic mission preachers sought to engender deep feelings of repentance manifested by an increased use of the sacrament of penance and a marked increase in devotional fervor.

Growth and Division Within Christian Churches

The ethnic and ideological complexity of America inspired an enormous growth and division within the churches. Nearly every Christian church divided over slavery during the Civil War, and most churches suffered some division over the evangelical impulse. As happened during the Reformation, divisions continued over internal church polity. The melting pot image of America never quite took hold of the ethnic imagination—at least not during the nineteenth century—and many specifically ethnic churches and church groups remained. The so-called Restoration movement attempted to unify like-minded people into one "Christian" church.

Roman Catholics remained united as a single church while most other Christian groups experienced major schisms. Some of those divisions were over what were considered to be innovations (Sunday school, or a paid professional ministry), some over major national conflicts (slavery), and some were continuations of earlier arguments (the appropriateness of evangelical preaching). In many churches most members were willing to accept a particular progressive teaching or arrangement and a small group split from them to be faithful to their understanding of the original vision of the group. Many churches split along North-South lines during the Civil War—American Baptists and Southern Baptists; the United Presbyterian Church (Northern) and the Presbyterian Church in the United States of America (Southern); the Methodist Episcopal Church (Northern) and the Methodist Episcopal Church of the South—and reunited in the twentieth century (though some groups are still attempting reunification).

Afro-American Christianity. A significant development in American Christianity was the formation of Afro-American churches. Slave owners in the South along with preachers from various Protestant denominations worked to convert black people to Christianity, and the Christian religion appears to have served many of the psychological and social needs of the slave population. We can, of course, find fault with a religion that tolerated slavery at all, and we may judge those sectors of American Christianity that were unable to see beyond the limitations of their own racial prejudices, but for now let us concentrate on the ways Afro-American Christianity developed.

Christian slaves in the South developed a set of hymns and spirituals that still speak powerfully to the black religious experience. The black preacher, who eventually emerged as a political as well as a religious figure, was a special kind of community genius. Since congregations of black Methodists and Baptists were almost always supervised, black preachers had to find ways to become strong community leaders without attracting hostile suspicion yet at the same time gaining the confidence of the local black congregation. Black churches were not granted independence until after the Civil War.

Besides Christian churches made up of slave populations, there were institutional churches made up of free blacks. The need for distinct black churches arose from the fact of second-class citizenship experienced by blacks in white churches. Methodists, Baptists, and others segregated black members of their own churches, forcing them to sit in balconies or to worship in separate buildings. In response to this situation some blacks formed their own denominations. Black Methodists, for example, formed the African Methodist Episcopal Zion church in 1776. Richard Allen (1760–1831), born a slave in Philadelphia, founded the African Methodist Episcopal church in 1816. These two churches, though not the only black denominations, comprise the congregations that serve a majority of Afro-American Christians today.

Within the variety of Christian responses to the challenges of the late nineteenth century, three significant movements occurred: the Holiness movement; its lineal descendant, Pentecostalism; and the so-called Restoration movement. We will look at each of these movements briefly before drawing conclusions about religious diversity in nineteenth-century America.

The Holiness movement. After the Civil War a series of Methodist revivals were preached stressing a return to holiness and emphasizing "entire sanctification." Wesley believed that there were two distinct blessings in the Christian life: justification (which changes the condition of one's life because God forgives one's sins and restores fellowship) and sanctification (which changes one's nature and helps one live a life of perfect love). Sanctification or Christian perfection does not mean freedom from mistakes or illness, according to Wesley, but is freedom from sin. The grace of God enables a person to love God so wholeheartedly that all that person's actions, thoughts, and words will be directed by love. The pivotal question is how sanctification is interpreted with regard to *time:* for the Methodists sanctification is a gradual process attained throughout the Christian life. Those who became part of the Holiness movement, however, believed sanctification was a sudden acquisition by the action of the Holy Spirit. Within the Holiness movement, people expected to receive entire sanctification—instantaneous holiness—at revival meetings. In 1867 a group of like-minded individuals formed the National Camp Meeting Association for the

Promotion of Holiness. From this came an interdenominational movement and the formation of separate Holiness churches.

The two most widely known Holiness churches are specific branches of the Church of God[12] (Anderson, Indiana, for example) and the Church of the Nazarene. The Church of God of Anderson, Indiana, is the *oldest* Holiness church, whereas the Church of the Nazarene is the *largest*. Holiness churches are usually grass-roots movements that are evangelistic and fundamentalist. They stand for what is known as the Four-Square Gospel: Jesus is the savior, the sanctifier, the healer, and the coming Lord.

Pentecostalism. The lineal descendant of the Holiness movement was the Pentecostal movement. Pentecostals believe in entire sanctification, but as a gradual—not instantaneous—process initiated by baptism in the Holy Spirit (often referred to as the Holy Ghost). Baptism with the Holy Ghost is manifested in the gift of *glossolalia,* according to Pentecostals: those who receive the Holy Ghost will speak in tongues. According to Pentecostals, the Christian experience at Pentecost—the coming of the Holy Ghost, the gifts of glossolalia, healing, and prophecy—should be a continuing and normal experience within Christianity.

Pentecostalism began in Kansas in the early part of the twentieth century. Charles Fox Parham (1873–1937), a preacher in the Holiness movement, convinced his followers that the baptism in the Holy Spirit required for salvation was essentially connected with speaking in tongues. One could determine whether or not one had received the Holy Ghost on the basis of a particular gift: only if the person spoke in tongues was it certain that he or she had received Spirit baptism. The most important source of Pentecostalism was the Azusa Street Revival held in Los Angeles, California, in 1906 by W. J. Seymour, a Holiness preacher.

Pentecostals are united in their belief that baptism in the Spirit and speaking in tongues are necessary signs of holiness; they are fundamentalist in their interpretation of Scripture, have strong dispensationalist leanings, and are strong believers in the imminent Second Coming of Christ. Pentecostals differ on matters of doctrine (some of them do not believe in the Trinity but see the Father, Son, and Holy Ghost as different manifestations of God in history), polity, and practice. The largest Pentecostal group is the Assemblies of God, an organization established in 1914. The United Pentecostal Church is the largest "Jesus name" (non-Trinitarian) group; baptism is administered in the name of Jesus Christ, not in the name of the Father, Son, and Holy Ghost.

A movement that has touched most other Christian churches and that is in some ways associated with Pentecostalism is Neopentecostalism or Charismatic Renewal. Christians in nearly all denominations, including Roman Catholics, have sought to experience the gifts of the Holy Spirit outside the context of classical Pentecostalism. These people are not usually motivated by a desire for the sign of glossolalia, but do hope to have some tangible experience of God, some manifestation of the Holy Spirit in their lives, without separating themselves from their particular churches. They do not agree with some of the doctrinal and behavioral principles of classical Pentecostals, but do share with them a desire for an experience of the Holy Spirit.

The Restoration or "Christian Church" movement. The Restoration movement or New Reformation of the nineteenth century was an attempt to combine efforts for Christian unity with a return to simple, New Testament Christianity. Some people believed that Christians were unnecessarily divided over issues of polity, practice, and creeds, so they espoused a noncredal New Testament–based Christianity. One leader of this movement was Barton Stone (1772–1844), who participated in the Cane Ridge Camp Meeting (1801) and was led to dissolve his Presbyterian congregation so that they could be "simple Christians"; James O'Kelly (c. 1735–1826) led a group of congregational Methodists to accept the Bible as their only creed. Other leaders were Thomas Campbell (1763–1854) and his son Alexander (1788–1866). Thomas Campbell left the Presbyterian church to found the Christian Association to promote unity among Christians. His son Alexander worked within Baptist associations and then founded a separate community that supported a rational, biblical, practical approach to Christianity. He avoided theological disputation and subtlety, on the one hand, and emotional revivalism on the other. All of these efforts aimed to restore ancient, primitive Christianity, to bring the New Testament church to life in the contemporary world. Furthermore, Restoration leaders hoped to appeal to simple New Testament piety and free Christians from the scandalous divisions that so many options appeared to foster. Their aim was to heal all conflicts.

Ironically, however, this Restoration movement experienced a division within itself almost immediately. Alexander Campbell called his followers the Disciples of Christ and their churches were known as Churches of Christ. A conservative splinter group opposing non–New Testament innovations like Sunday school, instrumental music in worship, and missionary activity took the name Church of Christ for itself and was recognized as a separate body in 1906. The hoped-for single "Church of Christ," therefore, was not to be. Disciples of Christ belong to the Christian Church, a different denomination from the Church of Christ.

Summary of Nineteenth-Century Christianity

The nineteenth century saw enormous growth and diversity within the Christian churches of America; by the end of the century a widespread spectrum of belief and practice was manifested in a multitude of American Christian groups.[13] Throughout this time and into the twentieth century, groups of Christians split and regrouped under different banners, a tendency that may attest to the dynamism within Christianity and the human need to join like-minded groups. By the middle of the twentieth century, many of the divided clusters had joined with others and merged to form large united churches like the United Church of Christ and the United Methodist Church. Some groups continued to maintain themselves as small churches. For the most part, however, the growth and diversity experienced in the nineteenth century gave way to movements of unity and cooperation in the twentieth century.

THE TWENTIETH CENTURY PREVIEWED

Optimism and a belief in human progress characterized the first part of the twentieth century. American Protestants entered into the spirit of the times with plans to improve themselves (by way of the temperance movement, for example), while Roman Catholics put an enormous amount of energy into building and maintaining their own school system and network of hospitals, newspapers, and charitable and religious institutions. The feeling of manifest destiny, which supported the idea of American democracy as capable of saving the world, was often given religious formulation by the churches, and a broad-based missionary movement was designed by the evangelical center of American Protestantism (see Chapter 9). All these noble adventures, begun in the enthusiasm of the new century, had been abandoned by the 1930s: the Eighteenth Amendment (Prohibition—passed to stop the consumption of alcohol) was repealed in 1934 because it had been a massive failure; American nationalistic fervor cooled when World War I ("the war to end all wars") did not end human warfare; and the worldwide missionary movement, begun in the nineteenth century, collapsed for lack of cooperation.

The 1940s focused the nation's attention on the Second World War and its aftermath. There was a resurgence of monastic life in the Roman Catholic church right after the war,[14] and renewed interest in religion in general. The 1950s were times of extraordinary success for almost all churches: more than 70 percent of the American population considered themselves to be religious and almost all Christian groups were busy building new churches, schools, fellowship centers, and other structures. If the 1950s were a boom time for religions, the 1960s were a down time. For a number of reasons (related to the war in Vietnam and its attendant unrest, both personal and social), church attendance declined markedly, fewer people supported their churches financially, and most churches went into debt. Most Protestant churches went into a decline, the Roman Catholic church began to experience the unsettling reform attempts of the Second Vatican Council,[15] and some of the newer Christian churches (Mormons and Pentecostals, for example) were growing at enormous rates. The 1970s and 1980s cannot be easily characterized, nor should they be at this point of insufficient historical distance, though we can relate some of the contemporary issues within American Christianity to older and perhaps deeper issues. But for background, we step back again to the beginning of the century and to the battle between two distinctly different religious views.

Fundamentalism Versus Liberalism: The Battle of the Century

As we have seen, Christians in the modern period did not divide neatly along denominational lines, but were inclined to group together on the basis of shared beliefs or theological convictions. Many of the beliefs and practices in nineteenth-century American Christianity had repercussions in most of the churches: Adventism, Evangelicalism, Pentecostalism all inspired the formation of separate churches, but they also precipitated groups within churches that did not split from those churches. The contemporary context, therefore, is genuinely pluralistic, and modern Christian churches often have a surprisingly wide range of opinion represented within them.

One of the main dividing issues in twentieth-century Christianity is *orthodoxy*. What are the "right" beliefs for Christians? As you can imagine, there are many answers to that question, all of them grounded on specific denominational histories. But let us make a broad generalization and divide Christians into two main groups: those who have welcomed the discoveries of the age and sought to use scientific insights and methods within Christianity, and those who have scorned or shunned new ideas in order to stay deeply in touch with the "old-time religion." Neither of these groups can be adequately described, but they stand at the limits of the argument, fundamentalists on the one hand and liberals on the other. Both words have been used as terms of derision and as badges of righteousness.

Orthodoxy is a question of right belief. What must a Christian believe? A certain theological orthodoxy had developed over many centuries and could, it was felt, be outlined in some basic (or fundamental) positions. Christians ought to believe in the Resurrection, in Christ as Savior and Lord of the world, in grace as a power of forgiveness and enablement (the power to do good), in the Trinity (three persons in one God, as defined by the ancient church), in the statements of the Apostles' Creed (see Appendix 5), in Original Sin and inherent spiritual weakness. To these central doctrines Protestants added some of the insights of the reformers: the priesthood of all believers, the salvation in Christ through faith alone, the sufficiency of Scripture as a religious authority, the sovereignty of God, and predestination. Catholics denied the Protestant insights and added instead the positions of the Council of Trent.[16] The argument I am now describing, however, is a Protestant one for the most part and what I say here relates to a debate within the Protestant church (one the Catholic church would face in a different way and solve in a different way later in the century).

Important for Christian orthodoxy was the theory of the atonement. The orthodox Protestant position up to the nineteenth century was that of substitutionary atonement. This doctrine says simply that human sinfulness demanded a payment, that Jesus paid the price (substituted for humanity), which satisfied the demands of divine justice, and that because of his work, death, and resurrection, people can be saved. All these points of orthodoxy derive from the Bible.

The orthodox view did not endure without challenges (in the Enlightenment, for example). Modern scientific discoveries were often at odds with established religious beliefs, and in the nineteenth century a whole new scientific method of textual analysis presented Christianity with its most difficult modern challenge. For a number of reasons, scholars became interested in biblical texts. As we have seen, some wanted to find the most accurate version of the Bible (the earliest translation, or the one least tampered with) and to revise the Bible people used in the light of new discoveries.[17] Some wanted to read the Bible differently. They were interested not so much in its devotional message as in trying to discover what the biblical authors really meant in the text. They studied the history and archaeology of the biblical period to see what they could learn about those people and were able, they thought, to shed new light on biblical stories and figures. Some of the conclusions of these scholars were threatening to traditional Christian beliefs. Most Christians had always believed that Moses wrote the first five books of the Bible, that the Gospel of John was a historically accurate picture of Jesus, and that no matter what else one could find in Scripture, there were no mistakes.

You can imagine how threatening it was (and still is to some Christians) to see these beliefs challenged. If Moses did not write the first five books of the Bible, then who did? What did one do with the theory of inspiration that said God dictated those first five books to Moses? If the Gospel of John was not a historically accurate picture of Jesus, what was? Who was the *historical* Jesus? Did he really work miracles? Did he know he was the Messiah? Did he really think the end of the world was coming? Are his ethics really meant to be lived by people now, or were they meant to be an interim ethic based on his belief that the world would soon end? Finally, if there were mistakes in the Bible, what happened to the whole concept of revelation, of God's authorship of Scripture? Surely, God did not make mistakes?

All these questions—originally posed by scholars in Europe—made their way into American Christianity and became the backbone of American Christian liberalism. The American context provided a congenial atmosphere for such questions: people were much readier to believe in natural human goodness than in theories of human depravity and predestination, and perhaps this new scientific method could provide a new way to understand and embrace the Christian faith.

The pivotal issue was the *authority of the Bible*. Let us review this issue a little bit. Before the Reformation there were profound differences of opinion about the Bible. Some parts of it were valued more highly than others. Luther judged the books of the Bible with reference to the norm of salvation by grace through faith, and so had little good to say about the Epistle of James with its emphasis on good works. He was not worried about the infallibility of the Bible. Later, however, people wanted to be able to place more authority in Scripture, to cite the authority of God (as written down in Scripture) against the competing authority of kings or popes or new religious views. In the seventeenth and eighteenth centuries some people went to extremes in their defense of biblical authority, arguing that even the *punctuation* of the Bible could not be questioned or changed.

Fundamentalists inherited these conservative views about biblical authority, and held fast to a belief that Scripture was infallible and inerrant. It is not fair to characterize all of them as extreme literalists or to picture them as closed-minded. The term *fundamentalist* comes from their belief that there is an irre-ducible minimum of beliefs without which one cannot claim to be a Christian, and one of those beliefs is in the inerrancy of the Bible.[18]

The heart of fundamentalism is a concern for salvation. The key question for them is simple and direct: "Have you been saved?" But how is one saved? According to orthodox Christian beliefs a person cannot save himself or herself; God must act to do it. And God has done it in Christ, who atoned for human sinfulness, but that atonement cannot work for a person unless she or he accepts Christ. Once one accepts Christ as the son of God and Savior, one is assured of heaven and receives the grace of God as a power to overcome sin. How does a person know this message or scenario to be true? Because God has said so: because it can be found in the Bible, which is God's word and so gives assurance to this position. Fundamentalists are concerned, therefore, to assert the iner-rancy of Scripture in order to protect what they see as the essential message of the gospel. James Barr explains fundamentalism as a religious position that seeks to tie Christianity to a conservative ideology. The fundamentalist insistence on biblical inerrancy, he says, insures that the Bible will speak in essentially conser-vative ways.[19]

An *extreme fundamentalist* believes that there are no mistakes in the Bible and that every word means exactly what it says: the Bible is to be read as fully and literally true. An *extreme liberal* admits that there are mistakes in the Bible, sees much of it as metaphor, and argues that the Bible should be read as an ethical guide for human life. Most of the people who tend to one or the other end of this spectrum are not extremists, and that makes the problem of interpre-tation more difficult. Conservatives or *neoevangelicals* are descended from the fundamentalist position, but have moved away from it in order to meet scientific and biblical criticism partway: they support their traditional views by way of scientific methods. They do not condemn biblical criticism as the work of the devil (as some extreme fundamentalists do), but neither do they accept the basic presuppositions of liberals. Neoevangelicals accept the supernatural world as a reality and are not constrained to explain divine intervention in the world; at the same time, they are willing to defend their views with reason and logic. They combine traditional orthodoxy with social activism and scholarship.

After a stormy period in the early part of the twentieth century, *neoliberalism* emerged in the 1940s. Harry Emerson Fosdick (1878–1969) elaborated some key tenets of it in a 1935 sermon: it is necessary to adapt Christianity to the modern world, but not by diluting the concept of God. Neoliberals are not overly opti-mistic about human nature (as earlier liberals, especially before the First World

War, may have been); they are willing to admit that the human situation is a predicament. People, they say, are sinful and there are no simple solutions; and people need more than ethics: they need to find themselves driven to God. Neo-liberals affirm the importance of the church as a living society and a divine institution (old liberals often looked at the church as no more than a social institution), and they affirm the necessity of repentance (some old liberals were not convinced of the reality of sin).

A tradition with some of its roots in liberalism but at the same time essentially convinced about the Protestant reformers' primary insights about God, human nature, and the Bible is *neo-orthodoxy*. Most neo-orthodox theologians have been suspicious of fundamentalism, yet convinced of the sovereignty of God, the power of sin, and the importance of the Bible for a realistic appraisal of human nature. The most important proponent of neo-orthodoxy was Karl Barth (1886–1968), a Swiss theologian who made a major impact on twentieth-century Protestant theology. The strongest American advocate of neo-orthodoxy was Reinhold Niebuhr (1892–1971). Neo-orthodoxy is socially and politically liberal yet theologically conservative. It requires a special social activism based on a committed Christian life. Neo-orthodox theologians have a renewed appreciation of the church as a collective group or community, and they support the concept of a worldwide church and the ecumenical movement.

CONCLUSION

I hope that from this chapter you have seen that the complexity of the arguments and the peculiarities of denominational history, even in American culture, make it nearly impossible to offer simple characterizations of particular groups. Today Christians face similar issues of biblical authority, orthodoxy, fundamentalism, and social activism, and they do so in a pluralistic context, often as part of larger social or political movements. Religious positions or controversies are no longer confined to denominational arguments, or even theological arguments: many of the ways Christians respond to their religious impulses today have worldwide consequences or roots. Add to this the vast size of some of these contemporary issues, and I hope you will see how much caution needs to be exercised before making sweeping statements about any Christian group.

Christianity—in America and in the world—is not simply made up of a variety of churches or denominations; it is also characterized by specific beliefs, questions, and actions. The purpose of this chapter has been to show how difficult it is to know exactly what we mean when we say that someone is a Methodist or a Catholic: there are wide differences of opinion within single denominations. It is also extremely hard to know what we mean when we say evangelical or liberal or fundamentalist. The words have been used by one group to dismiss the importance of another one. We should be careful and generous, therefore, when using them descriptively. When we move to contemporary issues (in Chapter 12) we may be inclined to see either fractionalization or richness, depending on our proclivities and our background. Whatever we see, we have seen it coming: the early church began in variety and diversity, it was politically involved as soon as it was able to be in a power position, it responded to serious controversy and reform from within, survived some challenges and reformed on the basis of others, and has demonstrated extraordinary adaptability.

CHAPTER 8 NOTES

[1] Nathan O. Hatch, *The Democratization of American Christianity* (New Haven: Yale University Press, 1989), p. 4. Hatch examines five mass movements that developed in the early nineteenth century—Mormonism, black churches, Baptists, Methodists, and the Christian movement—to show how they offered populist opportunities to *all* believers, not just to the educated or to the rich.

[2] For a description of a camp meeting and some of its religious exercises, see Alice Felt Tyler, *Freedom's Ferment: Phases of American Social History from the Colonial Period to the Outbreak of the Civil War* (New York: Harper & Row, 1944), pp. 35–42.

[3] Evangelicalism is theologically conservative Protestantism and so defines a wide-ranging group of Christian believers. There are also specifically evangelical churches: the Evangelical Covenant Church of America (1885), the Evangelical Free Church of America (1885), and the Missionary Church Association, a union of independent evangelical churches organized in 1898, are some examples of specifically evangelical denominations. An excellent book on contemporary young evangelicals is James Davison Hunter, *Evangelicalism: The Coming Generation* (Chicago: University of Chicago Press, 1987). Hunter, a sociologist of religion, found that the next generation of American evangelicals is a highly diverse group, less attached to some important fundamentalist aspects of religion and politics than one might imagine.

[4] Fundamentalism (discussed later in this chapter) is a post–Civil War movement that attempted to define those fundamental characteristics or beliefs that a Christian must adhere to. According to James Davison Hunter (see note 3), fundamentalists should be considered as a faction *within* Evangelicalism rather than as a separate movement.

[5] For a short, readable account of the communitarian impulse, see Mark Holloway, *Heavens on Earth: Utopian Communities in America 1680–1880*, rev. ed. (New York: Dover, 1966).

[6] Do not confuse this universalism with the universal mission discussed in Chapter 3.

[7] The Advent Christian Church (1860), for example, or the Church of God (Abrahamic), a non-Trinitarian group organized in Philadelphia in 1888.

[8] This summary of Mormon doctrine was passed on to me by my colleague Jan Shipps, who heard it from a president of the Mormon church. The word *man* here is intentional: women are saved along with their husbands. Single men and women can be saved but not "exalted"; they remain in the lowest heaven in a state of suspended animation. For an excellent picture of Mormon belief, see Jan Shipps, "Mormons: Looking Forward and Outward" in *Christian Century* 95 (16 August 1978), 761–66.

⁹For a provocative, pro-Americanist account of this chapter in American Catholic history, see Andrew M. Greeley, *The Catholic Experience* (New York: Doubleday, 1969).

¹⁰A short, engagingly written account of the Klan as experienced by a Catholic at the time is Robert Coughlan, "Konklave in Kokomo," in Isabel Leighton, editor, *The Aspirin Age: 1919–1941* (New York: Simon & Schuster, 1949), pp. 105–30.

¹¹For a historical analysis of the Catholic revivalist impulse, see Jay P. Dolan, *Catholic Revivalism: The American Experience 1830–1900* (Notre Dame, Ind.: University of Notre Dame Press, 1978).

¹²Church of God is a title used by more than two hundred separate denominations. German Americans touched by revivalism in the nineteenth century called themselves the Church of God, for example. Many members of the Holiness movement, as they formed churches, also called themselves the Church of God. You should be careful, therefore, when using this phrase to describe a particular group.

¹³Virtually all Christian churches experienced growth and division during the nineteenth century, but a full listing would be confusing and probably counterproductive. Let me give you some examples, however, so you have some sense of the diversity. A schism in the Roman Catholic church resulted in the Polish National Catholic Church (established as a separate group 1897–1900). Lutherans divided into more than the three main groups I discuss here—one can find many independent synods, like the Wisconsin Evangelical Lutheran Synod (1849). Radical Reformation churches split many times, usually over issues of purity or discipleship, but sometimes over what appear to be small matters (Black Bumper Mennonites, for example, think it is acceptable to own cars, but not adorned with chrome bumpers); it is not unusual to find many different kinds of Brethren, Amish, and Mennonite churches. Calvinist churches already had branches (Dutch Reformed and Presbyterian, for example), and those split, too, into other churches. Baptist churches tended to split easily over issues so that major arguments about revivalism, pacifism, the missionary movement, and so on all tended to produce separate Baptist groups (Hardshell or Primitive Baptists, for example, oppose sending missionaries anywhere). Methodists divided into Wesleyan Methodists, Free Methodists, Evangelical United Brethren, and so on, many of which were drawn back together with the establishment of the United Methodist Church. There are virtually hundreds of different Holiness and Pentecostal churches and thousands of independent churches that have no formal affiliation with anyone.

¹⁴The clearest impetus for this may well have been Thomas Merton's *The Seven Storey Mountain* (New York: New American Library, 1943). Merton (1915–68), a young, sophisticated writer, left it all behind to join a Trappist monastery in Kentucky; his autobiography had a tremendous impact on the American Catholic church and on monasticism in the postwar period.

¹⁵There are many books on the Second Vatican Council. One good introduction to the council itself is Gary MacEoin, *What Happened at Rome? The Council and Its Implications for the Modern World* (New York: Doubleday, 1967). One that captures the challenges for American Catholics is George Devine, *American Catholicism: Where Do We Go from Here?* (Englewood Cliffs, N.J.: Prentice-Hall, 1975).

¹⁶See Chapter 5 for a discussion of the Council of Trent.

¹⁷The scholars' version of the Bible is the Revised Standard Version (RSV). Many conservative Christians prefer the King James Version (KJV), the New American Standard Bible, or the New Internationalist Version because they take issue with some of the translations in the RSV.

[18]Although there is no single list of fundamentals, the most common set of beliefs recognized by fundamentalists includes biblical inerrancy, substitutionary atonement, the future Second Coming of Christ, full face value of the biblical miracles, and the divinity of Christ, including his physical resurrection. *The Fundamentals*, a series of twelve paperback volumes published between 1910 and 1915, probably gave the movement its name. Scholars disagree about the essential characteristics of fundamentalists. Ernest Sandeen, *The Roots of Fundamentalism: British and American Millenarianism 1800–1930* (Chicago: University of Chicago Press, 1970), places them within the context of nineteenth-century speculation about the end of the world. For him, fundamentalists are necessarily tied to biblical prophecies about the eschaton. George Marsden, *Fundamentalism and American Culture: The Shaping of Twentieth-Century Evangelicalism 1870–1925* (New York: Oxford University Press, 1980), understands fundamentalists as a distinct brand of evangelical Christianity set apart from other conservative Christians by their militant opposition to the modern world. James Barr (see note 19) focuses on their insistence on the inerrancy of the Bible as a key to understanding both their religion and their politics.

[19]See *The Scope and Authority of the Bible* (Philadelphia: Westminster Press, 1980), p. 68.

SUGGESTIONS FOR FURTHER READING

1. For more on specific denominations or general Christian history in America and the modern period, consult the bibliography at the end of the book.

2. A good documentary history of American religion can be found in Edwin S. Gaustad, editor, *A Documentary History of Religion in America*, 2 volumes (Grand Rapids: Eerdmans, 1982, 1983).

3. For an interesting introduction to some of the *impulses* of American religion in the early part of the nineteenth century, see Whitney R. Cross, *The Burned-Over District: The Social and Intellectual History of Enthusiastic Religion in Western New York, 1800–1850* (Ithaca, N.Y.: Cornell University Press, 1950).

4. For an introduction to the development of theology in America, see Deane William Ferm, *Contemporary American Theologies: A Critical Survey* (New York: Seabury Press, 1981), and its companion volume, *Contemporary American Theologies II: A Book of Readings* (New York: Seabury Press, 1982).

5. For a fascinating look at some parallels between nineteenth- and twentieth-century religions—Mormonism and Unificationism, for example, or Christian Science and Scientology—see Mary Farrell Bednarowski, *New Religions and the Theological Imagination in America* (Bloomington: Indiana University Press, 1989).

✦

CHAPTER 9

MISSIONS AND ECUMENISM

In Chapter 7 we reviewed some of the challenges of modernity and noted the responses of various Christian groups, and in Chapter 8 we looked at the extraordinary creativity of Christian development in nineteenth-century America. From both of these chapters we have become more aware of Christian diversity. We can no longer talk about Catholics, Orthodox Christians, and Protestants, but must now add territorial adjectives—Russian Orthodox and Greek Orthodox, for example—and words describing general intellectual postures like liberal and fundamentalist. In addition, we have seen the emergence of evangelical Christianity not only in terms of new communities, but as an important dimension of many mainline Protestant churches. Finally, we know that America was the soil for experimentation, division, and regrouping. Communitarian movements and new religions like Mormonism and Christian Science flourished, established churches like the Methodists and Presbyterians divided over painful issues raised during the Civil War, and general impulses to restore Christian unity inspired a regrouping of like-minded Christians into new denominations such as the Churches of Christ.

All of this new life shows that Christianity is a growing and dynamic religion, but it also leaves the impression that Christianity is hopelessly fractured. In this chapter we will examine two harmonious aspects of nineteenth- and twentieth-century Christianity, the cooperative adventure of the missionary movement and the impetus for interdenominational dialogue and understanding known as the ecumenical movement.

UNDERSTANDING THE MISSIONARY IMPULSE

From the earliest days of the Christian movement, evangelization was important. Jesus's words in Matthew 28:19–20 were interpreted as a clear command: believers were to "make disciples of all nations" with the confidence that Jesus would be with them always, even "to the close of the age." The very idea that the "close of the age" or end of the world was near inspired some of the earliest Christians to extend their message throughout the known world in an effort to gather as many as possible into the new community. We have already seen how hard Paul worked to make Christianity available to Gentiles and to preach the gospel throughout the Roman world. When it became clear that the world was not going to end soon, Christians still took the words of Jesus as a command and continued to spread their new faith wherever they went.

We have seen that the Christian empire under Constantine was distinguished by its power and beauty, as well as by its attention to philosophical debate and doctrinal definition. Another important feature of Constantine's patronage of Christianity was his support for missionaries, a practice continued by Orthodox Christianity. For example, Cyril and Methodius (d. 869 and 885), two brothers supported by the Eastern Orthodox empire, were known as the "apostles to the Slavs." Cyril gave up his post at the imperial university at Constantinople and Methodius relinquished his position as a provincial governor so that both could become priests and spread Christianity to the people of Moravia. They were able to succeed because they learned the Slavonic language. Their work on that alphabet enabled them to translate the Bible and the liturgy into Slavonic and to lay the groundwork for what would later become a flowering of Slavonic literature. For many Orthodox Christians today, Slavonic is the official liturgical language.

In the western part of the empire, as we have seen, missionaries were sent to the furthest reaches of the Roman world to bring Christianity to various barbarian tribes. We have noted the work of Patrick in Ireland, Boniface in Germany, and Augustine of Canterbury in England. When Western Christianity fell on hard times in the Dark Ages, the peoples of Europe were "re-Christianized" by monks. The labor force for missionary activity available to Western Christianity through monasticism cannot be underestimated. In addition to monks, new religious orders were important for continued missionary work. The Dominicans, for example, were founded by Dominic (c. 1170–1221) in 1216 for the express purpose of preaching and teaching in territories threatened by heretical interpretations of Christianity.

We have noted the impact of the resurgence of education under Charlemagne (known as the Carolingian Renaissance) in the ninth century, and the importance of schools, monastic life, and the universities for the maintenance of Christianity in the West. During the medieval period Christianity was available, it was thought, to everyone in the known world. Christians tended to think of their world as the center of the universe and their religion as the most perfect expression of religious consciousness in that world. If new territories opened up, the church was ready to win new peoples for Christ.

Two extraordinary occurrences opened new mission fields to late medieval Christianity: Marco Polo "discovered" China and Christopher Columbus "discovered" America.[1] Marco Polo (c. 1254–1324), an explorer from Venice, reached the magnificent court of Kublai Khan in 1275. He made other trips to China accompanied by missionaries, who were to bring Christianity to the Chinese. Their work was impressive and they reached what is now known as Beijing, but this early attempt to evangelize China did not flourish.

A Jesuit in China

Once the contact was made, however, European missionary—and economic—interest in the Orient was stimulated and the stage was set for later missionaries, notably for the work of the Jesuits in the seventeenth century led by Matteo Ricci (1552–1610).[2] Ricci had a marvelous facility for languages and made progress in China because, as he put it, he tried to "become Chinese in order to win the Chinese." Ricci let his hair grow into a traditional braid, dressed in local garb, spoke fluent Mandarin Chinese, and secured his place in the hearts of his audience by developing an interest in local literary classics. As a missionary, he was ahead of his time because his first goal was to adapt to the culture rather than imposing European ideals on it.

Ricci spent years in China talking more about Western inventions—like the clock—than about the life and death of Jesus. As he understood the situation, only patience would work as a missionary strategy. He was careful to gain the confidence of his audience before slowly introducing them to Christian stories, and he realized that Christianity could make progress in China only to the extent that it was adapted to Chinese cultural realities.

Typical of his pioneering spirit, he asked for permission to celebrate the liturgy in the vernacular—remember that the official liturgical language for Catholics was Latin—and he worked to translate the Bible into Mandarin Chinese. He hoped that Vatican officials would permit a translation of Christian documents and liturgy into Chinese and that they would make some accommodations to Chinese cultural expectations. Unfortunately, those hopes were misplaced. Ricci's mission to China was, finally, a dismal failure because Roman Catholic officials could not understand the need to make any accommodations. The story of the collapse of the Chinese mission in the seventeenth and eighteenth centuries is a sad one and too complicated to repeat here, but it is instructive because it helps us define one of the early problems of the missionary movement.

Ricci's instincts and methods are acceptable practice today: missionaries from all branches of Christianity first adapt themselves to the culture and only later begin to draw their listeners into Christianity. Missionaries encourage people to maintain their cultural identity so that their possible conversions to Christianity do not force them to abandon their heritage in order to become Christians.[3] In Ricci's time, however, such missionary adaptation was not possible. Roman officials were nervous about translating the Bible into Chinese because they feared that Christianity would become tainted with pagan Chinese beliefs. Vatican officials in charge of foreign missions insisted that new converts learn Latin in order to become priests and that native clergy follow the Western rules of celibacy, a practice that made no sense to the Chinese.

The whole situation was further complicated by competition from non-Jesuit missionaries who did not subscribe to the wisdom of missionary adaptation. Franciscans and Dominicans, for example, did *not* adapt themselves to the Chinese and so attempted to make Chinese converts into Europeans. Their strategies deeply offended Chinese officials. Christian missionaries were perceived as culturally imperialistic, as having no respect for the people to whom they ministered. The missionary movement in China, therefore, was closed and not opened again until the nineteenth century, when it flourished until political realities in the mid–twentieth century forced another dismissal of Christian missionaries from the territory.[4]

The New World

The second great discovery that opened new mission fields for European Christians was the "new world" discovered by Christopher Columbus and other explorers in the fifteenth and sixteenth centuries. When Pope Alexander VI "divided" the new world between Spain and Portugal in 1493, he split the responsibility for missionary activity between the two countries.[5] Explorers went to the new world to "conquer it for the greater glory of God" *and* to bring its treasures—gold, silver, precious stones—back to Europe. The story of missionaries in the new world—in present-day Mexico, Central America, South America, California, Canada, and the Mississippi Valley—is not a simple one. The missionaries sometimes treated native peoples as children or, worse, as slaves, forcing them into a new religion and into hard labor for Spain, France, or Portugal.

Some missionaries, notably Bartoleme de las Casas (d. 1566), protested against harsh treatment of native peoples and insisted that they be treated as children of God.[6] We will see the impact of these early missionaries and the importance of de las Casas when we deal with liberation theology in Chapter 12. At this point we need simply note that the same attitudes that led to the dissolution of the Chinese mission characterized the activity of many missionaries in the new world: they did not adapt themselves to the culture and life of the natives, but attempted to make Europeans out of the Indians in order to convert them to Christianity. The difference between the two settings was power: the Chinese empire was able to resist Christianity and to expel its missionaries, whereas the Amerindian tribes were easily conquered by the explorers. Native cultures and religions were often simply wiped out and Christianity forced on the people under threat of harsh punishment.

The history of Christian missions in the new world, as in China, is not a simple one: we can find stories of great heroism and compassion on the part of missionaries—the work of the Jesuits among the Hurons, for example—and we can find stories of exploitation and cruelty.[7] The only point I wish to make about this early modern period of Christian missionary activity is this one: missionaries did not always believe that they should adapt themselves to native cultures or respect native beliefs; in alliance with the explorers, their goal was often to *conquer* new peoples for Christ. However well-meant the ultimate goal—the belief that they were bringing the true faith to new peoples—the methods were often brutal. However successful the outcome—the overwhelming presence of Christianity in the Western Hemisphere—the price of that success can still raise questions for us.

Protestant Missionaries in the Nineteenth Century

For reasons that may be obvious, Protestants did not rush into missionary activity during the sixteenth, seventeenth, and eighteenth centuries. Besides being entirely taken up with establishing their new religious visions, their rejection of monasticism as an option for Christian life meant that they did not have the labor force for missionary conquest. Furthermore, the belief that God elected those who would be "saved" often enabled Protestants to see conversion as "God's problem," in no need of help from human agents. They tended to read the passage in the Gospel of Matthew as a directive of Jesus to the apostles rather than as a mandate for Christians at all times.

There were, of course, some notable exceptions. The Pietist movement had a strong missionary impulse, and the Moravians in the eighteenth century were distinguished by their missionary zeal, especially with Amerindians in the new world. John Wesley's rejection of predestination and his emphasis on salvation available to all who could respond to the invitation of Jesus tended to give Methodism a missionary mentality, and one can find some historical evidence for Puritan missionary activity, but the real heyday for missionary work in Protestant churches began in the nineteenth century.

The first great hero of the Protestant missionary movement was an Englishman, William Carey (1761–1834), a self-educated shoemaker and linguistic genius who converted to the Anglican church and later became a Baptist. Carey changed the typical Protestant attitude toward missionary activity at a time when the British empire was conquering new peoples in India and Africa. His book *Enquiry into the Obligations of Christians to Use Means for the Conversion of the Heathens* (1792) supported his understanding of the words of Jesus as a modern Christian duty. Jesus was not speaking only to the apostles, he argued, he was speaking to all Christians and sending them forth to bring the message of the gospel to the world. Carey inspired the Baptists to get interested in mission fields. He raised money to finance a trip to India, where he translated the Bible into Bengali and attracted converts to Christianity because he was able to speak to them in their own languages. Years later he became a professor of languages in Calcutta and produced important grammars in a variety of Indian languages.

Missionary enthusiasm characterized Protestant churches in general in the nineteenth century, notably in England and America. Young people especially were interested in the challenges of bringing God's word to peoples in the far corners of the globe and, like Carey, they heard Jesus's word directed to them. Hymns and tracts produced at the time inspired them to proclaim "the joyful sound of salvation" to the remotest regions of the world.[8] Evangelical Christians in particular believed that the best response they could make, in thanksgiving for their own Christian faith, was to bring the revelation of Christ to everyone. If Reformation Christians understood their lives as dedicated to love of neighbor, revivalist Christians in the aftermath of the Second Great Awakening understood that love of neighbor now extended everywhere. The hope that stirred them was that the world could be totally won for Christ, and they aimed to bring a moral revolution to the entire globe. Enthusiasm and optimism abounded and blended well with American ideas of manifest destiny: America was destined by God, many believed, to bring democracy to the world, just as Christians were enjoined to preach the gospel to all nations.

Carey's success, coupled with a general expansionary enthusiasm in the nineteenth century, led to the formation of a number of supportive societies. For example, the London Missionary Society was founded in 1795 as the first interdenominational missionary group, the one we may remember today for sending David Livingstone (1813–73), a Scottish missionary and explorer, to Africa. Because missionaries needed materials for their work, they established societies to produce Bibles and religious tracts. In many ways, the work of these groups was the first adventure in interdenominational cooperation.

The American Board of Commissioners of Foreign Missions was organized in 1810 to send Congregationalist missionaries to Southeast Asia. Its founding was stimulated by the interest of some remarkable young people at Williams College, notably Adoniram Judson (1788–1850), who felt that his call to ministry was, in fact, a vocation to carry the gospel to Burma. When he and his friends were commissioned, great enthusiasm spread to other groups. When Judson, stopping in India to see Carey, became convinced that the Baptist form of Christianity was more representative of New Testament practice, he became a Baptist and stimulated the formation of the American Baptist Missionary Union (1814). Like Carey, Judson was a linguistic pioneer who spent his early years in the mission fields translating the Bible into Burmese. Like Matteo Ricci in seventeenth-century China, he did not attempt to preach the gospel until he established cultural and linguistic links with the people.

During the nineteenth century, missionary societies were formed throughout Europe and the United States in all denominations. Mission Boards and Mission Societies attracted many zealous Christians and helped spread the gospel to Southeast Asia, the Pacific, China, Japan, and Africa. In many ways Christian missions came of age in the nineteenth century. They were not supported by the government and so were forced to rely on the devotion and financial sacrifices of believers. Missions were staffed and supported by lay people who saw their Christian destinies bound up with the conversion of the world.

Furthermore, mission activities tended to involve much more than the gospel: missionaries founded churches, schools, hospitals, and other institutions as they worked to understand the languages and grammars of new cultures. Much of what we know today about foreign languages and practices was first recorded by Catholic and Protestant missionaries in the field. Missionaries developed native leadership and introduced some innovations to native agricultural and trading practices.

Along with the success of the Christian missionary endeavor, however, there was also the scandal of diversity and competition. Christians were divided along denominational lines for many good historical and doctrinal reasons: they had different understandings of baptism and the Eucharist, different ideas about the ways churches should be structured (see Appendix 6), and differing points of emphasis in their interpretations of the gospel. Furthermore, they were not so far removed historically from a time when denominations persecuted one another in the name of truth. Their competitive tendencies, therefore, are understandable. At the same time, competition in the mission field was both scandalous and a little silly. New Christians in faraway places did not understand some of the doctrinal distinctions that divided European and American Christians and were shocked sometimes when groups fought with each other over their versions of the gospel. How could Christians talk about the "one body of Christ" yet continue to claim that one version of Christianity was better than another? The first realizations that cooperation might be a better strategy than competition were born in the hearts of nineteenth-century Protestant missionaries and they led to the beginnings of the ecumenical movement.

THE ECUMENICAL MOVEMENT IN ITS EARLY YEARS

Ecumenism comes from the Greek word *oikoumene*, which means "the whole inhabited world."[9] The ecumenical movement is usually defined as the attempt of Christian churches—all of them—to recover the unity of all believers. Ideally, ecumenism should enable Christians to rise above doctrinal and liturgical differences to achieve the unity imagined to exist in the early Christian movement. I have noted several times throughout this book that early Christianity was characterized by its differences, and I wonder whether such a unity is truly possible. At the same time, the idea of a unity of believers is an attractive one and has managed to gather modern Christians into a series of profitable conversations.

We have seen that Judaism at the time of Jesus was a diversified religion with many different expressions, and that religion in the Roman world tolerated a wide variety of belief and practice. Christianity, in the beginning, was one religion among many. With Constantine, however, Christianity began to assert itself as the one true religion with such power that other expressions of religious belief—paganism, for example—were condemned and uprooted. This idea that Christianity was the only true religion in the world, and that its European embodiment was its apex, led to the missionary attitudes of the early modern world.

Remember that up to the modern period, Christianity was not distinguished by its tolerance for disparate views. Medieval Catholicism perceived different expressions of Christianity as heresies and worked hard to uproot and destroy them. Reformation Christianity, both Protestant and Catholic, was not characterized by tolerance for diverse expressions either. Alternative versions of Christianity were judged to be false and dangerous, and seventeenth-century Christians put more effort into obliterating their enemies than they did into loving them. We have seen that although Puritans came to America for religious freedom, they interpreted that freedom to extend only to themselves: they showed no interest in making the new world safe for Catholics, Jews, Baptists, Shakers, or Lutherans. At the same time, other groups of Christians—George Fox and the Quakers in the seventeenth century, Alexander Campbell and the Disciples of Christ in the nineteenth century—were founded precisely because the divisions within Christianity inspired their founders to aim for a version of Christianity that would heal the wounds of division. Today, for the most part, Southern Baptists and Mormons have not been quick to be warmed by the fires of ecumenical fervor, and Catholics are cautious latecomers to ecumenical dialogue. These groups put a premium on their own particular understandings of Christianity and sometimes perceive efforts at unity as a dilution of the truth.

Nevertheless, there have been significant movements in modern Christianity to overlook differences in order to find some kind of unity of practice, or at the very least, unity of project. As we have noted, one of the largest Christian cooperative adventures of all times—the missionary movement—led logically to discussions about cooperation. Let us see how these impulses link together to form the beginnings of the ecumenical movement.

The missionary movement hoped to bring salvation to the whole world and stimulated some early interdenominational discussion in the nineteenth century. At the same time, evangelical Christians were crossing denominational lines during revivals, proving that Christians could worship together and experience God's grace in their lives even though they did not attend the same churches.

The Evangelical Alliance

The Evangelical Alliance, formed in London in 1846, was a coalition of interested individuals with no official connections with organized churches. The idea of an evangelical federation was extremely important for the beginnings of ecumenical dialogue. The American branch of the Evangelical Alliance, which because of the Civil War did not gather momentum until 1867, was meant to gather the efforts of evangelical Christians together for a number of social causes. Even before the Civil War, evangelical Christians often united for great causes. Recall that the conversion experience of Christians during the Second Great Awakening was both individual—a person was "saved" by accepting Jesus as a personal savior—and social. Christians were supposed to make their conversion felt in the world around them by supporting efforts to ban alcohol, slavery, and a host of other social ills. Little by little, the Evangelical Alliance became a powerful voice for missionary activity and an early advocate for ecumenical cooperation.

The journal of the Evangelical Alliance, *Evangelical Christendom*, called for cooperation among Christians, and the sponsorship of an annual week of prayer by this federation inspired the participation of more than 50,000 churches. Some members of the group saw evangelical cooperation as a sign that the kingdom of God was at hand, and all were committed to the principles of religious freedom. As such, the Evangelical Alliance provided strong theoretical support for Christian cooperation and stimulated some of the early discussions for the recovery of Christian unity. At the same time, the doctrinal foundations of evangelicalism—the emphasis on "born again" Christianity, for example—and its hostility toward Catholicism limited the ways this group could become an agent for full-blown Christian unity.

Increasingly, inspired by the *fact* of cooperation in groups like the Evangelical Alliance and stimulated by the scandal of diversity in various mission fields, Protestant Christians began to think in terms of national federations. Josiah Strong (1847–1916), one of the last great secretaries of the American branch of the Evangelical Alliance, resigned from that body to take a leading role in the formation of the Federal Council of Churches of Christ in America (1898). Unlike the Evangelical Alliance, which was a union of *individuals*, the Federal Council hoped to become a union of *churches* with an advisory function for member denominations. The Federal Council was formally convened in 1908 and united thirty-one major American denominations. By 1950, it had a membership of more than 32 million. The Evangelical Alliance brought a sense of common purpose to Christian life that enabled those with born-again experiences to work together in massive social movements whether or not they attended the same church. Their general commitment to social regeneration required cooperation.

The Student Movement

An important force for drawing these various enthusiasms together was the energy of nineteenth-century Christian students. Organized, in part, by the work of the revivalist preacher Dwight L. Moody, young Christian students grew interested in evangelization. Much as today's Inter-Varsity movement and Campus Crusade for Christ draw young people together for Christian purposes, student movements in the nineteenth century inspired a high level of Christian student activity. The young Scotsman who was the hero of the movie *Chariots of Fire* is a good example of the seriousness of many young people at the time.

A tremendously important young Methodist who dedicated his life to aspects of the missionary project was J. R. Mott (1865–1955), from Flint, Michigan. Mott was a leader in a fairly new movement, the Young Men's Christian Association (YMCA), founded in London in 1844 to win young men to Christ by uniting them in fellowship through their athletic activities. The YMCA—and later, the YWCA (founded in 1855)—were organizations designed to train the bodies and the minds of young people in order to make them conscious of the possibilities of Christian life. As an active student member, Mott became an officer and eventually rose to the position of secretary of its international committee. At an international convention in 1895, Mott founded and emerged as the first general secretary of the World Student Christian Federation (WSCF). He shared the general enthusiasm of its members, who hoped to win the world for Christ within their lifetimes.

The World Student Christian Federation was only one of the groups of students active in the nineteenth century. In England, the Student Christian Movement (SCM) was organized to enroll students in Bible study clubs. SCM was interdenominational and international. Imagine, therefore, what might happen if all three of these groups of devoted missionary enthusiasts—WSCF, SCM, and missionaries—were brought together for an international conference. They did meet together, at the Edinburgh World Missionary Conference in 1910. That meeting was a major turning point for interdenominational cooperation. Protestant and Anglican missionaries were eager to cooperate. They had begun to notice that the doctrinal and liturgical refinements separating them in England had little meaning in the mission fields and had begun to wonder what it would mean to work together. Their willingness to cooperate galvanized the students and led to the formation of the International Missionary Council, a coalition of missionaries and students all working for the evangelization of the world. This council, with its emphasis on missionary cooperation, sowed the seeds of the modern ecumenical movement.

ECUMENICAL COOPERATION: THE WORLD COUNCIL OF CHURCHES

The Edinburgh conference was a momentous event which stimulated interest among various church leaders. We have to stop for a moment to imagine the organizational structures of the churches at the time. Just as the Catholic church had the Vatican, a central office of church officials who decided policy questions and dealt with controversial issues of daily church life, most Protestant churches had bureaus—and bureaucrats—devoted to practical Christian life and to the expression of Christian belief. Two of these bureaus are of particular interest to us here: the Life and Work Bureau of a church routinely handled matters of practical Christianity, and the Faith and Order Bureau worked out new expressions of Christian doctrine and interpretation.

Little by little, these two church bureaus began to hold their own international conferences. The international meeting of Life and Work bureaus was held in 1925 to talk about ways to apply modern social and economic ideas to world Christianity. The international meeting of Faith and Order bureaus in 1927 opened discussion about the theological problems and basis of Christian unity. If the coming together of Christian students and missionaries produced amazing new energy for international Christianity and evangelization, what might it mean to combine the interests of these two major international bureaus? They both scheduled meetings in 1937: the Life and Work people gathered in Edinburgh; the Faith and Order people met in Oxford. The proximity of their separate meetings and their increasingly clear perception that cooperation was an ideal led them to the realization that they ought to be meeting together. Their plans for such a meeting were interrupted by the Second World War, but the seeds had taken root, and beginning in 1937, calls were increasingly heard for a "World Council of Churches."

The beginnings of the ecumenical movement were truly international. Church leaders in Sweden, Germany, and England, and representatives from most U.S. Protestant churches, along with leaders from Anglican and Eastern Orthodox churches, were eager participants in the discussion. All were passionate about the unity of the gospel and longed for a union of churches that would reflect the "one body of Christ." The great work of the 1927 Faith and Order conference was its "Call to Unity," a resolution, unanimously approved, that invited each Christian church to state its doctrines clearly so that all could be sensitive to the types and degrees of difference among them.

The World Council of Churches, which today has headquarters in Geneva, adopted a constitution at its first meeting in Amsterdam in 1948. It has been amended since then, but the WCC, which began with the cooperation of 144 church groups from forty-four countries, has lost none of its early enthusiasm. The council has met regularly since 1948 in various parts of the world and continues its interest in missionary activity. An important event at the 1961 meeting was the admission of Eastern Orthodox Christians to the WCC. It is ironic, in some ways, that this group was relatively late to be admitted to the body, since one of the early calls for ecumenical unity came from the Patriarch of Constantinople in 1920. Still, the fact that Orthodox Christians are members of the WCC, which now numbers more than 200 church groups, is important: Roman Catholics have still not joined, nor have most evangelical Christians.

In fact, many conservative Christians actively oppose the organization; some of them, who believe that the WCC is insufficiently attuned to Bible-based Christianity and too eager to adapt to changes in the modern world, even identify it with the anti-Christ. When the old Evangelical Alliance disbanded in 1944, many evangelical Christian groups joined the National Association of

Evangelicals, which has since joined the World Evangelical Fellowship as an alternative to participation in the WCC. Optimism about ecumenical unity, therefore, must be tempered with the facts: Catholics and conservative Christians have not been eager to be part of the World Council of Churches.

The World Conference on Faith and Order, now a department within the WCC, continues to work on major differences among the churches. As you can imagine, there are serious internal problems—such as the nature of the Eucharist and the possibilities for intercommunion—mixed with increasingly difficult external problems related to the ways Christianity can accommodate to the demands of modern culture or can address itself to the extraordinarily complex political realities in Third World countries. As we shall see in Chapter 12, the acceptance of Third World Christians as partners in dialogue about modern Christianity constitutes one of the most fruitful and difficult adjustments Christians are challenged to make in the modern world.

ECUMENICAL COOPERATION: PROBLEMS AND POSSIBILITIES

Ecumenical cooperation is not as difficult at the level of practical life as it appears to be at the level of belief. As long as doctrinal disputes can be avoided, in other words, it appears that ecumenical cooperation can become one of the shaping realities of modern Christianity. One of the early insights of the Faith and Order commission was a simple one: "Service unites, but doctrine divides." Some ecumenical leaders hoped that Christians could feature their unity of faith in Christ without focusing on doctrinal matters. In fact, however, Christians have serious differences, and the resistance of Southern Baptists and other evangelicals along with the caution of Roman Catholics is a vivid reminder of them. We should remember that American Lutherans were able to overcome most of their differences of perspective only in 1987. Many of the divisions in American Protestant churches that can be traced to the Civil War are still not healed, and churches that have managed to come to a unified understanding—United Methodists, for example—are today divided over other matters, like the proper role of the church in Central American countries.

Christians have been at odds for many years over issues like the number and nature of the sacraments, the sources of religious authority, the nature of the ministry, the nature of the church, and the goal of reunion itself. In 1952 the WCC listed four items that require special attention: the union of the church with Christ, the place of tradition, various modes of worship, and institutionalism were to form an agenda for ecumenical discussion for the next decades. Today the World Council of Churches recognizes the need for unity and makes major efforts to include groups that have resisted ecumenical dialogue, but representing the wishes of its membership, it also understands that unity, if it is ever to be achieved, must not gloss over the very real differences that divide Christians. The Roman Catholic church at the Second Vatican Council (1962–65) passed a decree on ecumenism that opened new possibilities for Catholic dialogue with Protestants and members of non-Christian religions, and that opening has been a major breakthrough for Catholics, but the problems are not reduced merely by a willingness to discuss them.

Ecumenism is not simply a matter of goodwill or congeniality. We need to remember that the ecumenical movement is a *search* for unity. Ecumenists often say that they hope to achieve a *restoration* of Christian unity, but we may wonder at that hope in light of the differences we have seen historically and will see in terms of contemporary challenges. It may be that the very richness and dynamism of Christianity demand the possibility of a range of liturgical and doctrinal expressions. At the same time, we should note that the possibilities for inter-denominational dialogue that the ecumenical movement has engendered constitute a genuine progressive step for Christianity in the modern world.

CONCLUSION

Chapters 7, 8, and 9 have suggested patterns of challenge and response for Christianity in the modern world. We have looked briefly at the nature of modernity to see the various ways Christians responded to the pressures of the Enlightenment and we have seen that some religious groups greeted modernity in a welcoming (liberal) fashion, while others reacted in a resisting (conservative) way. These general postures sometimes characterize entire churches: Southern Baptists tend to be conservative, for example, while Unitarians are understood to be religious liberals. Often we can find both liberal and conservative Christians within particular denominations.

We have also seen what can happen to Christianity in a totally new environment. The American context in the nineteenth century, with its millions of immigrants in a setting of church-state separation, led to experimentation and diversity. We have seen that Christianity refused to be defined by its European parameters and blossomed into a remarkable number of different expressions, including some totally new religions. Finally, we have noted the move toward cooperation and unity experienced by nineteenth- and twentieth-century Christians along with some caution and resistance to a unified Christianity.

The final section of this book is devoted to contemporary Christianity. As we might expect, Christians in today's world continue to find ways to unite their energies and to resist dialogue with one another. Contemporary Christianity needs to be understood in more than historical terms. We must recognize the fact that Christianity, whatever its hopes for unity, is extraordinarily diverse not only in its historical roots but in its responses to contemporary challenges.

The one conclusion we can draw from this section is that Christianity will not be forced out of existence by modern political and scientific theories. On the contrary, Christians have shown themselves to be creatively adaptive to the modern world in some cases and stubbornly resistant to it in others. All the developments that we have noted in this section—in response to modernity, in relation to the American adventure, and in light of calls for cooperation and unity—continue in the next as we attempt to understand Christianity within a different kind of framework.

CHAPTER 9 NOTES

[1] It is interesting and instructive to read first-person accounts of explorers to new worlds. Two classic texts in this regard take us to China and to Mexico. See *The Travels of Marco Polo*, translated and introduced by Ronald Latham (London: Folio Society, 1968), and Bernal Diaz, *The Conquest of New Spain*, translated and introduced by J. M. Cohen (London: Folio Society, 1974).

[2] A popular account of the history of the Jesuit mission in China is George H. Dunne, *A Generation of Giants* (Notre Dame, Ind.: University of Notre Dame Press, 1962). For a biblical parallel to Ricci's goal, see 1 Corinthians 9:20–23, where Paul explains *his* missionary strategy.

[3] Modern missionary theory has been distinguished by its attention to "missionary adaptation." In the Roman Catholic church, in particular, the documents of the Second Vatican Council are clear on this subject: missionaries are first enjoined to blend into the culture of the people to whom they wish to preach and to adapt their message to that situation. See the Vatican II document on the missions, *Ad Gentes* (1965), in any collection of the council documents. The Vatican Council document was stimulated, in part, by the modern experience of Catholic missionaries. A landmark book at the time, one that explains the history of previous mission theory and contrasts it with adaptation, was Alfonso M. Nebreda, *Kerygma in Crisis?* (Chicago: Loyola University Press, 1965).

[4] Stories of Christianity in India and Japan are also complicated histories of success and failure. For a look at Japanese missions, see R. H. Drummond, *A History of Christianity in Japan* (Grand Rapids: Eerdmans, 1971). For a general introduction to the situation in India, see S. C. Neill, *The Story of the Christian Church in India and Pakistan* (Grand Rapids: Eerdmans, 1970). You might also want to look up Francis Xavier (1506–52) in the *New Catholic Encyclopedia*. His work in India and Japan is the stuff of legend and he is remembered in Catholicism as the patron saint of the foreign missions. For a biblical parallel to Ricci's goal, see 1 Corinthians 9:20–23, where Paul explains *his* missionary strategy.

[5] The papal bull *Inter Cetera* was meant to settle the competition for trading and development in the new world. Since the pope was, therefore, involved in activity in the new world, he sent missionaries to that territory to protect the interests of the church. The problems that then confronted relations between church and state in the new world were extensions of old medieval church-state controversies. There is no need to know the details of this matter, but be aware that the situation was almost hopelessly complicated and that its ramifications have been carried down to the present day.

[6] For a brief introduction to the work of Spanish and French missionaries in the new world, see Jay P. Dolan, *The American Catholic Experience* (Garden City, N.Y.: Doubleday, 1985), pp. 15–68. Dolan shows that the Spanish program to "civilize" the Amerindians often led to the establishment of slave labor camps in which natives were worked to death and because of which entire populations began to disappear.

[7]You might want to look up information on some of the Jesuit missionaries to Amerindians: Isaac Jogues (1607–46) and his mission to the Mohawks, for example, or John de Brefeuf (1593–1649), sent to Canada as a missionary and one of the first to preach the gospel to the Hurons. Both of these men were killed by the Iroquois.

[8]A hymn often cited in this regard is "From Greenland's icy mountains," written by Reginald Herber, a minister, for a special worship service (1819) dedicated to missionary life. The hymn paints a picture of natives in India, Africa, and other parts of the world "calling for deliverance" and "bowing down to wood and stone" simply out of ignorance about the gospel. Herber wanted to inspire young Christians to bring "the lamp of salvation" to all nations so that Christ would be known everywhere and so could "in bliss return to reign." The attraction of missionary work, therefore, was strong: missionaries could enlighten those in darkness *and* hasten the Second Coming of Christ.

[9]Recall that early church councils were called ecumenical precisely because they aimed to include perspectives from Christian theologians and bishops from the whole known world (see Appendix 4).

SUGGESTIONS FOR FURTHER READING

1. The great source book for the history of the Christian missions is Kenneth Scott Latourette, *History of the Expansion of Christianity*, 7 vols. (London: Eyre & Spottiswoode, 1934–47). A shorter introduction is that of Stephen Neill, *A History of Christian Missions* (London: Penguin, 1964).

2. Two books that give some notion of the ways Christianity has changed religious life in Africa and has changed how missionaries think about their work are Lamin Sanneh, *West African Christianity* (Maryknoll, N.Y.: Orbis Books, 1983), and Vincent J. Donovan, *Christianity Rediscovered*, 2nd ed. (Maryknoll, N.Y.: Orbis Books, 1982).

3. An interesting introduction to Eastern Orthodox missionary theory is James J. Stamoolis, *Eastern Orthodox Mission Theology Today* (Maryknoll, N.Y.: Orbis Books, 1986). This is one of the first comprehensive surveys of Orthodox missiology published in the United States.

4. A comprehensive review of the literature on missionary context and practice is that of Charles W. Forman and Charles R. Tabor, "Recent Trends in Missiology," *Religious Studies Review* 13 (January 1987), 30–36.

5. A classic introduction to ecumenism is that of Robert McAfee Brown, *The Ecumenical Revolution: An Interpretation of the Catholic-Protestant Dialogue* (Garden City, N.Y.: Doubleday, 1967). Brown was an official Protestant observer at Vatican II. Two other general surveys are those of Samuel McCrea Cavert, *The American Churches and the Ecumenical Movement, 1900–1965* (New York: Association Press, 1968), and *Church Cooperation and Unity in America: A Historical Review, 1900–1970* (New York: Association Press, 1970).

6. For a picture of the modern ecumenical movement that shows some of the real practical problems involved, see Martin E. Marty, "The State of Disunion," *Commonweal* 115 (29 January 1988), 43–46. Marty's argument is that the ecumenical movement has slowed during the past two decades and is in need of some fresh leadership or new ideas.

❖ PART FOUR ❖

Contemporary Christian Life

NOW THAT WE have dealt with some aspects of the biblical background for Christianity, its history, and its general responses to the challenges of modernity, we will look at some of the ways Christians relate to the world and to their culture. And we will outline some of the contemporary problems Christians face in relation to the women's movement, Third World Christianity, modern fundamentalism, and modern liberalism.

Chapters 10 and 11 focus on some typical Christian responses to the world, particularly modern American culture, by showing variations of adaptation and resistance. The alternatives can be visualized as shown on the accompanying diagram, which is meant to suggest some of the differences among Christians in their attitudes toward the world and their culture. Many Christians experience a tension between the lure of the world on the one hand and the attractions of the church on the other. Let the jagged line between church and world define the field of interaction. How do modern Christians place themselves on this field?

Church /\/\/\/\/\/\/\ World

| Withdrawal | Nonconformity | Adaptation | Domination |
| (avoiding tension) | (coping with tension) | | (avoiding tension) |

We have already seen that the challenges of modernity generated responses that were sometimes positive and sometimes negative. In this section of the book, I will characterize these postures as those of resistance and accommodation and make some further distinctions. Some Christians resist the attractions of the modern world by *withdrawing* from contact with that world wherever possible. We will see that this attitude characterizes groups of Christians who may have nothing in common historically or doctrinally, but who *do* share some common assumptions about the ways Christians ought to relate to the surrounding culture.

Other Christians resist accommodation to modernity in a more active way: they take the field as combatants ready to assert what they understand to be essential Christian truths against the values of the modern world. I have called their position *nonconformity* because it is an attempt to define the field by way of the gospel rather than in the terms offered to it by the modern world. These groups are often linked by their beliefs that the words of Jesus about Christian behavior are to be taken literally. Accordingly, they tend to uphold pacifism, a simplified lifestyle, and racial harmony.

As we have seen, many Christians saw the challenges of modernity as calls for accommodation. Many Christians have adapted themselves to the modern world and do not see a great tension between the values of the gospel and the values of American culture. I have characterized their posture as *adaptation* because these groups tend to blend into the culture and find ways for the church to work within the American pluralistic system. Some adapted Christians are more liberal than others, but most share the conviction that Christian life does not require withdrawal from the world or active resistance to its principles.

Other Christians tend to adapt to the modern world in a different way. Like withdrawn Christians, they hope to avoid the tensions created by relations between the church and the world, but their preferred mode of action is different. I have characterized their position as that of *domination* because they attempt to resolve the tension by denying American pluralism and trying to dominate the society with their particular understanding of Christian life. Like withdrawn Christians, those in the position of domination hope to avoid the field of tension: withdrawn Christians flee from this tension, whereas domination Christians hope to obliterate it.

I will discuss those who resist the tension in Chapter 10 and those who cope with it in Chapter 11. I hope you will see that these categories are fluid and that one can just as well compare any set of postures. My purpose in arranging them as I have is simply to raise a series of rhetorical questions about the nature of the Christian life, and the relation of that life to modern political problems. The diagram will be explained more fully in Chapters 10 and 11. Chapter 12 will introduce a whole new set of contemporary questions and invite you to imagine how different groups of Christians respond to them.

CHAPTER 10

CHRISTIANS
AND THE WORLD

The Bible and history reflect a tension believers have often experienced between the demands of faith and the demands of life in the world. Christians have been warned to avoid the temptations of "the world, the flesh, and the devil." The meaning of these words—*world, flesh, devil*—has not always been clear, although people often have had more trouble describing *the world* than the other two. Sometimes *the world* is understood to include sinful enticements of the flesh and devilish preoccupations of pride, as well as temptations of power and greed. In this framework, a major tension exists between the values of the Christian faith or church and the values of the world, between the sacred and the secular. Some Christians regard the tension between the church and the world as no more than a reflection of the Christian belief in Original Sin; it simply points to an internal individual battle between good and evil desires. Whatever the understanding of the tension—and by all accounts the understandings are ancient—it has figured prominently in Christian experience.

A simple way of diagramming this idea is this:

Church /\/\/\/\/\/\/\/\/\/\ World

The jagged line represents tension. There are many different ideas about the nature of the church and the world. For purposes of our discussion, *church* is linked to the values of the Bible or Christian tradition, and *world* refers to the values of the surrounding culture. Individual denominations feel a pull from

187

both sides just as individual believers do; different religious denominations take significantly different positions within the tension. Because religion exists not in isolation but within a community of believers who live in the world, the community feels the tension between the attractions of the church (spiritual values, love of God and neighbor, specific moral values, and the hope of future happiness) on the one hand and the lures of the world (worldly values, material goods and power, love of oneself or one's culture, and satisfaction with the here and now) on the other. If the two poles of the tension can be said to set limits, the diagram of possibilities might look like this:

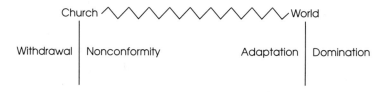

Here *church* is idealized and never perfectly realized and *world* encompasses a wide range of meanings, some positive and some odious. Most religious denominations work out their existence within the boundaries of the tension and take different positions within the middle area of the diagram. But this chapter describes two attitudes toward the world that support positions—radically different from one another—outside the limits of the tension.

The withdrawn position is placed on the *Church* end of the scale because the motivation for it usually derives from religious purity or perfection and a longing to achieve the ideal; domination is placed on the *World* end of the spectrum because its tactics and strategies often derive from worldly or political power. Both groups have definite attitudes toward the world—usually negative ones—and both seek to avoid or live outside the tension between the world and the church. Those who withdraw from the tension usually create their own worlds within the church and therefore widen the space between the limits of church and world. They respond to the tension by pushing the world far away. Those who take a position of domination usually extol the values of the world insofar as those values can be controlled by the church. They reduce the space between the church and the world—may even obliterate it—by imposing church values on the world.

WITHDRAWN COMMUNITIES

Groups that withdraw from the tension want little or nothing to do with the world; they think of themselves as removed from the world or standing entirely against its values. At least three forms of withdrawal are possible: physical, cultural, and psychological. Any of these forms may allow for some interaction with the world, but that interaction is perceived as an unwelcome necessity.

Members of all these groups are united in their belief that the secular world interferes with their religious lives.

Why would a religious group choose to withdraw from the world? There are at least two general aims: purity and perfection. Perfection is a positive striving toward a spiritual ideal; purity here means seeking to defend one's values and culture from the harmful ways of the world. Some believers, in order to keep their beliefs, practices, and lives free from taint, separate themselves from those who do not share their convictions and concerns. The less contact they have with people in the world, the more likely, they feel, their religious life is to remain constant and pure. Another reason for withdrawing to attain purity derives from a perception of the world as an evil place, a den of iniquity and a hotbed of temptation. According to this view, the world is the place of the flesh and the devil; it feeds on vice, narcotics, gambling, and prostitution; one keeps pure and out of the reach of temptation by staying away from the world.

A second aim of withdrawal is perfection. Some groups feel called to live a more rigorous, more communitarian, or more "perfect" life than can be lived in the world. Jesus commanded people to love one another, but also added these challenging words: "If you would be *perfect*" (Matt. 19:21) then sell all you own, give the money to the poor, and follow me. Some people have believed that following Jesus means withdrawing from the world. The monastic vows of poverty, chastity, and obedience (discussed in Chapter 4) have often been called counsels of *perfection* and they have been built on a strategy of withdrawal from the world. Some withdrawn communities have been separate religious entities and have been physically, culturally, and psychologically withdrawn from the world. Nineteenth-century communitarian groups (discussed in Chapter 8) were often withdrawn at all levels and lived out their specific interpretations of the Christian life as separate, intentional communities.

Physical Withdrawal: Monastic Communities

Many withdrawn groups are parts of larger communities of faith. Monastic communities represent a specific vocation within a particular kind of Christianity and are usually a small part of the larger religious group. They are separated from the larger group not by differing beliefs but as a special way of life within that larger community. Monks and nuns are a significant part of Orthodox Christianity, Roman Catholicism, and Anglicanism. The monastic vision has been discussed already (in Chapter 4) and need not be repeated here. Monastic life is an example of physical withdrawal from the world. Monks and cloistered nuns live in self-contained communities apart from the world and often in isolated places. Monasteries and convents have existed from very ancient times and some contemporary monasteries provide a way of life that has not changed much in centuries. Some modern monasteries are a blend of the old and the new: they trace their origins to ancient religious communities but also accept some contemporary ideas. Ecumenical monastic experiments embrace a variety of believers in physically withdrawn settings.[1] Monasteries usually are a world unto themselves, and often are self-contained places that provide for their own physical needs. Monastic separation from the world is supported by nonmonastic believers in the same denomination and is seen as one valid embodiment of the Christian life.

Cultural Withdrawal: The Amish

Sometimes a withdrawn community expresses the pure extreme of a particular religious viewpoint, which itself has undergone some significant changes; it is separated from the world and, in some senses, from its parent group. The Amish are an example of cultural withdrawal: they share a sectarian viewpoint with other Radical Reformation groups, but have separated from those groups precisely over the issue of involvement in the world.

A word about sectarianism. Sociologist of religion Ernst Troeltsch (1865–1923) distinguished between church and sect and characterized sect-type Christianity as emphasizing an individual religious experience, voluntary membership, and radical obedience to Christian ethics as specified in the words of Jesus.[2] It appeals to the life and beliefs of the primitive church and specific attitudes toward the world. Sectarians aim at personal fellowship and inward perfection and have no desire to dominate the world; they are indifferent or even hostile to the world and tend to be suspicious of worldly ways. Troeltsch's distinctions cannot adequately describe the American religious situation—some groups that otherwise fit his "sect" category are not withdrawn from the world and are not necessarily hostile to the political order—but they do serve to describe the Amish viewpoint.

In some senses the Amish have built a world of their own, but not for monastic reasons. Monks and nuns are often willing to adopt some of the conveniences of the modern world; their withdrawal does not necessarily reflect a negative judgment of surrounding culture, though their lives are decidedly simple. The Amish refuse to be part of the general society—the world—and they refuse to conform to cultural values or adopt modern conveniences. To their way of thinking, God's law has a specific rhythm that cannot be interrupted by the contrivances of the modern world. They do not drive cars but continue to use horses and buggies. They have nothing against the gasoline engine—indeed, they will ride in other people's cars, and one can sometimes see an Amish farmer using a horse-drawn wagon and a gasoline-powered cutting machine—but have a sense of life's pace that will not be hurried or overwhelmed by modern gadgets. They have no electricity—except in places where Amish bishops have deemed it acceptable as a way to cool milk and comply with state dairy laws—and are not disturbed by television and radio. The values of the world are not automatically adopted as their values, and their cultural and religious ways—styles of life, patterns of worship, language, and dress—have remained much the same for centuries.

The Amish are a small group; they have definite and rigorous qualifications for admission. Their idea of community is intimate and physical: they believe that one must identify with a concrete local group. They are, accordingly, perfectly sectarian, but have also chosen to remain culturally withdrawn—unconformed—as well. Some groups that were originally sectarian were slow to change and to adapt to new ways, but have adapted to the society in which they live. The Amish, on the other hand, are bound to their withdrawn position by their understanding of the world and its culture as inherently destructive of their religious life.

Psychological Withdrawal: Millennialist Christians

Many Christian groups—especially those with highly developed eschatological consciousness (those anticipating the end of the world in their lifetime)—are withdrawn from the world in mind and heart only. They live and work in the world, do not establish themselves as isolated communities (like monks and nuns), and are not hostile to modernity; yet they create worlds of their own in such a way that they exemplify psychological withdrawal. All these groups—Adventists, Pentecostals, Jehovah's Witnesses, some fundamentalist Christians, and Dispensationalists—share certain attitudes about the world: they perceive the world as an evil place and tend to see all others as outsiders in relation to their own world in the church.

Most of the individuals in these groups take a dim view of the world; it is a place of seduction by alcohol, drugs, or sex.[3] They work in the world but are mentally and behaviorally removed from it. A rousing hymn states the theme: "Take the world but give me Jesus, I won't go back [to the world and its vices], I won't go back." Testimony during religious services often takes a world-disparaging form: "When I was in the world I drank [or gambled or was unfaithful] but now that I am here [in the church] I am free from those things."[4] Preaching compares those in the church with those in the world in such a way that the worldly ones are invariably wicked, misguided, and not worthy to be part of God's entourage when Jesus comes again.

Most of these millennialist Christians live their lives within the framework of their organization: Bible study meetings, working for church concerns, social events within the churches, and various missionary enterprises (in the case of Jehovah's Witnesses, going door to door with a religious message) take up much of their lives outside work and family time. Their friends and family are (ideally) church members, and their reading and interests are very much defined by their religious preoccupations. Often television and movies are denigrated and drinking, smoking, and dancing forbidden entirely.

These groups are united primarily by their millennialist views. They eagerly await the end of the world and interpret political events and worldly happenings predictively, as part of God's plan. They build upon an apocalyptic scenario culled from the Bible, especially from some chapters in Daniel and from the

Book of Revelation. In the apocalyptic vision set forth in those books one can find a general plan: the world is dominated by an evil power (often shown as a beast or a tyrannical ruler); that evil power persecutes the saints and treats them shamefully; suddenly the saints are able to rise up and overthrow the beast or evil potentate; and the saints inherit the earth or reign in heaven. In that vision no one wants to be on the side of the world. *All* Christians are enjoined to remember that no one knows the day or the hour when Jesus will return and they are, accordingly, supposed to be always ready. In many millennialist groups, however, the readiness goes hand in hand with fear and/or assurance; in both cases the world figures heavily as an evil place.

Summary of Withdrawn Communities

All these various religious groups—monks and nuns, the Amish, Adventists, Pentecostals, Jehovah's Witnesses, dispensationalist Christians and some fundamentalist Christians—differ from one another theologically, historically, and in terms of doctrine and practice. But they are bound together by their relationship to the tension between the world and the church; they all seek to avoid that tension by withdrawing from the world. All see the necessity of being in some way separated from the world, but they differ about how and why that separation should occur. They are united in believing that the world interferes with their goals of purity or perfection, but they have different attitudes toward that interference and toward the world itself.

Monastic life is built on the notion of withdrawal from a *distracting* world. Monks and nuns do not hate the world, but choose to withdraw from it in order to "pray without ceasing" (1 Thess. 5:17)—to pray for the world and the people in it even while they pursue their own spiritual journeys. The religious traditions that support monastic life—Orthodox Christianity, Roman Catholicism, and Anglicanism—all believe that the world, created by God, is good and not evil. They may quarrel with specific worldly positions but they do not, by definition, hate the world. Monasteries stand as a witness to a specific way of Christian life. The desire to leave the world, monks and nuns believe, is the result of a distinct and special call by God to an individual; other individuals are called to life in the world.

The Amish withdraw from the world because the world is a *threatening* place where the time-honored ways of their ancestors are not respected. The world is a place of change—not fundamentally motivated by religious concerns—and their policy of cultural withdrawal is based on their own needs for preservation; they hope to conserve their culture and way of life, which they believe is better suited to the commands of Scripture. Many of them have a hostility toward the world and tend to see it as irredeemable and not worth bothering with; in that way they reflect something of the spirit of sectarianism. There is no need, in a sectarian model, to get involved with politics or other worldly preoccupations. The life that matters is the life of the church, and the church exists in the small group that lives out its convictions without reference to the world. The Amish do not make much attempt to draw others into their life despite the active missionary stance of their Anabaptist predecessors. To a great extent, one is born into an Amish way of life and then is asked to choose whether or not to accept it when one gets to be an adult. Often those who reject it must leave farm, family, and the whole way of life.

Millennialist Christians view the world under the influence of their apocalyptic understanding as an *evil* place dominated by evil powers. By virtue of their hopes and beliefs they tend to hate the world and to denigrate its ways. The world is not simply distracting or threatening to a specific way of life, it is evil and predatory and to be avoided at all costs. Unlike the Amish and monastic communities, most millennialist Christians proselytize with vigor. Withdrawal from the world is not a matter of vocation or of birth, but a matter of perceiving the state of things and asking for admission into the group that stands ready and waiting for the return of the Lord. Jehovah's Witnesses, especially, are tireless in their door-to-door ministry, and many other groups, such as Pentecostals, support a wide network of local and foreign missionary activity. Assurance of salvation and methods of increasing church membership differ among them, but they are all zealous to draw as many as possible into the church and away from the world.

All these groups build their own worlds in some ways. Monks and nuns build a physical world of their own in order to pursue their relationships with God apart from the distractions of the world. The Amish live in their own cultural world and live on their own terms and at their own pace so that their religious beliefs are not threatened by modern conveniences, language, and ideas. Millennialist Christians build their own worlds psychologically in their churches; the church is the social and religious center of their lives, a place safe from the dangers of the outside world.

DOMINATING POSTURES

Another way to avoid the tension between the church and the world is to obliterate it by making one's religious views predominate in a society. Those who master the tension do so by conquering the world with a religious point of view, by attempting to shape the life and values of the world in a particular religious way. If a society is dominated by Christian values, Christians do not feel the tension; the sacred so imposes itself on the secular that they become as one. Theocratic states operate on this principle: they are governments by God administered through a church or one of God's special agents. Calvin's experiment in Geneva is one historical example of domination; the medieval papacy of the Catholic church is another.[5]

Why would a religious group seek to avoid the tension by dominating the general society? There are probably many reasons, and most of them derive from negative views of the world or highly optimistic evaluations of human potential within the world. The medieval popes saw worldly princes as dangerous to the aims of religion; one way to understand the designs of Pope Gregory VII is through the slogan "Dominate or be dominated." Gregory inherited an abysmal situation[6] in terms of power politics, and the church-state arguments that plagued the Catholic church from the eleventh through the nineteenth centuries in some ways reflected his hope to dominate opposing rulers in order to make the world ready to hear the gospel. Some nineteenth-century religious leaders were so enamored of human progress and the power of the gospel that they hoped to build the kingdom of God on earth. This plan presupposes that the general society ought to be shaped into that kingdom, to be dominated by a particular religious view whether the society is willing to be shaped to that vision or not. Some groups want to assume political power for themselves in order to establish what they perceive as a more Christian society.

No one Christian group can dominate American society and there is little point in worrying about the renewal of medieval papal policies or Calvinist theocracies in the contemporary world. The *mentality* of domination, however, does survive in at least two ways: politically and financially. Since these ways take in a broad range of activity, they cannot be primarily associated with particular Christian groups and will be discussed here more as attitudes present in many different Christian communities and embodied in certain plans or movements. Like the discussion of the withdrawal mentality, this one gathers disparate groups together that otherwise would not be discussed in the same chapter, in an attempt to look at a range of Christian groups with a different lens.

Political Domination

Political domination as a religious strategy is a willingness to use political means to impose a religious viewpoint on everyone. Historically it was adopted by the Roman Catholic church and, later, by Calvinists, Anglicans, and Lutherans. One of the wrenching arguments of the Reformation was over the appropriateness of the Christian desire for political support of its views; much of the hostility of many Christians toward sectarian or Radical Reformation groups derives from the sectarian unwillingness to be allied with the political order. Groups that subscribe to political domination usually want some sector of the government or the society at large to conform to their particular religious interpretations; they hope to link a religious position to a political one and to pursue them as a single (usually religious) entity. We will look at three contemporary manifestations of the religious strategy of political domination here: liberation theology, the antiabortion amendment, and "Christian" political solutions.

Liberation theology. The theology of liberation is based on a reading of the Bible in which God is perceived as a liberator of captives (in the Exodus) and Jesus as identified with the poor.[7] According to this view, God's primary interest lies with the poor: they are the objects of divine concern in the Old Testament (see the Prophets, especially), and the ones to whom Jesus brings the message of salvation. It is argued that all Christians who want to imitate Jesus should work for the elimination of oppression, a task that may mean working to overthrow corrupt and exploitive political structures. Liberation theology is not entirely clear on its relation to violence: some who accept the premise that God has a preferential option for the poor also believe that nonviolent means are the only appropriate ones for a Christian; others believe that the abuse perpetrated by economic or political systems on the poor cannot be changed except through violent revolution. Whatever its position on violence, liberation theology is usually revolutionary: its adherents seek to replace an existing regime with a different, more "Christian" one. Liberation theology has found its most fervent adherents in Latin America—indeed, liberation theology may be seen as a creative contribution to world Christian thought from Latin America and parts of Africa—where totalitarian governments and multinational corporations are regarded as exploitive institutions that undermine more "Christian" socialist experiments. Liberation theology uses a combination of religious and political methods, methods that change according to the particular situation, to achieve its aim. The aim is consistent and clear: to bring what is perceived to be God's love for the poor into the political realm in order to create a Christian society.

The antiabortion amendment. Some religious groups use *constitutional* power to promote their views in order to dominate the entire society with them. The campaign on the part of a variety of Christians—Roman Catholic, fundamentalist, and conservative Christian churches—to secure a constitutional amendment against abortion is an example of this strategy.[8] The point to my inclusion of them here is not their belief that abortion is a sin, but their willingness to use political means to get all of society to behave according to their views. Other Christians may perceive abortion as wrong, but also see it as the proper concern of the church, not the state. The purpose of the amendment strategy is to make abortion a crime, to put the state in a position to punish those who commit what these Christians perceive as a grave sin.

"Christian" political solutions. Religious groups on both the right and left wings of the political spectrum can seek to enforce their religious views *politically* in the belief that society will be better if all people live according to their ethic—willingly or unwillingly. Some right-wing Christians—for example, members of the Moral Majority in the 1980s—identified their religious beliefs with conservative political views and linked Christianity itself with a specifically conservative political agenda. These Christians take political positions—against communism, against welfare, in support of capital punishment and conservative fiscal policy—and tie them up with God's will or the gospel. Their reading of the Old Testament and the words of Jesus leads them to a political-religious viewpoint that is essentially right-wing. On the other end of the spectrum, some

large church organizations—the World Council of Churches, for example—have sometimes supported left-wing political viewpoints. In certain circumstances they have identified their religious beliefs with select revolutionary movements, and have given financial support to aid victims of "liberation movements" (like the revolution in Zimbabwe). Their reading of the Old Testament and the Gospels leads them to a political posture that is left-wing. In both cases—from the right and from the left—churches and church members have been asked to endorse political viewpoints as if they were both the clearest readings of the gospel and the best course for worldly governments.

Financial Domination

Financial domination is the propensity to tie the Christian message to money in such a way as to control the society. What does one find in the Gospels about money? In the synoptic Gospels we find a story about a rich man who wished to follow Jesus. He had kept all the commandments and wondered what else he should do. Jesus told him to sell everything, give the money to the poor, and follow him, whereupon the rich man changed his mind and went away. His inability or unwillingness to do as Jesus asked inspired Jesus to say, "It is easier for a camel to go through the eye of a needle than for a rich man to enter the kingdom of God" (Mark 10:25). What do these words mean? If fidelity to God's law is bound up with justice, sharing, and concern for the poor—there is also Old Testament evidence for this—then it seems Jesus means that it is virtually impossible to have much money and be faithful to God. On a literal level the words mean what they say: being rich is dangerous and keeps one away from the kingdom of God. On an allegorical level, however, one can say that Jesus asked the young man to get rid of his *attachment* to money; one can be rich, but cannot be obsessed with riches.[9]

The question turns, to some extent, on what one thinks about poverty. On a practical level people cannot "feed the hungry" if they are poor themselves; on the other hand, Jesus seemed sometimes to have a particular concern for the poor. The Beatitudes reflect Christian ambivalence: in the Gospel of Luke, Jesus says, "Blessed are the poor" (6:20); in Matthew's gospel, Jesus says, "Blessed are the poor *in spirit*" (5:3).

We have already seen that poverty was accepted as a value in monastic life and understood as one of the counsels of perfection. In the Middle Ages new religious orders were established—the Franciscans, for example, founded by Francis of Assisi (1182–1226)—that valued poverty for its own sake; church laws protected the poor and reminded the rich of their obligations to all people who lived in poverty. Poverty became a pressing religious issue during the industrial revolution from the mid-eighteenth to mid-nineteenth centuries. As we have seen, the Salvation Army, founded by William Booth (1829–1912), was a specifically religious response to poverty in England.

American Christianity in the nineteenth and twentieth centuries took two fundamentally different positions on poverty: the Social Gospel and the Gospel of Wealth. One extolled collective responsibility and the other advocated self-help; both grounded themselves in an interpretation of Scripture. The Social Gospel, a theory associated with the teachings of Walter Rauschenbusch (1861–1918), offered a theological justification for collective responsibility for the poor. Poverty, Rauschenbusch believed, was a disgrace and a blight on the Christian conscience that ought to be addressed by Christians in terms of building the kingdom of God on earth. The Gospel of Wealth, rooted in American self-confidence and the work ethic, offered a theological justification for self-help: the poor were exhorted to change their lives and to pull themselves up by their bootstraps, and well-to-do Christians were absolved of obligations to change society or to work for the elimination of poverty. Both were religious responses to the social conditions of the nineteenth century and both were colored by strong feelings (in different directions) toward the rise of American capitalism. In some ways this argument about poverty and social ills reflected a fundamental argument in Christianity between personal salvation and the regeneration of society. Are Christians bound to look after the society in which they live, or are their efforts to be primarily directed at their own personal salvation? The conflict between the Social Gospel and the Gospel of Wealth did not settle that controversy: it continues down to our own day.

The Social Gospel. Rauschenbusch argued, in a series of books and articles, that capitalism and individualism had numbed the Christian conscience. Poverty was not a divine curse (as some had suggested), but was a result of human exploitation. The poor, said Rauschenbusch, were victims, and Christian men and women had an obligation to care for them. He believed that the church was the vehicle to be used for spreading the kingdom of God on earth, and he perceived the kingdom of God to be concerned primarily with social justice. Rauschenbusch tried to combine both sides of the argument: he did not think that external improvements by themselves were sufficient, but believed that social or collective concern was related to personal regeneration as well. A person was truly Christian only insofar as he or she was concerned both for personal salvation and for changing the societal structures of oppressed peoples.

The Social Gospel, as espoused by most of its adherents, belongs in the category of domination because it was a justification for imposing a specific vision of God's will on the churches and, through them, to "Christianize" all of society. Rauschenbusch's followers hoped to establish the kingdom of God on this earth, by which they meant they wanted the churches to change the social order by supporting a specific political program. The Social Gospel understanding of Christianity was essentially collective: it hoped to use the churches and the political structure to put this view (with its economic ideas) into practice in the general society, to create the kingdom of God on earth.

The Gospel of Wealth. Many Christians, however, had a quite different idea about responding to poverty. Led by their belief in individual salvation, they argued that one did not change social structures but tried, instead, to change human hearts. The Gospel of Wealth also reflected some other theories current in the nineteenth century, though its basic belief was in the necessity of individual salvation. The doctrine of predestination as accepted by some Christian churches led them to believe that God was interested only in the elect and that poverty was a sign that a person or a family was not part of God's chosen few. The work of Charles Darwin on the evolution of the species and the popular slogan about the survival of the fittest led many people to look upon the poor as morally unfit, a position known as Social Darwinism. Sociologists linked poverty with crime as surely as some church members associated it with sinfulness.[10] Some Christians saw poverty as a divine curse or punishment for sin, and if poverty was a divine curse, then it was the will of God, and working to eliminate poverty was tantamount to opposing God's will. These Christians took the words of Jesus, "The poor you will always have with you" (Matt. 26:11), as a mandate to leave the structures of poverty in place while, at the same time, exhorting the poor to move up out of them. Some Christian preachers saw riches as a sign of God's favor and the kingdom of God as a kingdom of wealth, as a place where the morally fit should be allowed to make money. Rich Christians acknowledged their great wealth as a sign of approval by divine providence.[11]

In contemporary terms, a version of the Gospel of Wealth is supported by some conservative Christians who think Jesus would have supported the American dream had he known about it. According to them, the economic system of America is bound up with God's plan: preachers assure their members that God wants them to be rich, that a believing Christian will never go under financially. In some ways they hope to demonstrate that it "pays to believe in Jesus." The sign of salvation for these preachers—who can be seen regularly on television—is prosperity. The Gospel of Wealth belongs in the category of domination because it adopts the financial values of the culture and equates them with the values of religion: it avoids the tension between the secular and the sacred by imposing religious approval on a particular economic system.

Financial perspectives from the left (collective) and from the right (individualist) both tend to associate economic positions with God's will. Both ground their beliefs in a reading of Scripture and believe that they have rightly interpreted the divine will. Both want the society at large to conform to an economic stance they regard as "more Christian."

Summary of Dominating Postures

All these religious attitudes—liberation theology, support of a constitutional amendment against abortion, varieties of "Christian politics," the Social Gospel and the Gospel of Wealth—differ from one another radically in terms of religious interpretation and ultimate goals. But they are bound together by their desire to eliminate the tension between the church and the world by imposing a specific religious perspective on the general society. All of them consider it appropriate for Christians to impose a particular viewpoint on all members of a society, though they employ different strategies in pursuit of that imposition. Most of them can be classified on either the right or left wing of the political spectrum, and in that way they reflect perennial arguments within the society.

Liberation theologians have been active mostly in Roman Catholic countries and reflect a serious pastoral problem within Roman Catholicism as that church relates to its members in Third World countries. It is usually a left-wing, socialist movement attempting to work out the doctrines and practices of the Roman Catholic church in repressive political climates. The coalition that supports a constitutional amendment against abortion is made up of conservative church members from a number of denominations. It is heavily Roman Catholic, but has strong support from Baptists, evangelical Christians, and fundamentally conservative Christian groups. Specifically "Christian" political ideologies manifest themselves as right-wing political attitudes in some sectors of the evangelical churches and have been active to some extent in the attempted politicization of such organizations as the Campus Crusade for Christ. They have taken on left-wing or radical political embodiments in large interchurch groups like the World Council of Churches. One of the results of this overt political activity among Christians has been a new wedge of divisiveness among Christians: they are no longer divided simply along denominational lines; now those denominational lines have political agendas as well. Some conservative or right-wing evangelical Christians tend to adopt the attitude of the Gospel of Wealth. Modern adherents of the Social Gospel theory tend to be left-wing or socialist Christians. All of them perceive their position as the one sanctioned and supported by the Gospels.

All these groups hope, in some way, to alleviate problems within society and all of them hope to do that on "Christian" grounds. Their strategies are those of domination: all hope society (or the political structure) will be run according to their reading of the Gospels.

QUESTIONS RAISED BY THE POSTURES
OF WITHDRAWAL AND DOMINATION

The reason for making these general interpretations of some Christian attitudes about the world is to see what kinds of questions can be raised by such radically different attitudes and ideas. All these groups, whether they adopt a strategy of withdrawal or domination, take their positions on the basis of their readings of Scripture. The life and words of Jesus provide the support they need for their positions. The very notion that such different attitudes are legitimate embodiments of the Christian vision, however, raises interesting questions.

Consider the question of the church and the world, especially in terms of political action. If the church is made up of members who believe that they in some way understand God's will and corporately reflect God's intentions, words, and actions, then we must first speculate a moment about God. According to the Bible and traditional Christian belief, God is perfect, eternal, invisible, and the source of absolute truth. How do these attributes correspond with the political order of the world? God is perfect, yet societies are imperfect; does an attempt to raise them to perfection—to an embodiment of divine will—invite frustration and violence? Or is it a real possibility that Christians have an obligation to pursue? God is eternal and invisible, yet societies are visible and continually changing; does a Christian political vision deny the necessity of change to societies? God possesses absolute truth, yet societies can reflect only relative truths; does a Christian approach to the situation obviate the room for disagreement that has historically been a part of all societies? These are general questions, but there are more specifically religious questions as well.

In What Sense Is Christianity Political?

The first question within this question is definitional: What does *political* mean? If it means "worldly" politics, some Christians would answer that Christianity is not at all political and should not be. These believers might cite the words of Jesus, "Render therefore to Caesar the things that are Caesar's and to God the things that are God's" (Matt. 22:21), and argue that Jesus was more interested in changing people's minds and hearts than he was in changing political structures. Others might wonder how it is so clear what things belong to Caesar and what things belong to God and argue from the Bible that God loves the weak, clothes the naked, visits the sick, comforts the afflicted, cares for widows and orphans, feeds the hungry, and buries the dead, and that Christians must work toward those ends—even politically—within the society.

If politics can be described broadly as the way people deal with the structures and affairs of the government (or state), then some people might argue that "Christian" politics do not correspond to the aims and tactics of traditional politics. The politics of Jesus, they might say, are revolutionary because they attempt to deal with political questions in fundamentally new ways. [12] Christians, according to this view, are enjoined to behave differently from everyone else: they are to follow Jesus's words and example by turning the other cheek, doing good to those who persecute them, and loving their enemies. If this is the case, then the political action of Christians becomes a way of life inherently different from and in some ways hostile to the political action of the state; the ethic of the church is an alternative to the ethic of surrounding society. On these grounds some Christians refuse to support wars and violence, and manifest their political consciousness precisely by embodying a different sort of society from the one embodied in the surrounding culture.

What Is the Church?

The same sorts of arguments arise with this question. Is the church an agent to promote societal change and to create a better life for all? Or is it the kingdom of the saved, the fellowship of personal regeneration, with no obligations to the larger society? Is the church a small body of believers who embody the kingdom of God and invite other people to become a part of it? Or is it a large organization that uses its power as an aggressive social agency? Does the church transcend the world in such a way that it must refuse to become involved in secular values and questions? Or is it necessarily involved in the world and somehow responsible for its values?

Is the church a prophetic fellowship that speaks out on injustice but leaves the remedy of injustice to secular agencies? Or are church members to take a prophetic stand within the secular world by working for specific political goals? Is the church a moral educator responsible for raising the consciousness of its members and other people by working for a better world? Or is the church the kingdom of God already come and yet still waiting to become the kingdom, the place in which one should be born again and wait for the coming of the Lord? Is the kingdom of God within the individual believer? Or is it a possible model for the general society? How does the kingdom come? Do believers create the kingdom on earth by virtue of their own works and political vision? Or is it entirely an act of God that makes human efforts worthless?

What Is the Christian Vision of Jesus?

We have already seen that presuppositions about Jesus color the way one interprets the Christian vision. The questions of who Jesus was and what he hoped for are crucial to this issue. Was Jesus primarily a man of prayer who inspired people to withdraw from the world in order to pray for it? Was Jesus a revolutionary interested in the political order? Was he concerned primarily with the individual believer? Or was his concern primarily for the future of his movement, and not for the general society? Did Jesus speak as a political figure and imply that Christians are competent to speak out on political issues? Or was Jesus manifestly not interested in political values, implying that Christians ought only to be interested in their personal relationships to God through him?

If believers take a purely social-reform approach to Christian life, do they ignore the underlying issues of temptation, greed, and evil in the human heart? Is a purely political approach naive, acting as if the elimination of poverty and injustice also eliminates people's grasping and selfish interests? Must one also seek spiritual elevation and moral earnestness? If believers take a purely evangelical approach to Christian life, is that enough? Is there a valid point in the historical example of converted Christians with good hearts and good intentions who continued to own slaves and to participate in the sweatshop abuse of women and children? Is there a way to both be personally converted to Jesus *and* to work toward a better society? Was Jesus socially conscious—eager for the welfare of the weak—as well as interested in the personal conversion of his followers? Does faith in Jesus require service in the world?

CONCLUSION

None of the questions this chapter raises about the relationship of Christians to the world can be answered simply. Those Christians who take a position of withdrawal or a position of domination have different answers, all of which are based on a careful reading of the Gospels and a thoughtful understanding of Jesus and his desires. How people can read the Gospels so differently is one of the continually perplexing questions in Christianity. The questions have not been raised here in order to confuse you, but as an attempt to broaden your understanding of the complexity of Christian belief and behavior. Other questions could also be raised, but there are enough here to indicate that there is no single Christian position on these issues, and that the arguments within the Christian community are worthy of consideration.

CHAPTER 10 NOTES

[1] One experimental group that has been in existence for more than twenty years is the Spiritual Life Association of America in Sedona, Arizona. It was begun by a Carmelite monk, William McNamara, as a contemporary ecumenical community of men and women living in the desert according to a modified monastic rule. See Walter Burghardt, "Without Contemplation the People Perish," *America* 127 (22 July 1972), 29–32.

[2] Troeltsch's work is dated and is not meant to be a last word here but is offered as a clear, general view. See *The Social Teachings of the Christian Church* (London: Allen & Unwin, 1931), pp. 331–43. For a more thorough understanding of the complexities of sectarianism, see Bryan R. Wilson, *Patterns of Sectarianism* (London: Heinemann Educational Books, 1967).

[3] One can find this view exposed by an ex-believer in Barbara Grizzuti Harrison, *Visions of Glory: A History and a Memory of Jehovah's Witnesses* (New York: Simon & Schuster, 1978). Like many ex-believers, Harrison has an axe to grind and you should read this book with a clear understanding of her presuppositions: it is *not* an objective history of the movement. I cite it here because she captures the "world-hating" posture clearly (see pp. 213–20).

[4] These quotations—from songs, sermons, and testimony—are ones I have picked up by attending various churches in southern Indiana, Mississippi, Ohio, and Texas over the last few years. I take them to be typical.

[5] A contemporary non-Christian example was Iran under the leadership of the Ayatollah Khomeini.

[6] For some indication of how bad a state the papacy was in when Gregory became pope, read about the House of Theophylact in E. R. Chamberlin, *The Bad Popes* (New York: New American Library, 1969), pp. 35–83.

[7] See the discussion of liberation theology in Chapter 12.

[8] Not all Roman Catholics support a constitutional amendment against abortion. Catholics for a Free Choice, with national headquarters in Washington, D.C., represents

those who do *not* agree with the position and strategy of the Catholic bishops on the abortion issue.

⁹This is the position of Clement of Alexandria (d. 215), one of the early Christian writers (see Appendix 3), whose sermon on the text from Mark 10:17–31 gives a symbolic or allegorical interpretation of the passage rather than a literal one.

¹⁰Robert Dugdale (between 1874 and 1876) devised a criminal theory that linked crime, poverty, and heredity. For a discussion of his theory in an unusual and fascinating setting, see Michael Lesy, *Wisconsin Death Trip* (New York: Random House, 1973), the conclusion (not paginated).

¹¹See, for example, Russell H. Conwell, *Acres of Diamonds* (New York: Harper Brothers, 1915). On another level, a rich person like Andrew Carnegie could satisfy his Christian duty *not* by giving money to the poor, but by endowing libraries where they could further their educations and lift themselves up.

¹²For a further explication of this position, see John Howard Yoder, *The Politics of Jesus* (Grand Rapids: Eerdmans, 1972).

SUGGESTIONS FOR FURTHER READING

1. For more about the influence of Social Darwinism, see Richard Hofstadter, *Social Darwinism in American Thought* (Boston: Beacon Press, 1967).

2. For a survey of social ethics with some of the texts and problems incorporated in this and the next chapter, see George W. Forell, editor, *Christian Social Teachings: A Reader in Christian Social Ethics from the Bible to the Present* (Minneapolis: Augsburg, 1966).

3. For a fascinating (though not simple) history of the influence of apocalyptic literature on people, see Norman Cohn, *The Pursuit of the Millennium* (Oxford: Oxford University Press, 1970). Related to this, and a book you should be aware of as both controversial and brilliant, is Robert Mapes Anderson, *Vision of the Disinherited: The Making of American Pentecostalism* (New York: Oxford University Press, 1979), which relates the rise of Pentecostalism to certain class and economic factors.

4. For more on the Social Gospel, see Charles H. Hopkins, *The Rise of the Social Gospel in American Protestantism 1865–1915* (New Haven: Yale University Press, 1967). You might be particularly interested in pp. 143–48, an analysis of *In His Steps,* a novel written by Charles Sheldon and made into a movie in 1936. Every chapter of the novel begins with a biblical quotation and the central question was: "What would Jesus do?" Would Jesus advertise liquor in local newspapers? Would Jesus report prize fights? The answer is always no, and Sheldon's point is that Christians are to walk "in his steps." The book and its examples are dated, but the question and the ways of posing it are current in some ways.

5. For a look at the religious right, see Edward E. Plowman, "Is Morality All Right?" in *Christianity Today* 23 (2 November 1979), 76–85. The religious right, especially the Moral Majority, has created a contentious environment for discussion and you should exercise caution when reading about it: finding objective studies in a heated atmosphere is difficult. Daniel C. Maguire, *The New Subversives: Anti-Americanism of the Religious Right* (New York: Crossroad/Continuum, 1982) is too negative. Jerry Falwell, *Listen, America!* (New York: Doubleday, 1980) is too positive.

CHAPTER 11

CHRISTIANS AND
THEIR CULTURE

T his chapter deals with two options some Christian groups have chosen in order to live *with* the tension between the world and the church, rather than outside it. The two groups may be represented on the diagram like this:

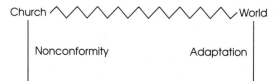

Recall that the jagged line represents tension between the values of the church and the values of the world, and that these interpretive descriptions allow us to raise some religious issues in ways that would not be possible if we were content simply to understand Christian groups in terms of denominational lines. Since the culture and values described here are American, the issues and examples have a particularly American flavor in most instances. The postures themselves, however, could be used to describe the varieties of Christian response to the world and church within other cultures as well.

Nonconformists consciously reject some of the values of the culture they live in, but are not so alienated that they withdraw from the tension. They understand themselves as embodying a small but persistent witness to the values of the gospel insofar as those values are at odds with the values of the society. Those who believe in adaptation tend to be part of large, established churches who have, for a number of reasons, accommodated themselves to the values of the society. They are not so identified with the general society that they wish to impose their values on everybody (the position of domination). They may lobby for a particular religious position—the abolition of the death penalty, for example—but they tend to do it in the framework of American pluralism, as in appealing to humanitarian values through a Washington-based lobby supported by a coalition of people who share similar views.

THE POSTURE OF ADAPTATION

Christians who choose to adapt have adjusted to their environment; they have conformed or modified themselves in order to be more intimately a part of the culture. In America, a pluralistic environment, one is free to adopt almost any religious posture. That has not always been the case, however, in America or in Christian history. The early Christians had a chance to adapt themselves to Roman culture—to be free to pursue their own religious preoccupations so long as they would occasionally offer sacrifice to the pagan gods—but they refused. Their understanding of Jesus and the gospel made them radical monotheists who would not offer sacrifice to pagan gods. They would not conform, adjust, or adapt. The response of the government to their intransigence was persecution; Christians were burned, maimed, tortured, and harassed. And the Romans made periodic efforts to destroy the movement altogether.

In times of persecution the choice for the Christian was stark: be faithful (and perhaps die miserably) or repudiate your beliefs (and be damned). Within this difficult choice some Christians discovered a compromise: they bribed officials to certify that they had sacrificed to the gods when, in fact, they had not. The early church came to regard this practice as apostasy. Deciding how to treat people who had denied their faith either directly or by using this method was an enormous pastoral problem in the third and fourth centuries. The compromise position illustrates the *mentality* of adaptation. In this line of reasoning one desires to be a Christian but does not understand Christianity as necessarily exacting such a great price; a believer ought to be able to adapt to the needs of the time, cooperate a little more with outside forces and so avoid persecution and martyrdom.

With Constantine the situation changed dramatically; his reign marked the beginning of the end of persecution and antagonism between church and state. Persecution—and the problems of adaptation under those circumstances—was not a major problem in the West again until the Reformation. We have already seen that one of the results of the Reformation was a series of religious wars in which Catholics and Protestants fought each other in the name of Christianity. Those wars and the peace that followed them raised a new set of questions about adaptation. What should a Roman Catholic in a Protestant country do? Or a Protestant in a Roman Catholic country? Should one withdraw and hide away or be a public witness to a particular religious view? Openly advocating a religious view different from the officially sanctioned one often ended in a gruesome public execution for the preacher. Should one move to a more congenial place? The mainline Reformation did not change the assumption that religion and culture were identified, but the Anabaptists did. They believed that Christian faith and the culture should not be identified; their sectarian stance was offensive to both Roman Catholics and Protestants precisely because it divided religion from culture.

Thus during the Reformation people began to find ways to adjust or adapt to their situation if they could not move away from it. Various religious undergrounds came into being and some groups had to hide in order to survive: in the mountain area of Switzerland and Italy, the Anabaptists took refuge from persecution from all sides. In America, religious pluralism eventually prevailed; the attempt by one group to dominate the religious life of all Americans failed. Still, in some areas religious persecution persisted, especially of non-English-speaking Christians and Roman Catholics. For a while both groups drew back into their own communities separated from the mainstream of American culture.[1] As time went on, however, and people were no longer barred by language or education from participation in the American experiment, more and more formerly isolated groups joined the mainstream.

Roman Catholics had special problems in adapting to American pluralism. They were separated from their Protestant neighbors until the mid-1960s on several levels: they celebrated their liturgy in a foreign language (Latin) and thus visitors usually did not know what was happening in Catholic worship. Their political loyalties were questioned because they owed allegiance to a foreign monarch (the pope); their behavior set them off from other people (they observed dietary laws and fasts). Catholics were also different from the rest of the culture because they were forbidden to practice birth control; they often had large families and were expected to marry within their faith. Some of those differences have been obliterated officially: Catholic liturgy is now celebrated in the vernacular and Catholics are no longer rigidly bound by dietary laws. Some differences have been minimized because individual Catholics, contrary to the official teaching of their church, have adapted to the culture around them: Catholics no longer tend to have large families and many are practicing birth control in opposition to official teaching but in conformity with their understandings of themselves within this culture.

Roman Catholics have adapted to American culture partly as a result of persecution and bigotry; persecuted groups often labor to prove that the surrounding culture is unjustified in discriminating against them. Other religious groups are increasingly adapting to American cultural values because they are losing their ethnic distinctiveness. Some Radical Reformation groups like the Mennonites are no longer simple rural folk; many have become professionals and have moved to urban areas where they have lost the trappings of their ethnic distinctiveness.

Adaptation is the posture many groups throughout Christian history have adopted. In the American context of religious pluralism, adaptation involves taking on an attitude of religious toleration: groups recognize that people of other beliefs may possess no less truth, may in fact be just as likely to be "saved." In the context of the American dream of upward social mobility, these Christians live comfortably within the culture.[2] Finally, adapted church groups cooperate with the government and often perceive their own aims as compatible with those of the government.

THE POSTURE OF NONCONFORMITY

Nonconformity is a failure or refusal to conform or adapt to the established order. Nonconformists believe that the church must be clearly distinguishable from the state. Sometimes, they believe, the values of the church are in conflict with those of the world; at those points they must not conform to the surrounding culture. They share some of the assumptions of the adapted Christians. They may recognize that people in other religions can be "saved" (endorsing religious pluralism), and they may sometimes be active in political matters, sometimes cooperating with government agencies in pursuit of a specific goal. Their main point of difference lies in their willingness to criticize the policies and pursuits of the establishment, whether that establishment is political or religious or both.

Unlike adapted groups, nonconformists do not assume that their religious beliefs are compatible with the values of the general society or the policies of the government. Unlike withdrawn groups, they are not so pessimistic or apolitical as to write the culture off as entirely evil or irrelevant to their belief. Rather, they accept and adopt some aspects of the culture, but maintain the importance of some critical distance from it, emphasizing the need to discern between what suits their convictions and what undermines or runs counter to them.

These postures are easier to describe in terms of specific issues than they are in isolation. Nonconformity changes as the society changes: in the second century it might have meant sure martyrdom; in the seventh it might have inspired a monastic life; in the thirteenth century, nonconformists might have joined the communities of Francis of Assisi in order to live in "holy poverty," and in the sixteenth century, nonconformity might have meant risking one's life in pursuit of the Anabaptist vision. In the twentieth century, nonconformity means a number of different things depending on the cultural context and the religious alternatives available.

RELATIONSHIP OF THE TWO POSTURES TO VITAL ISSUES

The positions of adaptation and nonconformity are clearer when understood in relation to specific issues within the culture. No more than a sampling of groups and their responses to issues can be presented here; this treatment is not intended to be complete. Here we discuss these two different attitudes as they relate to concrete problems of war, poverty, and racism.

Problems of War and Peace

Was has historically been part of the human experience; hostility and violence seem to be a constant of the human condition. How might one think about war? On the one hand one could hold that every war that serves someone's legitimate interests is acceptable: war is simply another way of doing politics and if the cause is justified, then the means used to pursue that cause are necessarily justified as well. On the other side of the question one could say that all wars are wrong: every war, even a war of self-defense, is unacceptable because bloodshed is always evil. The two extremes of the argument are these: war is always right and war is always wrong.

Most Christian churches have adopted a position somewhere between these opinions. Peace, they say, is to be preferred, but is not always possible. Because we live in a sinful world, sinful, unscrupulous people will attempt to involve a society in dangerous, criminal ventures. Experience shows, the argument continues, that only violence can stop violence. Here Christian participation in war is permitted, but only under certain circumstances. The theory of *just war* specifies the conditions under which Christians may wage war. To be justified in waging war, a group:

1. Must have just cause (one side must persist in unjust aggression).
2. Must exhaust all peaceful means first (so war is a matter of legitimate self-defense regretfully taken up when negotiations have failed).
3. Must have reasonable hope of success (a tiny country should not sacrifice its people in a hopeless war against a superpower).
4. Must use proportionate means (one side cannot use guns when the other side is just using swords and spears).
5. Must observe noncombatant immunity (violence may not be directed against civilians).

Almost all American Christian groups have adopted this theory in some form, and members have distinguished themselves in every American war as soldiers, chaplains, nurses, and so on. Adoption of just-war theory is one form of adaptation because it enables Christians to sanction warfare.[3]

The nonconformist position on this issue is taken by the "peace churches," those that consider pacifism and nonresistance a Christian obligation. The historic peace churches have been Anabaptist groups (Mennonites, Amish, Hutterites), the Religious Society of Friends (Quakers), and Churches of the Brethren. In recent years they have been joined by Christians from other churches who are convinced that the peace churches have a valid reading of the Bible and a valuable position of witness on this question.[4] Peace churches are opposed to Christian participation in all war, no matter what the circumstances. They argue that experience does *not* teach us about the efficacy of violence but about its uselessness; violence, they argue, breeds violence. Jesus meant what he said about loving one's enemies and turning the other cheek. They say that nonviolent means have never really been tried and taken seriously. More important, the peace churches argue that Christians must be nonviolent whether nonviolence works or not: their position is not based on a pragmatic judgment about the possible good outcomes of the position, but is based on Jesus's words and his way of dealing with violence. These people believe that being faithful is more important than determining by violent means what kind of government they will live under.

Many members of the peace churches are absolute pacifists: they will not fight in a war, nor will they contribute to the war effort in any way (for example, they will not take a desk job in the army, which then frees someone else to carry a gun). Some may help the wounded, but they are as willing to nurse the "enemy" as their compatriots. Some peace church agencies were severely criticized for providing vitamins and medicine to children in North Vietnam during the Vietnam War. Peace church members have been involved in relief work in the aftermath of war: Mennonites, Quakers, and Brethren poured into Europe after the Second World War in order to clean up the rubble, distribute food and clothing, tend the wounded and homeless. Quakers won the 1947 Nobel Peace Prize for their work in relief, reconstruction, and international services during the war.

Some peace church people now are trying to discover the meaning of peacemaking in a country that is not at war but that spends half its budget for national defense. A New Call to Peacemaking movement sponsored by the historic peace churches has been established to introduce conversations about peace into all the churches. Consciousness raising about issues of war and peace has also spilled over into issues of nuclear weapons and the arms race. Pacifist Christians have been active in nonviolent demonstrations at plants where nuclear weapons are constructed; some are engaged in various forms of tax resistance, to show their opposition to what they regard as excessive defense spending. They publish pamphlets and books on the peace issue and work to raise the consciousness of other Christians on issues of peace. Members of the peace churches have traditionally provided counseling services for young people about draft resistance and conscientious objection.

In all these ways the peace churches do not conform to the cultural assumption that war is sometimes necessary. As such they witness against a major government policy and against those churches that accept and support that policy. Christians with a pacifist position have not always been welcome in American culture, especially in times of war. Their position assumes a willingness to spend time in jail, and during every American war some members of peace churches have spent time in prison and some have been harassed by their neighbors. Because of the efforts of the historic peace churches, the American government made a legal provision for alternative service and conscientious objection.

Problems of Poverty and Lifestyle

The poverty issue surfaced in the last chapter in the discussion about financial domination. Scripture focuses on two concerns: the needs of the poor and the appropriateness of accumulating personal wealth. Some Christians have tied the message of Scripture to wealth and capitalism, while others have linked it with socialism and a distribution of goods and properties. Christians use Scripture to justify both extremes. But what about poverty itself? If one maintains that feeding the poor is a primary New Testament value, then one can argue that some private wealth is necessary to perform this service. Christian churches can have money and individual Christians can accumulate wealth as long as they attend to their obligations to the poor. Nonconformists see the issue not simply as one of caring for the poor; they regard accumulating personal wealth as contrary to their calling. The questions, from their perspective, cannot be separated: Christians have an obligation to help the poor by identifying with their state; Christians should stand as a witness against the American values of accumulation and upward social mobility. Nonconformist Christians identify with the poor, moving into their neighborhoods, living at their standard of living.

One Christian denomination founded specifically to minister to the poor is the Salvation Army (discussed in Chapter 8). Two other groups that illustrate this position are both affiliated with larger Christian groups. The People's Christian Coalition, sometimes called the Sojourners Fellowship because the magazine they publish is called *Sojourners,* is rooted in the American evangelical tradition.[5] The Catholic Worker Movement is rooted in American Catholicism.[6] The Sojourners group is relatively young; it began in the early 1970s and moved to Washington, D.C., in 1975. The Catholic Worker Movement was founded in 1934 and enjoyed a considerable success at one time, but had dwindled in recent years; it continues, nevertheless, to pursue its goals. Both groups read the Gospels in such a way that they believe it is necessary to identify with the poor, not just provide food for them. Both groups have been active in peace movements, oppose nuclear armament, and serve as advocates for causes of social justice.

The Sojourners Fellowship began when a small group of young evangelical seminarians in Chicago prayed together and began to look for a place to live according to their interpretations of the gospel: in poverty, helping the poor, widows, orphans, and other disenfranchised peoples. After some initial experiments in the Chicago area they moved to Washington, D.C., found a large house near the so-called riot corridor (a slum neighborhood, mostly black and very poor), and moved in there as a group. They did not immediately design programs or enlist government aid, but simply went out into the street each evening and invited people without places to go to come in for dinner and a place to sleep. Their community has grown, as has their magazine's circulation. Members live in several households in one neighborhood, in a conscious attempt to offer an alternative to American values of consumption, accumulation, and upward social mobility. Accordingly, they feel called to demonstrate and write against the arms race and American defense policies. In addition to spirituality and Christian nurture, their magazine deals with poverty, peace, the arms race, political repression, and so on. The publication has become a forum for other like-minded groups; their movement is not unique, but exemplifies one type of nonconformity in the area of poverty and lifestyle.

The Catholic Worker Movement was founded by a young, well-educated Roman Catholic convert and a French peasant with ideas about agrarian reform and Christian poverty. Dorothy Day (1897–1980) had been a young socialist at the University of Illinois who rejected religion as poppycock even as she continued to read evangelical sermons. She was drawn to the Roman Catholic church because of its teachings about poverty—the social encyclicals of the late nineteenth century[7]—but found those teachings were not often implemented within the church. She could not understand piety that did not help poor people. Peter Maurin (1877–1949), a French agrarian anarchist disdainful of modern technology and urban middle class values, gave her the impetus she needed; together they founded the Catholic Worker Movement.

They set out to practice a kind of Catholicism that did not conform to the general norm: they were socialists when most Catholics were staunchly anti-Communist, pacifists when Catholics were strong supporters of the just-war theory, and they opposed big government when some of the principles of the New Deal echoed modern Roman Catholic social theory.[8] Their fundamental principle, derived from their reading of the New Testament, was subsidiarity: what a small group can do, it should do; people ought to do what they can to look after one another, however small the scale. Catholic Workers perceive government policies like Social Security as an indictment against churches, which are not fulfilling their obligations to the poor, widows, orphans, and the elderly. With headquarters in New York City, they operate a soup kitchen and shelter in the Bowery. They publish a newspaper, *The Catholic Worker,* that has sold for a penny per copy since its beginnings.

Both Sojourners and the Catholic Worker Movement are examples of nonconformity in poverty and lifestyle. Both have moved into poor neighborhoods in order to identify with the people to whom they are ministering. For both groups, community life and prayer are an important part of their Christian self-understanding. That prayer life takes evangelical form in the Sojourners community and traditional Roman Catholic form with the Catholic Workers.

Churches with more conventional views have addressed the issues of poverty in a different way. They set aside a portion of their budget to give to the poor, unite in groups to establish programs for the forgotten members of society, and support missions in poor neighborhoods to care for and preach to the poor. They do not feel compelled, however, to move into those neighborhoods or to identify with the poor by living at the same income level. Ecumenical groups have funded organizations to lobby for legislation for the poor and the powerless; their organizations in Washington try to influence congressional decisions on the one hand and raise the consciousness of Christians within their constituent churches on the other.

Problems of Racism

The belief that one race is inherently inferior to another has sometimes led Christians to violent exploitation of other peoples. The postures of nonconformity and adaptation can be delineated on the issue of racism—especially white discrimination against blacks—in its most virulent form, slavery. From the seventeenth through the nineteenth centuries black Africans were systematically uprooted from their own civilizations and religions and sold into slavery. Their culture was destroyed and their religion replaced with a form of Christianity designed as a means of social control. The New Testament injunction, "Slaves, obey . . . your earthly masters" (Col. 3:22) was pushed to its limits as a theoretical justification for slavery. Nevertheless, people soon began to ask, "If slaves have been baptized into the body of Christ, does that mean they must be set free?"

Only one nonconformist group made a concerted protest against slavery. Quakers were the first Christians to condemn slavery systematically; they were united and firm in their protest. When Thomas Jefferson and George Washington still owned slaves, a Quaker preacher, John Woolman (1720–72), traveled up and down the colonies speaking against it. Quakers formed an important part of the underground railroad, which provided an effective escape route to the North for runaway slaves.

By the mid-nineteenth century, American Christians were at a moral impasse about slavery. Three major American churches split precisely over the issue: Methodists, Baptists, and Presbyterians divided along North-South lines when each group adopted the predominant position of its culture on the issue. John Wesley, founder of the Methodists, opposed slavery, but by the 1840s, American Methodists had divided over the right of the clergy (especially bishops) to own slaves.

We have already seen that one product of the Second Great Awakening was an informal coalition of evangelical Christians united by their conversion experience and prepared for a life of action. The American Bible Society and the American Temperance Union were two projects supported by the evangelical alliance. The American Anti-Slavery Society was also part of the evangelical alliance, but it did not succeed in uniting all evangelical Christians for the abolitionist cause. The great revivalist preacher Charles Grandison Finney sympathized with antislavery views and influenced the revivalist movement significantly. One of his disciples, Theodore Dwight Weld (1803–95), became a leader of the antislavery movement and a founder of the Anti-Slavery Society. Agents selected by the society spread abolitionist views along with evangelical Christianity. Weld influenced politicians in the North and shaped public opinion on the issue. His book *Slavery As It Is* (1839) inspired Harriet Beecher Stowe's novel *Uncle Tom's Cabin* (1852). Those two books were the most important antislavery works written in the United States. Stowe's novel is clearer in its opposition to slavery than to racism in general. She assumes racism will continue: freed blacks will want to be *separate*. In this view neither the gospel nor abolition requires fellowship with blacks. Stowe could, therefore, imaginatively enlist white evangelical preachers in the cause of abolition without challenging them to speak for integration.

The division within the churches reflected a division within the society. Apart from the Quakers, the abolitionist cause had few advocates in the eighteenth century. The American constitutional principle that all men are created equal did not apply to slaves; each slave counted as only three-fifths of a human being in early census figures. The liberal positions of the time were shaped by antiblack stereotypes almost as much as by proslavery arguments. Liberals aimed at finding a cure for blackness (as if it were a disease) or a way to surmount the problems of black genetic "inferiority." The religious viewpoint was shaped, in part, by an acceptance of slavery as part of God's plan: God created black people for a reason—to be slaves. Many ministers argued that blacks could not be set free because freedom would violate a divine design. (This argument, as we have seen, was later extended to the problem of poverty).

By the early nineteenth century, people began to be more bothered by slavery; the situation approached crisis proportions. A swelling tide of humanitarian reform inspired solutions to the slavery problem: some people thought blacks ought to be free to emigrate elsewhere to form their own colonies; others joined in the abolitionist movement and hoped to free all slaves and so destroy the institution of slavery. Finney and the American Evangelical Alliance adopted an antislavery position and disciples like Weld carried it forward. The revivalist movement was strong in the 1830s, a period when the seeds of division began to take root. The Nat Turner rebellion in 1831 unleashed latent fears in the South and precipitated a tightening of the slave code. William Lloyd Garrison (1805–79), a strong abolitionist, founded *The Liberator,* a proabolition newspaper. His editorial policy led to increased hostility between North and South.

By the end of the 1830s the South had rallied to support slavery both theologically and with their own distinct form of revivalism. The splits within the Methodist, Baptist, and Presbyterian churches reflected this growing gap between South and North.

Southern Christians used the Bible to support slavery. Since slavery was mentioned in the New Testament and not specifically condemned there, the churches argued that baptism meant only that slaves were set free in the Lord. Their freedom consisted in the ability to obey their masters willingly and cheerfully in order to secure a place for themselves in heaven. Segregation was extolled as a sensible arrangement and projected into the future. One white minister told a slave congregation they would reach heaven if they were docile and obedient, but that even in heaven they would not mingle with the master and mistress; they could look forward to a heaven with a dividing wall.[9] Northern Christians also supported their abolitionist views with the Bible. The theological stance of both Northern and Southern Christians reflected their differing cultural and political beliefs.

In the twentieth century, American Christians—North and South—have not distinguished themselves for their antiracist beliefs. A number of specifically black churches were formed in the eighteenth and nineteenth centuries within mainline Protestant Christianity in America. Black churches often existed as segregated adjuncts, represented as such. Catholics, too, supported a policy of separation with black seminaries, church organizations, convents, and schools. For most Christians no obvious "Christian" alternative to segregation presented itself; the culture only assumed a position of "separate but equal" after Supreme Court rulings. The churches did not lead people to consider black equality or integration. When Martin Luther King, Jr. (1929–68) led civil rights protests in the 1950s in the name of Christianity, church leaders cautioned that his protests and actions against segregation were "unwise and untimely."

Racism is supported by negative presuppositions about other people. One modern religious experiment that has attempted to challenge those fundamental presuppositions is the Koinonia Partners of Americus, Georgia.[10] The Koinonia group, a nonconformist experiment in Christian living, was founded in 1942 by Clarence Jordan, a Baptist with a degree from Southern Baptist Theological Seminary and experience working in inner-city churches in Louisville, Kentucky. The Koinonia community has a twofold goal: to live together as an integrated fellowship sharing wealth and labor and to assist local farmers by introducing scientific farming methods so that poor farmers can make their land more fruitful. The group had to withstand mounting hostility in the 1950s when racism and segregation were particularly sensitive issues. Their locally supported chicken and egg business had to shut down because of racial prejudice and they began a mail-order pecan business, which had a broader base of support. The mail-order operation allowed them to extend *koinonia*—fellowship—to Christians all over the world. The partnership with those Christians, they said, reflected their own partnership with God. Koinonia continues to exist as a commune in partnership with people; their activities include child development, small industries, and providing housing for people. Their common life involves a wide variety of people in a fellowship they believe to be similar to the kingdom of God they await. Their first interest is not to inspire people to live in communes, but to encourage them to adopt a new way of seeing other people.

QUESTIONS RAISED BY THE POSTURES OF NONCONFORMITY AND ADAPTATION

Although these brief glimpses into the problems of war, poverty, and racism do not shed light on the issues as such, they clarify the distinction between nonconformist and adapted Christianity. Examining the postures within the context of specific cultural issues permits a view of their interconnectedness with society. Some of the general questions raised in the last chapter are important here as well; the same questions about the churches and the political order are raised within the framework of these alternatives of nonconformity and adaptation.

In What Sense Is Christianity Political?

Christian understanding of the church's role in the political order varies according to the definition of politics different groups adopt. Nonconformist Christians take politics to be broader than the accepted life of the society, its government, and public institutions. Their political stance rests on the assumption that the Christian community is inherently different from the state; in some cases the church provides an alternative to the established order. Christians in this group limit their cooperation with the state on the grounds that its values and policies are sometimes different from and even hostile to the values of the church. Their loyalty to the distinctive witness of the church, they believe, prevents them from fully endorsing the values of the culture. Christians in churches that are more adapted accept more of the values of the culture; they tend to see the aims of the state as coextensive with the aims of the church. Adapted Christians usually see no reason, *in principle,* to oppose the goals and policies of the state; they minimize areas of possible conflict between the aims of the society and those of Christian truth.

Whether Christianity is concerned primarily with personal regeneration or with restructuring the society is not the fundamental issue between nonconformity and adaptation. The argument, to some extent, is part of Christianity in whatever form it takes; both nonconformist and adapted Christians would see need for both personal regeneration and efforts for social change. The difference between the positions lies in the way they conceptualize the church and its role in society. Nonconformists tend to see the church as fulfilling an important prophetic function in society; they regard the church as the locus of strong social critique and as a witness to a radical alternative. Adapted Christians tend to see the church as moral educator and helper; they are often more willing to proceed slowly toward change because they regard the church as an institution in fundamental cooperation with the state. Their confidence in social structures is manifested by their willingness to change society through their votes and through participation as candidates for public office.

What Is the Church?

Sociologists of religion sometimes distinguish between "church-type" and "sect-type" Christianity.[11] According to this distinction, sectarian Christians identify the church as a small group of believers whose values differ from those of their culture; their lifestyle is often rigorous and they do not expect to attract many followers or to see their views adopted by the society in general. Christians with a nonsectarian perspective see the church as a large institution whose values contribute to the stability of the society as a whole. They expect the church to be socially acceptable, with many followers, and to exert a positive influence on society. They expect to see their views sanctioned by the culture in which they live.

Were the words of Jesus, which are taken seriously by many sectarians—about loving one's enemies, for example—meant to apply for all times? Or were Jesus's ethics meant to be for the interim: did Jesus expect the world to end so soon that he formulated positions to be adhered to only for the short period between his death and the end of the world? These serious theological questions and issues of scriptural interpretation are reflected in the differences between the nonconformist and adapted positions on some of the issues outlined above.

The questions raised by an argument between sectarian and nonsectarian perspectives often lead to self-righteous judgments on the part of one group or the other. Both groups can perceive themselves as the locus of true Christian conviction. Sectarians often see themselves as more righteous or more faithful to the commands of Jesus; they may condemn the nonsectarian position as secular and perceive the churches as interested in the salvation of the world on the world's terms. Sectarians may see the church as no longer motivated by divine ideals, but by the business of the world, while sectarians provide the witness of the faithful remnant. Nonsectarians often understand themselves as more realistic interpreters of the gospel because they do not present the message of Jesus in such stark terms; they may condemn sectarians for being socially ineffective and alienating. Church-type Christians may see sectarians as narrow and unnecessarily hostile to the world while the churches provide an effective Christianity attractive to modern society. Church-type Christianity can be universal, reach out to large numbers of people, and bring its influence to bear on social and political problems. Sectarian Christianity can remind people of the demand for personal commitment. Together they reflect the range of opportunities within the Christian experience.

How Should the Bible Be Interpreted?

As with the options described in the last chapter, adapted and nonconformist Christians support their positions with their reading of the New Testament. Does their use of the New Testament to support fundamentally differing views mean that the message of the New Testament is not clear with regard to racism, violence, and poverty? Does the New Testament itself reflect differences or disagreements already present in the early Christian community? Or is the New Testament perfectly clear on every issue and do some Christians willfully misunderstand it? Did the cultural context in which the Bible was written shape its message? Does their cultural context shape the way North Americans read the Bible?

Most Christian groups agree that Scripture is normative, but how, exactly, does it bind people? Are only the general principles found in Scripture—for example, to love God wholeheartedly and one's neighbor as oneself—binding? Or are specific injunctions addressed to a particular cultural context—"A woman ought to have a veil on her head" (1 Cor. 11:10)—equally binding? How does one discriminate? Should Christians conform their behavior to descriptive statements in the Bible—for example, that Abraham had slaves? Or are they bound only by prescriptive statements like the Ten Commandments? How do they decide about these matters? Must Christians do only what the Bible commands? Or may they do anything not specifically forbidden—for example, since Jesus said nothing about slavery, can one assume owning slaves is acceptable?

Are some parts of the Bible more important than others? In the Old Testament, God urges people to go to war and often supports their efforts to conquer another nation; in the New Testament, Jesus enjoins his followers to love their enemies and to put away their swords. How do Christians decide which texts are more important in times of war? Most Christians use the New Testament as an interpretive key to the Old Testament: they see God's words and actions in the lives of the Jewish people as pointing directly toward Jesus. Does that mean that the words of the New Testament must always supersede those of the Old Testament? Within the New Testament how does one resolve differences in wording, as between being poor and being poor "in spirit"? Are some parts of the New Testament more important than others? Are the words of Jesus more binding than the teachings of Paul?

All these questions occur in the differences between nonconformist and adapted perspectives on particular issues. They are usually answered within the context of the believing community's historical experience and tradition. Can those answers change? Will textual criticism and biblical scholarship help people answer these questions more clearly? Or does biblical scholarship threaten the inerrancy of the Bible? Will cultural attitudes be the major interpretive framework in which such questions are answered? Or is it possible to read the text purely, without being influenced by the cultural context? Does a literal reading of the New Testament lead to clear interpretations? Or does that reading tend to reduce issues to a simplicity they do not have?

CONCLUSION

None of the questions raised in this chapter or the previous one can be answered simply; they reflect ancient disagreements and contemporary problems of interpretation. The four postures outlined—withdrawal, domination, nonconformity, and adaptation—do not describe particular groups in an iron-clad way, but suggest some pressing theological issues underlying a wide range of Christian belief and behavior. As Christians continue to be challenged by problems within the world and their culture—nuclear power and weapons, sexism, multinational corporations in Third World countries, worldwide poverty, the emergence of new nations in Asia and Africa—most will not find simple solutions. They will continue to seek answers within the tension between the church and the world and beyond its bounds.

CHAPTER 11 NOTES

[1] Religious persecution was part of the American scene almost from the beginning, and was energetically anti-Catholic throughout much of the nineteenth century in various nativist movements, as mentioned in Chapter 8. See John Higham, *Strangers in the Land—Patterns of American Nativism 1860–1925* (New York: Atheneum, 1977).

[2] There may even be an "American civil religion": a general kind of religious ethos that transcends specific denominations. For a statement of this social theory, see Robert Bellah, "Civil Religion in America," *Daedalus* 96 (1967), 1–21; also, G. C. Bedell et al., *Religion in America*, 2nd ed. (New York: Macmillan, 1982), pp. 14–68.

[3] One modern consideration turns on how to apply just-war criteria to the possibility of nuclear war. An opinionated but thorough book on this subject is William V. O'Brien, *The Conduct of a Just and Limited War* (New York: Praeger, 1981). For an interesting application of just-war theory to modern situations, see J. G. Davies, *Christians, Politics and Violent Revolution* (Maryknoll, N.Y.: Orbis Books, 1976).

[4] The peace movement has grown in other churches since the war in Vietnam, and nuclear war discussions have activated Christians in almost all denominations. One group that is causing quite a stir with its emerging protest against nuclear arms is the Roman Catholic church. In 1976 the American Catholic bishops in a pastoral letter questioned

the morality of modern war; in 1979 they declared that a nation could not, in conscience, use or *intend to use* a nuclear weapon. This latter position raised serious questions about deterrence and American military policy, and the Catholic bishops received both criticism and support for their views. In 1981 a committee headed by Archbishop Joseph Bernardin of Cincinnati (later Cardinal Archbishop of Chicago) began to draft a pastoral letter on nuclear war: the committee represented a broad spectrum of Roman Catholic opinion on the issue, held fourteen hearings, interviewed thirty-six witnesses (including the Secretary of Defense), and began to draft the letter. In June 1982 word leaked out that the pastoral letter was decidedly "dovish" in tone and emphasis, and the controversy surrounding the issue grew more intense. By the end of 1982 the bishops had become a hot topic for the media; see, for example, the cover story in *Time*, 29 November 1982, 68–78. For the text of the bishops' pastoral, see U.S. Catholic Bishops, *The Challenge of Peace: God's Promise and Our Response* (Washington, D.C.: National Conference of Catholic Bishops, 1983).

[5] An article about the beginnings of this community can be found in the magazine *Sojourners* 6 (January 1977), 14–31. Looking through the magazine will help you see the kinds of concerns they have and also will give you some indication of the other like-minded groups that have sprung up in the United States in recent years.

[6] The best study of the movement is William Miller, *A Harsh and Dreadful Love* (New York: Image, 1974). An excellent introduction to Dorothy Day is through her autobiographical works, especially *The Long Loneliness* (New York: Curtis Books, 1952).

[7] Leo XIII (pope from 1878 to 1903) wrote a ground-breaking social encyclical (letter to the whole world) in 1891, *Rerum Novarum;* it set a pattern for Roman Catholic social thought for the next fifty years. See Aaron I. Abell, *American Catholicism and Social Action: A Search for Social Justice 1865–1950* (Notre Dame, Ind.: University of Notre Dame Press, 1963), for a history of Catholic social thought and for some indication of why Dorothy Day might have found such things exciting.

[8] One Roman Catholic social reformer, Monsignor John Ryan (1869–1945), was the author of the American Catholic Bishops' Program for Social Reconstruction (written in 1919); many of the suggestions it offered were also part of President Franklin Roosevelt's program. Ryan's biography is subtitled *The Right Reverend New Dealer.*

[9] See Martin Marty, *Righteous Empire: The Protestant Experience in America* (New York: Dial Press, 1970), p. 33.

[10] A good book on Koinonia, with pictures, is William Hedgepeth, *The Alternative: Communal Life in New America* (New York: Macmillan, 1970).

[11] I am using the same general distinction I used in Chapter 10 from Ernst Troeltsch; see note 2 to that chapter.

SUGGESTIONS FOR FURTHER READING

1. For documents on American religious history that will deepen your understanding of both Protestant and Roman Catholic adaptation, see George Bedell et al., *Religion in America*, 2nd ed. (New York: Macmillan, 1982).

2. For a critical look at religious lobbies, see Allen D. Hertzke, *Representing God in Washington: The Role of Religious Lobbies in the American Polity* (Knoxville: University of

Tennessee Press, 1988). Hertzke asks whether religious lobbies are staffed by selfless reformers or sanctimonious meddlers. Do they serve the poor or do they speak for elites? He interviewed lobbyists from mainline Protestant, evangelical, fundamentalist, Roman Catholic, and peace churches, and Jewish communities.

3. Any of the peace churches—Quaker, Brethren, Mennonite, for example—will be able to give you information on current activity within the peace movement, not only within their churches but worldwide. In addition, you might find significant peace groups within churches traditionally associated with just-war theory. The Roman Catholic church, for example, is part of an international peace movement, Pax Christi International. The American branch, Pax Christi USA, publishes a quarterly journal and coordinates local peace activists in Roman Catholic churches.

4. For more on the black Christian experience, see C. Eric Lincoln, *The Black Church Since Frazier*, and Franklin E. Frazier, *The Negro Church in America*, combined in a single volume (New York: Schocken Books, 1963). See also C. Eric Lincoln, *Race, Religion and the Continuing American Dilemma* (New York: Hill & Wang, 1984). Shorter introductions to black Christianity can be found in Albert J. Raboteau, "Black Christianity in North America," in Charles H. Lippy and Peter W. Williams, editors, *Encyclopedia of the American Religious Experience* (New York: Scribner's, 1988), pp. 635–49.

❖

CHAPTER 12

CONTEMPORARY
CHRISTIANITY

Our understanding of Christianity began with a look at the religious experience of the ancient Hebrews, noticing that their beliefs about God's personality and desire encompassed two different concepts. On the one hand, God
was the transcendent creator, remote, powerful, and resplendent, a God who
came with fire and thunder to deliver commandments and to instill feelings of
awe. On the other hand, God was the immanent partner, close, protective, and
involved, a God who came with compassion to offer a covenant relationship and
engender feelings of friendship. We noted that throughout the Hebrew Bible,
God acted both to judge and to uphold the people. We can see, therefore, that
there is room for different points of emphasis when one attempts to interpret
God's will in today's world.

In the New Testament, Jesus had harsh things to say to those who exploited
the poor and the weak, and he had comforting words for the afflicted. Furthermore, as we have seen, the wording of the New Testament allows for different
interpretations of the divine design in relation to specific social problems. Although the early Christians understood themselves to be in partnership with the
Holy Spirit, they were continually involved in a struggle to define themselves in
relation to the world around them. Christian history, as we have seen, has been
marked by a continual adjustment to new circumstances and has been informed
at various times by particular readings of Scripture. We should not be surprised,

221

therefore, that contemporary Christianity is also defined by its struggles to relate to the world and to culture. Nor should we be astonished to find that widely variant interpretations of Christianity can all be based on the Bible.

The goal of this last section of the book has been to show how Christians can disagree on fundamental issues in good faith. I have not attempted to prove that one group is right and another wrong, but to suggest that the bases for disagreement have long historical roots and proceed from dearly held assumptions about the nature of God, the power of biblical authority, and the definition of the church. When we looked at the challenges of modernity (Chapter 7), we noted two general reactions that define a wide spectrum of response: welcoming the insights of modernity and resisting them.

Contemporary Christianity is distinguished, in part, by new articulations of these two postures in response to a set of new challenges raised by Christians themselves in the latter part of the twentieth century. This chapter will examine the general distinction between liberal and conservative Christianity (which we examined as the liberal-fundamentalist debate in Chapter 8), and look at some particularly vexing issues and opportunities offered to Christianity from the women's movement, electronic technology, and Third World theologians. By the end of the chapter, I hope, you will be better equipped to make some judgments for yourself about the future of Christianity.

LIBERAL AND CONSERVATIVE CHRISTIANITY

As we have already seen, modernity engendered at least two widely different responses on the part of Christians. In broad terms, we can define these positions in relation to one another knowing, as we do, that they come from the different experiences of both groups in the nineteenth and twentieth centuries. Both liberals and fundamentalists are dedicated to the preservation of Christian truth as they understand it, but that understanding is shaped by their relation to the modern world.

I am using intentionally general terminology in this section as a caution against assigning labels to particular groups of Christians. Liberal Christianity can mean a number of things in practical terms and one can find liberal Christians in most mainline Protestant churches, in Roman Catholicism, Orthodox Christianity, and Anglicanism. The kinds of concerns—for the elimination of racism, world hunger, injustice—that inform the World Council of Churches, along with that body's desire for ecumenical dialogue, characterize many of the desires of liberal Christians. Conservative Christianity can also mean a number of things in practical terms: some conservative Christians are fundamentalists[1] and some are not. One can find conservative Christians also in most mainline Protestant churches as well as in Roman Catholic, Orthodox, and Anglican churches. Evangelical Christians are usually considered to be conservative, but as we saw in the last chapter, one can identify liberal evangelicals as well. The kinds of concerns taken up by the World Council of Churches are generally *not* embraced by conservative Christians, and many prefer to associate with the National Association of Evangelicals.[2] Caution must be exercised, however, when attempting to assign labels.

Liberal Christianity

In general, liberals are comfortable with ambiguity and understand Christian life to be complex and their conclusions tentative. They are influenced by the principle of continuity or development and tend to be optimistic, or at least open-minded in relation to the world around them. The central authority for their faith is their relation to Christ, but that relationship is often rooted in experience and some trust in reason. Liberals, in general, are often attracted to the immanent images of God in the Bible and tend to blur classical distinctions between the natural and supernatural worlds. Accordingly, they see no need for extraordinary interventions of the divine into human life. Miracles for them are not proofs of God's existence and power. On the contrary, a person's experience of Christ shapes a belief in God, and a person's belief in God enables him or her to see the miraculous power of God displayed in ordinary life. According to them, revelation is contained in a special way in the Bible, but it is also available in the stuff of everyday life. Human experience and human existence provide clues about the nature of God, and revelation is considered to be a dynamic, ongoing event in the unfolding of human history.

The world is therefore not perceived as a hostile environment for Christians. Liberals tend to be open to new theologies, new understandings about God, and they tend to welcome dialogue and pluralism. Convinced by nineteenth-century theologians that Christianity is a communal experience, liberals often perceive the nature of the Christian life in social terms and tend to see the mission of the church as connected with the regeneration of society.

American liberal Christians do not believe that America is the new promised land. If America has a mission to the world, it is because the country has many problems of its own and is also blessed with resources that could be used to help the distressed peoples and situations of the earth. In terms of their political agenda, liberals often sound like secular humanists: they appeal to human rights, and are convinced that the problems of the world need to be solved by human ingenuity. Some critics today say that liberal Christianity is declining in America precisely because it cannot differentiate itself from secular humanism, but I wonder whether that is a fair judgment.[3] Liberals distinguish themselves from their secular counterparts primarily by virtue of their religious belief. Their Christian faith, they say, is a primary motivating power for them and gives them the strength to act creatively in the world. When they stress goals of social justice for the world, they are moved by the words of the biblical prophets and the example of Jesus. The Bible, for them, galvanizes social reform, and they cite the influence of biblical power on reformers like Martin Luther King, Jr.

Liberal Christians tend to be social activists with an agenda that leans to the left. Issues of nuclear power and disarmament, along with ecological concerns, and a general support for the goals of the World Council of Churches define many of their fields of interaction. In terms of the diagram introduced in this section, liberal Christians might be found in nonconformist or adapted positions. At the same time, a prayerful concern for liberal social agendas can be found in withdrawn monastic communities. Finally, specific groups, like the American Catholic bishops, who take the posture of domination on the issue of abortion, have a long history of creative response to issues of social justice. The bishops released a pastoral letter on nuclear war in 1983 and one on the economy in 1986. Both of these documents, while not ultimately grounded in the principles of liberal Christianity, do take positions that are attractive to liberal Christians. Where one can find liberals, therefore, is not easily predictable and sometimes needs to be addressed on a case-by-case basis. Still, the general outlines of this position should give you some basis for determining the general attitude.

Conservative Christianity

In contrast to liberals, conservative Christians prefer certainty and understand Christian life to be clear, its conclusions fixed. They are influenced by the principle of a divine plan for humanity and tend to be pessimistic about and sometimes suspicious of the world around them. The central authority for their faith is their relation to Christ, a bond that is rooted in God's invitation in the Bible. According to them, God disclosed a plan of salvation to the peoples and authors of the Bible, and guaranteed its essential rightness through divine inspiration. One can trust the Bible to be free from error and so has only to trust in God's word as found in the Bible.[4]

Conservatives, in general, are often attracted to images of divine transcendence and tend to highlight the classical distinction between the natural and supernatural worlds. Accordingly, they expect extraordinary interventions of the divine into human life. Miracles, indeed, are a proof of God's existence and can be defined as extraordinary: everyday life may have glimmers of the divine in it, but God's power is especially evident in the miracles recorded in the Bible, and, for some, in miraculous healings and manifestations in the lives of Christians today. According to them, revelation is contained in the Bible and is not to be found in contemporary history or ordinary events.

Human experience, far from providing clues to divine attributes, proves the constant need for God by its continual manifestations of sinfulness. The world is, in many ways, an alien environment for the Christian. Conservatives tend to resist any new theology, preferring what they sometimes call "the old-time religion." They may be open to dialogue with others, and they live in a pluralistic society, but they often regard their position as the only true one and see no need to absorb the insights of other religions. Convinced by reformers and revivalists that Christianity is a matter of individual conversion, conservatives often perceive the Christian life in individual terms and tend to understand the mission of the church as connected with the evangelical impulse to draw all people into a personal relationship with Jesus.

American conservative Christians may adopt the rhetoric of America as the new promised land, the new Eden where God has given humanity a chance to gather everyone into the kingdom. America is the home of God's chosen people and God's preferred way of life; the task set for the country is the evangelization of the world, an event that will hasten the Second Coming of Christ at the end of the world.

In terms of their political agendas, religious conservatives often sound like political conservatives: they appeal to capitalism, strong defense initiatives, and anti-Communist rhetoric. They also tend to understand that the problems of this world will, eventually, be solved by God's intervention. Critics sometimes say that fundamentalist Christians who support conservative political positions are more interested in preserving the status quo than they are in religion, but I wonder whether that is a fair judgment. Conservative Christians distinguish themselves from conservative secular politics primarily by virtue of their religious belief. Their Christian faith, they say, inspires them to act and gives them the strength and wisdom to oppose the directions of the modern world. When they stress goals of individual salvation and preservation of the American way of life, they are moved by God's covenant with them and their belief in America as a new promised land.

Fundamentalist Christians are sometimes social isolationists, preferring to put their energies into the work of personal salvation, and sometimes are political activists. As activists, they tend to gather around issues of American military superiority, anti-Communism, and a general contempt for the goals of the World Council of Churches. In terms of the diagram on p. 185, some conservative Christians can be found in the withdrawn position, where one would expect them to be interested primarily in personal regeneration and opposed to social activism. Some, whose theology is often not so conservative, might be found in the nonconformist position: Evangelicals for Social Action, for example, have taken strong positions both on the biblical basis of their lives and against poverty and world hunger.[5] One can find conservative Christians in the adapted groups of American Christianity, and sadly, can find fundamentalists who exploit a Gospel of Wealth reading of the Old Testament to support their own personal financial gain.[6]

Finally, one can find fundamentalists in the position of domination. Jerry Falwell's association with the Moral Majority in the 1980s was a marriage of fundamentalist Christianity with a dominating political perspective, and Pat Robertson's use of "The 700 Club" as a launching pad for his political ambitions is an example of the ways fundamentalist Christianity can take on the political goals of the new right.[7] As was the case with liberal Christians, one cannot always predict where conservatives will line up on the diagram, but this general description should provide you with some clues for identification and rationale.

CONTEMPORARY ISSUES

Christians today, like their counterparts in other times, face issues of biblical authority, ministry, mission, and the definition of the church itself. As you can imagine, liberal and conservative Christians respond quite differently to challenges raised in these areas and I can now trust you to predict how various groups will react and to explain why they react as they do.

A simple listing of contemporary *moral* problems that demand Christian consideration will show us that questions about the ordination of homosexuals,[8] the legitimacy of a pro-choice position on abortion,[9] and the mandate to eliminate nuclear weapons[10] all promise to make the practical realities of Christian life highly volatile in the future. My purpose in this chapter, however, is not to engage in extensive discussion of complex moral issues. I prefer to draw your attention to the kinds of issues we have been discussing throughout the book, ones that present perennial challenges to Christians by raising questions about ministry, church, and mission.

We will look at three complex issues and connect each one with a specific kind of definitional problem. They all have long, complicated histories which I can only allude to in this book. I hope, however, that they will interest you enough that you will do some further study and try to grasp the nuances involved. I will discuss ministry in terms of the women's movement by focusing on questions of women's ordination. I will discuss the nature of the church in terms of the so-called electronic church and use the opportunity to say something about Christian broadcasting. Finally, I will discuss the mission of the churches by way of an introduction to Third World liberation theologies. By the end perhaps you will have what I have hoped for throughout this book, a sense of the great dynamism of Christianity and its continuing bustle of life in the contemporary world.

The Women's Movement and the Problems of Ministry

Any organization that exists within a particular culture is usually impelled to deal with the challenges and questions of that culture. Modern women are raising critical questions which have enormous consequences for the Christian churches. The problem is sexism, the systematic cultural and institutional denial of opportunity to women simply because of their sex.[11] Sexism is an especially difficult problem because discussions about it often engender strong resistance: some want to deny that there is a problem at all, and others, though recognizing the cry for justice, are often shocked at some of the directions taken by feminist critics.

At the heart of the matter for Christian women is the issue of biblical authority that we have encountered many times throughout this book. If women are treated as second-class citizens by religious denominations *on the basis of the Bible*, what does that say about biblical authority? Does God intend for women to be secondary? Did God create women as helpmates for men with no opportunities beyond motherhood or (in Catholic teaching) the convent?

Some church leaders (mostly male) would say that, indeed, God did create women with natures and attributes that are different from those of men: men are strong, rational, naturally inclined toward philosophical speculation, and meant to rule, whereas women are weak, emotional, naturally inclined toward bodily life (motherhood), and meant to be ruled. This division pleases some women and many men, and has the advantage of being consistent with the kinds of opinions one can find in the Bible. At the same time, feminist interpreters in the churches point out that we can find a rather different perspective in the words and behavior of Jesus toward women. Jesus invited women into discipleship, appeared to have a special understanding of their lives, treated them with unusual dignity, and made his first post-resurrection appearance to a woman. It appears, therefore, as if a tension is present even in the New Testament about the proper role and place of women: the example of Jesus tends to lead to the conclusion that the new community is a discipleship of equals, whereas *some* of the other writings in the New Testament, including some of those attributed to Paul, lead to the conclusion that women may not speak in public, hold any office in the church, or have any life of their own apart from the protection and direction of their husbands. The fact that the New Testament can be read in different ways on this issue should not surprise us.

Feminist critics of Christianity can begin to be understood in terms of three aspects of their early work. First, they noticed that women are virtually invisible in the texts—biblical and historical—and that they appear to have been omitted on purpose. Second, they showed that the sparse amount of material that *can* be found about women is not flattering: women are described as essentially erotic, lustful, and revolting; as the "devil's gateway," probably not made in the divine image; not persons in the fullest sense of the word; remembered, if at all, as whores, virgins, wives, or mothers in relation to famous men; as naturally defective, misbegotten males suspended in a state of eternal childhood in which they long for domination and in which they need to be subject to male control; as unfit for ordination, too unclean or impure to walk in sacred space; and as sexually insatiable and mercilessly nagging.[12] Much of this material can be found in the writings of the ancient Christian fathers (see Appendix 3) and in the works of medieval theologians, but the fact that it still influences some of the arguments against women's ordination and full participation in positions of church leadership makes it a continuing source of anger and pain for many Christian women. Third, feminists began to find some of the women who have been "lost" to Christian history, restoring the visibility of some of the important and unusual women whose lives changed the shape of Christianity.[13]

Feminists have challenged the male God-language of the Bible, attempted to create new theologies meant to reinterpret traditional Christian doctrines like the Trinity, and tried to find new ways to imagine their interaction with the divine in symbolic and practical terms. One salient issue is that of women's ordination and the continuing challenge it raises for the churches.

Women have always been the major practitioners of Christianity, but they have only recently taken some role in the leadership of the church. Eighty-four denominations now ordain women and nearly as many do not. Whether women ought to be ordained is a question that divides Christians even within denominations: fundamentalist Southern Baptists forbid it, moderate Southern Baptists allow it, and the American Baptist church ordains women as a matter of policy. Although women were not admitted to divinity schools in any significant way until the 1950s, by 1987 nearly 30 percent of all seminary students were women. It appears, therefore, that many Christian churches have met the criticisms of the women's movement and now welcome the leadership of women as well as men.

Those appearances, however, can be deceiving. One of the problems faced by churches that ordain women is the placement of those women. Many of them are *not* called as the primary ministers of churches, but are relegated to secondary positions as hospital chaplains, assistant ministers, and as ministers of education. The mere fact of ordination, therefore, does not eliminate the challenge.

The problems faced by the churches that do *not* ordain women are different. Roman Catholicism is a case in point. The refusal of Catholics to ordain women is based on the idea that the priest represents Christ and so must resemble him physically, an argument that has been denied and criticized by Catholic feminists and theologians.[14] The desire for reunion between Roman Catholic and Anglican churches, a process that has absorbed great time and energy in both churches for the last hundred years, is now in jeopardy because of the Anglican decision to ordain women to the priesthood. Finally, the appeal to "tradition" made on the part of Roman Catholic officials, an appeal shared by Orthodox Christians, raises the whole question of the validity of tradition and introduces questions about the ways tradition has been used to support the power structures of the church rather than to enhance the life of the faithful. The question of women's ordination, therefore, raises challenges about the authority of the Bible, the role of tradition, the credibility of church leadership, and the need for new attitudes toward women in the churches.

It also raises the question of ministry. What is a minister or priest supposed to do in a congregation? If the minister represents God, then is the presence of women ministers an invitation to find and use images for divine-human interaction that stress female images of the divine? If the minister is the authority figure in the community, does the presence of women in the ministry contradict Paul's injunctions about women not having power over men? Does it mean that Paul was wrong about this issue? Or might it suggest that Christians need new ways to understand and exercise power? How will the participation of women ministers affect the ways congregations think about God? Will the presence of more women in church leadership change the nature of the church in some way?

If you think women in ministry *will* change patterns of worship and articulations of religious language, how do you envision such a change? If you think that such a change might "ruin" Christianity as we have known it, *how* do you think it might have that outcome? If you think that such a change might "improve" Christianity as we have known it, *how* do you think it might do so? The questions are not simple, because they touch the very core of Christian worship and challenge Christians to think more deeply about the ways they pray, sing, preach, and, in general, relate to God. The questions will not disappear: in many ways, the challenge of the women's movement in Christianity sets part of the agenda for the churches into the next century.

Technology and the Nature of the "Electronic" Church

When we consider the challenges of modern technology, we are in a zone where, it appears, we cannot appeal to the Bible. Jesus had nothing to say about radio and television, and neither did the ancient Christian writers. They did, however, give the church a task to preach the gospel to all nations, to make disciples out of all peoples. Has modern media technology made that task possible in new ways? Or has the church's use of radio and television changed the ways Christians can envision the nature of the church? Is the church a community of believers united in fellowship in a particular place, associated with a larger institutional structure, or is it a collection of those who have a personal relationship with Jesus whether they gather together in a local congregation or not? Is the gospel necessarily connected with Christian political activism?

In the early 1920s, an innovative program manager at KDKA, Pittsburgh, invited a local minister to broadcast a short message over the radio. The minister and the idea were both highly successful: by 1926 nearly all of the 600-plus radio stations in America supported some kind of religious broadcasting. In the competitive radio market, program directors began to look for preachers with "personality" who could draw large audiences and build national reputations. Catholic audiences tuned in to two priests, the controversial Charles Coughlin and the man who would later become a television personality as well, Fulton Sheen; mainline Protestant churches had special shows like "The Lutheran Hour." The real supporters of this new form of ministry, however, were fundamentalists.

Recall the fact that fundamentalism was engaged in some major religious battles in the 1920s, and also remember that the heart of fundamentalism is its emphasis on evangelism. Radio appeared to be a great medium for preaching the gospel to all nations, and a perfect way to disseminate the work of independent churches and Bible institutes. For example, the Moody Bible Institute in Chicago had its own radio station and was the strongest fundamentalist voice in the Chicago area in the 1930s. A young, powerful new preacher from North

Carolina, Billy Graham, was clearly a man who was going places and who knew how to use the media for an evangelical advantage. Finally, Charles Fuller, whose program, "The Old-Fashioned Revival Hour," was carried nationally on the Mutual Radio network, was reputed to have the largest audience of any preacher on the airwaves.

Fuller's success was amazing: he began with a local program in Los Angeles, pioneered the use of audience participation with a weekly phone-in segment, and finally entered into radio ministry full time, supported by his listeners' contributions. You should know that he managed to do this during the Depression: people who had little hope and less money made donations that financed expensive air time and finally resulted in the capital necessary for founding the Fuller Evangelical Seminary.

In the mid-1950s, the strategies of radio evangelism were translated to television. Preachers began to build national audiences with a blend of "old-time religion" and commercial appeals. Oral Roberts, Rex Humbard, and Billy Graham, all with different styles, became phenomenally successful and began to change the ways people looked at the church. People were no longer confined to local congregations, but could now participate in a kind of national evangelical consciousness by way of their contributions and support for these new ministries.

In the mid-1960s, computer technology added new dimensions to the picture. Computers could be programmed to store names, addresses, and personal information. If smart advertisers saw the advantages of appealing to the American public by way of "personalized" letters, so did television evangelists. Preachers began to hire writers, to use combinations of religious entertainment and the gospel to increase their audiences. They found that they could get massive financial support for building projects and began to appeal for funds to build hospitals and colleges (such as Oral Roberts University and Jerry Falwell's Liberty Baptist College).

If television in the 1960s seemed full of dreadful news—assassinations, the Vietnam War, an energy shortage, the toppling of traditional values by a permissive "new" morality—it was also able to transmit the comforting message of evangelical Christianity. Preachers offered hope and certainty, and evangelicals had a distinct advantage over other Christian groups. Unlike Catholics, Anglicans, and Lutherans, whose worship is not designed for broad appeal, and mainline Protestants who rely on the fellowship of local congregations, television evangelists were able to go directly to people's hearts. Their message was simple: they asked people to "get right with God," settle differences with their loved ones, and accept themselves. These simple, moving messages, delivered with technological sophistication and strong emotional preaching, made the television evangelists enormously popular.

That popularity drew the attention of conservative politicians in the 1970s: Richard Vigeurie, head of the largest political mailing organization in the United States; Tim Le Haye, president of the American Coalition for Traditional Values; Morton Blackwell, head of the Leadership Institute, and others began to steer some television evangelists into politics.[15] President Ronald Reagan appeared at a massive rally of conservative Christians in Dallas in 1980, telling them that he understood that they could not endorse *him*, but assuring them that *he* endorsed *them*.

Increasingly, a new generation of television evangelists called for Christians to get involved in politics. Jerry Falwell founded the Moral Majority as a means of gathering support for conservative political causes. Pat Robertson, the founder of the popular television program "The 700 Club," ran for President of the United States. Jimmy Swaggart preached against moral evil in general and explained to his revival audiences that President Reagan was fighting an uphill battle without their support. Money began to pour in for political causes—more than $1 billion in 1986—and conservative politicians began to sense that they had only begun to tap the resources available to them through a coalition of conservative religious and political activists.

Predictably, the political issues held dear by television evangelists have taken on religious descriptions. The Strategic Defense Initiative and the death penalty, for example, are said to be "Christian" causes. There is nothing new about this claim: during the Civil Rights campaign in the 1960s and in support of action against the Vietnam War, liberal Christians claimed that their views best represented Christian principles. The question of who speaks for American values and who speaks for Christianity is not one that we need to solve. We need only realize that the question has become increasingly complicated by the emergence of the conservative Christians as political activists. At this point, we will leave the political issues aside and focus on the challenges raised to the concept of church.

Does the very existence of the "electronic church" draw people away from local congregational participation? Or does the stimulation of television evangelism—in its political and nonpolitical forms—inspire Christians to become more active at the local level? Has the "electronic church" challenged other churches to adopt particular political profiles? If the political agenda of television evangelists is designed to celebrate and reshape American values, does it force other churches to fall into line with it, or to articulate alternative versions of a "Christian America?" Has the technology involved in direct mail solicitation and other innovations given the "electronic church" an unfair advantage financially? Does the survival of Christianity depend on increased use of such tactics by other groups?

Finally, what does the success of the "electronic church" tell us about the nature of the church? *Is* television a proper medium for evangelization? Can we expect Christianity to change dramatically because of the stimulation of television evangelism? How does the success of the "electronic church" raise questions about the nature of the Christian community? Like the challenges raised by the women's movement, problems associated with the religious interaction with electronic technology will not disappear. The questions I have posed here are, in many ways, only the beginning and should alert you to an increasingly interesting arena of debate that promises to have continuing impacts on the churches.

Third World Challenges to the Nature of the Christian Mission

When we looked at some of the early Christian missionary endeavors in the new world in Chapter 9, we began to wonder whether some of the methods employed by the missionaries were geared more to conquest and exploitation than to preaching and discipleship. We need to keep that question in mind as we take another look at liberation theology (see Chapter 10) in a Third World perspective.

Liberation theology was born in a context of poverty and oppression in Latin America. Its special method, *praxis*, developed by Brazilian educator Paulo Freire,[16] tends to focus on actions rather than words. Based on a reading of the Bible in which God's special concern rests with the poor and oppressed peoples of the world, liberation theology holds that God's most significant actions in the Bible are those involved with deliverance or liberation (from oppression, slavery, exile, sin). According to this view, God has a special relationship with the poor and marginalized members of any society.

Liberation theology, therefore, starts with a commitment to the poor and to their struggle. In this way, the early missionary Bartolome de las Casas can be considered a hero for liberation theologians, but their work is based primarily on the life of Jesus. Like Social Gospel preachers in the nineteenth century, liberation theologians argue that God does not will poverty. On the contrary, through the life and example of Jesus, God has called Christians to work for the elimination of all forms of oppression.

Non-conformist Christians like members of the Sojourners community and the Catholic Worker Movement follow the impetus of the liberation perspective when they identify with the poor in order to minister to them. Liberation theologians claim that their commitment to the poor gives them a new perspective from which to read the Bible and gives their theology an edge that is both critical and prophetic. Like liberal Christians, they understand salvation in social terms and tend to define spirituality in activist terms. Liberation theology is not, however, an isolated view of Christian social action meant to inspire a particular kind of relationship with oppressed peoples. Its theologians claim that it is a whole new way to understand Christianity and its doctrines.

Liberation theology articulates an experience of God as involved in the human problems of the world. As liberation theologians read the Bible, they see that God entered into human history after the Fall and offered humanity a series of covenants and promises of deliverance. When people in bondage cried out, God liberated them and made them responsible for establishing peace and justice on the earth. If the ancient Israelites forgot their mission, God reminded them through the prophets. Jesus's mission was to the poor, and he spent his life trying to counteract human selfishness. According to liberation theologians,

God intervened from *outside* in the Old Testament and from *inside* in the New Testament. Jesus is located inside human history in a dramatic way; and he was sent to teach humanity that religious responsibility is a matter not of keeping specific laws but of accepting God's love so that Christians are prepared to lay down their lives for their neighbors. The ethics preached by Jesus are meant to be followed in the lives of ordinary Christians.

Liberation theology grew in predominantly Catholic soil and was inspired in part by some of the modern social teachings of the Catholic church.[17] At the same time, many of the themes raised by liberation theologians have been found in Protestant Christianity, especially in the meetings of the World Council of Churches.[18] Furthermore, the liberationist perspective can be applied to any group that has experienced oppression. Black theology, for example, reads the Bible from the perspective of racist oppression, and James Cone argues that only a black understanding of Scripture and faith is authentic.[19] Women's groups have also identified with liberation perspectives. For the most part, those oppressed groups who find solace in liberation theology tend to take the exodus motif in the Old Testament as a metaphor for their relationship to God. To their way of thinking, God is involved in their suffering and active with them in the struggle to overcome oppression.

In contemporary Christianity, liberation theology has the potential to build up and to divide communities. This volatile capacity is especially evident in responses to Christian missionary activity and reminds us that most denominations are made up of Christians from both liberal and conservative perspectives. At the present time, for example, several Protestant churches are sharply divided over the proper role for their missionaries in Latin America. Should they be there to identify with the poor and help them build a more just society, or are they sent primarily to preach the gospel and to move their listeners to personal regeneration? Does a Christian have to choose between these two possibilities? Can a missionary fulfill the intentions of Jesus by simply asking people to change their hearts? Or must missionaries also involve themselves in helping people change the circumstances of their lives?

The Roman Catholic church is also divided on the issue. The participation of priests and sisters in the Nicaraguan revolution in 1979, for example, was based on their liberationist reading of the Gospels; yet the Vatican has sharply criticized active political involvement on the part of its clergy and has attempted to frame its social justice agenda in less partisan ways. Are the issues at stake for Catholics different from those raised by Protestants? How does Catholicism explain its clear interests in the lives of impoverished peoples along with its official refusal to allow its priests to participate in politics? What kinds of work should nuns and priests be doing in Africa, Asia, and Latin America? What are the connections between the work of Christian missionaries and the ways Christianity is perceived by Third World peoples?

One of the sharpest criticisms of contemporary Christianity from a Third World perspective has been that of Tissa Balasuriya, a Sri Lankan Catholic priest. He argues that modern Christianity is morally bankrupt and suggests a "new mission," what he calls a "mission in reverse." Third World Christians, who understand how to live the gospel, should go as missionaries to industrialized countries where Christians have abandoned the teachings of the gospel in favor of policies of exploitation.[20] Christians in America and Europe are also increasingly challenged to new understandings by their dialogue with African Christians, an area we cannot even begin to describe here.

Christians in Europe and later in America took seriously the words of Jesus to carry the gospel to all nations. Their missionary work was sometimes accompanied by a desire to preach their culture and politics as well, a policy which, as we have seen, was disastrous in seventeenth-century China, and relatively successful in the Americas, though at murderous cost to native religions and cultures. Christianity was linked with the expansion of the British empire in Africa and India in the nineteenth century, and with American ideas about manifest destiny in the Pacific and other places. Many of the peoples in those places have struggled throughout the twentieth century—and in some cases are still involved in revolutions—to establish their political independence. It should not be surprising that they also hope to find and articulate a religious independence as well.

Christianity is no longer a religion that has an essentially American and European character. On the contrary, Christians throughout the world are bringing their own perspectives, their own forms of celebration, their own music and styles of preaching, and their own evaluations of the proper roles for Christians in the pressing social questions of the day.

What, then, is the role of the missionary in today's church? As you can imagine, Christians have different answers. Conservative Christians agree that one should interpret the gospel and the invitation to salvation in a way that does not attempt to undermine or reconstruct the society, whereas liberal Christians believe their goals should be dictated in part by the grave social ills of the country and that their work should begin with and always include ways to improve the living conditions of the people there. At this point, you should be able to make some reasonable predictions about the ways various Christians might respond to the challenges of modern Christian missionary activity, and you are no doubt aware that worldwide Christianity is a dynamic and complex phenomenon.

CONCLUSION

Christianity is an extraordinarily rich religion, rooted in ancient texts and traditions that continue to be upheld and followed. We have seen throughout this book that Christianity has always understood its obligations to be "faithful" to the life, work, and words of Jesus while at the same time attempting to adjust itself to new circumstances, cultures, and peoples. As I have mentioned several times in this book, conflict and controversy characterize any living religion:

Christians have always argued heatedly over important issues as they attempted to figure things out in ways that they believed would preserve the integrity of the early church even as they responded creatively to new situations.

The general distinction I have made between liberal and conservative Christians is not a modern one. From the beginning there have been those whose energies have been primarily invested in guarding the tradition from the encroachment of new ideas, just as there have been those who have been inspired to seek new articulations and open new possibilities. In the New Testament, the church in Jerusalem presided over by James represented a dedicated following of traditional patterns, whereas the new churches founded by Paul were examples of a radically different way of interpreting the intentions of Jesus. Throughout Christian history we can locate these two different modes of operation: conservatives cling to traditional understandings, while liberals press for adaptations and adjustments. Both groups are necessary for the creative survival of Christianity and will continue to set the parameters of argument within the Christian churches.

This chapter has been an attempt to recapitulate these two governing attitudes within the churches while raising some of the vexing issues that, I believe, will remain under discussion by Christians well into the next century. The women's movement, the possibilities of technology, and the pressing problems of Third World liberation will all continue to raise challenges for Christianity that involve practical matters like ministry, church membership, and the nature of mission. At the same time, underneath those practical matters will be important conceptual issues like the personality of God, the authority of the Bible, and the understanding of a faithful Christian life. The questions should not surprise us, and the arguments they will inspire should not disturb us. If there is one thing to take away from our study of Christianity it is this: Christianity unfolds in history like a great story, full of passion and promise, intrigue and integrity, still capable, after all this time, of astonishing itself.

CHAPTER 12 NOTES

[1] George Marsden defines fundamentalism as a distinct brand of evangelical Christianity uniquely shaped by the experiences of early twentieth-century America and notes that fundamentalists are united by a militant opposition to modernism in any of its forms. See *Fundamentalism and American Culture: The Shaping of Twentieth-Century Evangelicalism 1870–1925* (New York: Oxford University Press, 1980). Ernest Sandeen, however, interprets fundamentalism as a longstanding millennialist movement related to end-of-the-world speculation in nineteenth-century England. See *The Roots of Fundamentalism: British and American Millenarianism 1800–1930* (Chicago: University of Chicago Press, 1970).

[2] Some denominations try to take a middle road position by retaining membership in the National Council of Churches while at the same time serving as official observers

on the council of the National Association of Evangelicals. This creative position was adopted in 1988 by the American Baptist church, the (relatively speaking) liberal cousin of the Southern Baptist church.

[3]Wade Clark Roof and William McKinney, *American Mainline Religion: Its Changing Shape and Future* (New Brunswick, N.J.: Rutgers University Press, 1988), argue that there is no such thing as "mainline Protestantism" in contemporary America. Their perspective is sociological, based on survey data and statistics, so they sometimes miss religious nuances, but they raise some important questions when they conclude that liberal Christians can regain strength only if they sharpen their religious identity. For a different view of the matter, see James Davison Hunter, *Evangelicalism: The Coming Generation* (Chicago: University of Chicago Press, 1987), an examination of student opinion at evangelical colleges. Hunter concludes that young evangelical students are moving decidedly to the left on moral and theological issues, which may suggest that liberalism is attractive to normally conservative Christians.

[4]The whole question of biblical inerrancy is currently at the heart of serious debates within fundamentalist circles. Efforts by the most conservative elements within the Southern Baptist church to gain control of the whole denomination have led to the formation of a "loyal opposition" within that church. The issue at stake is interpreting not only the doctrine of biblical inerrancy but the Reformation doctrine of the "priesthood of all believers." Baptists have used that doctrine in the past to guarantee autonomy for local congregations: the church as a whole can make recommendations and suggest policy, but local churches are free to make their own choices about ministry and other internal matters (see Appendix 6). The victory of the right wing, led by the Reverend W. A. Criswell of Dallas, Texas, has led to a position in which, it appears, the leaders are attempting to dictate policy to all local churches, especially on issues such as the ordination of women. The response of some moderate Baptists to this move has been the formation of the Southern Baptist Alliance (1987). The whole situation is complicated and bears further scrutiny. A recent book hostile to the Criswell forces is Joe Edward Barnhart, *The Southern Baptist Holy War* (Austin: Texas Monthly Press, 1986). A more objective presentation of the issues is the Bill Moyers television special "The Battle for the Bible: The Southern Baptist Debate over Inerrancy," originally broadcast on PBS 16 December 1987.

[5]See, for example, Ronald J. Sider, *Rich Christians in an Age of Hunger* (Downers Grove, Ill.: Inter-Varsity Press, 1977). Sider is one of the founders of Evangelicals for Social Action. The principles of that group, based on the Bible, state that the family is a divinely willed institution; that every human life is sacred; that religious and political freedom is a God-given right; that God has a special care for the poor and requires economic justice in society; that sin is both personal and social; and that God requires Christians to be peacemakers and stewards of the earth's resources.

[6]I have in mind, of course, the scandal of Jim and Tammy Bakker, who give fundamentalists a bad name. For a look at the greed, secrecy, and scandal that marked their downfall, see "God and Money," the cover story for *Time* magazine, 3 August 1987. For a provocative analysis of the *religious* implications, see Frances FitzGerald, "Reflections: Jim and Tammy," *The New Yorker* 66 (23 April 1990), 45–89.

[7]It might be instructive to watch "The 700 Club" on television to see how the Bible is used to support such political goals as the destruction of the Sandinista revolution in Nicaragua. Whether Robertson is right or wrong politically is not the issue here: we must pay attention to the ways the Bible is cited in favor of his positions and against any alternatives. See also "Power, Glory, and Politics," the cover story in *Time* magazine, 17 February 1986.

8This issue is currently a divisive one in several denominations. In December 1987 a group of Methodist ministers gathered in Houston, Texas, and issued the so-called Houston Declaration, which they then sent to Methodist ministers all over the country. One aim of the document was to exclude practicing homosexuals from the ministry, so the quadrennial General Conference (see Appendix 6) in 1988 looked to be a contentious event. The conference voted to reject practicing homosexuals from the ministry, but the atmosphere was not as bellicose as some had predicted, and the issue promises to return for further consideration at a later time. In January 1990, two Lutheran parishes in San Francisco ordained practicing homosexuals, bringing homosexuality to the forefront in the Lutheran church.

9This issue is currently vexing all the churches. Some fundamentalist groups are united in their opposition to any and all abortions, and some mainline churches are split on the issue. The Roman Catholic church has an official policy against abortion and American bishops have thrown their political support to antiabortion candidates, but there is also a pro-choice movement within the Catholic church and one cannot consider the matter fully resolved.

10The 200th General Assembly of the Presbyterian Church (U.S.A.) in 1988 approved a document that might have placed Presbyterians in the forefront of mainline churches on nuclear war issues. The final document was considerably amended, however, and the approved statement is not as strong as the original, but it does raise an important issue in a major denomination. The American Catholic bishops' pastoral on nuclear issues was also considerably amended between its first draft and final passage. Both groups continue to find opposition to these "official" policy statements within their own congregations.

11An introduction to the women's movement in general, and its impact on Christianity in particular, can be found in my *New Catholic Women: A Contemporary Challenge to Traditional Religious Authority* (San Francisco: Harper & Row, 1985; paperback, 1987). Although the book concentrates on the issues faced by Roman Catholic women, it is a general survey and can be applied to women in almost any denomination.

12One small, useful sourcebook for this list is Elizabeth Clark and Herbert Richardson, *Women and Religion: A Feminist Sourcebook of Christian Thought* (New York: Harper & Row, 1977).

13Two books are helpful here: Rosemary Ruether, editor, *Religion and Sexism: Images of Women in the Jewish and Christian Traditions* (New York: Simon & Schuster, 1974), and Rosemary Ruether and Eleanor McLaughlin, editors, *Women of Spirit* (New York: Simon & Schuster, 1979).

14Leonard and Arlene Swidler, editors, *Women Priests: A Catholic Commentary on the Vatican Declaration* (New York: Paulist Press, 1977). For an extensive review of the problem and the literature, see Chapter 4 of my *New Catholic Women*, cited in note 11.

15A controversial film by Antony Thomas, *Thy Kingdom Come*, was produced in 1986 to trace the evolution of Christian right-wing politics and to expose the scandal of the Jim and Tammy Bakker enterprise. It was shown on public television on the program "Frontline" in a shortened version in 1988. Many parts of this film are excellent: one can get a sense of why many people are drawn to the message of evangelical Christianity, and why political appeals work with them. At the same time, Thomas's biases are clear: he is appalled by the whole notion of Christian politics. One needs to exercise critical judgment, therefore, when watching this film.

16See his book *Pedagogy of the Oppressed* (New York: Continuum, 1970).

17See, for example, Pope John XXIII's encyclicals *Mater et Magistra* (1961), which focused on Christianity and social progress, and *Pacem in Terris* (1963), devoted to peace on earth.

[18]The 1961 meeting of the WCC in New Delhi dramatized the problems of world hunger and poverty, and a 1966 meeting of church leaders of the WCC in Geneva concluded that the gospel is revolutionary by nature and that Christians ought to be involved on the side of social revolution. A meeting of Roman Catholic and World Council of Churches leaders in Beirut (1968) discussed Pope Paul VI's encyclical *Populorum Progressio* and urged Christians to be politically active on behalf of peace and world development. The world conference of the WCC in Uppsala in 1968 was focused on the needs of the world and concluded that those who were complacent in the face of vast social injustice were guilty of heresy.

[19]*A Black Theology of Liberation* (Philadelphia: Fortress Press, 1970).

[20]*Planetary Theology* (Maryknoll, N.Y.: Orbis Books, 1984).

SUGGESTIONS FOR FURTHER READING

1. A feminist critique of Christianity is not new. See, for example, Elizabeth Cady Stanton, *The Woman's Bible* (Seattle: Coalition Task Force on Women and Religion, reprint 1974), which was originally published in the 1890s. Many Christian women who worked in the antislavery campaigns or in the temperance movement later were drawn to issues of women's rights. Although religion was not the overwhelming concern in the early years of the nineteenth-century women's movement, it was a significant one and continues to be one today. For a survey of religious attitudes toward women in the Catholic church, see Mary Daly, *The Church and the Second Sex*, 2nd ed. (New York: Harper & Row, 1975), originally published in 1968. Daly was the first to raise the modern cry against sexism in the churches. For an interrelation of feminist and liberation theologies, see Rosemary Ruether, *New Woman, New Earth: Sexist Ideologies and Human Liberation* (New York: Seabury Press, 1975). Ruether has published widely in this field from a variety of perspectives, so it may be to your advantage to look into other books by her.

2. The women's movement within the churches is not unified. One can find a wide range of perspectives even among those who agree that "something ought to be done." An evangelical woman's perspective on feminist theology is Virginia Ramey Mollenkott, *Women, Men, and the Bible* (Nashville: Abingdon Press, 1977). An introduction to the work of women in the World Council of Churches can be found in Susannah Herzel, *A Voice for Women* (Geneva: World Council of Churches, 1981). Herzel reports on the Women's Department in the WCC (which began in 1948) and describes the lives and work of some of the pioneering women in that department as they worked in villages and towns throughout the world. Both Mollenkott and Herzel assume that women in the churches should remain within their institutions and work toward full justice for men and women within the churches. Some feminists, however, believe that women ought to abandon Christian churches altogether in search of other alternatives. An overview of feminist thinking about Judaism and Christianity which begins by raising questions about traditional theological categories and ends with the argument that "women need the Goddess" is Carol P. Christ and Judith Plaskow, editors, *Womanspirit Rising: A Feminist Reader in Religion* (New York: Harper & Row, 1979). Conservative Christians often take the position that feminism is not necessary in the churches because the Bible already provides mutually supportive roles for the sexes as they relate to one another. See Ronald B. Allen, *Liberated Traditionalism* (Portland, Ore.: Multnomah Press, 1985).

3. The "electronic church" phenomenon has caused considerable discussion on various issues which you find most readily in the periodical literature: for example, Jeffrey K. Hadden, "Soul Saving Via Video," *The Christian Century* 97 (28 May 1980), 609–13. Books have only begun to appear on this topic. For a historical introduction, see Razelle Frankl, *Televangelism: The Marketing of Popular Religion* (Carbondale, Ill.: Southern Illinois University Press, 1987). For a look at American televangelism by a British critic who tends to lean toward the left, see Peter Elvy, *Buying Time: The Foundations of the Electronic Church* (Mystic, Conn.: Twenty-Third Publications, 1987).

4. The *political* implications of television evangelism emerged for the first time in the early 1980s, often most clearly apparent in the connection between Jerry Falwell and the Moral Majority. See "Born Again Politics," *Newsweek* 96 (15 September 1980), 27–36, and Frances FitzGerald, "A Disciplined, Charging Army," *The New Yorker* 57 (18 May 1981), 53–141. Pat Robertson's run for the presidency of the United States focused the political issues on him. See "Gospel TV: Religion, Politics and Money," *Time* 127 (17 February 1986), 62–70, and David Edwin Harrell, Jr., *Pat Robertson: A Personal, Political, and Religious Portrait* (San Francisco: Harper & Row, 1988).

5. The main publisher of works on liberation theology is Orbis Books in Maryknoll, New York. All the following books have been published by Orbis. An oversimplified but accessible introduction can be found in L. John Topel, *The Way to Peace: Liberation through the Bible* (1973), pp. 146–56. A clear book about developments in the Roman Catholic church in Latin America for the past thirty-five years is Edward L. Cleary, *Crisis and Change: The Church in Latin America Today* (1985). An introduction to the *diversity* of the movement is Deane William Ferm, *Third World Liberation Theologies: An Introductory Survey* (1986). A book that explains how liberation theology is a whole new way of doing theology (as opposed to a version of social ethics) is Victorio Araya, *God of the Poor: The Mystery of God in Latin American Liberation Theology* (1987). Finally, a good introduction by two practitioners is Leonardo and Clodovis Boff, *Introducing Liberation Theology* (1987).

6. For more on black liberation theology see James Cone, *For My People* (Maryknoll, N.Y.: Orbis Books, 1984), and the excellent work of J. Deotis Roberts, *Liberation and Reconciliation: A Black Theology* (Philadelphia: Fortress Press, 1971).

APPENDIX 1
THE ORDER OF THE BOOKS
IN THE OLD TESTAMENT

The Christian Old Testament is a reordering of the books in the Hebrew Bible. The Hebrew Bible is divided into three parts: the Law (Torah), the Prophets, and the Writings. The Christian Old Testament eliminates the distinction between the Prophets and the Writings and puts the Prophets at the end, to serve as an introduction to the New Testament. Notice that the order of the books changes the tone and emphasis. Because of the differences in intention and theological signification, it is not correct to say that the Old Testament is the same thing as the Hebrew Bible.

Roman Catholics formerly used an Old Testament that contained books found in neither the Hebrew Bible nor the Protestant Old Testament. Why? Because Roman Catholics based their Old Testament on the Greek translation, while Protestants used the Hebrew version. In the Douay (Roman Catholic) Version of the Old Testament, which most Roman Catholics no longer use, one can find books that appear in the Apocrypha in the Revised Standard Version (Tobit, Judith, the Wisdom of Solomon, Ecclesiasticus, Baruch, and 1 and 2 Maccabees).

HEBREW BIBLE		PROTESTANT OLD TESTAMENT	ROMAN CATHOLIC OLD TESTAMENT (DOUAY VERSION)
Genesis	⎫	Genesis	Genesis
Exodus	⎪	Exodus	Exodus
Leviticus	⎬ the Law	Leviticus	Leviticus
Numbers	⎪	Numbers	Numbers
Deuteronomy	⎭	Deuteronomy	Deuteronomy
		Joshua	Josue
Joshua	⎫	Judges	Judges
Judges	⎪	Ruth	Ruth
Samuel	⎪	Samuel	Kings
Kings	⎪	Kings	Paralipomenon
Isaiah	⎪	Chronicles	Esdras
Jeremiah	⎪	Ezra	Nehemias
Ezekiel	⎪	Nehemiah	*Tobias
Hosea	⎪	Esther	*Judith
Joel	⎪	Job	Esther
Amos	⎬ the Prophets	Psalms	Job
Obadiah	⎪	Proverbs	Psalms
Jonah	⎪	Ecclesiastes	Proverbs
Micah	⎪	Song of Solomon	Ecclesiastes
Nahum	⎪	Isaiah	Canticle of Canticles
Habakkuk	⎪	Jeremiah	*Wisdom
Zephaniah	⎪	Lamentations	*Ecclesiasticus
Haggai	⎪	Ezekiel	Isaias
Zechariah	⎪	Daniel	Jeremias
Malachi	⎭	Hosea	Lamentations
		Joel	*Baruch
Psalms	⎫	Amos	Ezechiel
Proverbs	⎪	Obadiah	Daniel
Job	⎪	Jonah	Osee
Ruth	⎪	Micah	Joel
Song of Songs	⎪	Nahum	Amos
Lamentations	⎬ the Writings	Habakkuk	Abdias
Ecclesiastes	⎪	Zephaniah	Jonas
Esther	⎪	Haggai	Micheas
Daniel	⎪	Zechariah	Nahum
Ezra	⎪	Malachi	Habacuc
Nehemiah	⎪		Sophonias
Chronicles	⎭		Aggeus
			Zacharias
			Malachias
			*Maccabees

* Books not found in the Hebrew Bible or in the Protestant Old Testament.

APPENDIX 2
SYNOPSIS OF THE BOOKS
OF THE OLD AND NEW TESTAMENTS

This list is a synopsis of the *content* of the books of the Old and New Testaments, Revised Standard Version, and is for handy reference. New Testament writings have been dated along the lines suggested by Norman Perrin in *The New Testament, An Introduction*. In some ways there are too many opinions about the origins of New Testament books; in Pauline scholarship, especially, one can find endless argumentation about authenticity and dating. Students who want more precise information should refer to a wide variety of reference works and recent scholarship and should, in any case, be advised that the system adopted here is a starting point, not a final word.

THE OLD TESTAMENT

GENESIS ("origins"): The first of the Five Books of Moses, recounting the beginnings of the world and the creation of humanity, the story of Noah and of the Patriarchs—Abraham, Isaac, and Jacob—ending with the death of Joseph.

EXODUS ("a way out"): The second of the Five Books of Moses, recounting the oppression of the Jews in Egypt, their deliverance by Moses, the covenant at Sinai, and the establishment of the Tabernacle, the movable community shrine.

LEVITICUS (Levites = assistants to the priests): The third of the Five Books of Moses, containing the legislation dictated to Moses by God after the establishment of the Tabernacle, dealing primarily with ritual purity.

NUMBERS: The fourth of the Five Books of Moses, relating the history of the Jews in the desert from the second to the fortieth year of their wanderings.

DEUTERONOMY ("repetition of the Law"): The last of the Five Books of Moses, containing Moses's review of the events since Sinai, a repetition of the Ten Commandments, and Moses's final admonitions to Israel.

JOSHUA: An account of the history of the Israelites in their conquest and division of Canaan from the death of Moses to the death of Joshua, his successor (ca. 1220 B.C.E.).

JUDGES: Describes the acts of ancient heroes and heroines of Israel from the death of Joshua until the time of Samuel (ca. 1050 B.C.E.); it includes the stories of Samson, Deborah, and Gideon.

RUTH: Story of a non-Israelite woman, Ruth, married to a Hebrew. After his death she returns to Judah with her mother-in-law to live with the Israelites. Through her marriage to Boaz, Ruth becomes great-grandmother of King David.

1 AND 2 SAMUEL: Relate the history of the Jews from the end of the period of Judges to the last days of King David (972 B.C.E.), focusing on the biographies of Samuel, Saul, and David. These books depict the Davidic monarchy as a divine institution, established to represent God's rule on earth.

1 AND 2 KINGS: Contain the history of the Jews from the reign of Solomon (c. 970 B.C.E.) to the fall of Jerusalem (587 B.C.E), and can be seen as a continuation of the Books of Samuel. Kings recount a period of Israel's glory, division, decline, and fall.

1 AND 2 CHRONICLES: Contain genealogical lists of Israelite tribes, a history of David's rule, and an account of Solomon's rule, emphasizing the building of the temple and ending with the destruction of the temple and the exile to Babylon. Chronicles picture the events in Israel's history as divine judgments.

EZRA: Relates the events after the return from the Babylonian exile (538 B.C.E.), including the beginning of the rebuilding of the temple.

NEHEMIAH: A continuation of the Book of Ezra, recounting the reconstruction of Jerusalem.

ESTHER: A story of the deliverance of the Jews of Persia through the influence of Esther on the King of Persia, her husband.

JOB: Relates the story of a righteous man who suffers as a result of God's testing his faith. It points to the mystery of human suffering and the inadequacy of human knowledge in things pertaining to the purposes of God.

PSALMS ("poems sung to stringed instruments"): A collection of Hebrew poetry (150 psalms) that contains deep religious feeling and conviction. Many of the psalms are attributed to King David. This book contains some of the most beautiful poetry in the Bible.

PROVERBS: A collection of maxims on how an individual can survive and prosper.

ECCLESIASTES ("members of the assembly"): A somewhat pessimistic book that concludes that "all is vanity," and that one should resign oneself to suffering and injustice. It claims that there is no correlation between righteousness and happiness.

SONG OF SOLOMON: Contains love poems written in dialogue form that have been read as describing love between persons, love between God and Israel, or love between Jesus and the church.

ISAIAH: First of the major prophets, who protested strongly against moral laxity. Isaiah emphasizes that God will punish but not exterminate Israel for its sins and that there will come times of redemption and comfort.

JEREMIAH: Second of the major prophets, containing bitter prophecies addressed to foreign nations and some biographical material on the prophet himself. Jeremiah's ministry began around 627 B.C.E. and ended sometime around 580 B.C.E.

LAMENTATIONS: Contains elegies and mournings over the destruction of Jerusalem and the temple by the Babylonians.

EZEKIEL: Third of the major prophets who prophesied at the time of the destruction of the temple (587 B.C.E.). Ezekiel contains rebukes spoken before the destruction of Jerusalem and prophecies of disasters, consolation, and the coming of the new kingdom.

DANIEL: Contains two parts, the first of which recounts the miraculous experiences that happen to Daniel and his pious friends during the Babylonian exile, the second containing apocalyptic visions.

HOSEA: First of the minor prophets (so called because of the brevity of the books compared to Isaiah, Jeremiah, and Ezekiel), containing comments on the relationship between God and Israel and oracles rebuking Israel, followed by promises of salvation.

JOEL: Second of the minor prophets; describes a locust plague and the "Day of the Lord," when Israel will be restored to God.

AMOS: Third of the minor prophets, focusing on social morality as the determining factor in the history of Israel.

OBADIAH: Fourth of the minor prophets, consisting of one chapter condemning Edom (a country in southeast Palestine) for refusing to help Jerusalem in its hour of need.

JONAH: Fifth of the minor prophets, relating episodes in Jonah's life illustrating the power of repentance and divine mercy for all creatures.

MICAH: Sixth of the minor prophets, containing prophecies against the oppression by the ruling classes and speaking of a future king of Israel who will bring peace.

NAHUM: Seventh of the minor prophets, containing a masterful foretelling of the fall of Nineveh, the capital of Assyria.

HABAKKUK: Eighth of the minor prophets, consisting of an outcry against the evil in the world, God's reply, a prayer, and a description of the "Day of the Lord."

ZEPHANIAH: Ninth of the minor prophets, containing mainly prophecies dealing with the last days, declaring the coming of the "Day of the Lord" when the wicked will disappear and the poor will inherit the land.

HAGGAI: Tenth of the minor prophets, calling for a rebuilding of the temple.

ZECHARIAH: A contemporary of Haggai, Zechariah shares his zeal for the rebuilding of the temple.

MALACHI ("my messenger"): Twelfth and last of the minor prophets, rebuking Israel for its sinfulness, complaining of mixed and broken marriages, and envisioning the "Day of the Lord" to be preceded by Elijah's coming.

THE NEW TESTAMENT

GOSPEL OF MATTHEW (written between 70 and 90 C.E.): A synoptic gospel, regarding Jesus as the new Moses, emphasizing Jesus as the fulfillment of the Hebrew Bible and as the bringer of the new law or covenant.

GOSPEL OF MARK (written between 70 and 90 C.E.): Likely the earliest synoptic gospel, viewing Jesus as the Son of God who must suffer and die. Mark emphasizes Jesus as a man of action and focuses very little attention on Jesus's teachings.

GOSPEL OF LUKE (written between 70 and 90 C.E.): Synoptic gospel emphasizing the universality of Jesus's work and message. Here Jesus is the merciful one who forgives all humanity.

GOSPEL OF JOHN (written between 80 and 100 C.E.): John emphasizes the mystery and divinity of Jesus more than the synoptics do. God's love for humanity is a central theme of this gospel.

THE ACTS OF THE APOSTLES (written between 70 and 90 C.E.): The first history of the movement of Christianity, recording outstanding events in the spread of the Gospels from Jerusalem to Rome. It pictures the apostles as guided and empowered by the Holy Spirit.

THE EPISTLE TO THE ROMANS: Written by Paul around 57 C.E. and considered the first work of Christian theology. The intention of this letter is to announce Paul's coming to Rome and to prepare the Christians there for his arrival. In Romans more than in any other letter, Paul discusses the meaning of Christian salvation, the powerlessness of people, and the fullness of God's redeeming work.

THE FIRST EPISTLE TO THE CORINTHIANS: Also written by Paul around 55 C.E. to the church at Corinth, dealing with the Eucharist, love (*agape*) as the highest of spiritual gifts, and the meaning of the Resurrection.

THE SECOND EPISTLE TO THE CORINTHIANS (written c. 56 C.E.): Dealing principally with Paul's personal position as an apostle in relation to the activities of the church at Corinth.

THE EPISTLE TO THE GALATIANS: Written by Paul around 54 C.E., emphasizing the futility of trying to live by the Jewish Law and reestablishing the importance of justification by faith.

THE EPISTLE TO THE EPHESIANS: Attributed to Paul, emphasizes the universality of salvation for Jews and Gentiles alike; probably written between 70 and 90 C.E.

THE EPISTLE TO THE PHILIPPIANS: Written by Paul while in prison (c. 52–5 C.E.), thanking the Philippians for their assistance during his imprisonment and asking them to continue to follow Christ's example of charity and humility.

THE EPISTLE TO THE COLOSSIANS: Attributed to Paul (70–90 C.E.), stressing faith in Christ as all-sufficient redeemer. The author warns against the doctrines of the Gnostics and reestablishes the church's position on God, creation, and the church.

THE FIRST EPISTLE TO THE THESSALONIANS: One of the earliest letters written by Paul (c. 51 C.E.), assuring the Thessalonians that both the living and the dead will partake in the glory of the Second Coming of Christ.

THE SECOND EPISTLE TO THE THESSALONIANS: Not written by Paul but later (70–90 C.E.), warning the Thessalonians not to neglect their everyday duties while they await the Second Coming.

THE FIRST EPISTLE TO TIMOTHY: The first of the pastoral Epistles, discussing the practices of false teachers and methods of combating these practices; probably written between 90 and 140 C.E.

THE SECOND EPISTLE TO TIMOTHY: The second of the pastoral Epistles, again concerning false teachers, and reminding Timothy of the fidelity to tradition and the patience required of all apostles; probably written between 90 and 140 C.E.

THE EPISTLE TO TITUS: The third and last of the pastoral Epistles, discussing the duties of apostles and the need to struggle against false teachings; probably written between 90 and 140 C.E.

THE EPISTLE TO PHILEMON: Written by Paul while under house arrest (61–63 C.E.), asking Philemon to forgive a runaway slave who has been received by Paul as a Christian, and who is to be seen as a brother in Christ.

THE EPISTLE TO THE HEBREWS: Written before 96 C.E., it focuses on the idea that Christianity is the final and absolute religion because Jesus is the true high priest and the final mediation between God and humanity. Hebrews reestablishes the ineffectuality of the law.

THE EPISTLE OF JAMES: Written between 90 and 140 C.E., this is the first of the general Epistles (not written to a specific church or person, but to Christians in general) and deals with the superiority of deeds over theory, just treatment of the poor, the danger of evil speech, and the value of humility and sincerity.

THE FIRST EPISTLE OF PETER: The second of the general Epistles, written between 90 and 140 C.E., emphasizing a life of hope in Christ, which entails faith in the redemptive work of Christ and submitting to the will of God.

THE SECOND EPISTLE OF PETER: The third general Epistle (written between 90 and 140 C.E.), warning Christians against false teachings, exhorting them to hold fast to their faith, and assuring them of salvation.

THE EPISTLES OF JOHN: The fourth general Epistle (actually contains three very short letters written between 80 and 100 C.E.), emphasizing that "God is love," that morality, fellowship, and charity are extremely important in the Christian life, and that all false teachings are to be avoided.

THE EPISTLE OF JUDE: The fifth and last of the general Epistles (written between 90 and 140 C.E.), reminding Christians that God's forgiveness of sins is not an excuse for immoral actions, that God does punish disobedience, and that Christians have duties of prayer, faith, and love for God.

REVELATION OR THE APOCALYPSE: The last book of the New Testament (written between 90 and 100 C.E.), it describes the final struggle between good and evil and the eventual triumph of Christ and the church; it is written in highly symbolic language.

APPENDIX 3
EARLY CHRISTIAN WRITERS

Bishops and theologians in the early Christian community whose opinions on matters of doctrine and practice carried great weight are often referred to as "the Fathers." Because this designation makes it appear as if women made no contributions to the development of tradition in the early church, a point disputed by feminist theologians, I use the terminology *early Christian writers* here instead.[1] Little by little there came to be an appeal to tradition, especially to these early writers, for a consensus on disputed questions within Christianity. When the New Testament did not provide enough of an answer on an issue, people consulted the opinions that had been developing in the church in the works of these great theologians. According to a commonly accepted notion, these respected writers were those characterized by orthodoxy in doctrine, holiness in life, and approval of the ancient church. This last point is important: their authority is ancient. There are several groupings of early Christian writers, the most important of which are Greek, Latin, and Syrian.

The tasks of these writers varied according to the place and time in which they were working. In the early church, they functioned mostly as apologists: as those who *explained* Christianity to a hostile world or to an emperor who was considering persecution of the Christians. As the church grew in numbers and power and in problems, they wrote

[1] It is not easy to find church "Mothers," as it is not easy to find women in any historical period. Nevertheless, one can name a few: Egeria, Perpetua, Proba, and Eudokia. For translations of their works, critical commentary, and an introduction to the issue of early Christian literature by women, see Patricia Wilson-Kastner et al., *A Lost Tradition: Women Writers of the Early Church* (Washington, D.C.: University Press of America, 1981).

on various disciplinary matters—marriage, divorce, paying of taxes, fighting in wars—and on theological questions—the divinity of Christ, the place of Mary in the Christian church, and so on. When the church became the dominant institution in the Western and Eastern worlds, they devised elaborate systems of theology—the doctrine of the Trinity, for example.

One can read them for an understanding of a particular period, or for some introduction to the customs and beliefs of a particular region at a particular time. One can also find in them rich sources of spiritual writing and prayer. They provide the Christian church with much of its ancient history on several levels: cultural, religious, political, and moral.

The following brief outline mentions some of the important names and issues. An outline as sketchy as this is not meant to teach so much as to entice. Some people think that the only Christian writing from the ancient world is the New Testament. I hope that this list of topics and writers will show you that there was extraordinarily energetic argument, speculation, and writing going on in the early church.

A SELECTIVE OUTLINE OF THE LITERATURE

I. *Primitive Ecclesiastical Literature*
   A. Creeds developed in the period after the death of the apostles, the most famous of which is the *Apostles' Creed*.
   B. Teachings about discipline and behavior, the most famous of which is the *Didache*.
   C. Early writings associated with particular people that stressed the Christian philosophy of martyrdom, attitudes toward marriage, sin, penance, and so on. Some of the most famous writers were *Clement of Rome, Ignatius of Antioch,* and *Polycarp of Smyrna;* the most famous document was a work on penance and the forgiveness of sins called *The Shepherd of Hermas*.

II. *Apologetic Literature of the Second Century*
   A. Works that were written to an emperor precisely to show that Christians were not dangerous to the state and should therefore not be persecuted. Some of the most important literature of this type was written by *Aristedes of Athens, Justin Martyr, Tatian, Athenagoras of Athens, Minucius Felix,* and *Theophilus of Antioch,* all of whom wrote toward the end of the second century.
   B. Works that explained Christianity in philosophical terms and tried to make a case for Christianity that was philosophically respectable: good examples of this type of literature can be found in *Justin* and *Athenagoras*.
   C. Some apologetic literature was cast in the form of a dialogue. The most famous dialogues were written by *Justin* (a Greek) and *Minucius Felix* (a Roman).

III. *Heretical and Antiheretical Literature of the Second Century*
   Various types of what was later judged to be heretical literature were written during the second century.
   A. Philosophical or religious works dealing with particular interpretations of Christianity. The most famous literature of this kind is *Gnostic literature*.
   B. Stories about Jesus and his life that were not judged to be apostolic and therefore

were not included in the canon of the New Testament. These are called *apocryphal Gospels*.

C. Works dealing with the final age, the end of the world: *apocalyptic literature*.

The Christian church, as a whole, opposed much of this writing. The theologian remembered especially for his writings against Gnosticism is *Irenaeus of Lyons*.

IV. *The Beginnings of Christian Theology*

A much more elaborate Christian theology developed during the second and third centuries. The church moved into various philosophical cultures and interacted with them, writers were exposed to different ideas (especially to Stoicism and Neoplatonism), and problems were raised not only by heretics but by the faithful—problems about Jesus, the way to live a Christian life, immortality, and so on. Early theologians tried to develop theological positions working mostly from the Bible and their own experience. This writing has great richness, a variety of opinions and solutions to problems. It is important to see that there was no single Christian answer to a problem, but a variety of creative responses.

A. Writing in Greek were the famous theologians of the Alexandrian school, *Clement of Alexandria* and *Origen*.

B. Writing in Latin were apologists and controversialists like *Tertullian*, writers on church-state politics like *Cyprian*, and writers concerned with the internal matters of the Christian church like *Hippolytus*.

V. *The Golden Age of Christian Literature*

As problems of doctrine and discipline became more difficult, the writings became more complex. When Christianity was no longer a persecuted religion, Christian writers were able to pursue their theological peroccupations more directly. Much of the writing was more overtly philosophical and specific to particular controversies or problems: the person and nature of Christ, the foundations of a theology of grace, the doctrine of Original Sin and justification, the development of a sacramental system, and so on. In the writings of this period one can find catechists (those who devised systems to teach people about Christianity), mystical writers (those who attempted to discern and articulate a theology of religious experience), preachers, theologians, and bishops, all interested in specific ecclesiastical problems.

A. Writing in Greek were *Eusebius of Caesarea* (a church historian), *Cyril of Jerusalem* (a catechist), *Gregory of Nyssa* (a spiritual writer), *John Chrysostom* (a renowned preacher), *Basil* (an ecclesiastical writer), and theologians like *Athanasius, Theodore of Mopsuestia*, and *Cyril of Alexandria*.

B. Writing in Latin were those interested in political questions like *Ambrose*, and theologians like *Hilary of Poitiers* and *Augustine*. Some of the writers of the Latin church were also popes, notably *Leo I* and *Gregory I*.

APPENDIX 4
ECUMENICAL COUNCILS

A council is a formal meeting of bishops and representatives of the Christian churches convened for the purpose of regulating doctrine and discipline. Councils can be held on a local or regional level (sometimes called synods) as well as on a worldwide, universal level. The great councils in the history of Christianity have been the *ecumenical* (from the Greek word meaning universal) councils, meetings that include bishops from the whole, universal church. Decrees of a council are considered the highest authority the Christian church can give. Roman Catholics and Eastern Orthodox Christians recognize the dogmatic decrees of ecumenical councils as truly authoritative, authentic interpretations of the gospel; for them, the dogmatic decrees of the council represent the mind of the whole church.

Some Christians do not recognize any councils; they believe Christianity to be a matter of New Testament faithfulness alone, or base their Christianity on an experience of Jesus that does not need doctrinal definitions. Thus not all Christians recognize a need for or the importance of councils. Those Christians who *do* accept ecumenical councils are divided into two groups: some Protestants and Eastern Orthodox Christians accept the first seven ecumenical councils as authoritative and have some interest in the Second Vatican Council; they reject the rest of the councils on the grounds that they were not truly ecumenical but were only local Roman synods. Roman Catholics accept twenty-one ecumenical councils and reject the Council of Pisa on the grounds that it was not authentic; many scholars accept the validity of the Council of Pisa and it has been included in this chart.

#	COUNCIL AND YEAR HELD	PROBLEM	WHICH MEANS	COUNCIL'S RESOLUTION
1	Nicaea I 325	Arianism	There is only one God, so Jesus is not God (creator) but a creature.	Jesus is the son of God and is God, of the same divine essence as the Father.
2	Constantinople I 381	Apollinarianism	The Logos takes the place of the human mind in Jesus; he is not then fully human.	Jesus is divine, as Nicaea said, but also fully human. Also, Holy Spirit is divine.
3	Ephesus 431	Nestorianism	If Jesus is human and divine, then there are two persons in Christ, and Mary is mother of Jesus, not mother of God.	There are two natures (in hypostatic union) but only one person in Christ. Mary is the Mother of *God*.
4	Chalcedon 451	Monophysitism	The hypostatic union taken to an extreme so that there is only one nature (*mono physis*) in Christ.	There are *two* natures, as Ephesus said, and they are unmixed and unconfused.
5	Constantinople II 553	Three Chapters	Emperor issued a condemnation of three positions; pope refused to go along with this interference.	Council accepted the edict of the emperor, implicitly going against the pope.
6	Constantinople III 680	Monothelitism	Emperor attempts to win back the monophysites with the theory that Christ had only one will.	There are two wills and two energies in Christ, fully coordinated, divine and human.
7	Nicaea II 787	Iconoclasm	Emperor issued edict (726) against images and icons in churches.	Iconoclasm is condemned; veneration of images is permitted.

These first seven councils are accepted as authoritative by Orthodox Christians, Roman Catholics, and some Protestants.

#	COUNCIL AND YEAR HELD	PROBLEM	WHICH MEANS	COUNCIL'S RESOLUTION
8	Constantinople IV 870	Photian Schism	Complicated political problem involving papal authority in patriarchal appointments. Photius was the patriarch of Constantinople.	A council, actually held in Rome, deposed Photius and restored Ignatius as the patriarch of Constantinople.

Greeks do not recognize the Roman solution so held their own council in Constantinople in 880, which favored Photius as patriarch.

9	Lateran I 1123	Investiture	Can an emperor choose and invest a bishop or an abbot? A political struggle for power in West between pope and emperor.	Settled by the Concordat of Worms (1122) and council called to confirm it.
10	Lateran II 1139	Arnold Brescia	Arnold was an early reformer, against worldly popes and sinful priests; argued that sinful priests cannot administer sacraments.	Arnold and his views condemned.
11	Lateran III 1179	Papal elections	Emperor Frederick I, in political struggle with pope, had supported an antipope and caused a schism.	Schism ended; principle from now on was that the college of cardinals would always elect pope.
12	Lateran IV 1215	Doctrine and discipline	Church in high point of its power was plagued with questions and problems of doctrine and discipline.	Most important of Lateran councils; defined doctrine of the Eucharist and transubstantiation.
13	Lyons I 1245	Frederick II	Emperor in contest with the pope for supreme political power in Europe.	Council deposed emperor; a complicated chapter in history of church-state relations.
14	Lyons II 1274	Reunion with Greeks	Greek Orthodox church thought it politically wise to ask for reunion with Roman church.	Greeks pledged obedience to the pope, ended old schism; the peace lasted until 1289.
15	Vienne 1311–12	Templars	A twelfth-century military-religious order, highly influential and wealthy; Philip IV of France wanted their lands.	Convened during Avignon papacy; Templars condemned; Philip took their land.
16	Pisa 1409	Schism	Two men claiming to be the legitimate pope; church had been divided on the issue from 1378.	Healed the schism (temporarily) by deposing both popes and electing new one.

17	Constance 1414–18	Schism	Three men all claimed to be the rightful pope; European Christendom completely split on issue.	Ended the schism and declared that councils are superior to popes and councils ought to meet often.
18	Florence 1438–39	Reunion	Greek Orthodox church sought support of West against the Turks; also sought to discuss theological differences.	Reunion voted for but not ratified by Orthodox synods; important council for theology of the Trinity.
19	Lateran V 1512–17	Reform	Convoked by pope to invalidate the decrees of the Council of Pisa (1409), which was an antipapal power council, but not recognized by Roman Catholic church as ecumenical.	Touched on some minor areas of needed reform, but main causes of the Reformation were left untouched.
20	Trent 1545–63	Protestants	Called to respond to reformers, to define Roman Catholic doctrine, and tighten up teaching and theology.	Very important for Roman Catholics as it defined most doctrine and discipline that would hold up to twentieth century.
21	Vatican I 1870	Infallibility	Called to deal with various issues of doctrine and discipline, but also to define the limits of papal power.	Pope declared primate of the universal church and infallible in matters of faith and morals when speaking *ex cathedra*.
22	Vatican II 1962–65	Renewal	Called by John XXIII to evaluate contemporary church and to bring the Roman Catholic church up to date.	Issued documents for modernization of doctrine and practice; accepted ecumenism and principle of religious freedom.

APPENDIX 5
CREEDS AND CONFESSIONS

The word *creed* comes from the Latin word *credo*, which means "I believe." A creed summarizes the beliefs or lists the doctrines agreed upon by a particular church. For a number of reasons Christians have developed statements that outline their doctrinal positions. Some heretical groups in the early church claimed that Christians could, in good conscience, believe almost anything: some groups said that Jesus did not really rise from the dead, but just "seemed" to die and rise; others denied any link between Jesus and the God of the Bible. In response to the confusion created by heretical groups, Christians developed a systematic list of official beliefs. Creeds helped them clarify their own positions and oppose heretical teachings with an official statement. Early creeds were used for religious instruction and often were used in liturgical celebration as well.

One early summary of beliefs is the Apostles' Creed, so called because it contains the essential Christian doctrines as they were understood and believed in the apostolic church. The Apostles' Creed was not written by the apostles (as legend has it), but dates back to the old Roman Creed. In its present form, it probably did not exist before the middle of the seventh century, though there is evidence that it developed from the baptismal creed used in the Roman church in the second century. The Apostles' Creed is short and was apparently easy to learn; it summarizes early belief about the Father, Son, and Holy Spirit, the life and mission of Jesus, and the life of the church.

THE APOSTLES' CREED

I believe in God, the Father, almighty, creator of heaven
    and earth.
I believe in Jesus Christ, his only son, our Lord.
He was conceived by the power of the Holy Spirit and born
    to the Virgin Mary.
He suffered under Pontius Pilate, was crucified, died and
    was buried.
He descended to the dead.
On the third day he rose again.
He ascended into heaven and is seated at the right hand of
    the Father.
He will come again to judge the living and the dead.
I believe in the Holy Spirit, the holy catholic church,
    the communion of saints, the forgiveness of sins, the
    resurrection of the body, and the life everlasting.

Creeds have been important in history as a means of further refining the basic beliefs of Christians. After the Reformation, creeds distinguished the acceptable beliefs of one group from those of another. The following list describes some of the more important creeds in the history of Christianity; they are specific to certain groups of Christians.

THE NICENE CREED (325; revised at the Council of Constantinople, 381): The official creed of Roman Catholics and Orthodox Christians, and accepted by some Protestant churches. It is often used during the liturgy as a common expression of beliefs. In the eleventh century the word *filioque* ("and the Son") was officially added to the creed by Christians in the West; this addition has long been a source of dispute between Roman Catholics and Orthodox Christians (see Chapter 4).

THE ATHANASIAN CREED (written between 381 and 428): Attributed to but probably not written by St. Athanasius, it sets forth the doctrines of the Trinity and the Incarnation and states that people who do not believe these things will be condemned to damnation. It was used until recent times only in Western Christian churches.

THE SCHLEITHEIM CONFESSION (1527): Lists points of agreement among Radical Reformation groups that fixed the direction of the Anabaptist movement. It includes insistence on adult baptism, separation from the world, refusal to swear oaths, and pacifism.

THE AUGSBURG CONFESSION (1530): The Lutheran confession of faith written, for the most part, by Philip Melanchthon. The first part lists essential Lutheran doctrines, the second part lists the abuses in the Roman church that needed to be remedied.

THE HELVETIC CONFESSIONS (1536 and 1562): Confessions of faith written in the Swiss Reformed Church. The first contained twenty-seven articles that embodied many of Zwingli's teachings yet, at the same time, sought reconciliation with Luther's positions. The second is a long discourse on the main Reformed teachings and expresses disagreement with Roman Catholicism and Lutheranism.

THE HEIDELBERG CATECHISM (1563): A Reformed confession of faith that is more concerned with Christian life than with theological formulations. It was accepted by the Reformed churches in Europe and approved by the Synod of Dort (1618–19). The catechism was designed to correspond to Paul's Epistle to the Romans: human misery in sin, redemption, and new life were key themes.

THE THIRTY-NINE ARTICLES (1563): A set of doctrinal formulas accepted by the Church of England. It is not so much a creed as it is a brief summary of acceptable doctrines. Royal supremacy over the church is clearly enunciated.

THE BOOK OF CONCORD (1580): The assembled confessions of the Lutheran church. It is a doctrinal standard that defines Lutheranism and its norms. It includes the accepted creeds (Nicene, Athanasian, and Apostles'), the Augsburg Confession, some of Luther's writings, and the Formula of Concord (drawn up in 1577 to restore unity among German Lutherans).

THE WESTMINSTER CONFESSION (1648): Profession of Presbyterian faith as set forth by the Westminster assembly. It is thoroughly Calvinist in its theology and expounds leading articles of the Christian faith from the creation to the last judgment.

THE CAMBRIDGE PLATFORM (1648): Not a doctrinal confession, but a plan for organization and practice in American Congregational churches; it includes provisions for the autonomy of local churches, covenanted membership, and the obligation to foster fellowship with other congregations.

MORMON ARTICLES OF FAITH (1842): In response to a question by a Chicago newspaper editor about Mormon beliefs, Joseph Smith listed thirteen articles of Mormon doctrine including belief in the inspiration of the Bible and the Book of Mormon, continuing revelation, and the literal gathering of Israel in the restoration of the ten tribes on the American continent.

CONFESSION OF 1967 (Presbyterian): A contemporary statement of faith designed for the union of American Presbyterian churches. The confession is biblical and is based on the themes of reconciliation, especially on issues of war, poverty, and various forms of discrimination. It represents a major doctrinal shift within Presbyterianism.

Creeds and confessions are not part of all Christian churches. Anabaptists, Quakers, and Seventh-Day Adventists have excluded creeds as rules of faith within their churches; one can be a member without accepting a particular creed. Some of these Christians may accept a statement of common beliefs to foster cooperation among themselves—some American Mennonites, for example, accept the Dordrecht Confession of Faith—but they do not impose that statement on their members. Many Baptist and Congregational churches rely only in part on general credal statements and prefer each local church to draw up its own covenant. Other churches use ancient creeds in their worship services and yet work to develop modern confessional statements; the Korean Conference Creed (1905) of the Methodist church is an example. The Disciples of Christ were founded on the phrase "No Creed but Christ."

Christianity was fragmented during the Reformation when new churches emerged and a variety of creeds were written. Major Protestant churches called their credal formulations *confessions*. The experience of fragmentation continued and, to some ways of thinking, grew worse in America. Because there were so many different creeds with contradictory statements about the nature of God or the mission of the church, some people were confused and grew suspicious of creeds in general. The rejection of all creeds played a major part in the foundation of churches whose roots were in revivalist movements. Primitivists, sometimes called Seekers, tended to move away from all organized religion in hopes of finding enlightenment elsewhere; they believed in the gifts of the Holy Spirit and the experience of Jesus, but not in written, fixed formulations of belief.

Anticredalism is opposition to any creed used as a rule of faith and is the opposite of confessionalism, the position that adherence to a creed is necessary for life within a church.

Most Christian churches have some agreed-upon principles of behavior or practice; most have some way to define the membership requirements of their church. Not all churches have creeds, however, nor do they all desire to have them.

APPENDIX 6
A SUMMARY OF STRUCTURAL ARRANGEMENTS

Christians believe that the Holy Spirit is present in the church, but they differ about the locus of that presence and its implications for church authority. They also differ in their interpretations of New Testament passages on issues of organizational structure and authority: some believe that Jesus intended to entrust the church to one chief apostle who would govern the community with the cooperation of the other apostles; others believe that the early church, in fact, operated in local, autonomous groups where leadership was found within the congregation; still others noted that many of the early communities were organized along the lines of the old Jewish synagogue, where a group of elders administered the daily life of the church.

One of the key arguments during the Reformation concerned the nature of the church: for Catholics the church is a highly organized institution founded by Christ with definite patterns of authority modeled on Peter, whereas for Protestants the church is a more loosely structured community of believers who share salvation through faith. For the most part, Christianity has adapted itself to three common polities—episcopal, congregational, and presbyterian—and to some less usual ones.

THE EPISCOPAL STRUCTURE

Episcopal comes from the Greek word for overseer and is translated into English as *bishop*. The episcopal system, therefore, is church government by bishops. The episcopal (or hierarchical) structure is a pyramid. According to the underlying assumptions of this model, authority in the church flows from the top down, from the bishop to the priests to the members of the congregation at the bottom of the pyramid.

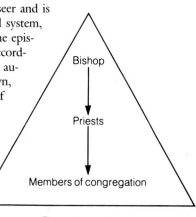

The episcopal polity

Traditional episcopal churches—Roman Catholic, Orthodox, Anglican, and Old Catholic—are based on apostolic succession. They believe that their bishops are successors of the apostles and share in the power and authority Christ bestowed on the apostles. In this system, the clergy are divided into a hierarchy of order and powers: bishops possess the fullness of sacramental power (they can celebrate *all* the sacraments) and usually preside over extended territories (dioceses) made up of many local parishes. Priests share in the sacramental power of the bishop in a *limited* way (they cannot ordain new priests, for example) and preside over local congregations (parishes) within the diocese. Because of priest shortages, some parishes are administered by *deacons*, who have very limited powers (they can preach and baptize) and work cooperatively with a supervising priest. For the most part, however, the traditional episcopal system is defined by the shared powers of bishops and priests.

The Roman Catholic church has a chief bishop, the pope (the bishop of Rome), whose authority extends over bishops and then on down the lines of the structure. All bishops—including the pope—are supposed to embody three of Christ's titles in their work: they are to be *priests* (sanctifying the church and possessing full sacramental powers), *prophets* (teaching and interpreting doctrine and discipline), and *kings* (ruling or administering their territories).

Nontraditional episcopal churches—Methodist, Nazarene, and some Lutheran and Evangelical churches, for example—deny the importance of literal apostolic succession, but understand bishops as historically important figures within Christian churches since New Testament times. Other Christian groups—the Amish, for example—are presided over by bishops whose functions are purely administrative. Such bishops make no claim to apostolic succession or to special powers.

It is not always clear, therefore, what the word *bishop* means. In some Christian churches it defines special sacramental powers that are associated with the apostles. In others it is a title of biblical and historical importance which defines an administrative function. In some hierarchical churches, the title is not used at all: those who function as administrative leaders call themselves overseers or superintendents. Their church structure, however, is still called episcopal.

In some churches the title of bishop has survived without any of the hierarchical structures or powers. One can find Lutheran bishops—sometimes even those who claim apostolic succession—who are basically administrators: they do what all bishops do—ordination and visitation—but they have no more power than pastors. In some Christian churches bishops have special powers and function as spiritual leaders. Moravian bishops function more as spiritual advisers than as administrators. Amish bishops preside over a church district, that is, over the families that can be accommodated at a preaching service held in a home (sometimes a barn). That bishop has full powers to lead the congregation; administer Communion, baptism, and marriage; declare excommunications; receive members back into the church; and ordain and supervise ministers. There is no central organization in the Amish church—each district is a self-contained unit—but bishops sometimes have unofficial meetings to discuss pressing problems.

Some Christians—Methodists and some Evangelicals—retain the title of bishop and some prefer to call their administrators superintendents (the Nazarenes, for example). Oftentimes their polities are mixtures of congregational and presbyterian models, but their retention of the office or title of bishop suggests that their primary structure is episcopal, even though it might be a modified form. Church structures change and adapt to new situations, so one can always expect changes in the ways churches operate. The important thing to note in the episcopal structure is its hierarchical model and the way that authority is understood as flowing downward.

THE CONGREGATIONAL STRUCTURE

The congregational polity, modeled on the New Testament concept of a house church (a small local group of believers gathered together in a home in the name of Jesus), makes the local community supreme. The ministers, deacons, elders, and other officers all come from within the congregation. The gathered group of believers *is* the church and as such is guided by the Holy Spirit. Those who espouse congregational polity often defend private judgment and interpretation of Scripture, but they believe that the gathered body of believers is a place where matters of worship, belief, and, practice are discussed and decided.

The congregational structure is circular. According to this model, Jesus sent the Holy Spirit to the church, to the gathered Christian believers, not to a few leaders and administrators. The Holy Spirit guides the local church, and authority flows throughout the congregation. The local church does not need external or hierarchical authority, since the power of the Spirit is present in all and since the word of God in the Bible is equally accessible to everyone. While congregations may appoint pastors, deacons, elders, or teachers, those offices designate people's differing functions and gifts; they do not create differences of status within the community.

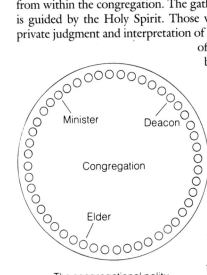

The congregational polity

Two types of congregational polity need to be distinguished. Pure or independent congregationalism is just that: the local church sets its own theology, doctrine, practice, and internal life without responsibility to any other group. Associational congregationalism recognizes local church autonomy but also acknowledges the need to relate to the larger body of believers. In associational congregationalism, theology and doctrine are guarded by the developed tradition: the local congregation is *not* free to determine its own theology and doctrine. Independent Christian churches, in storefronts and in suburban neighborhoods, follow a pure congregationalism. Most traditional congregationalist churches—Baptist, United Church of Christ, Brethren, Mennonites—adhere to an associational congregationalism and provide ways for their members to meet with other church members so that decisions about behavior and interpretation are made within a broader-than-congregational frame of reference.

The first Baptist Association in the United States was formed in Philadelphia in 1707 to promote doctrinal unity, to settle disputes, to help churches find suitable ministers, and to promote missionary activity. Associations have no juridical power and Baptists are not required to cooperate with them. Baptists are also united in conventions—state or national organizations of cooperation—like the Southern Baptist Convention. They meet annually and may make recommendations about an issue—the ordination of women, for example—but the local church is still free to follow its own lights on the matter. No association or convention has any legal power over the congregation.

Some churches with a congregational polity operate on a consensus model for making decisions: every member of the local congregation must agree to a policy before the church pursues it. When difference of opinion arises, members listen to all dissent; their belief in the Holy Spirit's presence in the local community suggests to them that a dissenting voice is as valuable in a discussion as one of agreement. Other churches have congregational structures and representatives elected by the congregation to make decisions, present them to the church, and proceed if a majority vote favors the proposal. In Mennonite and Brethren churches, annual conferences can be attended by all members of the denomination. The purpose of the annual conference is fellowship, growth in mutual understanding, and deliberation on matters of discipline. In all these cases, the locus of the continuing presence of the Holy Spirit is the congregation; the church is understood to be the gathered community.

THE PRESBYTERIAN STRUCTURE

According to the model followed by Presbyterian and Reformed churches, authority rests with a group of elected elders (the Greek word for elder is *presbyter*), not with a single authority (a bishop) or with a local congregation. The presbyterian model, based on New Testament offices like elder and deacon, combines some characteristics of both episcopal and congregational structures in an attempt to reflect the organization of the early Christian community. According to Calvin, the genius behind the presbyterian model, the church possesses divine authority but is also *semper reformanda*, always needing to be reformed. Accordingly, the church has no final and perfect form, no structure presented to it by divine design. One can, however, work out from the New Testament a set of offices and functions within the church.

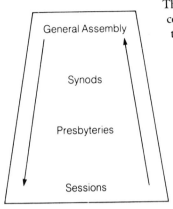

The presbyterian polity

The presbyterian model, which is basically an elected constitutional government, is best represented by a trapezoidal figure. It has an authoritative body at the top (like the episcopal structure), but also provides for local initiative and governance (like the congregational model). Authority circulates within the structure and moves from the bottom up (by way of suggested agenda) and from the top down (by means of decisions of the general assembly agreed upon by the presbyteries).

In this model, the local church is called a *session* and is administered by a pastor, called a *teaching elder*. All ordained ministers are teaching elders, but not all are pastors. In addition to the teaching elders, each session also has a number of *ruling elders* (from three to twenty depending on the size of the session) elected by the congregation. The pastor is the moderator of the session and it is the job of the session to maintain the spiritual government of the local church. The session can receive and dismiss members, examine and ordain ruling elders, and supervise the educational work of the church. Session meetings *must* occur at least four times each year, but may occur more frequently.

A number of sessions (at least twelve) together form a *presbytery*, or a district body. The presbytery has legislative, executive, and judicial powers and is a kind of corporate episcopacy. The presbytery receives candidates for ministry and sanctions the call of a congregation to a minister by ordaining or installing him or her. The presbytery can dismiss, judge, and remove ministers and can organize and divide local sessions if they appear to be too large for effective Christian life. All delegates sent to synods and to the general assembly are elected by the presbytery, which also initiates the business of the general assembly. The questions and issues decided higher up, therefore, are generated from the district level. If the general assembly proposes some change in government, the proposal has to be passed by a certain percentage of the presbyteries.

Presbyteries in a given geographical area make up a *synod*, a regional body which is an American refinement of presbyterianism. The synod meets annually to coordinate projects and facilitate cooperation among churches. The synods are less important in practice than the presbyteries, but they provide some important resources to enable the presbyteries to carry on with their work.

The *general assembly* is a national body made up of members elected by the presbyteries. It represents the whole church and is responsible for matters of faith and order. It institutes and supervises agencies for education, missions, and ecumenism. The general assembly can advise the presbyteries, but all changes in traditional documents or beliefs have to be passed by the presbyteries, and all questions of policy and items for discussion must be initiated by a presbytery. There is a World Alliance of Reformed Churches, but it has no jurisdiction. The main juridical body within this system is the general assembly, working in cooperation with the presbyteries.

OTHER POLITIES

Some Christian communities—including many nineteenth-century communitarian groups —are founded by a single charismatic individual and often disband when that leader leaves or dies. Other groups founded by charismatic leaders—the Church of Christ, Scientist, for example—continue to be "led" by that individual. Christian Scientists have no local or regional organization: all policy and teaching decisions come from the "mother church" in Boston. But the mother church has no power to make changes or to introduce new ideas; it follows the *Manual of the Mother Church* written by Mary Baker Eddy. Decisions are administered according to her will and direction.

Mormons follow the organization of the early church as they understand it; their structure includes apostles, a prophet, and elders. Their chief officer is the First President, who is also a "priest of the order of Melkisedek" (see Heb. 5:6 and Gen. 14:18); he is assisted by two counselors. The president is also a prophet who Mormons believe receives the ongoing revelation of God. He is elected for life. Assisting these officers is the Council of the Twelve Apostles, chosen on the basis of revelations received by the president. New decisions arise from new revelations: for example, black males were admitted to full priesthood in 1978, when the prophet received a revelation that said they could be included.

Quakers began with a belief about the centrality of an inner light in each person, not mediated by church membership, sacraments, or a particular polity. By 1668, however, George Fox developed the *Rules for the Management of a Meeting* and an organizational scheme to go with it. Friends meet weekly for worship and monthly for business; the monthly meeting is either local or regional. Quarterly and yearly meetings take in wider geographical areas and include more people. No voting occurs at meetings because the Quaker doctrine of the inner light upholds the notion that members seek to discover God's will by deliberation. The decisions of the yearly meeting have the highest authority within the church. Friends have also organized for specific purposes beyond the scope of the local meeting. The American Friends Service Committee, for example, unites Quakers in peace and humanitarian efforts throughout the world.

Not all Christians are comfortable with these models; contemporary dissatisfaction with all these polities may lead to experimentation with new models. Some Christians display an anti-institutional bias and others have a strong desire for interdenominational fellowship and worship; some form groups around specific issues of social justice. Within this mixture of discontent and desire some Christians have abandoned old structures altogether in favor of new ones or modified ones, and others have supplemented old polities with new experiments in Christian living. New experimental structures include small groups that meet weekly for worship and fellowship; house churches that gather members together for worship and sharing in homes rather than the more formal atmosphere of church buildings; "floating parishes" where people meet to celebrate the Eucharist in smaller, more informal settings; and Christian communal groups, like the Koinonia Partners in Georgia. Any of these might be interdenominational; most of them have some form of congregational polity.

APPENDIX 7
HISTORICAL TIME LINE

Sometimes it is helpful to see when, in the context of the long line of history, certain events occurred. The following time line is general and has a greater concentration of events in earlier times than it does in modern ones. It is not meant to be all-inclusive, but to give a general sense of things, especially in less well-known periods.

Time Before the Common Era (B.C.E.)

c. 1700	God's call to Abraham
c. 1200	Exodus from Egypt/covenant at Sinai
c. 1013—972	David, king of Israel
587	Babylonian exile
538	Return to Palestine
470—321	Great Greek philosophers—Socrates, Plato, Aristotle—in Athens
168	Maccabean revolt and Jewish control of Palestine
63 B.C.E.—14 C.E.	Augustus, emperor of Rome from 27 B.C.E.
63	Romans conquer Palestine and capture Jerusalem
c. 4	Jesus born in Palestine

Time in the Common Era (C.E.)

29—33	Preaching and crucifixion of Jesus
c. 35—107	Ignatius of Antioch
50s	Paul's epistles written; earliest New Testament literature

54–68	Nero, Roman emperor
64	Death of Peter (crucified in Rome)
c. 70–90	First gospel (Mark) written
70	Temple in Jerusalem destroyed
80–150	Remaining New Testament books written
120–220	Age of apologists; first reasoned defenses of Christianity
c. 150–215	Clement of Alexandria
c. 160–225	Tertullian
c. 185–254	Origen
c. 251–356	Anthony ("the first hermit") living in Egyptian desert
c. 260–340	Eusebius, father of church history and biographer of Constantine
284–305	Diocletian, emperor in Rome
296–373	Athanasius, theologian important at Council of Nicaea
303	The Great Persecution under Diocletian; all Christian churches ordered to be destroyed and all Scriptures burned; persecutions began with Nero in 64 and occurred periodically until 313.
306–37	Constantine reunites empire and moves capital to Constantinople
313	Constantine, emperor, issues Edict of Milan; Christians no longer persecuted
318	Pachomius (c. 290–346) founds first monastery in Egypt
325	Council of Nicaea called by Constantine to settle Christological problem
330–76	Bishop of Rome (pope) has no political rival in West
330–79	Basil the Great, established monastic rule for Orthodox church
340	Monasticism moves to the West
347–407	John Chrysostom, preacher and theologian in Orthodox church; his liturgy is in general use in Orthodox church
354–430	Augustine, preacher and theologian in Western church
372	Huns reach the Danube basin
382–400	Jerome (c. 342–420) translates Bible into Latin: the Vulgate
395	Empire divided permanently between East and West
406	Vandals invade Gaul
410	Visigoths sack Rome
425	First monasteries in Ireland and England
430	Vandals in Africa (Augustine's *City of God* published in 426)
440–61	Leo I pope; meets Attila at gates of Rome in 452
476	Roman Empire in West ends
482–511	Clovis, king of the Franks; converts to Christianity in 496
496	Pope in alliance with Franks
c. 525	Benedict founds his monastery at Monte Casino; begins Benedictine Rule
530–800	Golden Age of monastic preservation of classical manuscripts
532–37	Hagia Sophia, great Orthodox cathedral, built in Constantinople
590–604	Pope Gregory I lays claims for papal absolutism
596	Augustine, first archbishop of Canterbury, sent to England as missionary

664	Synod of Whitby; English church in agreement with papacy on all issues
673–735	Venerable Bede, father of English history
723	Boniface (680–754) sent as missionary to Germanic tribes
726	Beginning of Iconoclast controversy in Orthodox church
c. 742–814	Charles I (Charlemagne), first emperor of Holy Roman Empire
774	Charlemagne conquers Lombards; becomes king of Franks and Lombards
c. 780–885	Carolingian Renaissance; new learning, culture, schools
800	Charlemagne crowned emperor by Pope Leo III
863–85	Cyril (826–69) and Methodius (c. 815–85) sent from Constantinople as missionaries to Bohemia
887	Carolingian empire ends; new invasions (Norsemen) begin
910	Monastery founded at Cluny; base for monastic reform in West
936–73	Otto the Great, emperor who revives royal authority over popes
966–72	Renaissance under patronage of Otto the Great
1027	"Truce of God" established; attempt to restrict feudal warfare
1033–1109	Anselm, theologian responsible for theory of substitutionary atonement
1054	Schism between Orthodox and Roman Catholic churches
1073–85	Gregory VII, reforming pope who strengthens claims of papal absolutism
1077	Emperor Henry IV begs pope's forgiveness at Canossa
1079–1142	Peter Abelard, philosopher/theologian, applies reason to mysteries of faith
1095–99	First Crusade
1100–60	Peter Lombard, beginnings of Scholastic theology
1132–1202	Joachim of Fiore, apocalyptic preacher and reformer
c. 1182–1226	Francis of Assisi, founder of Franciscan friars
1198–1216	Innocent III pope; height of papal power
1202–04	Fourth Crusade; Western soldiers conquer and pillage Constantinople
1215	Magna Carta signed in England between King John and English nobles
1215	Transubstantiation defined as article of faith at a Lateran Council
1216	Dominican friars founded
c. 1217	Death of Peter Waldo, founder of "heretical" Waldensians
1225–74	Thomas Aquinas, the "angelic doctor," author of the *Summa Theologica*
1265–1321	Dante, author of *The Divine Comedy*
1265	Marco Polo visits China
1294–1303	Boniface VIII pope; humiliated and defeated by French king, Philip IV (compare to king begging papal forgiveness in 1077)
1304	Clement V first Avignon pope
1330–1400	English mystics: Julian of Norwich, Richard Rolle, Walter Hilton
c. 1330–84	John Wycliffe, English reformer, associated with Lollard movement

1337	Hundred Years' War (between France and England) begins
1340–1400	Geoffrey Chaucer, author of *The Canterbury Tales*
1348–50	Black Plague decimates European population
c. 1372–1415	John Hus, Czech reformer, burned at Council of Constance
1377	Avignon papacy ends
1378	Great Western Schism begins with one pope in Avignon and another in Rome
1409	Council of Pisa called to end schism
1414–18	Council of Constance ends schism, does not reform church
1450	Invention of printing press
1453	Constantinople captured by Turks; overland trade route no longer safe and people begin to search for a new route to the east, which begins age of explorers: Magellan, Balboa, Columbus, and others
1453	Byzantine refugees bring priceless art and manuscript treasures to West
1454	Gutenberg Bible printed
1484–1531	Ulrich Zwingli, Swiss reformer
1495–98	Leonardo da Vinci paints *The Last Supper*
1504	Michelangelo's *David* finished
1509–64	John Calvin, French reformer
1513	Machiavelli's *The Prince* published
1513–72	John Knox, Scottish reformer
1517	Luther (1483–1546) posts his Ninety-five Theses on church door; mainline Protestant Reformation begins
1521	Luther condemned by the Diet of Worms
1536	Tyndale's English Bible printed
1540	Jesuits founded to defend Roman Catholicism and pope
1542–1621	Robert Bellarmine, Roman Catholic reformer
1545–63	Council of Trent called to reform Roman Catholic church
1552–1610	Matteo Ricci, Jesuit missionary to China
1555	Peace of Augsburg settles religious disputes in Germany
1558–1603	Elizabeth I queen of England from 1558
1559	First Index of Forbidden Books established by Roman Catholic church
1564–1616	Shakespeare
1564–1642	Galileo
c. 1582	Congregationalist churches established in England
1612	First Baptist church formed in England
1618–48	Thirty Years' War; Peace of Westphalia (1648)
1620	Pilgrims land in America
1624–91	George Fox, founder of the Quakers
1642–1727	Isaac Newton, physicist and scientist
1674–1748	Isaac Watts, one of the foremost English hymn writers
1685–1750	Johann Sebastian Bach
1700–60	Count Zinzendorf, patron of the Moravians
1703–58	Jonathan Edwards
1703–91	John Wesley

1720–72	John Woolman, Quaker reformer
1740s	Great Awakening
1756–91	Wolfgang Amadeus Mozart
1774	Mother Ann Lee (1736–84) leads a group of Shakers to America
1776	Declaration of Independence signed
1776–91	Dawn of religious freedom for American Catholicism
1782–1849	William Miller, founder of Adventist movement
1788–1866	Alexander Campbell, founder of Disciples of Christ
1789	French Revolution
1801	First camp meeting in America, at Cane Ridge, Kentucky
1805–44	Joseph Smith, founder of Mormon church
1821–1910	Mary Baker Eddy, founder of Christian Science
1824	First performance of Beethoven's *Ninth Symphony*
1833–45	Oxford Movement in Anglican church
1842	Launching of American Protestant Association against Catholic church
1844	YMCA founded
1848	Karl Marx publishes the *Communist Manifesto*
1852–84	Three Baltimore councils define program of American Catholicism
1856–1939	Sigmund Freud, founder of psychoanalysis
1861–1918	Walter Rauschenbusch, pioneer of Social Gospel movement
1865	Salvation Army founded
1869–70	First Vatican Council declares papal infallibility
1886–1968	Karl Barth, neo-orthodoxy in Protestant theology
1892–1971	Reinhold Niebuhr, American neo-orthodoxy
1914–18	First World War
1925	Scopes trial in Dayton, Tennessee; extreme fundamentalism
1939–45	Second World War
1948	World Council of Churches established in Amsterdam
1962–65	Second Vatican Council called to modernize Roman Catholic church

GLOSSARY

ABRAHAM: Father of the Jewish people; first of the three patriarchs, Abraham, Isaac, and Jacob. See Genesis 17:5. Abraham = father of many.

A.D.: *Anno Domini,* "in the year of Our Lord," is a way of dating events according to the Christian calendar. In this book I use C.E. (common era) instead.

ALEXANDER THE GREAT (356–23 B.C.E.): King of Macedon, one of the greatest leaders and conquerors of all time.

ALTAR CALL: Invitation by a preacher for members of the congregation to come up to the altar. People respond for a number of reasons: to repent and be saved, to help others accept Jesus, to pray for themselves, to confess their sins, or to ask for special prayers from the minister and others.

ANGELS (Gk = messenger): Found in Bible and New Testament, usually as God's messengers. Three angels are named: Michael, Gabriel, and Raphael.

ANSELM (1033–1109): Archbishop of Canterbury, teacher, and theologian; first to develop theory of substitutionary atonement.

ANTIOCHUS IV (d. 163 B.C.E.): Attempted to hellenize Judea and crush Judaism, a policy that instigated the Maccabean revolt.

APOCALYPTIC (Gk = uncovering): Type of Jewish and Christian literature dealing with the end of the world. Writing characterized by obscure symbols, visions, and vivid imagery.

APOCRYPHA (Gk = hidden things): Biblical books for which divine authorship is questioned (as opposed to canonical books). There are fifteen books or portions of books in the Apocrypha: 1 Esdras, 2 Esdras, Tobit, Judith, Additions to the Book of Esther, The Wisdom of Solomon, Ecclesiasticus (also called the Book of Sirach), Baruch, The

Letter of Jeremiah; The Prayer of Azariah and the Song of the Three Young Men, Susanna, Bel and the Dragon (all three of these are additions to the Book of Daniel); The Prayer of Manasseh, and 1 and 2 Maccabees.

APOLOGIST/APOLOGETICS (Gk = speak in defense): Early Christian writers (c. 120–220) known as apologists defended Christianity against hostile or misleading characterizations; they explained its doctrines and practices. Modern apologetics is a defense of Christianity on intellectual grounds; it argues for the reasonableness of religious faith in general and for Christianity in particular.

APOSTASY (Gk = revolt): Denial of one's beliefs. In Christianity, a deliberate turning away from God and the Christian faith, the opposite of conversion.

APOSTLE: Envoy or "one sent." Refers to prime missionaries of Christianity and to the twelve men chosen by Jesus as his primary followers.

APOSTOLIC CONSTITUTIONS: Late fourth-century work comprised of eight books of administrative rules for Christians (clergy and laity) and directions for worship. Attributed to, but not written by, the apostles.

ARMINIANISM: Theological system inspired by Jacob Arminius (1560–1609). The emphasis is on the freedom of a person to accept grace (versus the Calvinist notion of irresistible grace), though it also includes beliefs in universal atonement, conditional predestination, and human freedom. It has sometimes been used to describe liberal or rational tendencies in Christian religion. One needs to exercise caution, therefore, before applying the term to a person or group.

ASCETICISM (Gk = exercise): A system of practices designed to develop virtues and combat vice, used by Greek philosophers, Christians, and various Eastern religions.

ATONEMENT: Sometimes written as *at-one-ment* to indicate the reconciliation between God and people through the death and resurrection of Jesus. Christians agree that there is a need for reconciliation, but they argue about how atonement ought to be understood. There has been a long history of interpretation from the New Testament to the present. Substitutionary atonement, for example, was considered to be one of the Christian fundamentals when fundamentalists tried to define the minimum beliefs one should have to be Christian.

ATTILA (d. 453): King of the Huns. He was going to invade Rome (452) but changed his mind either because of the diplomacy of Pope Leo I or because of lack of provisions.

AUGUSTINE (354–430 C.E.): Bishop of Hippo (North Africa) and one of the most important early Christian writers. His influence on later religious thinkers was enormous.

AUGUSTUS (63 B.C.E.–14 C.E.): First Roman emperor, reigning when Jesus was born.

BARTH, KARL (1886–1968): Swiss theologian associated with neo-orthodoxy, the attempt in the twentieth century to lead Protestants back to the original principles and intentions of the Reformation.

BASIL THE GREAT (330–379): Greek theologian who wrote monastic rule still used in Orthodox monasticism.

B.C.E.: Before the common era. A designation of time equivalent to B.C. but not centered on a theological claim as is B.C. (before Christ).

BENEDICT OF NURSIA (c. 480–550): Founder of the Benedictines, he wrote first monastic rule used in the West.

BERNARD OF CLAIRVAUX (1090–1153): A monk and abbot of the monastery at Clairvaux in France who is renowned for his theological and mystical writings.

BIBLICAL CRITICISM: An approach to the study of the Bible which applies a variety of interpretive tools—literary, historical, textual—to the words, composition, and meaning of the Bible. Christians have always searched for various levels of meaning in the Bible and have often used the scholarly tools available to them at the time. In the modern world, those tools are many. Biblical criticism is opposed by those who believe in absolute *inerrancy* of the Biblical text.

BISHOP (Gk = episcopos; Eng = episcopal): In Greek the word literally means overseer; bishops were the administrative officers of the early community. In some Christian churches they are the highest order of ministers and can be distinguished from other ministers by their power to ordain priests/ministers.

BOOK OF COMMON PRAYER: Authorized liturgical book of the Church of England. Its various editions and revisions reflect the doctrinal battles within the Tudor Reformation.

BYZANTIUM: Site of present-day Istanbul. Constantine had a new city built there in 330, and renamed it Constantinople when he moved the capital of the Roman Empire there in 333.

CALIGULA (12–41): Roman emperor who claimed to be a god and attempted to erect a statue of himself in the Jewish temple in Palestine.

CAMP MEETINGS: A form of revivalist meeting used on the American frontier. It originated as a form in Kentucky in 1801 during the Second Great Awakening. Camp meetings were designed to attract many people and were held outdoors; various ministers preached and conversions were often accompanied by emotional exercises and manifestations.

CANON: The Greek word means straight rod; it usually means a kind of measuring stick. In Christian language it means the official list of biblical books that are recognized as inspired. Canonical books must be distinguished from apocryphal books (books about which there is some question as to authenticity). Also, an ecclesiastical title used to refer to nonmonastic clergy belonging to a cathedral (the chief church in a diocese). Canons participate in officially sanctioned religious life in a way that is technically different from monks, nuns, and friars. Canon law is a phrase for church law.

CATHERINE OF SIENA (c. 1347–80): Saint, mystic, and doctor of the Roman Catholic church. As a religious reformer she used her influence to help end the Avignon papacy.

C.E.: The common era. It corresponds to what Christians call A.D. (anno Domini, meaning "the year of our Lord").

CELIBACY: Being unmarried. This condition is accepted by priests in the Roman Catholic church as necessary for ordination. In the Orthodox church men may marry before ordination, but not after; bishops must not be married.

CHARISMATIC (Gk = gift of grace): Possessing gifts of the spirit. In the New Testament various gifts are mentioned that help a Christian to advance spiritually. In 1 Cor. 12:8–11 these gifts (*charismata*) are listed as wisdom, knowledge, faith, healing, miracles, prophecy, discernment of spirits, tongues, and the interpretation of tongues. They are sometimes called the gifts of the spirit and thereby associated with Christians who have a special relationship to the Holy Spirit.

CHARLEMAGNE (c. 742–814): King of the Franks, crowned emperor of the West in 800 by Pope Leo III.

CHRISTOLOGY: The study of the person and nature of Christ. The questions about the human and divine nature of Christ were especially important in the early years of the Christian movement (see Appendix 4).

CLEMENT OF ALEXANDRIA (d. 215 C.E.): Greek theologian who first attempted a synthesis between Platonic and Christian thought.

COMMUNION OF SAINTS: Mentioned in the Apostles' Creed (see Appendix 5). To some Christians it means sharing together in the Eucharist and to others it is a description of Christian fellowship here on earth. Traditionally, however, it refers to the spiritual union between Christ and each believer and, by extension, describes the spiritual union that exists among all believers on earth and in heaven.

COMMUNITARIAN: Nonmonastic communities motivated by ethical or religious ideals. In the nineteenth century there were a wide variety of religious communitarian groups in America.

CONFESSION: In one sense, confession means to acknowledge or to admit one's sins for the purpose of being forgiven. The sacrament of penance provides one possibility: the sinner confesses his or her sins to a priest, who is empowered (through his ordination) to forgive those sins in God's name. Confession also means to profess one's faith: a formal statement of beliefs is sometimes called a creed and sometimes a confession. A *confessional group,* therefore, is one with a common creed: it follows the established practices and adheres to the established credal statements of that group.

CONGREGATIONAL: A type of ecclesiastical government where authority flows throughout the congregation (see Appendix 6).

CONSTANTINE (d. 337 C.E.): First Christian Roman emperor. He conquered under the Christian sign of the cross and issued the Edict of Milan (313), which stated that Christianity would be tolerated in the empire and put an end to persecution.

CONSTANTINOPLE: Capital city of the Roman Empire under Constantine and his successors, formerly called Byzantium. Called also the "new Rome." Three ecumenical councils were held there.

CONSUBSTANTIATION: An explanation about the Eucharist associated with Martin Luther which differs from transubstantiation. Consubstantiation proposes that after the consecration of the elements, both the body and blood of Christ *and* the bread and wine exist together in union with one another.

CONVERSION (Gk = *metanoia* is one root, meaning radical turning of the heart and will): Several meanings: (1) turning from sin to God in faith and repentance (the controversy here is whether this turning is entirely an act of God, of the person, or a cooperation between them); (2) drawing closer to God by living a more dedicated Christian life; (3) changing from nonbelief to belief, as in conversion from atheism; (4) sometimes used by Roman Catholics to describe the experience of someone who has turned from one church to the Catholic church; thus *convert* is the word often used by Catholics to describe a Protestant now become Catholic.

COUNCIL OF TRENT: Roman Catholic council held periodically from 1545 to 1563 to respond to Protestantism. Until the Second Vatican Council (1962–65), Trent was the most comprehensive statement of Catholic belief and practice.

COUNSELS OF PERFECTION: Traditionally the vocations to poverty, chastity, and obedience, which form the basis of nearly all monastic and religious life for Roman Catholicism, Orthodox Christianity, and Protestant religious orders.

COVENANT: An agreement entered into voluntarily by two or more parties. God established a covenant with Abraham and with the Jewish people at Sinai; Christians believe a new covenant began with Jesus.

COVENANT THEOLOGY: Used, especially by the Puritans, to explain the election and perseverance of the saints. It was an important part of the religious, political, and social understanding of both Presbyterian and Congregational Puritans.

CRANMER, THOMAS (1489–1556): Archbishop of Canterbury at the beginning of the English Reformation, chiefly responsible for the *Book of Common Prayer*.

CREED: Summary of basic doctrines of faith. See Appendix 5.

CRUSADES (from the Latin word for cross; the Crusaders wore a cross on their official clothing): A series of military expeditions launched from the eleventh to the thirteenth centuries by Christians for the recovery of the Holy Land (Jerusalem) from the Muslims. The first one was called by Pope Urban II in 1095. There were nine of them altogether. The fourth Crusade (1202–04) ended with the capture and pillaging of Constantinople. The word *crusade* came to be used for other expeditions—against heretics, for example—sanctioned by the pope.

DARK AGES: Usually refers to the period between the collapse of the old Roman Empire (in the fifth century) and beginning of a stable society (about 1000 C.E.). The Dark Ages is often associated with the barbarian invasions, unstable government, and minimal levels of education and progress.

DAVID (d. 972 B.C.E.): King of ancient Israelites, one of the great national heroes of Judaism. Some Jews expect the Messiah to come from the house of David.

DEACON (Gk = servant or minister): Mentioned in the New Testament and recognized in many Christian churches as an office or ministry (often attached to reading the gospel, visiting the sick, and so on). The role and nature of the deacon vary according to polity.

DEAD SEA SCROLLS: A collection of texts discovered in 1947 that tell scholars something about the Qumran community, a group of Essenes who lived around the time of Jesus.

DEIFICATION: In Eastern Orthodox mysticism and theology, it usually means divinization: becoming divine by way of a profound union with God.

DEISM (Lat *deus* = God): Belief in a Supreme Being who created the world and then left it to its own discoverable and reasonable natural laws. The Deist God is not personal and does not reveal religious truths or work miracles.

DENOMINATIONALISM: A denomination is a specific church group united in polity and belief. *Denominationalism* has several meanings: (1) refers to the variety and independence of various churches; (2) refers to the notion that there are and ought to be many differing church bodies; (3) refers to the movement to unite local churches into one larger body. In this third sense denominationalism has been opposed by those who clearly favor congregational polities or who value their own distinctness. Antidenominationalism is resistance to any centrally organized church body.

DEVOTIONS: Acts of prayer or religious fervor meant to focus one's energies on a relationship with God. In the Middle Ages many Christians believed that their eternal salvation depended on how faithfully they had said certain prayers, kept certain feasts, and performed certain religious acts. Devotions sometimes required very small efforts: uttering a pious phrase like "Have mercy on me, O Lord," or saying special prayers on Sundays. Some devotions, however, required major commitments and could even endanger one's life, such as making a pilgrimage to Jerusalem. At the end of the fourteenth century, a movement arose called *devotio moderna* (modern devotion) which laid great stress on one's inner life and required the practice of meditation. The most popular book of this movement was Thomas à Kempis's *Imitation of Christ*. Many of the reformers, upset by some devotional excesses and/or convinced that such practices were of no use in obtaining salvation, condemned devotional practices and enjoined their followers to trust in God's mercy and to realize that they would be saved on the basis of faith alone, not because of their "good works" or devotions.

DIDACHE: An early collection of moral precepts and directions for the celebration of the Eucharist and administration of baptism, written somewhere between 50 and 150 C.E. in Greek. Also contains directions for bishops and deacons.

DIOCESE: A unit of territorial administration in churches with episcopal structures (see Appendix 6). A diocese is under the jurisdiction of a bishop and is usually a relatively large territory. The Romans divided the empire into provinces called dioceses in order to insure smooth and effective government. Christians adapted the system to suit their ecclesiastical purposes.

DOCTRINE: A system of beliefs or dogmas; teaching of a particular group.

DUALISM: Any philosophical system that tries to explain things in terms of two distinct and irreducible principles; in religion, good and evil or light and darkness, both of which are equally powerful.

ECUMENICAL COUNCIL (Gk = universal): Universal meeting of bishops, whose authority was accepted as official. See Appendix 4.

ECUMENISM: From the Greek word for universal or worldwide. Ecumenism is an attempt to realize greater Christian unity by interchurch cooperation.

EDICT OF MILAN: Passed by Constantine (313) granting religious toleration to Christians.

ELDER (Gk = presbyter): An office in the presbyterian structure that is divided into teaching elders (ordained ministers) and ruling elders (elected from the congregation). Some Christians translate the word *presbyter* as priest rather than elder (see Appendix 6).

ENGLISH CIVIL WAR: Conflict between King Charles I of England and a significant group of his subjects. It lasted from 1642 to 1648 and was focused on Charles's monarchical views versus the demands of the Parliamentarians. Many of the king's opponents were Puritans.

ENLIGHTENMENT: A term applied to scientific and philosophical thought in the eighteenth century characterized by belief in natural law and order, confidence in human reason, and a rational approach to religious questions.

EPISCOPAL: A type of ecclesiastical government where authority rests with bishops and flows down from them through priests to members of the congregation (see Appendix 6).

ERASMUS, DESIDERIUS (c. 1469–1536): Usually referred to as Erasmus of Rotterdam. Renowned humanist scholar and priest; famous during the Reformation for his Latin translation of the New Testament (from Greek) and for his debates with Martin Luther on the freedom of the will.

ESCHATOLOGY (Gk = last discourse or last things): The doctrine of the last things or end of the world; eschatology is concerned with the end of the individual soul, all other people, the church, and the world. It is treated in the Old Testament and New Testament, but is most thoroughly treated in apocryphal books.

ESSENES: Small Jewish ascetic sect at the time of Jesus. Essenes lived pious, communal lives in the desert, where they purified themselves in preparation for the Messiah. Community of goods, celibacy, and purification through baptism were some of their practices.

ESTABLISHED CHURCHES: Those churches whose practice and doctrines are supported by the state in some way. The Church of England is "established": the church is supported by and to some extent controlled by the state.

EUCHARIST (Gk = thanksgiving): Christian practice that repeats the action of Jesus at the Last Supper. Christians partake of the bread and wine in memory of Jesus. Some Christians believe the bread and wine is truly the body and blood of Christ; others believe it is a symbol of the body and blood; still others believe it is a memorial fellowship meal.

EUSEBIUS (c. 260–340): Bishop of Caesarea and so-called father of church history. Wrote official biography of Constantine.

EXCOMMUNICATION: An ecclesiastical punishment whereby a person is excluded from communion with the church; that is, the excommunicated person may not partake of the sacraments or, in some cases, speak to anyone in the community.

EXEGESIS (Gk = to narrate or explain): The process of explaining a text, usually a biblical one, by way of translation, paraphrase, or commentary. An exegete applies interpretive skills to a text in order to understand it more deeply. Exegesis has been done from ancient times—commentaries on Scripture predate Christianity, and Christianity itself has a long and varied history of exegesis—but it changes as exegetical skills (linguistic, archaeological, historical, spiritual) develop over time.

EXILE (the Babylonian captivity): In the history of Israel, the period from the fall of Jerusalem (587 B.C.E.) to the reconstruction in Palestine of a new Jewish state (538 B.C.E.).

EXODUS: Second book of the Hebrew Bible (or Old Testament). In Jewish history, the Exodus was the flight from Egypt led by Moses (including the miraculous crossing of the Red Sea and God's victory over the Egyptians).

FAITH: For some Christians an attitude of trust in God's mercy; people may be saved through Christ by faith. For other Christians *faith* refers to a body of beliefs and is more like a creed or set of doctrines believed by people. For still others, intellectual assent to a body of beliefs.

FALL: The moment when Adam and Eve disobeyed God's command not to eat of the tree of knowledge, thus forfeiting the original blessedness that they had enjoyed. Theologically, a fall from a state of harmony to one of discord with the will of God. See Genesis 3.

FILIOQUE (Lat = and the Son): Words added to the Nicene Creed by Western Christians so that it reads "the Holy Ghost . . . proceeds from the Father and Son." Long a source of friction between Roman Catholics and Orthodox Christians.

FLAGELLANTS: Groups of people who, in medieval times, scourged themselves in public procession or in town squares in order to lead people to repentance and to do penance themselves for their own sins and the sins of the world.

FORTY-TWO ARTICLES: Collection of Anglican doctrines issued in 1553 but never enforced (due to the restoration of Roman Catholicism under Queen Mary I). They form the basis of the present-day Anglican doctrinal formulation, the Thirty-nine Articles.

FRANCISCANS: The order of friars founded by Francis of Assisi (1182–1226), distinguished by complete poverty.

FRIARS: Religious beggars living an officially sanctioned, vowed religious life. Friars were called *fraters* (brothers); they were usually distinguished by the color of their cloaks (Gray Friars, Black Friars, and so on).

GENTILE (Hb = the nations): A term applied to non-Jews.

GENTILE MISSION: Refers to Saint Paul's spreading the gospel message not just to Jews, but to Gentiles; to anyone who would believe in Jesus as the Christ.

GLOSSOLALIA (Gk = tongue talking): The ability or gift of speaking "in tongues," which may mean speaking in a real language unknown to the speaker (one might, for instance, speak Chinese under the influence of the Spirit), or in an unknown language (which then may or may not be interpreted to the congregation). In Pentecostal churches, speaking in tongues is considered a sign of baptism in the Spirit.

GNOSTICS (Gk = knowledge): The term is used to describe a variety of early Christian heretics whose interpretation of the Gospels and the Christian life was based on secret knowledge; in order to be saved, they said, one had to know the secret signs and words. Recent research on the manuscripts found at Nag Hammadi in Egypt has given us a more thorough understanding of the Gnostics, who were heretofore known mostly through the condemnations of their opponents. Many of the apocryphal gospels were written by Gnostics.

GOSPELS ("good tidings"): Any of the first four books of the New Testament preaching the "good news," namely, that there is salvation through the birth, life, passion, death, and resurrection of Jesus. The four Gospels in the New Testament are Matthew, Mark, Luke, and John.

GRACE: In Christian theology it means God's favor or supernatural assistance. People receive grace so that they may be sanctified. Christians admit the need for some kind of divine help in their lives, but there has been much disagreement about what exactly this help is, how it comes to people, how people accept it, whether it is there all the time or only for specific acts.

HEBREWS: See *Jews*.

HELENA (c. 255–330): Mother of Constantine. According to a later tradition, she found the true cross in Jerusalem.

HELLENISM: The culture, ideals, and pattern of life of ancient Greece. As a system it competed with Christianity and challenged it to develop a philosophical language.

HERESY: Formal denial of a defined doctrine.

HERMIT (Gk = desert): Individual who, for religious motives, retires from the general society and goes out to a lonely place in order to focus on an intense relationship with God. In the early church these people went into the deserts of Egypt and Syria.

HEROD: Dynasty reigning in Palestine at time of Jesus. Herod the Great (d. 4 B.C.E.) gave the family its name, and was king of Judea. His son Herod Antipas (d. 39 C.E.) executed John the Baptist and was reigning at the time of Jesus's death.

HOLY SPIRIT (HOLY GHOST): Theologically, the third person of the Trinity; biblically, a manifestation of God's power in this world. The Holy Spirit was promised by Jesus, and Christians believe it is present in the church in some way.

HUMANISM: A philosophical and literary movement that extolled human capabilities. In its Renaissance form it signaled a return to classical antiquity. It inspired some of the scriptural research that led to the Reformation.

HUSSITES: Followers of John Hus, they were Czech nationalists who resisted armed attempts to squelch their religious protests. One of their main tenets was the reception of the Eucharist under both species; that is, they believed that people should receive both the bread and the wine. A Czech flag still used today has eucharistic symbols on it.

ICONOCLAST CONTROVERSY (Gk iconoclasm = image breaking): Opposition to religious use of images, from the fourth to the ninth centuries a raging battle in Orthodox Christianity. In the Reformation some Protestants (especially Puritans) considered the use of religious images idolatrous.

ICONOSTASIS: Screen in Orthodox churches that separates the sanctuary from the rest of the church.

ICONS (Gk = image, picture): Flat pictures of God and saints venerated in Orthodox churches.

IGNATIUS OF ANTIOCH (c. 35–107): Bishop of Antioch and martyr. In an age of doctrinal questioning, he argued that the best way to safeguard true beliefs was through the teaching and ruling authority of the bishop.

IMMANENCE (Lat. *in manere* = to dwell in): God's dwelling in and being active in the world. The doctrine of immanence sees the world as, in some sense, containing God within it (see *transcendence*).

INCARNATION: Christian doctrine that the eternal Son of God took flesh; Jesus Christ as both fully divine and fully human.

INDEX: Officially, *Index Librorum Prohibitorum* (Index of Forbidden Books). A list of books considered to be dangerous to the faith and morals of Catholics, drawn up by a censoring agency established by the church in the sixteenth century. The Index was abolished in 1966.

INDULGENCES: Remission by the church of temporal punishment due for sin. Based on the merits of Christ and the saints, the medieval Catholic church reasoned that it could grant indulgences drawn from a treasury of merits available to help sinners on earth.

INERRANCY: The belief that there are no errors in the Bible that are not corrected within the Bible itself. According to this view, the Bible is literally true and available to anyone who can read the text. See *biblical criticism*.

INFALLIBILITY: The ability to speak on religious matters without making a mistake. There have been arguments about biblical infallibility; that is, to what extent the Bible is infallible. Roman Catholics believe that the pope is infallible when speaking *ex cathedra* (from the chair): when the pope is speaking to the whole church, on matters of faith and morals. The issue of papal infallibility is a matter of continued debate within Roman Catholic Christianity; some argue that the calling of Vatican II indicates that infallibility is not entirely vested in the pope, but in the church as it meets in ecumenical council.

INQUISITION: The official persecution of heresy by designated ecclesiastical courts; established in the thirteenth century. Called the Holy Office from 1908 to 1965, when it became the Congregation for the Doctrine of the Faith with the function of promoting faith and morals, not just safeguarding them.

INSPIRATION (Gk = breath, spirit): Doctrine that Scripture was written under the influence of the Holy Spirit. How it works is a matter of some dispute and speculation among Christians.

ISRAELITES: See *Jews*.

JESUS: Theologically, the son of God and second person of the Trinity; biblically, the savior who died and rose from the dead; historically, a carpenter from Nazareth born in the reign of Caesar Augustus.

JEWS: Three terms must be distinguished here. *Hebrew* refers to the Semitic people not yet formed into the nation Israel. *Israelites* refers to those Hebrews who were part of the nation Israel formed under the leadership of Moses and Joshua around 1200 B.C.E. Jews, as a term, derives from the last surviving Israelite tribe, Judah, and is a term applied to these people after the exile (587 B.C.E.). In chronological order, then, one speaks of the Hebrews up to the Exodus, of the Israelites from the Exodus to the exile, and of the Jews after the exile. In a more embracing sense, however, Judaism traces itself back to the days of Abraham, Isaac, and Jacob, and Jews are descendants of Abraham and Sarah.

JOHN THE BAPTIST: Cousin of Jesus who after retiring into the desert emerged to preach repentance and to baptize in preparation for the Messiah. He baptized Jesus.

JOHN XXIII: Name taken by two popes: (1) Baldassare Cossa (d. 1419), who was elected pope by the Council of Pisa (1409) and was an antipope (that is, was pope in contest with two other men who also claimed to be the rightful pope); he called the Council of Constance; (2) Angelo Roncalli (1958–63), who called the Second Vatican Council, which reformed and modernized the Roman Catholic church.

JUSTIFICATION (Lat = make just; Gk = pronounce just): A person's passage from sinfulness to righteousness (or justice). Also, that act whereby God makes a person just (conveys grace to a person's soul); or the act whereby God, because of the sacrifice of Christ, treats a person mercifully—as though that person were just or righteous. Christians share the belief that justification is bound up with rebirth or regeneration, but they disagree about what that rebirth means, how it is accomplished and how, exactly, it affects the person.

JUSTIN MARTYR (100–65 C.E.): Christian apologist who tried to convert people to Christianity by way of philosophical argument.

LITURGY (Gk = work of the people): Used to describe worship in general and the Eucharist especially.

LOLLARDS: Followers of John Wycliffe in England.

MACCABEES: Jewish family of second and first centuries B.C.E. that brought about restoration of Jewish political and religious life.

MARTYR (Gk = witness): During persecution, used for those who suffered for their religious beliefs; finally restricted to those who died for them. Martyrs are honored as saints by the church.

MARY (Hb = Miriam): Mother of Jesus. She occupies a place of honor—principal saint—in Roman Catholic and Orthodox churches. Theological statements about her acknowledge her virginity and title Mother of God. During the Reformation, Protestants reacted against what they interpreted as excessive devotion to Mary. Her place in the devotional life of the church is a serious issue between Roman Catholics and Protestants.

MASS: A name—along with Lord's Supper and Holy Communion—for the celebration of the Eucharist. It is usually used by Roman Catholics, but has also been used by Anglicans.

MENDICANT FRIARS: Members of religious orders that were forbidden to own property. Unlike monks, they worked or begged for a living and were not required to spend their lives in one monastery.

MESSIAH (Hb = anointed one): In Judaism, a man sent by God to restore Israel and reign righteously for all people. Christians consider Jesus to be the Messiah and interpret the Messiah as a suffering savior (see Isaiah 52–55).

MILLENNIALISM (Gk = thousand): Based on Revelation 20:1–10, the belief that Christ promised faithful believers a thousand years of bliss, and will return to establish it.

MOSES (thirteenth century B.C.E.): Leader and lawgiver of the Jewish people. Called by God to take the Jews to Mount Sinai, where God made a covenant with them.

MYSTERY (Lat = *sacramentum*) RELIGIONS: In Greek and Roman religion, secret cults that required elaborate initiations, purification rites, and accepted occult ideas.

MYSTICISM: A form of religious experience that emphasizes the possibility and desirability of a direct and intuitive apprehension of divinity. A mystic is one who strives for this direct personal union with God.

NATIVISM: Intense suspicion or dislike of foreigners, often directed against Catholics by American Protestants in the nineteenth century.

NEOPLATONISM: Ancient mystical philosophy based on doctrines of Plato. It had a lasting effect on the development of Christian mysticism.

NEW TESTAMENT: The Christian portion of the Bible: twenty-seven books.

NICENE CREED: Official statement of beliefs from the Council of Nicaea (see Appendix 4).

OLD CATHOLICS: Catholics who split off from Roman Catholicism in the nineteenth century as a protest against papal infallibility. Old Catholics are a coalition of small national churches whose liturgy and edifices appear to be Roman Catholic, but whose beliefs deny many Roman Catholic doctrines (especially those about Mary).

OLD TESTAMENT: The Christian name for the Hebrew Bible, as rearranged by Christians.

ORDINANCES: Nonliturgical churches—for example, Baptists and Mennonites—rejected the word *sacrament* and adopted the word *ordinance* because they thought *sacrament* had medieval connotations of magic.

ORIGEN (c. 185–254 C.E.): Christian philosopher and scholar, one of the first theological geniuses of the Christian church. Attempted to synthesize Neoplatonism and Stoicism with Christian creed so as to provide a Christian view of the universe.

ORIGINAL SIN: In Christian theology, the sin of Adam and Eve. The effect of it is the fundamentally graceless nature of human beings; that is, all people are regarded as having a sinful nature.

ORTHODOXY: Right belief (as contrasted with heresy). The word is used for the ancient Greek Christian church (Orthodox Christianity: Greek Orthodox, Russian Orthodox, and so on). It can also refer to adherence to traditional or established belief (as opposed to liberalism or innovation).

OTTO I (the Great) (912–73): Holy Roman Emperor from 962, reviving the Carolingian claims.

PARLIAMENTARIANS: Group opposed to King Charles I in the English Civil War; many of them were Puritans, and the English Civil War is sometimes referred to as the Puritan Revolution.

PASSOVER: A Jewish feast of highest importance. In the Bible it is an act of deliverance from the Egyptians, where an angel of death passed over the Hebrews in the last of the great plagues (Exodus 12).

PATRIARCH: One of the progenitors of the Jewish people, especially Abraham, Isaac, and Jacob. In the Christian church, a title of certain exalted bishops. In the early church there were five great patriarchates: Rome, Constantinople, Alexandria, Antioch, and Jerusalem.

PAUL (d. 64 or 67 C.E.): Apostle to the Gentiles. Born and reared a Jew, he converted to Christianity after an "experience of the risen Lord." Author of major epistles in the New Testament, great missionary, and early theologian.

PEACE OF AUGSBURG (1555): Settled the religious battles in Germany with the formula *cuius regio eius religio:* the people in a given region must follow the religion of the ruler of that region (those who opposed their ruler's religion should move to a more congenial place).

PEACE OF WESTPHALIA (1648): The general settlement ending the Thirty Years' War.

PEASANTS' REVOLT: An uprising of German peasants in 1524–26. Although their grievances were economic, the peasants were urged on by some religious reformers and others who were impatient for change. Their list of demands included some religious reforms, but their methods were variations of mob violence. Luther called for their extermination.

PENANCE: In Orthodox and Roman Catholic churches, a sacrament of the forgiveness of sins. It can also mean a punishment of some sort (as in one "doing penance" for sins).

PENTECOST (Gk = fiftieth): In Judaism, a spring feast fifty days after Passover, commemorating the Sinai covenant. In Christianity, the feast celebrating the coming of the Holy Spirit to the apostles and into the church.

PENTECOSTAL: Member of a church that requires baptism in the Spirit manifested by *glossolalia*, speaking in tongues. Today one can find Pentecostal Christians in non-Pentecostal churches as well; for example, there is a Pentecostal movement in Roman Catholicism.

PERSECUTIONS: Sporadic but systematic attempts on the part of Roman authorities to destroy Christianity. Began with Nero (64 C.E.) and ended with the Edict of Milan (313).

PETER (d. 64 C.E.): Most prominent of the twelve apostles of Jesus. Traditionally, the first bishop of Rome.

PHARISEES: One of two great political parties (with Sadducees) in Jerusalem at time of Jesus. They were extreme in their attempt to keep all that was Jewish away from what was non-Jewish; they were liberal in accepting both written law (Torah) and oral law (tradition).

PILGRIMAGE: Journey to a holy place in order to obtain divine help or to honor God or the saints. Many religions encourage pilgrimage, and the desire to visit the place where a holy person actually lived appears to be common to many religious people. Christians went on journeys to shrines (holy places) all over Europe. Chaucer used the occasion of a pilgrimage to the shrine of Thomas à Becket (archbishop of Canterbury who was murdered in 1170) as the setting for *The Canterbury Tales* (fourteenth century). The most important pilgrimage, however, was the one to Jerusalem: many Christians undertook the dangerous journey to the places where Jesus had lived and died, and many have left moving accounts of their journeys there. At the same time, shrines were notorious for abuses: then as now, entrepreneurs were able to take advantage of people by selling fake relics, manufacturing incredible tales of miracles, and generally helping the pious to part with their money. Erasmus wrote a famous satire about pilgrimage, "A Pilgrimage for Religion's Sake," in 1526 precisely to make fun of the abuses and to support those Reformation thinkers who believed that the whole concept of pilgrimage was unnecessary and perhaps even harmful to one's religious life. Pilgrimages still occur in Christianity, mostly within the Roman Catholic tradition.

PIUS V (1504–72; pope from 1566): Recognized as a saint in the Roman Catholic church, he was an austere and zealous reformer, instrumental in promoting the reforms of the Council of Trent. In 1570 he excommunicated Elizabeth I, queen of England, and greatly aggravated the position of Catholics there.

PLAGUES OF EGYPT: In the Bible, the troubles visited on Egyptians by God so that the pharaoh would let the Jewish people go out of Egypt. There were ten plagues. See Exodus 7:19–12:36.

PLATO (427–347 B.C.E.): Greek philosopher. One of the most important and influential thinkers in the history of the world.

PLURALISM: The belief that no single theory can explain the universe, which, according to pluralists, is composed of many principles. In religion it is the coexistence of a variety of religious forms and beliefs.

POLITY: Church structure or government (see Appendix 6).

POMPEY (106–48 B.C.E.): Rival of Julius Caesar. Conquered Jerusalem for Rome in 63 B.C.E.

PONTIUS PILATE: Roman procurator of Judea when Jesus was crucified. According to the New Testament, he evaded responsibility for Jesus's death because he feared Jewish high priests' power.

POPE/PAPACY (Lat = father): Title restricted to the bishop of Rome since the fourth century.

PREDESTINATION: The idea that God decrees beforehand for all eternity the fate of individual souls. Some Christians believe that God predestines people to both heaven and hell; others say that God predestines to heaven but reprobates to hell. Predestination is deduced on the basis of divine foreknowledge.

PRESBYTERIAN: A type of ecclesiastical government where authority rests with a group of elected elders (see Appendix 6).

PRIEST (Gk = presbyter): As a special ministry (apart from elder) priesthood does not appear in the New Testament, but by the second century the office of the priest had developed to include a share in the powers of the bishop, specifically powers to celebrate the Eucharist and to forgive sins.

PROPHETS (Hb = called by God): Prophets were those called in the Old Testament to speak God's word to the people (usually to urge them back to the terms of the covenant). Sometimes prophets predicted future events, but their main function was to speak for God, not to be seers.

PROVIDENCE: The doctrine that the world is divinely administered; that God, in some way, rules the world; and that the events that occur in the world are understood and controlled (or allowed) by God. The doctrine of providence need not destroy free will.

PURGATORY: A Roman Catholic doctrine that says there is a state of life after death which is neither heaven nor hell, but a place where one can suffer or work out the temporal punishment due to sins committed on earth. Accordingly, Catholics tend to pray for the dead while Protestants, in general, do not. The theory for purgatory is relatively straightforward: if one must be perfectly purified in order to go to heaven but dies before achieving such purification, there must be another chance to do so. Purgatory is predicated on ancient beliefs about the divine attributes of justice and mercy. God's justice demands purification and so *could* refuse heaven to anyone who was not perfectly purified before death, but God's mercy will not permit such a refusal of heaven to those who truly long for heaven and simply need more time. The doctrine of purgatory has been a longstanding disagreement between Catholics and Protestants since the Reformation.

RATIONALISM: Theory that reason alone (unaided by experience) can arrive at some basic truths about the world. In religion it is often opposed to revelation: it holds that religion can be understood on the basis of reason alone and that revelation is unnecessary.

REFORMATION: A complex series of changes occurring in Christianity from the fourteenth to the seventeenth centuries.

RELICS: Material remains of a saint, or sacred objects that touched the body.

RENAISSANCE: From the word for rebirth, it was a development of Western civilization from the fourteenth to the sixteenth centuries that marked the passage from medieval to modern times. In it there was a new importance given to individual expression, culture, and worldly experience.

RESURRECTION (Lat = rising again): Rising from death to life. In Christianity, the resurrection of Jesus is the central fact of Christian experience. Christians believe that all believers will rise from the dead at the end of the world.

REVIVALISM: A form of evangelical preaching that is highly emotional in style, characterized by its focus on sin and salvation, and designed to bring listeners to a conversion experience.

SABBATARIANS: Those who observe Saturday as the Sabbath, or those who observe the Sunday Sabbath rigorously, by abstaining from all work and recreation on Sundays.

SABBATH (Hb = repose): Last day of the week in Judaism, first day of the week in Christianity. Observed on Saturday as a day of rest for Jews. Observed on Sunday as a celebration of the Resurrection for Christians.

SACRAMENT (Gk = mystery): An outward sign instituted by Christ to draw people into relationship with God. Historically there have been arguments about how many sacraments there are, whether or not they give grace, and what they mean. Some Christians prefer the term *ordinances,* and others may "have communion" but never use the words *sacrament* or *ordinance.* Most Christians—except Quakers and the Salvation Army, who have no sacraments—accept baptism and the Lord's Supper (Eucharist or Communion) as sacraments and some accept the forgiveness of sins. Roman Catholics and Orthodox Christians accept seven sacraments: baptism, confirmation, reconciliation, the Eucharist, ordination, matrimony, and the anointing of the sick.

SADDUCEES: Jewish sect or party made up of the priestly aristocracy (the Jewish establishment); political collaborationists with the Romans who accepted only written law (Torah).

SAMARITANS: Descendants of non-Jewish colonists who settled in Samaria in the eighth century B.C.E. They accepted only the first five books of the Bible and were considered by the Jews to be heretics.

SANCTIFICATION: Once a sinner has been turned to God through conversion and justification, there remains the possibility and task of drawing closer to God or to Christian perfection. Sanctification is a "second step" or second blessing.

SANCTUARY: That part of the church that contains the altar. In some churches the altar is called a table and the sanctuary contains the table, the Bible, and a pulpit (for preaching). In Roman Catholic, Orthodox, and many Anglican churches the sanctuary contains a tabernacle: a locked, enclosed space built into the high altar where the consecrated bread (called the Blessed Sacrament) is kept. In Orthodox churches the tabernacle and sanctuary are behind the iconostasis. In all churches where the Blessed Sacrament is kept one can find a sanctuary light or candle always lighted to indicate that the Blessed Sacrament is present there.

SANHEDRIN: Ancient Jewish legal and religious institution that operated as a court of law for Jews.

SATAN (Hb = adversary): A devil or demon, the great adversary of people and enemy of God.

SCHISM (Gk = to tear): A rift in the unity of the church.

SCHOLASTICISM (SCHOLASTIC THEOLOGY): The educational system of the medieval schools, which consisted in methods of disputation and philosophical and theological speculation. It was stimulated by the discoveries of Aristotelian logic in the eleventh century and led to logical speculation and systematization of Christian faith on every conceivable level.

SIN: In religion, an unethical act, disobedience to a personal God. There is disagreement about what constitutes a sin, but agreement that it is a rebellion against God.

SOCIAL DARWINISM: The application of the teachings of Charles Darwin (1809–82) about organic evolution to society so that poverty, crime, and disease can be explained in relation to survival of the fittest.

STOREFRONT CHURCHES: Some evangelical churches have an outreach to inner city areas by means of churches set up in abandoned stores; some religious individuals with a mission of their own to preach about Jesus also are sometimes drawn to downtrodden, urban settings. The churches set up in abandoned stores are called storefront churches; they do not form a denomination and often have little in common in terms of preaching, doctrine, and practice.

SYNOD: A formal meeting of religious leaders, usually of a particular region. To be distinguished from an ecumenical council, which involves the leaders of the church from all regions of the world.

SYNOPTICS (Gk = to see together): The books of Matthew, Mark, and Luke in the New Testament are considered synoptic Gospels: they bear greater similarities to each other than any of them do to the Book of John.

TALMUD (Aramaic from Hb = learning): The vast body of Hebrew oral tradition containing the elucidations, elaborations, and commentaries of the rabbis. Accepted as authoritative by orthodox Jews.

TEMPERANCE MOVEMENT: An effort to get people to abstain from drinking alcohol (totally or partially), which grew particularly strong in nineteenth-century America with help of the WCTU (Women's Christian Temperance Union) and the Anti-Saloon League. Their efforts (and others) led to the Eighteenth Amendment, prohibiting the sale and consumption of alcohol (Prohibition).

TESTIMONY: An account of the power of Jesus in one's life shared with fellow believers. It is distinguished by some Christians from witness, which is an account shared with nonbelievers. Testimony is meant to support the faith of one's fellow believers.

THEISM (Gk *theos* = God): Intended to oppose the concept of atheism, the conscious rejection of God's existence. Theism is the term for a philosophical system that accepts a transcendent and personal God. Unlike Deism, theism accepts the possibility of miracles and revelation.

THEOPHANY: An appearance of God in some visible form, temporary and not necessarily material.

THEOPHILUS (late second century): Bishop of Antioch and apologist.

THIRTY-NINE ARTICLES: The doctrinal positions of the Anglican church (see Appendix 5).

THOMAS À KEMPIS (c. 1380–1471): Spiritual writer, author of *The Imitation of Christ,* one of the most famous manuals of spiritual devotion in Christian literature. The book tells Christians to seek perfection by following Christ as a model.

TIBERIUS (42 B.C.E.–37 C.E.): Second Roman emperor (14–37 C.E.), in power when Jesus was killed.

TORAH (Hb = teaching): Hebrew name for the first five books of the Bible: Genesis, Exodus, Leviticus, Numbers, and Deuteronomy. Believed to have been handed down to Moses on Sinai, it contains laws of moral and physical conduct and love of Jewish people.

TRANSCENDENCE (Lat *trans* = across; *scandare* = to climb): The transcendence of God is his existence prior to and above the world. God is different from the world. See *immanence*.

TRANSCENDENTALISM: A literary, philosophical, and religious movement that flourished in New England from about 1836 to 1860. It originated with a small group of intellectuals who were against the teachings of Calvin and against the option offered by the Unitarians. They developed their own doctrine, which featured the divinity of human beings.

TRANSUBSTANTIATION: One explanation—along with transignification and consubstantiation—of how the bread and wine used in the celebration of the Eucharist are transformed into the body and blood of Christ. It was adopted as the official teaching of the Roman Catholic church in the thirteenth century, but arguments about it continue within Catholicism and Christianity in general.

TRINITY: One of the central doctrines of Christianity, the belief that there are three divine persons existing in one God. Various explanations have been given for the way God exists as one substance and three distinct persons, but the Trinity is generally said to be a mystery—that is, a belief that cannot be understood or explained simply in terms of human reason. The biblical basis for this belief is the working of God as creator, redeemer, and sanctifier and the words of Jesus about God as his father along with his promise to send the Spirit to abide with the church forever. Christians, with few exceptions, baptize members into the church in the name of the Father, the Son, and the Holy Spirit, an ancient formula which recognizes three distinct persons in one God.

TYPOLOGY (Gr = example): A method of scriptural interpretation used by some early writers to show how Jesus could be understood by way of Old Testament figures.

UNAM SANCTAM: The papal bull (or letter) issued by Pope Boniface VIII in 1302 during his quarrel with Philip IV of France. In it the pope defined the four marks of the church as being one, holy, Catholic, and apostolic, and argued that "outside the church there is no salvation."

UNIATE CHURCHES: Churches of Eastern Christendom that are in communion with Rome, yet retain their own languages, church laws, and rites.

VATICAN: Modern papal residence in Rome. By the Italian Law of Guarantees (1871) and the Lateran Accords (1929), the Vatican, the Lateran cathedral, and the papal villa at Castel Gandolfo were granted extraterritoriality (not subject to the Italian government). Vatican City—including the library—is a separate city-state within Italy.

VATICAN II (1962–65): Council called by the Roman Catholic church in order to respond to liturgical and pastoral needs of Catholics in the twentieth century. It made some significant changes in Catholic practice and attitude as well as in theological understanding.

VOLUNTARISM: The theory and practice whereby church membership is a matter of personal choice, not civil control or some other form of coercion.

VULGATE: Latin version of the Bible compiled and translated by Saint Jerome in the fourth century to provide one authorized version of the Bible to Christians (instead of the many versions in circulation at the time). It was adopted by the Roman Catholic church as the only official version, a position opposed by the reformers.

WALDENSIANS: Followers of Peter Waldo (d. 1217), who, like Francis of Assisi, gave his money to the poor in order to live in holy poverty according to the Gospels. When the Waldensians began to preach without permission from the local clergy, they were condemned. They continued to preach—often against abuses in the church—and were hunted down and burned as heretics.

WISDOM LITERATURE: Those biblical books that deal with what we might call profound common sense, instructions about life and conduct passed on from teacher to disciple, often dealing with moral conduct. The Wisdom books in the Old Testament include Job, Proverbs, and Ecclesiastes.

WITNESS: An account of the power of Jesus in one's life shared with nonbelievers. It is distinguished by some Christians from testimony, which is an account shared with fellow believers. The purpose of witness is to bring people to an awareness of Jesus by virtue of one individual's faith and example.

ZEALOTS: A revolutionary party extremely concerned with national liberation of the Jews from the Romans. They expected the Messiah to be a warrior-king.

ZEUS: In Greek religion, the supreme god, who ruled other gods and people from Mount Olympus.

SELECTED REFERENCE WORKS

Bowden, Henry Warner. *Dictionary of American Religious Biography.* Westport, Conn.: Greenwood Press, 1977.

Brauer, Jerald C. *The Westminster Dictionary of Church History.* Philadelphia: Westminster Press, 1971.

Brown, Raymond E., Fitzmyer, Joseph A., and Murphy, Roland E. *The Jerome Biblical Commentary.* Englewood Cliffs, N.J.: Prentice-Hall, 1968.

Buttrick, George Arthur, ed. *The Interpreter's Bible.* 12 vols. New York and Nashville: Abingdon Press, 1952–57.

———. *The Interpreter's Dictionary of the Bible.* New York: Abingdon Press, 1962.

Canney, Maurice A. *An Encyclopedia of Religions.* Detroit: Gale Research, 1970.

Cross, F. L., ed. *The Oxford Dictionary of the Christian Church.* 2nd ed. Oxford: Oxford University Press, 1978.

Douglas, J. D., ed. *The New International Dictionary of the Christian Church.* Rev. ed. Grand Rapids: Zondervan Press, 1978.

al Faruqi, Isma'il Ragi, and Soper, David E. *Historical Atlas of the Religions of the World.* New York: Macmillan, 1974.

Feiner, Johannes, and Vischer, Lukas, eds. *The Common Catechism: A Book of Christian Faith.* New York: Seabury Press, 1975.

Gehman, Henry Snyder, ed. *The New Westminster Dictionary of the Bible.* Philadelphia: Westminster Press, 1970.

Hastings, James, ed. *Encyclopedia of Religion and Ethics.* 12 vols. New York: Scribner's, 1961.

Langer, William L., ed. *An Encyclopedia of World History.* 4th ed. New York: Houghton Mifflin, 1968.

Leith, John H. *Creeds of the Churches.* Rev. ed. Richmond, Va.: John Knox Press, 1973.

Leon-Dufour, Xavier, ed. *Dictionary of Biblical Theology.* New York: Desclee, 1967.

Lippy, Charles H., and William, Peter W. *Encyclopedia of the American Religious Experience.* 3 vols. New York: Scribner's, 1988.

Macquarrie, John. *Dictionary of Christian Ethics.* Philadelphia: Westminster Press, 1967.

Manschreck, Clyde L., ed. *A History of Christianity: Readings in the History of the Church from the Reformation to the Present.* Englewood Cliffs, N.J.: Prentice-Hall, 1964.

Meagher, Paul Kevil, ed. *Encyclopedic Dictionary of Religion.* 3 vols. Washington, D.C.: Corpus Publications, 1978.

Meagher, Paul K., O'Brien, Thomas C., and Aherne, Consuelo Maria. *The Encyclopedic Dictionary of Religion.* Baltimore: Catholic University of America Press, 1987.

Melton, J. Gordon, ed. *A Directory of Religious Bodies in the United States.* New York: Garland Publishing, 1977.

———. *The Encyclopedia of American Religions.* 2 vols. Wilmington, N.C.: McGrath Publishing, 1978.

Neill, Stephen, ed. *Concise Dictionary of the Christian World Mission.* Nashville: Abingdon Press, 1971.

New Catholic Encyclopedia. 17 vols. New York: McGraw-Hill, 1967–79.

Palmer, R. R., ed. *Atlas of World History.* New York: Rand McNally, 1970.

Petry, Ray C., ed. *A History of Christianity: Reading in the History of the Early and Medieval Church.* Englewood Cliffs, N.J.: Prentice-Hall, 1962.

Piepkorn, Arthur Carl. *Profiles in Belief: The Religious Bodies of the United States and Canada.* 4 vols. New York: Harper & Row, 1977–9.

Schaff, Philip, ed. *The Creeds of Christendom.* 3 vols. New York: Harper Brothers, 1877.

Seeberg, Reinhold. *Textbook of the History of Doctrines.* Grand Rapids: Baker House, 1952.

Weiser, Francis X. *Handbook of Christian Feasts and Customs.* New York: Harcourt Brace Jovanovich, 1952.

Who's Who in Religion. 2nd ed. Chicago: Marquis Who's Who, 1977.

SELECTED BIBLIOGRAPHY

Abell, Aaron I. *American Catholicism and Social Action: A Search for Social Justice 1865–1950*. Notre Dame, Ind.: University of Notre Dame Press, 1963.

Ahlstrom, Sydney E. *A Religious History of the American People*. New Haven: Yale University Press, 1972.

Albanese, Catherine. *America: Religions and Religion*. Belmont, Calif.: Wadsworth, 1981.

Albright, Raymond W. *A History of the Protestant Episcopal Church*. New York: Macmillan, 1964.

Anderson, Bernhard W. *Understanding the Old Testament*. 4th ed. Englewood Cliffs, N.J.: Prentice-Hall, 1986.

Anderson, Gerald H., and Stransky, Thomas F., eds. *Mission Trends No. 3: Third World Theologies*. New York: Paulist Press, 1976.

———. *Mission Trends No. 4: Liberation Theologies*. New York: Paulist Press, 1979.

Anderson, Hugh, ed. *Jesus*. Englewood Cliffs, N.J.: Prentice-Hall, 1967.

Anderson, Robert Mapes. *Vision of the Disinherited: The Making of American Pentecostalism*. New York: Oxford University Press, 1979.

Bainton, Roland H. *Early and Medieval Christianity*. Boston: Beacon Press, 1962.

———. *The Reformation of the Sixteenth Century*. Boston: Beacon Press, 1952.

Balasuriya, Tissa. *Planetary Theology*. Maryknoll, N.Y.: Orbis Books, 1984.

Barnhart, Joe Edward. *The Southern Baptist Holy War*. Austin: Texas Monthly Press, 1986.

Barraclough, Geoffrey. *The Medieval Papacy*. New York: Harcourt, Brace & World, 1972.

Barrett, Charles D. *Understanding the Christian Faith*. Englewood Cliffs, N.J.: Prentice-Hall, 1980.

Barrett, C. K. *The New Testament Background: Selected Documents*. London: SPCK., 1956.

Bedell, George C., Sandon, Leo Jr., and Wellborn, Charles T., eds. *Religion in America,* 2nd ed. New York: Macmillan, 1982.

Benson, Peter L. and Williams, Dorothy L., *Religion on Capitol Hill*. San Francisco: Harper & Row, 1982.

Benz, Ernst. *The Eastern Orthodox Church—Its Thought and Life*. New York: Doubleday, 1963.

Boff, Leonardo and Clodovis. *Introducing Liberation Theology*. Maryknoll, N.Y.: Orbis Books, 1987.

Boff, Leonardo. *Jesus Christ Liberator: A Critical Christology for Our Time*. Maryknoll, N.Y.: Orbis Books, 1979.

Bornkamm, Günther. *The New Testament: A Guide to Its Writings*. Philadelphia: Fortress Press, 1973.

Bouwsma, William J. *John Calvin: A Sixteenth-Century Portrait*. Oxford: Oxford University Press, 1988.

Braithwaite, W. C. *The Beginnings of Quakerism*. 2nd revised ed. by Henry J. Cadbury. Cambridge: Cambridge University Press, 1970.

Brown, Raymond, et al. *Peter in the New Testament: A Collaborative Assessment by Protestant and Roman Catholic Scholars*. Minneapolis: Augsburg, 1973.

Brown, Robert McAfee. *The Ecumenical Revolution: An Interpretation of the Catholic-Protestant Dialogue*. Garden City, N.Y.: Doubleday, 1967.

Burkholder, J. R., ed. *Kingdom, Cross and Community: Essays on Mennonite Themes*. Scottdale, Pa.: Herald Press, 1976.

Chadwick, Owen. *The Reformation*. London: Penguin, 1972.

Chamberlin, E. R. *The Bad Popes*. New York: New American Library, 1969.

Cogley, John. *Catholic America*. Revised by Roger Van Allen. Kansas City, Mo.: Sheed & Ward, 1986.

Constantelos, Demetrois J. *Understanding the Greek Orthodox Church*. New York: Seabury Press, 1982.

Coutts, John. *This We Believe: A Study of the Background and Meaning of Salvation Army Doctrines*. London: Challenge Books, 1979.

Cragg, Gerald R. *The Church and the Age of Reason 1648–1789*. Grand Rapids: Eerdmans, 1964.

Cullman, Oscar. *The New Testament: An Introduction for the General Reader*. London: SCM Press, 1968.

Daly, Mary. *The Church and the Second Sex*. 2nd ed. New York: Harper & Row, 1975.

Devine, George. *American Catholicism: Where Do We Go from Here?* Englewood Cliffs, N.J.: Prentice-Hall, 1975.

Dickens, A. G. *The Counter Reformation*. New York: Harcourt, Brace & World, 1969.

———. *Reformation and Society in Sixteenth-Century Europe*. New York: Harcourt, Brace & World, 1966.

Dickson, Kwesi A. *Theology in Africa*. Maryknoll, N.Y.: Orbis Books, 1984.

Dillenberger, John, and Welch, Claude. *Protestant Christianity Interpreted Through Its Development*. 2nd ed. New York: Macmillan, 1988.

Dolan, Jay P. *The American Catholic Experience: A History from Colonial Times to the*

Present. Garden City, N.Y.: Doubleday, 1985.

Donovan, Vincent J. *Christianity Rediscovered*. 2nd ed. Maryknoll, N.Y.: Orbis Books, 1982.

Donovan, Vincent J. *The Church in the Midst of Creation*. Maryknoll, N.Y.: Orbis Books, 1989.

Duckett, Eleanor. *The Wandering Saints of the Early Middle Ages*. New York: W. W. Norton, 1964.

Dulles, Avery. *Models of the Church*. New York: Doubleday, 1974.

Durnbaugh, Donald F. *The Believers' Church: The History and Character of Radical Protestantism*. New York: Macmillan, 1968.

Ellis, Jane. *The Russian Orthodox Church: A Contemporary History*. London: Croom Helm, 1986.

Ellis, John Tracy. *American Catholicism*. Rev. ed. Chicago: University of Chicago Press, 1969.

Ellis, John Tracy, ed., *Documents of American Catholic History*. Milwaukee: Bruce Publishing, 1956.

Ellwood, Robert C., and Partin, Harry B. *Religious and Spiritual Groups in Modern America*. 2nd ed. Englewood Cliffs, N.J.: Prentice-Hall, 1988.

Elvy, Peter. *Buying Time: The Foundations of the Electronic Church*. Mystic, Conn.: Twenty-Third Publications, 1987.

Everyday Life in Bible Times. Washington, D.C.: National Geographic Society, 1976.

Falwell, Jerry. *Listen, America!* New York: Doubleday, 1980.

Ferm, Deane William. *Contemporary American Theologies: A Critical Survey*. New York: Seabury Press, 1981.

———. *Contemporary American Theologies: A Book of Readings*. New York: Seabury Press, 1982.

———. *Third World Liberation Theologies: An Introductory Survey*. Maryknoll, N.Y.: Orbis Books, 1986.

Ferm, Robert L., ed. *Issues in American Protestantism: A Documentary History from the Puritans to the Present*. Gloucester, Mass.: P. Smith, 1976.

FitzGerald, Frances. "A Disciplined, Charging Army." *The New Yorker* 57 (18 May 1981), 53–141.

Fitzmyer, Joseph A. *Pauline Theology: A Brief Sketch*. Englewood Cliffs, N.J.: Prentice-Hall, 1967.

Flannery, Austin, ed. *Vatican Council II: The Conciliar and Post-Conciliar Documents*. New York: Costello Publishing, 1975.

Forell, George W., ed. *Christian Social Teachings: A Reader in Christian Social Ethics from the Bible to the Present*. Minneapolis: Augsburg, 1966.

Freemantle, Anne, ed. *The Papal Encyclicals in Their Historical Context*. New York: New American Library, 1963.

Frend, W. H. C. *Martyrdom and Persecution in the Early Church: A Study of Conflict from the Maccabees to Donatus*. New York: Doubleday, 1967.

Gager, John G. *Kingdom and Community*. Englewood Cliffs, N.J.: Prentice-Hall, 1975.

Gallup, George Jr., and Castelli, Jim. *The American Catholic People: Their Beliefs, Practices, and Values*. Garden City, N.Y.: Doubleday, 1987.

Gaustad, Edwin S., ed. *A Documentary History of Religion in America to the Civil War*. Grand Rapids: Eerdmans, 1982.

Gibellini, Rosino, ed. *Frontiers of Theology in Latin America*. Maryknoll, N.Y.: Orbis Books, 1979.

Gottschalk, Stephen. *The Emergence of Christian Science in American Life*. Berkeley: University of California Press, 1974.

Grant, Robert M. *Augustus to Constantine: The Thrust of the Christian Movement into the Roman World*. New York: Harper & Row, 1970.

Greeley, Andrew M. *The Catholic Experience*. New York: Doubleday, 1969.

Grollenberg, Lucas. *A Bible for Our Time*. London: SCM Press, 1979.

Gutierrez, Gustavo. *A Theology of Liberation*. Maryknoll, N.Y.: Orbis Books, 1973.

Hammell, Patrick J. *Handbook of Patrology*. New York: Alba House, 1968.

Harrell, David. *All Things Are Possible: The Healing and Charismatic Revivals in Modern America*. Bloomington: Indiana University Press, 1975.

Harrison, Barbara Grizzuti. *Visions of Glory: A History and a Memory of Jehovah's Witnesses*. New York: Simon & Schuster, 1978.

Hedgepeth, William. *The Alternative: Communal Life in the New America*. New York: Macmillan, 1970.

Herzel, Susannah. *A Voice for Women: The Women's Department of the World Council of Churches*. Geneva: World Council of Churches, 1981.

Higham, John. *Strangers in the Land—Patterns of American Nativism 1860–1925*. 2nd ed. New York: Atheneum, 1977.

Hill, Bennett D., ed. *Church and State in the Middle Ages*. New York: John Wiley, 1970.

Hill, Samuel S. *The New Religious Political Right in America*. Nashville: Abingdon Press, 1982.

Hoekema, Anthony A. *The Four Major Cults: Christian Science, Jehovah's Witnesses, Mormonism and Seventh-Day Adventists*. Grand Rapids: Eerdmans, 1965.

Hofstadter, Richard. *Social Darwinsim in American Thought*. Rev. ed. Boston: Beacon Press, 1967.

Hollenweger, W. J. *The Pentecostals*. Minneapolis: Augsburg, 1972.

Holloway, Mark. *Heavens on Earth: Utopian Communities in America 1680–1880*. Rev. ed. New York: Dover, 1966.

Hope, Marjorie, and Young, James, eds. *The Struggle for Humanity: Agents of Nonviolent Change in a Violent World*. Maryknoll, N.Y.: Orbis Books, 1977.

Hopkins, Charles H. *The Rise of the Social Gospel in American Protestantism 1865–1915*. New Haven: Yale University Press, 1967.

Hordern, William. *A Layman's Guide to Protestant Theology*. Rev. ed. New York: Macmillan, 1968.

Hostetler, John A. *Amish Society*. 3d ed. Baltimore: Johns Hopkins University Press, 1980.

Hubbard, Geoffrey. *Quaker by Convincement*. London: Penguin, 1974.

Hudson, Winthrop S. *Religion in America: An Historical Account of the Development of American Religious Life*. 3rd ed. New York: Scribner's, 1981.

Hunter, James Davison. *Evangelicalism: The Coming Generation*. Chicago: University of Chicago Press, 1987.

Jeschke, Marlin, *Discipling the Brother: Congregational Discipline According to the Gospel*. Scottdale, Pa.: Herald Press, 1972.

Johnson, James Turner. *Can a Modern War Be Just?* New Haven: Yale University Press, 1984.

Johnson, Luke Timothy. *The Writings of the New Testament: An Interpretation*. Philadelphia: Fortress Press, 1986.

Jules-Rosette, Bennetta. *African Apostles: Ritual and Conversion in the Church of Maranke*. Ithaca: Cornell University Press, 1975.

Kastner, Patricia Wilson, et al. *A Lost Tradition: Women Writers of the Early Church*. Washington, D.C.: University Press of America, 1981.

Kater, John. *Christians on the Right: The Moral Majority in Perspective*. New York: Seabury Press, 1982.

Kee, Howard C. *Jesus in History: An Approach to the Study of the Gospels*. 2nd ed. New York: Harcourt Brace Jovanovich, 1977.

Kee, Howard C., Young, Franklin W., and Froehlich, Karlfried. *Understanding the New Testament*. 4th ed. Englewood Cliffs, N.J.: Prentice-Hall, 1983.

Kohmescher, Matthew F. *Catholicism Today: A Survey of Catholic Belief and Practice*. New York: Paulist Press, 1980.

Küng, Hans. *The Council, Reform and Reunion*. New York: Doubleday Image, 1965.

Land, Gary, ed. *Adventism in America: A History*. Grand Rapids: Eerdmans, 1986.

Lernoux, Penny. *Cry of the People*. New York: Doubleday, 1980.

Lincoln, C. Eric, and Frazier, E. Franklin. *The Black Church Since Frazier* and *The Negro Church in America*. New York: Schocken Books, 1975.

Loetscher, L. A. *A Brief History of the Presbyterians*. 3rd ed. Philadelphia: Westminster Press, 1978.

Lohfink, Gerhard. *The Bible, Now I Get It: A Form-Criticism Handbook*. Garden City, N.Y.: Doubleday, 1979.

Lohse, Bernhard. *Martin Luther: An Introduction to His Life and His Work*. Philadelphia: Fortress Press, 1986.

Lohse, E., ed. *The New Testament Environment*. Nashville: Abingdon Press, 1976.

McAvoy, Thomas T. *A History of the Catholic Church in the United States*. Notre Dame, Ind.: University of Notre Dame Press, 1969.

McBrien, Richard P. *Caesar's Coin: Religion and Politics in America*. New York: Macmillan, 1987.

———. *Catholicism*. 2 vols. Minneapolis: Winston Press, 1980.

MacEoin, Gary. *What Happened at Rome?: The Council and Its Implications for the Modern World*. New York: Doubleday, 1967.

McDonnell, John J. *The World Council of Churches and the Catholic Church*. Toronto: Edwin Mellen Press, 1985.

McGiffert, Arthur Cushman. *A History of Christian Thought*. New York: Scribner's, 1961.

McKinley, Edward H. *Marching to Glory: The History of the Salvation Army in the United States of America 1880–1980*. San Francisco: Harper & Row, 1980.

Maguire, Daniel C. *The New Subversives: Anti-Americanism of the Religious Right*. New York: Crossroad/Continuum, 1982.

Malherbe, Abraham J. *Social Aspects of Early Christianity*. 2nd ed. Philadelphia: Fortress Press, 1983.

Manschreck, Clyde L. *A History of Christianity in the World*. Englewood Cliffs, N.J.: Prentice-Hall, 1974.

Marsden, George. *Fundamentalism and American Culture: The Shaping of Twentieth-Century Evangelicalism 1870–1925*. New York: Oxford University Press, 1980.

Marty, Martin E. *Protestantism in the United States: Righteous Empire*. 2nd ed. New York: Scribner's, 1986.

Mead, Sydney. *The Lively Experiment: The Shaping of Christianity in America.* New York: Harper & Row, 1963.

Meeks, Wayne A. *The Moral World of the First Christians.* Philadelphia: Westminster Press, 1986.

Meeks, Wayne A., and Wilken, Robert. *Jews and Christians in Antioch in the First Four Centuries of the Common Era.* Missoula, Mont.: Scholars Press, 1978.

Meyendorf, John. *The Orthodox Church: Its Past and Its Role in the World Today.* 3rd rev. ed. Crestwood, N.Y.: St. Vladimir's Seminary Press, 1981.

Miller, John H., ed. *Vatican II: An Interfaith Appraisal.* Notre Dame, Ind.: University of Notre Dame Press, 1966.

Moore, William T. *A Comprehensive History of the Disciples of Christ.* New York: F. H. Revell, 1909.

Morgan, Edmund S. *The Puritan Dilemma: The Story of John Winthrop.* New York: Little, Brown, 1958.

Murphy, Francis X. *Politics and the Early Christian.* New York: Desclee, 1967.

Ndiokwere, Nathaniel I. *Prophecy and Revolution: The Role of Prophets in the Independent African Churches and in Biblical Tradition.* London: SPCK, 1981.

Neill, Stephen. *A History of Christian Missions.* 2nd ed. revised by Owen Chadwick. New York: Penguin, 1986.

Nelson, E. C. *The Lutherans in North America.* Philadelphia: Fortress Press, 1980.

Norwood, Fredrick A. *The Story of American Methodism.* Nashville: Abingdon Press, 1974.

O'Brien, David J. *The Renewal of American Catholicism.* Oxford: Oxford University Press, 1972.

O'Brien, William V. *The Conduct of a Just and Limited War.* New York: Praeger, 1981.

O'Dea, Thomas F. *The Mormons.* Chicago: University of Chicago Press, 1957.

Outler, Albert. *Methodist Observer at Vatican II.* Westminster, Md.: Newman Press, 1967.

Payne, Daniel A. *The Semi-Centenary and the Retrospection of the A.M.E. Church.* New York: Books for Libraries Press, 1972.

Peel, Robert. *Christian Science.* New York: Holt, Rinehart & Winston, 1959.

Perrin, Norman, and Duling, Dennis. *The New Testament, An Introduction: Proclamation and Parenesis, Myth and History.* 2nd ed. New York: Harcourt Brace Jovanovich, 1982.

Pike, Edgar R. *Jehovah's Witnesses.* New York: Philosophical Library, 1954.

Plowman, Edward E. "Is Morality All Right?" *Christianity Today* 23 (2 November 1979), 76–85.

Pobee, John S. *Toward an African Theology.* Nashville: Abingdon Press, 1979.

Ramm, Bernard. *After Fundamentalism: The Future of Evangelical Theology.* San Francisco: Harper & Row, 1983.

Rauschenbusch, Walter. *A Theology for the Social Gospel.* Nashville: Abingdon Press, 1945.

Reynolds, Stephen. *The Christian Religious Tradition.* Encino, Calif.: Dickenson, 1977.

Rice, Richard. *The Reign of God: An Introduction to Christian Theology from a Seventh-Day Adventist Perspective.* Berrien Springs, Mich.: Andrews University Press, 1985.

Roof, Wade Clark, and McKinney, William. *American Mainline Religion: Its Changing Shape and Future.* New Brunswick, N.J.: Rutgers University Press, 1987.

Rosenberg, Stuart E. *The Christian Problem: A Jewish View.* New York: Hippocrene Books, 1986.

Ruether, Rosemary. *Contemporary Roman Catholicism.* Kansas City, Mo.: Sheed & Ward, 1987.

Ruether, Rosemary, and Keller, Rosemary Skinner, eds. *Women & Religion in America.* 3 vols. New York: Harper & Row, 1981–86.

Russell, Letty M. *Human Liberation in a Feminist Perspective.* Philadelphia: Westminster Press, 1974.

Schall, James V. *The Distinctiveness of Christianity.* San Francisco: Ignatius Press, 1982.

Schmemann, Alexander. *The Historical Road of Eastern Orthodoxy.* Crestwood, N.Y.: St. Vladimir's Seminary Press, 1973.

Senn, Frank C., ed. *Protestant Spiritual Traditions.* New York: Paulist Press, 1986.

Shute, Anson D. *Born Again Politics and the Moral Majority.* New York: Edwin Mellen Press, 1982.

Sider, Ronald J. *Rich Christians in an Age of Hunger.* 2nd ed. Downers Grove, Ill.: Inter-Varsity Press, 1984.

Sojourners 6 (January 1977), 14–31.

Spivey, Robert A., and Smith, D. Moody. *Anatomy of the New Testament.* 4th ed. New York: Macmillan, 1989.

Sweet, Leonard I. *The Evangelical Tradition in America.* Macon, Ga.: Mercer University Press, 1984.

Sweet, William W. *The Baptists: A Collection of Source Materials.* New York: Holt, 1931; reissued Cooper Square Press, 1964.

———. *The Congregationalists: A Collection of Source Materials.* Chicago: University of Chicago Press, 1939; reissued New York: Cooper Square Press, 1964.

———. *The Methodists: A Collection of Source Materials.* Chicago: University of Chicago Press, 1946; reissued New York: Cooper Square Press, 1964.

———. *The Presbyterians: A Collection of Source Materials.* New York: Harper Brothers, 1936; reissued Cooper Square Press, 1964.

Synan, Vinson. *The Holiness-Pentecostal Movement in the United States.* Grand Rapids: Eerdmans, 1972.

Thielicke, Helmut. *I Believe: The Christian Creed.* Philadelphia: Fortress Press, 1965.

Time cover story on American Catholic bishops and nuclear war. 120 (29 November 1982), 68–78.

Topel, L. John. *The Way to Peace: Liberation Through the Bible.* Maryknoll, N.Y.: Orbis Books, 1979.

Trueblood, David E. *The People Called Quakers.* New York: Harper & Row, 1966.

Walter, Williston, and Norris, Richard A., Handy, Robert T., and Lotz, David W. *A History of the Christian Church.* 4th ed. New York: Scribner's, 1985.

Weaver, J. Denny. *Becoming Anabaptist: The Origin and Significance of Sixteenth-Century Anabaptism.* Scottdale, Pa.: Herald Press, 1987.

Weaver, Mary Jo. *New Catholic Women: A Contemporary Challenge to Traditional Religious Authority.* San Francisco: Harper & Row, 1985.

Webber, Robert, and Bloesch, Donald, eds. *The Orthodox Evangelicals: Who They Are and What They Are Saying.* New York: Thomas Nelson, 1978.

Weinstein, Donald, ed. *The Renaissance and the Reformation 1300–1600.* New York: Free Press, 1965.

Whalen, William J. *Minority Religions in America.* New York: Alba House, 1971.

Wilken, Robert L. *The Myth of Christian Beginnings: History's Impact on Belief.* New York: Doubleday, 1971.

Williams, Peter W. *Popular Religion in America: Symbolic Change and the Modernization Process in Historical Perspective.* Englewood Cliffs, N.J.: Prentice-Hall, 1980.

Wilmore, Gayraud S., and Cone, James H. *Black Theology: A Documentary History 1966–1979.* Maryknoll, N.Y.: Orbis Books, 1979.

Wilson, Bryan R. *Patterns of Sectarianism.* London: Heinemann Educational Books, 1967.

Yoder, John Howard. *The Politics of Jesus.* Grand Rapids: Eerdmans, 1972.

INDEX